Writing Choices

Andrew J. Hoffman

San Diego Mesa College

Allyn and Bacon

Boston ■ *London* ■ *Toronto* ■ *Sydney* ■ *Tokyo* ■ *Singapore*

To Cathy,
my beloved wife

Vice President, Humanities: Joseph Opiela
Series Editor: Carla Daves
Developmental Editor: Carol Alper
Editorial Assistant: Andrea Geanacopoulos
Marketing Manager: Lisa Kimball
Production Administrator: Deborah Brown
Editorial-Production Service: Susan Freese, Communicáto, Ltd.
Text Designer/Composition: Denise Hoffman, Glenview Studios
Composition/Prepress Buyer: Linda Cox
Manufacturing Buyer: Suzanne Lareau
Cover Administrator: Linda Knowles
Cover Designer: Studio Nine

Copyright © 1997 by Allyn & Bacon
A Viacom Company
160 Gould Street
Needham Heights, MA 02194

Internet: www.abacon.com
America Online: keyword: College Online

Library of Congress Cataloging-in-Publication Data
Hoffman, Andrew
    Writing choices / Andrew J. Hoffman.
      p.   cm.
    Includes index.
    ISBN 0-205-19818-X (alk. paper)
     1. English language—Rhetoric—Problems, exercises, etc.
  2. English language—Grammar—Problems, exercises, etc.   I. Title
    PE1413.H556   1997
    808'.042—dc21   96-46886
                                     CIP

Printed in the United States of America

10 9 8 7 6 5 4 3 2 1   01 00 99 98 97 96

Contents

3

The Building Blocks: Basic Structures of the Paragraph   41

4

Telling It Like It Is: Narration, Description, and Example in Paragraphs   71

5

The Thing Itself: Definition and Classification Paragraphs   99

6

Similarities and Differences: Comparison and Constrast Paragraphs   123

7

Reasons and Results: Cause and Effect Paragraphs   148

8

How Things Work: Process Paragraphs   171

9

What's Your Point? Creating the Thesis Sentence   189

10

Building from Within: Moving from Thesis to Essay   207

11

Adapting the Essay to Your Purpose: Using and Combining Rhetorical Modes   230

12

Arguing Your Point:
Logical Support and Logical Fallacies   249

13

How to Say It: Style   276

14

Under the Gun:
Writing Essay Examinations   303

Reviewing the Rules:
A Guide to Grammar, Spelling, and Punctuation   323

Preface for the Instructor

The principle guiding *Writing Choices* is a simple one: Students can improve their own writing by understanding the choices they make during the writing process. Once they are more aware of their choices, they can learn to exercise control over those choices. With this sense of control, students can become more confident, more capable writers. The ultimate goal of *Writing Choices* is to help students become self-sufficient in their writing. Learning about their choices will provide them with that self-sufficiency.

Writing Choices blends the competing demands of process-oriented and product-oriented instruction. The book will help students become more aware of the presence of choices by teaching students the stages of the writing process: from generating ideas and choosing a topic, to drafting and revising, to rewriting in response to criticism and editing. Students are also instructed in the structures of the paragraph and the essay. They are taught the traditional rhetorical modes at the level of the paragraph, and they are shown how to use and combine these modes at the level of the essay. Grammar and punctuation instruction is included in each chapter, as well.

Features

Users of *Writing Choices* will benefit from the following important features:

■ Writing is presented as a skill that can be learned. Toward that goal, the book presents different parts of the writing process as a series of manageable tasks. Tasks grow progressively more difficult throughout the book.

■ Students' choices at each stage of the writing process are emphasized. Examples of different writing choices are included, followed by a discussion of the effectiveness of the different choices.

■ Frequent examples illustrate important points of instruction so that students can readily see how the instruction applies to the kinds of writing they actually do.

■ The tone of the book is friendly and helpful. The emphasis is not so much on *correct* and *incorrect* but on *effective* and *ineffective*. The style of the book encourages, not threatens, students.

■ Each chapter includes a journal-writing prompt to serve as a prereading exercise and as a potential source for writing ideas.

■ Exercises and writing assignments reinforce instruction in each chapter. They increase in length and difficulty as students master succeeding tasks of writing.

■ Students are helped through the writing process by a series of questions and guidelines that they can work on by themselves (Start-Up Suggestions and Self-Revision Questions) or with a peer-editing group (Peer-Editing Guidelines).

■ A questionnaire (Your Choices) accompanies each student writing assignment; it asks students to recall the choices they made throughout the writing process.

■ Beginning with Chapter 3, an extended example of student writing is included in each chapter, showing each stage of the writing process. Extensive commentary accompanies each example to analyze the choices the student faced in his or her particular writing situation.

■ Each chapter has a Computer Exercise suitable for use in a computerized or computer-aided instruction classroom. These exercises take advantage of the enormous potential for collaborative learning in such classrooms.

■ A brief lesson in grammar or punctuation is included in each chapter so that students can reinforce the fundamentals needed for successful writing.

Organization

Writing Choices is organized in the following fashion:

■ In Chapters 1 and 2, students are taught how to prepare for writing courses. They learn about generating ideas through prewriting exercises and how to search outside themselves for ideas.

■ Chapter 3 introduces the basic structure of the paragraph. Students are also introduced to the concept of *coherence* in a paragraph, the use of abstract and concrete language, and the need for both general ideas and specific details.

■ Chapters 4 through 8 introduce the traditional rhetorical modes at the level of the paragraph. Using this approach, students can learn the important qualities of each mode before using it in longer works.

■ Chapter 9 is devoted solely to the thesis sentence. Students are shown what is necessary for a thesis sentence, how to write one, and why some thesis sentences are effective and others are not.

■ Chapter 10 introduces the essay as developed from the thesis sentence. All major structural aspects of the essay, including introductory and concluding paragraphs, are discussed. Different methods of developing the main body paragraphs are included.

■ Chapter 11 shows students how to take the knowledge learned about rhetorical modes at the paragraph level and apply it to the essay. This chapter shows how most essays combine rhetorical modes to prove their theses.

■ Chapter 12 introduces logical thinking and logical fallacies. The fundamentals of argumentation are included, as is a discussion of induction and deduction.

■ Chapter 13 concentrates on matters of style. By this point in the book, students are ready to start using language in a more sophisticated way. The chapter discusses several helpful suggestions and presents problems to avoid.

■ Chapter 14 is devoted to the timed essay. Since many students end a developmental course with a required competency exam, this chapter includes suggestions on how to prepare for such an exam and strategies that may prove to be successful.

■ Reviewing the Rules: A Guide to Grammar, Spelling, and Punctuation is a handbook designed to supplement the grammar instruction in each chapter. It provides brief, practical instruction in areas in which students often need help, such as run-on or comma splice sentences, sentence fragments, subject-verb agreement, pronoun-antecedent agreement, and case errors. Additional exercises are included, as well.

■ The Readings reflect a wide variety of topics and authors. As writing models, these readings can serve as an excellent source of class discussion; they can also provide the basis for additional student writing.

■ A Glossary defines all terms introduced in the book.

Acknowledgments

I would like to thank many people for assisting me in writing this book. Carla Daves, my sponsoring editor at Allyn and Bacon, believed in this project with such determination and force that I could not let her down. Carol Alper, my developmental editor, stepped into the project, rolled up her sleeves, and did the detail work that needed to be done. She did a super job in helping me get the manuscript into final form. Assistant Andrea Geanacopoulos was an important resource, as well. My special appreciation goes to Sue Freese and Denise Hoffman for their work in producing this book. It is they who have shaped the book into its final form.

I am grateful to the many instructors in colleges and universities who took the time to review earlier versions of this book and offer their helpful suggestions. Among those who contributed to this book were the following: Cathy C. Cole, Tulsa Junior College; Pauline Corse, Chaffey College; Nancy Cox, Arkansas Tech University; Clifford Gardiner, Augusta College; Elisabeth B. Leyson, Fullerton College; Patricia A. Malinowski, Finger Lakes Community College; Karen J. Patty-Graham, Southern Illinois University; Judy Ryan, Fresno City College; Elizabeth Sawyerr, Howard University; Roberta C. Straight, University of New Mexico, Los Alamos; Robert E. Yarber, Emeritus, San Diego Mesa College; and Nancy Yee, Fitchburg State College.

I would like to single out Robert E. Yarber for special thanks. Bob saw this textbook when it was just a few pages of notes and a scratch outline, and for many months afterward, he counseled me in the writing of this book. His advice, based on thirty years of experience in the classroom and in writing textbooks, proved invaluable. I am especially indebted to Bob for his editing of the Reviewing the Rules section of this book.

Of course, no instructor can write a textbook without having been influenced in the classroom. My students at San Diego Mesa College have contributed to this book in many ways. I especially want to thank two of my classes that used an early draft of this book as their textbook. Many of them contributed their own writing to serve as examples. I want to single out Deanetta Ali, Jocelyn Prewitt, Susan Moore, and Adam Stephens-Bren for allowing their work to be used, along with their names.

Finally, I wish to thank my family. My boys, Sean and Alex, are too young even to read, but they accepted that sometimes Daddy had to leave them to work on the book. Daddy regrets the time away and promises to make it up to them. My gratitude also is given to my wife, Cathy, to whom this book is dedicated. Cathy is not only a terrific wife and mother, but she is also an outstanding English instructor. Her ideas about teaching can be found on nearly every page of this book. Thank you.

A. J. H.

Preface for the Student

Imagine that you have been presented with a giant wedding cake, prepared by a master pastry chef and covered with delicate icing that has been shaped into flowers and angels. The cake has three levels, each exquisitely beautiful, and the whole thing looks as if it could feed a hundred guests. Then you are told, "Now go in the kitchen and make another one just like it!"

Unless you are already an expert at cake making, chances are good that your own attempt would fall short. That's because the pastry chef has years of training and experience in making cakes. The chef probably has a few helpful recipes, as well.

This is the same situation you may face when you are given a writing assignment at school. All too often, you are told *what* to do but not *how* to do it.

Writing Choices teaches the process of writing—the recipe, if you will—but it also teaches the techniques of writing. After all, even a recipe isn't always enough; you also have to know how to do the things the recipe requires.

This book begins by discussing how to write paragraphs, the basic building blocks of the essay, and shows you how paragraphs are formed differently for different purposes. From there, you move to writing short essays—the kind you will be expected to write in a freshman composition course. You will also discover how to avoid mistakes in reasoning and how to improve your writing style. You will learn how to write the timed essay exams you may face at the end of the semester.

Writing Choices reflects the philosophy that your writing is guided by the choices you make. To expose you to the process of writing, and thereby help you become aware of the choices you make in that process, the following features are found in each chapter:

Journal Exercises

Each chapter begins with journal-entry questions to help you start thinking about the issues the chapter covers. You should do each Journal Exercise in a notebook that you set aside specifically for this purpose. Do the Journal Exercise *before* you read the rest of the chapter. That way, your journal writing will not be influenced or prejudiced by what you read later. These Journal Exercises are a part of the prewriting stage of writing, which is discussed in greater depth in Chapter 2.

The Rhetoric

Each chapter discusses an aspect of writing in both a theoretical and practical manner so that you know both the *why* and the *how*. Numerous student writing samples are included to show you how other writers like yourself have handled the issues discussed in the chapter.

Student Writing Assignment

Starting with Chapter 3, each chapter has at least one Student Writing Assignment, which is intended to take you through the writing process, from prewriting to final draft. You will see that the process is divided into four parts: Start-Up Suggestions, Self-Revision Questions, Peer-Editing Guidelines, and Your Choices.

The first steps involve work you do yourself. The Start-Up Suggestions section helps you begin the writing process by offering ideas to consider before drafting a paragraph or essay. The second section, Self-Revision Questions, is a list of questions to ask yourself as you work through the early drafts of your writing. These questions are designed to make you more aware of the structural and rhetorical tasks you face.

The Peer-Editing Guidelines are intended to be used by groups of three to five students. On days when you are peer editing, make sure you have enough copies of your paragraph or essay for all of the members of your group. Each member will read your writing and complete the questions in the guidelines. Then he or she will return your writing to you with the questions answered, so that when you are rewriting your paragraph or essay, you will have additional input. Of course, you will do the same for all of the other members of your group. In this way, all of you will have had several readers for your work before your instructor sees the final draft.

After you complete the final draft, answer the questions from Your Choices. This section asks you to examine the reasons behind the choices that you made in the drafting and revising of your work. The purpose is to emphasize that you are in control of your writing and to expose you to how you have already exhibited that control. Increasing self-awareness in the writing process may help you produce writings that more accurately communicate your thoughts.

Computer Exercises

Each chapter has a Computer Exercise for use in computer-aided instruction (CAI) classrooms. Students in these classrooms work on computer terminals that are networked, sometimes through a central computer controlled by the instructor. If you are in such a classroom, you will be able to use these Computer Exercises to reinforce the lessons of the chapter. These exercises rely on the CAI classroom's ability to transfer files from student to instructor, instructor to student, and student to student. Some CAI classrooms feature programs that enable you to conduct in-class conferences with each other. In this case, you can form writing groups without leaving your chairs. Other computer-equipped classrooms feature personal computers without the capability of sharing files. In such a classroom, you can share files by saving them on diskettes and passing the diskettes back and forth.

The Computer Exercises reinforce instruction about the steps of the writing process. You can use the exercises as one stage of the writing process for your student writing assignments. Please note that some of the Computer Exercises will require you to work with another student, called your *writing partner*. Be aware that you may also share your work with the entire class, as well.

Student Writing Sample

Each chapter closely analyzes a student writing sample as it passes through each stage of the writing process, from the prewriting stages through drafting to making the final revisions. Tracking this sample allows you to see revision as an integral part of every writing assignment, rather than as a separate or extra task. The Student Writing Sample will also provide you with a model of how to use the Start-Up Suggestions, Self-Revision, Peer-Editing Guidelines, and Your Choices sections.

Grammar Review and Exercises

Each chapter includes instruction in a particular aspect of grammar or punctuation. The discussions are clear and simple. You will find several examples and a short exercise to practice what you learned. For a more extensive discussion of grammar and punctuation, consult the grammar handbook included in this book.

Grammar Handbook

Reviewing the Rules: A Guide to Grammar, Spelling, and Punctuation is an easy-to-use handbook designed to supplement the grammar instruction included in the earlier chapters. Reviewing the Rules covers more areas of how to use language, gives additional examples of correct usage, and provides more exercises to help you learn.

Readings

The Readings section has articles and essays that cover a range of subjects, styles, and rhetorical modes. Each writing sample is introduced with questions to consider before the reading, followed by the reading itself. Afterward, there are questions for written response that require you to deal closely with the writing sample as well as questions that ask you to think beyond the writing sample to the larger issues it raises. These questions are designed to be the basis for additional written work.

Glossary

The Glossary gives definitions of all the terms in *Writing Choices* that are presented in bold type the first time they are used. This handy reference covers terms related to matters of composition, structure, style, logic, grammar, and punctuation.

A Final Word

Ultimately, your success as a writer will be determined long after you've completed your college writing classes. Learning how to write well is a long, sometimes difficult task. This book will help you beyond your days in the classroom by teaching you to recognize the choices you face in every writing task. Once you are aware of these choices and learn how to manage your writing to respond to them, you will be on the path to writing with control, clarity, and power.

A. J. H.

1 Your Choice

Getting a Handle on Your Writing

When you walk into an English class, are you afraid that:

- *Writing is a gift or talent that only a few people can master?*
- *You have nothing to write about?*
- *Your personal experiences, job history, and past school work will not help you to write well?*
- *You will not need English skills in your future career, so this class will be a waste of your time?*
- *You cannot express in writing what you can say in conversation?*
- *What you write will sound trivial or silly?*
- *Your grammar skills are too poor to allow you to write well?*
- *Your new English instructor will require your essays to be written differently from how you have learned to write them in the past?*
- *Grading is entirely subjective, so you have no control over the grades you earn?*
- *You will be told to write essays but never told how?*

Writing Choices is designed to ease your fears and help you tackle the difficulties of writing. The ultimate purpose of writing is, after all, communication. Communication allows for the exchange of ideas, the discovery of ourselves and others, and the progression toward goals. The ability to communicate is power.

Learning How to Write

A common experience for many students such as you is to see writing as a mystical process that only a few men and women can understand or control. Students often feel powerless in front of a fresh sheet of paper or a blank computer screen and will spend their time tapping pencils or staring at a blinking cursor, waiting for inspiration to grab them. Some view writing as unpleasant and burdensome, and they dread seeing their best efforts marked by an instructor's red pen.

Writing, however, should be seen as a craft, one that you can learn through instruction and practice. In this respect, writing is like shooting a free throw or playing a guitar. You may not become another Michael Jordan or Bonnie Raitt, but you can learn the *fundamentals* of shooting or playing. These fundamentals help you control the ball or guitar. Do not, however, make the mistake of thinking that these fundamentals will always come quickly or easily. Just as no one learns the fundamentals of shooting a basketball or playing the guitar overnight, no one learns how to write well without putting in time and hard work.

In writing, control comes when you realize that language is a tool for communication and that underlying all writing are choices. You make choices about how you will use language—its form, content, tone, and word choice. You choose your topic, your attitude about the topic, and any message you have about that topic. Writing is like making your own furniture: you choose what to build, the materials you will use, and the plan you will follow, and then you spend hours of careful, hard work crafting the piece, making sure to include your own distinctive touches. In the end, you will have created a product that you can be proud of and that others can appreciate and use.

EXERCISE 1.1

Describe your experiences from past English classes. What good experiences did you have? What bad ones? What distinguishes a good English class from a bad one?

The Decision to Write

You make your first choice when you decide to write. When you write a letter to a friend to describe an exciting concert you went to see, you have made a choice. You also make choices when you write a list of groceries to buy, things to do, or books to read over the summer. At work, you may decide to write a proposal to expand your department's budget for computer software and training. That proposal could earn you a promotion. At home, you may write a biography of your grandmother, who worked in a factory on the home front while her husband fought in the Pacific during World War II. You choose to preserve important family history for posterity.

At school, the decision to write is often connected to success in a class. Many instructors, not just English instructors, require written work: there are lab reports in the sciences, papers in history and the social sciences, proposals and reports in business, and creative writing in the performing arts. Indeed, most academic disciplines require written work at one time or another, and if you fail to write well, you will have a difficult time succeeding, no matter what your chosen field.

So, your decision to write may be subject to some coercion: you write because the instructor requires it. Nevertheless, even if a requirement of a course is written work, you still have many choices. Remember that the decision to write is only the first choice in the writing process.

Influences on Your Writing: Internal and External Forces

Internal Forces

All writing is influenced by forces both internal and external to the writer. The **internal forces** are those things that make up who you are: your family background and spiritual beliefs; your life experiences that have shaped you; your academic goals; your interests outside of school; your reading for both pleasure and information; and your goals, fears, and desires. These aspects of who you are create a unique personality—one that, if harnessed properly, will give your writing a distinctive shape and tone.

Writers who ignore the internal factors tend to write boring, dull, and unimaginative prose. They try to make their writing fit some preconceived mold that they may only vaguely understand. Perhaps they use unfamiliar terms, trying to be sophisticated without recognizing that sophistication is the ability to handle complicated ideas smoothly, not the ability to use a thesaurus. Other writers never take risks. They write about topics that have already been discussed at great length, and they bring no new insight or expression to those topics. They try to write safe essays that will guarantee a passing grade, and the results are usually uninspired.

Prewriting

One way to reach your internal forces and bring them into your writing is by **prewriting.** There are many different prewriting techniques, including brainstorming, listing, mapping, freewriting, asking questions, clustering, outlining, and keeping a journal. (You will be introduced to these methods in Chapter 2.) These techniques are designed to free your imagination, help you tap into your past experiences or interests, and recognize how a myriad of ideas can be brought into coherent order. Prewriting can help you find fresh topics for writing or even provide fresh points of view on older topics.

External Forces

External forces are those outside yourself. These forces include **purpose, audience,** and **subject.** They determine the length, style, word choice, and writing strategy you will use.

Purpose

Why you write may have everything to do with what you write. You may wish to entertain your reader by writing a short story. Perhaps you choose to inform your reader about new discoveries in cancer research. Maybe you choose to persuade your reader to adopt your opinion about the benefits of legal immigration. To entertain, to inform, or to persuade—these are generally considered the three purposes in writing. Of course, most writing has a certain measure of all three purposes, but usually one is the dominant or main purpose.

Different patterns of development are used to advance your purpose, particularly when your main purpose is to inform or to persuade. You may decide to define the term *justice,* or you may classify *sisters* into three basic types. At times, you will write to compare or contrast two different subjects, such as *parents* and *grandparents.* On other occasions, you will write to show causes, such as what events led to the fall of the Berlin Wall, or effects, such as how the Civil Rights Movement changed race relations in the United States. You might need to describe a process, such as how nuclear fusion occurs within a star. You may even analyze an event or issue to better understand it, such as why voters rejected a particular proposition in the last election.

Whatever your intent, your writing needs to accomplish its purpose. If you lack a clear sense of understanding how to achieve your purpose, your writing will be incoherent and muddled. You will not have accomplished what you set out to do, which is to communicate.

Audience

Do you talk to your grandparents the same way you talk to your friends at school? You probably don't because you realize that people use language differently, depending on such matters as age, education, personality, and occasion. In fact, you can get yourself in trouble if you lack a good sense of audience. Your writing may offend, bore, irritate, or simply confuse your audience if you use words or expressions that are inappropriate.

In school, instructors require the use of standard English, and some demand that you use a formal style rather than an informal style. *Formal* means you must limit the use of contractions; avoid first- and second-person pronouns (such as *I* and *you*), unless the writing is about the author's personal experiences; and take on a serious tone. Even if some instructors will accept informal English, many will not accept the slang expressions that appear in everyday conversation. You will probably be shocked to discover how often you use slang instead of standard English. (A more detailed discussion of slang, informal, and formal English will appear in Chapter 13.)

Instructors also expect you to develop a good understanding of effective grammar and punctuation, be able to spell properly, and know how to use a dictionary. *Grammar* simply means the rules that govern the ways in which words can be used in a sentence. If you are not able to use grammar effectively, you will not be able to communicate well. If you can communicate in a dialect but not in standard English because of weaknesses in grammar or punctuation, you risk losing credibility with your audience. Punctuation, like spelling, is important when writing English. Failure to develop the skills necessary in these areas will only weaken your ability to inform or persuade your audience.

A sense of audience includes understanding what knowledge can be assumed on the part of your reader. When you write for an instructor, you can assume that he or she is familiar with material that has been discussed in class. Do not, for instance, write an essay about Mark Twain's *The Adventures of Tom Sawyer* that merely retells the story, because your instructor can be expected to be familiar with it already.

(One exception to this would be if your assignment is to write a *summary* of the book; then you would retell the story.) On the other hand, an instructor will not know much about your personal life. Therefore, any personal experience you use in your writing will need to be explained in sufficient detail. For this reason, some instructors prefer that you not use personal experience in your writing assignments.

Subject

The more you understand your subject, the better your writing will be. Think about it: Have you ever had to take a test that you were not ready for? You probably guessed, blustered, and stumbled through, knowing all along that you did not understand the material. The same thing can happen in writing. If you try to write on a subject you know little about, you are likely to paste together whatever information you can remember and fill out the essay with fluff and bluff. The result will lack substance, coherence, and imagination. In a case such as this, your essay might be quite long, as you attempt to make up in length what your writing lacks in content.

At this point, one important distinction needs to be made between two terms that appear frequently in this book: *subject* and *topic*. Your **subject** is the broad area of inquiry. Your **topic** is the narrow focus into or limited aspect of the subject. For instance, if your subject is *television* (a broad area of interest), your topic might be *the effect of television violence on young viewers* (a limited aspect of that broad area of interest). Thus, even if an instructor provides you with a subject to write about, you must still narrow that subject down to a particular topic that you can then address.

JOURNAL EXERCISE

Get a binder and some lined paper. This will be your writing journal. You will be asked to write in this journal at different times in each of the chapters. Do all your journal exercises and prewriting assignments in this journal. Over the course of the term, your journal will become a valuable resource as a record of your thoughts.

For your first journal exercise, write about the writing you have done thus far; the choices you have made; the influences on your writing; and the purposes, the audiences, and the subjects of your writing.

In a CAI classroom: Start a file named "Journal" in which you will store all your journal exercises and prewriting assignments. You should be able to do everything in a computer file that you can do on paper except for mapping and clustering.

What Can You Do Now and Why?

Perhaps you feel that it is too late for you—that if you have not learned how to write well by now, you never will. Maybe you fear that poor grammar skills, weak spelling, or punctuation errors are set like concrete in your writing. Nothing could be more wrong. Grammar, spelling, and punctuation are skills that can be learned. Nevertheless, just as with shooting a basketball or playing a guitar, these skills do not come easily, especially if you have already acquired some bad habits. One or two grammar lessons do not always make errors go away, just as a few broad strokes of the pen and a last-minute rewrite will probably not create a good piece of writing. Even using a computer program that checks spelling and grammar is not enough. Technical competence in the matters of grammar, spelling, and punctuation—like good writing—is the result of long, hard effort.

Even if a piece of writing contains no technical errors, it still may not be a good example of writing. What makes good writing? For one thing, good writing starts with good ideas. Without good ideas, there is nothing to say. The difficulty is that good ideas are not always readily available. How do you find them?

Reading

Most good writers are also good readers. In fact, most professional writers grew up as voracious readers and continue to read as much as they can. Reading gives writers models to imitate, provides them with new information or attitudes about subjects, and shows them what subjects have already been discussed so widely and thoroughly that they should be avoided. Reading educates writers in the traditions of writing and shows how other writers tackled their own problems.

Read on your own. Reading only what has been assigned in school is seldom enough. Pick up newspapers or magazines and scan them for interesting articles; find nonfiction books on subjects that intrigue you; start reading a novel by an author you have heard of but never read. Broaden your reading experiences.

Learn to read with a pencil in your hand. You should become actively involved in what you are reading, and that means taking notes and asking yourself questions. Passive readers just accept the material in front of them; active readers get involved with it. So, go ahead and write in your books. Jot down questions in the margins, underline significant passages, and scribble in definitions of new words. By writing in your books, you make them your own. (Of course, do not deface materials that do not belong to you! Instead, place Post-it notes to yourself in the book, which can be removed later.)

Start reading more now, even if it is just a half hour a day. The results will not be instantaneous, but after a period of extensive, active reading, you will find that writing will come a lot easier.

Talking and Listening

Talking is something most of us can do, and most of us do quite a bit more of it than reading or writing. But what do we talk about? If your conversations always tend toward personal gossip, you may find that you are not learning very much about the world outside of you, your friends, and your family. Talking with others is a great way to learn, and not just about who went where with whom! Instead, talk about what you have learned in school, what you are struggling with, and what you would like to learn more about.

When you talk about the subjects you are reading in school, do not forget to listen, as well. You may be pleasantly surprised at what happens. A conversation with fellow students, family members, or friends can lead you in directions you never imagined. If you have to write an essay about the Vietnam War, you may be surprised to learn that your uncle served a tour of duty there, and he may have many interesting stories to tell. A discussion about a political or social issue may bring out arguments or points of view that you never before heard expressed. Even a conversation with your instructor could lead in directions that are helpful to your writing. However, if you just talk and never listen, none of this may occur.

Observing

A common misconception is that writers must travel extensively to find material. American poet Emily Dickinson rarely traveled far from her home in Amherst, Massachusetts, yet she wrote some of the most insightful and powerful poetry in American literature. What is necessary is that writers be able to observe the world, notice the things that are happening, both large and small, and make some sense of that world. Look out a window and watch the world go by—this is the material writers work from the most. Writers try to see what is happening with people, places, and ideas.

Train yourself to be more observant. When you walk into a room, look around and then close your eyes. How much of what is in the room can you recall? What is on the walls, on the floor, the ceiling? Notice how people dress, walk, and talk. Are they dressed in expensive designer clothes or thriftshop seconds? Do they move quickly or slowly? Do they speak loudly and with confidence or in shy, muted tones?

As a writer, you also need to observe things that go beyond the physical reality and into the realm of ideas and emotions. Is someone sad or happy? Is the general mood among your circle of friends upbeat, or is there a general malaise or depression settling in? Are people seeking spiritual values, or are they rejecting them? A good writer looks at the world and tries to discover just exactly what is happening now and what may happen soon.

EXERCISE 1.2

Write a letter to yourself in which you talk about the kinds of things that you can do to make yourself a better writer.

The Benefits of Writing

Many a student rebels at the thought of taking a writing class. "After all," she may say to herself, "I don't need writing. It's not going to help me in the future because I'm going to be a _____."

That blank space, whatever it is, will almost assuredly require some measure of writing skills. But even if a certain occupation has no obvious requirement for writing skills, students benefit in other ways from learning how to write well.

Thinking

The acts of thinking and writing are closely related. After all, try to think without using language. It is very difficult. You use language to convey your most basic thoughts as well as sophisticated acts of reasoning. School and work, even when they do not require writing, require thinking. Because language is so closely related to the process of thinking, your ability to control language will also help you control your thinking. That is, you can learn better to recognize how you reason, what logical steps your reasoning is taking, and what mistakes or logical fallacies you may make in your reasoning. Precision in the use of language leads to precision in thought.

Learning

As you write, you discover. You may learn about yourself or the subject at hand, but the process of writing is one that continually forces you to create, examine, and re-create. You will be surprised at how often you will examine the depth of your knowledge and, in turn, how often you will need to learn more in order to write the essay you want. This process of discovery is integral to the act of writing.

Because writing involves thinking, learning how to write well will help all areas of study that require the use of reason and logic. If you consider that most subjects in school require reason and logic, that is an impressive benefit. Writing also communicates that improved thinking to others.

Using the Computer in Writing

Once a rarity, computers can be found in virtually every workplace and school in the United States and in a great number of homes, as well. That means more students are coming to college already familiar with computers, and they expect to use computers to help them in many classes, including English. Colleges and universities have responded by creating computer labs. Also, classrooms have been designed to take advantage of computers' abilities to process and share information. These classrooms are not labs or workrooms devoted to allowing individual students to work apart from each other; instead, they are designed to be classrooms where instructors teach and students share their writing.

COMPUTER EXERCISE

Create a computer file for the computer exercises in this book. You may wish to name your file "CompEx" or any other distinctive name.

Each time you open your file, be sure to enter the date for each new entry. This way, you can keep one file with all your computer exercises for the term arranged chronologically.

For your first exercise, write in your file what you hope to learn this semester. Discuss with your classmates and your instructor how the course may or may not meet those expectations.This is particularly effective if your classroom is equipped with an overhead projection system or a broadcast function that allows each student's screen to be seen by others.

Suggestions for College Success

Going to college can be a demanding experience. One of the most difficult aspects of college for many students is that the resources and structures they depended on in high school to keep them on track are no longer there. College instructors expect students to work on their own, be prepared for each class, and meet deadlines. The following are some suggestions on how to succeed in a college course:

1. Read the syllabus and keep it handy. The syllabus describes the course and lets you know what will be required of you all semester. Be prepared for each class by reading your assignments and completing your written work. Pay special attention to the dates on which papers are due or exams are scheduled. Many instructors will not accept late papers or give make-up exams.

2. Bring a notebook to class every day. Make sure you label each class session with the date. Learn to record the most important material that is presented in each class. If you try to record every word the instructor says, you will miss out on participating in the class. On the other hand, do not fall into the trap of taking no notes at all. If your instructor will allow

(continued)

you to tape record each class, that can be helpful, as well, but it should not replace notetaking completely. Also, devote a section of your notebook to keep any handouts you receive and store all the material you have done for a class. Do not throw anything away until the course is over!

3. Bring your textbooks to class every day. Many times, instructors refer to the textbooks even when no reading material has been assigned that day.

4. Read your books with a pen or highlighter in hand. Underline important words, phrases, or sentences. Write notes to yourself in the margins. In this way, you will become more actively involved in what you are reading, and rereading will be much more productive.

5. Read your assignments more than once whenever possible. Rarely will you absorb all the meaning from a text from just one reading. Particularly difficult passages may require several readings. When you receive assignments that require written responses, be sure to follow the directions. Ask questions if you need anything clarified.

6. Use a dictionary, not just when you write to look up spellings but also when you read to look up the meanings of words. This is one of the best ways to improve your reading comprehension and expand your vocabulary.

7. Participate in class! Sit near the front of the classroom, and contribute to discussions whenever appropriate. Get to know other members of your class and exchange phone numbers. This way, if you miss a class, you can find out what happened while you were absent and will be prepared when you return. If you return to class unprepared, you essentially miss that class, as well.

8. Join with other members of your class to form study groups that meet on a regular basis to discuss issues raised in class, go over homework assignments, and prepare for exams. The most productive study groups build on what each person in the group can contribute. Avoid groups in which only one person seems to be doing all the work. What you are looking for is a support system that works for all members of the group.

9. Discover what additional academic services are available to you on your campus. Know how to use your school's library and the various services it offers. Your school may have a tutoring center or a computer center that you can use, too. These services exist to help you, so use them.

10. Use your instructor as a resource. Many instructors hold office hours outside of class time just to help students. When you have questions or concerns that you cannot resolve by yourself, go to your instructor during his or her office hour. Do not be afraid to make that extra effort. Your instructor wants you to succeed.

EXERCISE 1.3

Continue the list started in Suggestions for College Success by adding your own ideas about how students can be more successful in college.

GRAMMAR INSTRUCTION AND EXERCISES:
Parts of Speech

After each word listed in a dictionary is an abbreviation, such as *n* or *adj* or even *interj*. Following each of these abbreviations are the definitions of the word. What do the abbreviations stand for, and why are they important?

These abbreviations represent different parts of speech. A part of speech determines how a word is used, how it is formed, where it is placed in a sentence, and what its function is. Each word in the English language belongs to at least one part of speech. It is generally recognized that there are eight parts of speech: nouns, pronouns, verbs, adjectives, adverbs, prepositions, conjunctions, and interjections.

You should remember that many words can function as more than one part of speech. That is why a dictionary may include several definitions of a word, arranged by the part of speech. For example, the word *rose,* as a noun, refers to a type of flower, but as a verb, it is the past tense for the word *rise.*

Nouns

Nouns name people, places, things, or ideas. **Common nouns** are the names of general people, places, or things. **Proper nouns** are the names of particular people, places, things, or ideas. **Collective nouns** are used for groups of people or things. For example:

Dr. Jones sailed to **Hawaii** last **year.**

Proper noun   Proper noun   Common noun

The **class** was unruly until the substitute **teacher** threatened

Collective noun   Common noun

the **students** with **homework.**

Common noun   Common noun

Sometimes verbs can function in sentences as nouns and are referred to as **verbals.** Gerunds (the *-ing* form) and infinitives (the *to* form) are two types of verbals. Here are two examples:

Swimming is an excellent form of exercise. I have been **swimming**

three times this week.

Swimming is a noun in the first sentence but not in the second.

Brad likes **to hike** in the hills behind campus.

To hike is a noun because it names an activity.

Verbals may also function as adjectives or adverbs. (See pages 352–54 for further discussion of verbals. See page 324 for further discussion of nouns.)

Pronouns

Pronouns are words that substitute for nouns. Pronouns that substitute for the names of people or things are called **personal pronouns.** Sometimes personal pronouns show possession (such as *my, mine, his,* *her, hers, their,* or *theirs*). The personal pronouns in the following sentences are printed in bold type:

> Mr. Arnold, the lawyer, told Virginia **she** had to get married before **her** thirtieth birthday in order to receive **her** inheritance.

> Raymond took **his** son to the park where **they** had a picnic.

> Investing in the stock market frightened **him**, so Dr. Zumwalt bought gold and silver instead.

Another type of pronoun is a **relative pronoun**. Relative pronouns introduce dependent clauses and include words such as *that, these, those, which, where, when, who,* and *whom.* Note the relative pronouns in the following sentences:

> The detective determined **that** the robbery had been done by rank amateurs.

> The carpenters **who** work for my uncle learned their craft in Germany.

> She hid her jewelry **where** no one could find it.

(See pages 336–37 for a discussion of dependent clauses. See pages 325–27 for further discussion of pronouns.)

Verbs

Verbs are words that describe actions or states of being.

> The doctor **touched** the sore spot.
> > Action

> Kyle **discovered** the point of the lecture after reviewing his notes.
> > Action

> My good friend Joseph Ho **is** a physician.
> > State of being

(See pages 327–28 for further discussion of verbs.)

Adjectives

Adjectives modify or describe nouns or pronouns.

> The **tiny** infant wailed loudly.

> Jason took off his **dusty** boots before entering the house.

> The **last** one to leave the room should turn off the lights.

Sometimes proper nouns can serve as adjectives.

> The **Notre Dame** football team is the best-known college team in the country.

> **Giorgio Armani** sunglasses have proved to be quite popular this year.

(See pages 328 and 367–70 for further discussion of adjectives.)

Adverbs

Adverbs modify verbs, adjectives, and even other adverbs. Often adverbs can be made from adjectives by adding the suffix *-ly*. For instance:

> Yvonne is a **quick** runner.
>
> Adjective

> Yvonne runs **quickly**.
>
> Adverb

Adverbs explain the where, when, and how of a sentence.

> Jacob **successfully** runs a business with over fifty employees.

> There was **certainly** no guarantee that Rosa would be admitted to a prestigious college.

> **Clearly**, Jessica was next in line for a promotion.

(See pages 328–29 and 367–70 for further discussion of adverbs.)

Prepositions

Prepositions show the relationships between nouns or pronouns and the rest of sentences. Often the relationship involves time or space.

> We will meet **after** my last class.
>
> The oil filter fell **underneath** the car and rolled **to** the center of the garage.
>
> The customs officials searched **through** the luggage to find suspicious bags.

(See pages 329–30 for further discussion of prepositions.)

Conjunctions

Conjunctions are words that link words, phrases, or clauses. Conjunctions include two types: coordinating and subordinating. The **coordinating conjunctions** link equivalent parts of sentences. For example:

> Jack **and** Jill went up the hill.
>
> You had better eat your peas, **or** you won't get any dessert.
>
> Abbie wanted a better grade, **but** she wasn't willing to spend more time studying.

The **subordinating conjunctions** relate dependent clauses with independent clauses. (See pages 336–37 for a discussion of dependent and independent clauses.)

> Linh wanted to buy the blouse **because** the colors were just right for her.
>
> **Although** Richard is an expert at computer networks, he still has trouble programming his own VCR.
>
> **After** James had worked so hard on the exhibition of his paintings, he was depressed by the negative reviews.

(See pages 330–31 for further discussion of conjunctions.)

Interjections

Interjections are words or expressions that show emotion or feeling but are not part of the grammatical structures of sentences.

> **Ow**! I stubbed my toe!

> **Oh**, he's not sure what to do about that problem.

> Don't you love this music, **huh**?

(See page 331 for further discussion of interjections.)

EXERCISES   Using your dictionary, identify which parts of speech the following words can be. All the words listed can be used as more than one part of speech. For each part of speech possible for the word, write a sentence using the word as that part of speech.

> **For example:** *turn*

> "It's my **turn** to sing," said Patti.
>   Noun

> **Turn** the car around.
>   Verb

1. part
2. fence
3. well
4. race
5. cool
6. row
7. travel
8. orange
9. real
10. six

2 The Gathering Process

Finding Ideas and Prewriting

Here are some reasons students give for not wanting to learn to write:

- *"I don't need to know how to write. When I have my career, my secretary will do the writing for me."*
- *"If I need to say something to a friend, I never write letters. I just pick up the phone and call."*
- *"In the future, video communication will make writing obsolete."*
- *"In my field, no one does much writing. It's hands-on ability that counts."*
- *"I know my writing is terrible, so I just avoid classes that require essays."*
- *"The only thing I need to learn to write is my signature so I can sign checks."*

No matter what your major or career choice is, you will need to write. Perhaps you will need to fill out a report, write a proposal, or draft a letter to a customer—tasks that obviously require writing skills. Less obviously, you may need to explain in writing how to operate dangerous machinery or justify why you should get a pay increase. Even outside of school or work, writing is important, not only because it enhances your communication skills, but it also improves your thinking skills. However, to understand how all this works, you need to know what the writing process is and how to harness it.

The Impetus to Write

The writing process starts with the decision to write. What can provoke this decision? You may not even be aware of how often you find yourself writing outside of school. For example, consider the following:

■ **Personal diaries** are records of the daily events in one's life. Keeping your personal diary allows you to see what you did on any given day. Reading someone's diary can, in fact, tell you much about the person and his or her times. *The Diary of a Young Girl* by Anne Frank, for instance, has become a source of inspiration and insight into the horrors of the Holocaust in ways that history textbooks seldom are able. Some people keep personal planners that essentially serve the same purpose but use hour-by-hour notations to record meetings, phone calls, and important events.

■ A **journal** differs from a diary in that a journal records your thoughts. Journal writing is less concerned about recording the daily events of your life than your reflections about the world in which you live. Indeed, keeping a journal over the course of years can give insight into your own emotional and intellectual development. Many well-known people, such as former New York governor Mario Cuomo, have kept journals for most of their adult lives.

■ **Letters** are a way to communicate in business as well as in your personal life. Unlike conversations over the phone or in person, writing letters allows you to think about your topic, to carefully word your language, so that the receiver of your letter can in no way misunderstand you, as can happen so frequently in conversation. Before the era of electronic communications, letter writing developed into something almost like an art form. The personal letters of famous people are often collected and published because they can be so revealing, such as the correspondence between George and Martha Washington during the Revolutionary War. Today, you might find that some employers require a cover letter in addition to a résumé and job application, or you may need to file a letter of complaint or grievance in some business matter. E-mail is a form of letter writing, too!

■ **Listing** might seem like a mundane task, hardly worth noting here, but consider how often you make a list. You make lists of groceries you need to buy, things you need to do on the weekend, greeting cards that need to be sent, and people you want to invite to a party. If you realize that the activities involved in listing include critical and creative thinking skills, you may see the value of listing. After all, you must think critically to decide which food items to purchase, keeping in mind what is in your refrigerator, what foods you are low on, and what you will need in the coming days. You also need to think creatively about new food combinations you might like to try or how to account for the tastes of a finicky eater in the family.

■ **Creative writing** is an activity you may have started as a young child—inventing rhymes to put silly, new twists on the lines "Roses are red, violets are blue . . ." or sketching out a play for friends or family. Perhaps today you write poems for personal fulfillment or in hopes of publishing them. You might dream of writing the great American novel or the script of an Oscar-winning film. Indeed, creative writing can be either an enjoyable hobby or a serious profession.

As a student, your most common motive for writing is usually to complete an assignment from your instructor. At first, this hardly seems promising—especially if you take the attitude that you are writing under duress, strictly looking to get a good grade or, more commonly, to avoid a bad one. With this attitude, you seek to muddle through the process and produce a piece of writing without making too many mistakes.

Instead, if you look at each assignment as an opportunity to show what you have learned or to advance your point of view on a topic, you can create a paragraph or essay that is exciting, intelligent, and fun to read. Good writing does not come easily. This may confuse or surprise you. After all, since good writing is so easy to read and understand, it must have been easy to write, right? Most professional writers work hard at their craft, learning how to organize their thoughts and choose their words so that the writing only seems effortless. When you see only the polished, final product, it is easy to become discouraged when you compare professional writing to your own. If you look at how good writing is created, however, you can follow the same steps to create your own good writing.

Searching for Good Ideas

Good writing begins with good ideas. But how do you get good ideas? Many people think that if they just think hard, ideas will come. However, sitting in a room, staring at a blank wall is the worst way to find inspiration. You need to search actively—begin by looking at yourself.

Your Own Interests

Remember that your writing is a reflection of who you are. Putting on a mask and pretending to be someone you are not can make for very flat writing. What do you like to do? Your own activities can be a source of inspiration. Going to the movies, hitting the club scene, or playing with children are all activities that can lead to possible writing topics. What you need to do is be aware of what is happening around you. This may lead you to write about the scarcity of good roles for women in the movies, what new slang is being used by the young and the hip, or how games teach children constructive behavior.

One of the things you need to do when you are confronted with a writing topic is to ask questions such as What do I think about the topic? How does this interest me? Is there something from my own experience that I can relate to this topic? When prewriting is discussed later in this chapter, you will see several different techniques you can use to help generate ideas based on your own interests or personal experience.

The Electronic Media

Write about what's hot. If you do not know what the leading issues of the day are, turn on the television, listen to the radio, or surf the Internet. You can learn what topics have caught the imagination of the public. Why should this concern you? For starters, the presence of a great deal of discussion about an issue means that something important may be in the air: a new medical breakthrough, an election campaign, or an important development on the international scene. Perhaps the media are talking about fads: a new musical group, strange clothing fashions from Paris, or the latest diet craze. The news may even be gossipy: a popular movie star's naughty behavior, a lottery winner's fall into poverty, or which members of royalty are getting married and which are getting divorced. Not all these topics, of course, are suitable for classroom assignments, and sometimes topics can suffer from overexposure. These are best left untouched. But if you have a sense of the general issues of your time, you can add your own voice to the discussion.

Bookstores and Newsstands

Browsing through bookstores or newsstands is a pleasant and enjoyable diversion for many people, yet you may not recognize that this can also help you search for writing topics. Newspapers, magazines, and books often cover the same kinds of topics found in the electronic media, but they are usually able to give these topics a more thorough, detailed look. Remember, too, that there is a time factor involved with print media: newspapers have the most current information, magazines drag a little behind, and books, because of the length of time involved in writing and publishing them, are sometimes over a year behind. But with each of these media, the greater time delay is compensated for by the presence of more detail, analysis, and historical perspective.

Check out what is in your local newspaper—not only are important news topics covered, but interesting feature articles often include in-depth analyses of these topics. Human-interest stories can relay touching and emotional stories about people's experiences, such as a tragic story of a young woman struggling with ovarian cancer or a lighthearted look at the newest activities at a local seniors center.

Take a look at the cover of a magazine—it might suggest the latest hot topic that bears further investigation. Is there a growing trend among young people toward a certain look? Is a "has-been" entertainer making a surprising comeback with a new audience? Magazines tend to cover more popular topics and are accessible to almost any reader; journals are more specialized. Journals are written for audiences with advanced education and experience in particular subjects. Both types of periodicals can, however, be valuable to you in your search for topics. Not all magazines are equal—some tend to be breathy, uncritical tributes to their subjects, such as Hollywood gossip rags or fashionably faddish magazines.

Sit down with a book and glance through it. What is it about? Who wrote it? Why was it written? Is it interesting to you? A dedicated reader can get virtually lost in a bookstore while exploring the worlds that exist inside the covers of each and every book. Some bookstores even encourage this behavior by including coffee stands, lounge chairs, and even live (but quiet) entertainment. Take advantage! Study the best-seller lists, both fiction and nonfiction. Look at the discount tables. Buy a few books to take home and enjoy. Let the work of other writers inspire you in your own writing.

Libraries

Libraries are a writer's best friend, and librarians run a close second. Perhaps you think of the library as a dull, stuffy place that only drudges find appealing. Look again. A library contains information on nearly every topic under the sun. It is hard to imagine a better source of ideas and information. You can browse through the stacks, looking at book titles, or seat yourself in the magazine section and scan the titles there. Find out where the newspaper and magazine rack is; learn to use the catalog system, whether it be on cards or on computers; and investigate the periodical indexes available to you. You can even scan the listings in the *Library of Congress Subject Headings* reference guide to see how many subjects, topics, and subtopics exist in the library. Acquaint yourself with your campus library early in the term so that you can take advantage of it immediately.

Classrooms

Take note of the issues that come up in class. What has the instructor talked about or lectured on? What have students discussed? What have you read about? Many times, simply paying attention to what is going on in class can give you ideas for writing. Do not just copy or imitate what people are talking about—use it as a springboard for your own ideas. If your instructor has assigned reading on the dangers of swimming alone, that may lead you think about the dangers of swimming while intoxicated, which could lead you to contemplate the role of alcohol abuse in boating accidents. Your final product may even include a call to regulate the consumption of alcohol in motor boats in the same way that drinking alcohol in automobiles is regulated.

Always be on the lookout for new ideas. The world of human experience is very large indeed, and unless your instructor has given you a specific topic or has defined limits for an assignment, you will need to be aware of and explore the possibilities.

Generate a list of ideas that you might want to write about. Search through your own activities, inspirations, and interests. Visit a bookstore or library. Access the Internet or build on an idea you heard about in another class. When ideas come to you, remember them, and add them to your list.

Prewriting Techniques

As you search for topics, try to stretch your imagination. Once you think you have found a topic, think about what you already know and feel about it. This may seem odd: Don't you know what you know? Aren't you aware of how you feel? These questions point to an important problem that all writers face: How do you explore the depths of your own knowledge, understanding, and emotion beyond what is in your conscious thought? Much information is stored away in your brain's long-term memory and cannot be recalled without something to bring it to your attention. Fortunately, there are ways of doing just that. These techniques, to one degree or another, involve the use of creative thinking skills and critical thinking skills.

Brainstorming

Brainstorming is a technique that maximizes your creative thinking skills by using free association. **Free association** occurs when you think of one topic and that leads you to think of another. For instance, if you start with *white* as your topic, your next thought might be *black* or *snow* or *light*. When you brainstorm, you write down the ideas as they occur to you. You can do so in a haphazard fashion, paying no attention to the physical orientation of your writing on the page, or you can do so in an orderly fashion down the side of a page, creating a list.

The first technique, writing in a haphazard fashion, will lend itself to mapping. **Mapping** involves drawing lines between items from your brainstorming that seem to be connected in some meaningful way. The more you are able to draw lines and connect entries, the more your ideas are interrelated. Mapping also gives you a good sense of what you seem to know a lot about. The more entries you have on a given idea, the easier it will be to write about that idea. Consequently, mapping also helps point out what you do not know. When you examine your mapping, you may find orphans, or ideas that are unrelated to any other idea. These could be areas that you might want to explore further in another brainstorming session.

Figure 2.1 is an example of brainstorming in a haphazard fashion. This is done on the topic of *nutrition*.

FIGURE 2.1
Sample of
Brainstorming
(Topic: *Nutrition*)

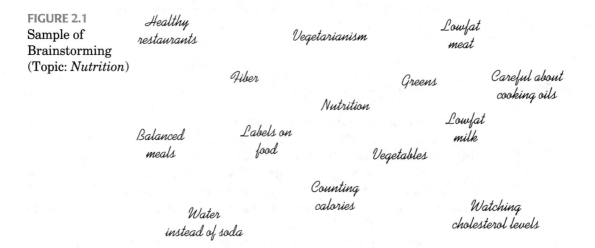

Figure 2.2 shows the results of mapping the brainstorming shown in Figure 2.1.

FIGURE 2.2
Sample of
Mapping
(Topic: *Nutrition*)

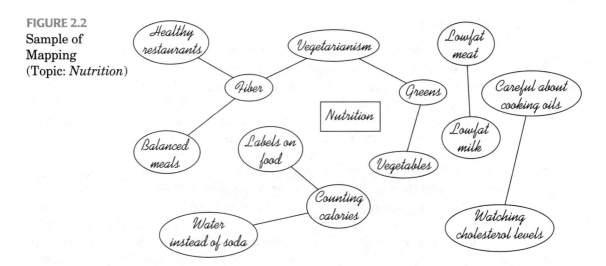

EXERCISE 2.1

Brainstorm for ten minutes by writing down everything you can think of about one of the following topics. After you have completed your brainstorming session, create a map by grouping various items together.

car problems   fresh foods
musical groups   furniture
fashions   computers

Listing, which is another type of brainstorming, is an excellent way to discover what you know. When you create a list, the length of the list will make you aware of just how much you do or do not know about a subject. Usually, you begin a list with a general topic, such as *the environment.* You might come up with a list like this:

dirty beaches need cleaning

air pollution from cars

recycling

costs of cleaning

the rain forest disappearing

costs to businesses

tearing up undeveloped land

Greenpeace

spotted owl controversy

oil spills—like in the Persian Gulf War

Creating such a list not only allows you to see what you know, but it also can lead you into other areas. For instance, the item *recycling* could be used as the general topic for a new, more specific list, starting the process over again. Another possibility is to group together similar items on the list, in much the same manner as mapping.

EXERCISE 2.2

Brainstorm for ten minutes by making a list on one of the following topics. After you have created your list, check to see if you can group various items together. Did you find that you were able to generate several related ideas? Are there items on the list that could be used as other topics for brainstorming?

childhood friends	status symbols
travel destinations	home repairs
religious customs	contents of your backpack or purse

Freewriting

Freewriting is similar to brainstorming in that it, too, relies on free association. As in brainstorming, you begin with a general topic to consider. The difference is that instead of just writing down isolated ideas in a vertical list or in phrases scattered about on a page, you write a continuous flow of ideas that runs left to right across the page, just as when you normally write. Unlike your normal writing, however, you do not worry about rules of grammar, spelling, punctuation, or sentence formation, and you do not stop to erase mistakes or consider what you are writing. Do not be concerned about matters of correctness; focus only on writing down ideas as fast as they come to you. The technique requires that you write without stopping so that free association can occur. If you do stop to analyze your material, you are using a fundamentally different thought process—one that pulls from your critical thinking side, not your creative thinking side.

Another key to successful freewriting is to freewrite only for a predetermined period of time. Do five-minute sessions to start until you get used to the technique; then try it for ten or fifteen minutes. You should either have a timer, such as on an alarm watch or kitchen clock, or have someone time you. You do not want to have to stop to look at your watch—that only subverts the process. Only if you are free of worry and concern will you be able to freewrite.

Here is an example of a freewriting session done on the topic *the death penalty*. The errors have been left in to show that correctness is not a concern in freewriting.

I just saw <u>Dead Man Walking</u> last night and boy did it make me think a lot about the death penalty I mean I've always been for it because I figure they get what they've got coming after killing people like that and I think I still feel that way but last night I was really upset because the movie really showed how the guy was a human he really was'nt a good guy and he was guilty he'd really done a horrible, horrible thing I don't have any kids yet I think about the times at night when your alone and someone could come up and kill you but the death penalty did'nt stop those kids from getting killed it just added another death that's what the movie said anyway I think the death penalty is more revenge than anything else although why is revenge such a bad thing? after all shouldn't we want revenge, blood for blood, all that? People want to feel like something happened to that guy and prison just isn't enough in some ways it punishes the family of the prisoner though because the prisoner is as good as dead in prison anyway I think that part hit me the hardest that and how hard it is to die

Once you have completed your freewriting, you are ready for a looping exercise. **Looping** is a variation on any prewriting technique in which you use part of what you have written in one prewriting session as the basis for the start of another session.

When you loop with freewriting, begin by reading what you have written in your first session. See what you like and dislike. Underline interesting passages. You then use these underlined passages as the general topic for a second freewrite. Write the passage as the first words of a new freewrite. Reset your time and start again.

Freewrite for five minutes on one of the following topics. Once you have finished, read over your freewriting and underline the passage you like best. Then freewrite for another five minutes, this time using your underlined passage as your new topic.

high school dropouts	photography
holiday decorations	cooking for one
babies	video games

Asking Questions

The adage says, "The only stupid question is the one you don't ask." Learning begins with asking questions, especially questions you cannot answer without further investigation. Whenever you confront a new topic, you should write down all the questions you have regarding it. If the topic is one you are familiar with, then your questions are likely to be very specific and detailed; if you are not familiar with your topic, you may find yourself asking very broad, general questions.

When you ask questions, you can work either in your journal or on a separate sheet of paper, just as in brainstorming or freewriting. Again, a good technique is to work within a set time limit. Devote five, ten, or fifteen minutes and begin writing down questions in a list. The questions do not have to be in any logical order—just write down the questions as they come to mind. Free association may take your questions into areas you have never thought about before. Here is an example of a list of questions generated for the topic *space exploration:*

Why explore space?
What is happening now in space exploration?
What will happen in the future?
Is it worth the cost?
What have we learned from the past?
Is the money better spent elsewhere?
Was going to the moon really worth the money, time, and effort?

What did we learn from the Challenger disaster
  in 1986?
Are we willing to risk more lives? For what?
Will international cooperation make space exploration
  cheaper for the United States?
Will the public benefit from new space technology? How?

This student has generated a number of different topics about space exploration. Indeed, he could examine this list and see ideas regarding the goals, costs, risks, and history of space exploration. He could loop by using one of her new topics, such as the *cost of space exploration,* as the basis of a new list.

Whenever you review your list of questions with an eye toward writing a paragraph or essay, ask yourself what other questions someone might ask *you,* not just the questions you ask yourself. Anticipate the questions an instructor might ask about the topic. Be prepared to have these questions take you in new directions.

EXERCISE 2.4

For five minutes, write down all the questions you can think of on one of the following topics. Review your list to see which questions might lead to good writing topics.

graffiti vandals   prison life
horse racing   American history
pagers   credit cards

Clustering

Clustering allows you to explore the relationships between a general subject and specific topics within that subject. The technique begins somewhat like brainstorming. Take a blank sheet of paper, write your general subject in the center of the page, and draw a circle around it. Then, leading from the circle, draw a line outward and write down a word or phrase associated with that general subject. Do that for as many items as you can think of that are directly associated with the general subject. Then, from *those* topics, draw lines outward and write down words or phrases associated with those topics. Notice, as you do

FIGURE 2.3
Sample of
Clustering
(Topic: *Pastimes*)

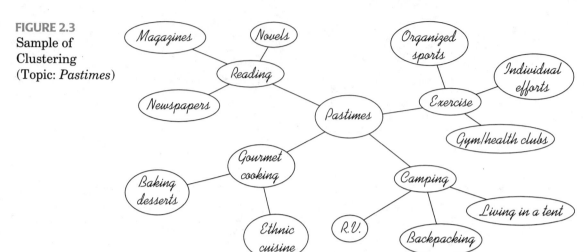

this activity, that your ideas become more and more specific the further you move from the circle. Also, by using this method of association, you have already grouped your ideas into major divisions and subdivisions. Examine Figure 2.3 to see an example.

In this example, the general subject is *pastimes*. As you can see, the writer came up with several first-level ideas associated with pastimes, including exercise, reading, gourmet cooking, and camping. Breaking off from that level are several other specific topics. For instance, on the *exercise* branch are *organized sports, individual efforts,* and *gym/health clubs.* Each of these could be developed further.

To continue the pattern of thought, you can also loop with clustering. You do this by selecting one of your specific items to be the new center. For instance, you might take *exercise* to start a new clustering, or you could decide to begin on an even more specific level and start with *gym/health clubs.* Such a clustering might lead to Figure 2.4. As with brainstorming or freewriting, the looping technique can be used at any level to generate more ideas.

FIGURE 2.4
Sample of
Specific
Clustering
(Topic: *Pastimes*)

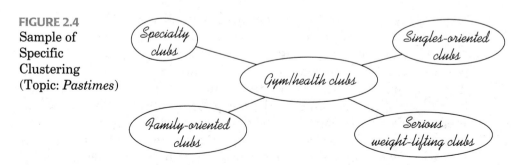

EXERCISE 2.5

Make a cluster diagram on one of the following topics. Then examine the diagram you created, choose one of the specific topics, and make a second cluster diagram with it as the new topic at the center.

professional sports	movies
the dangers of smoking	clothing
ethnic foods	mother/daughter relationships

Outlining

Outlining, which is the most formal of the prewriting techniques, is usually not the first technique to be used. **Outlining** is a way to understand the relationship that your ideas have with each other and the overall topic. That means that you normally have already been generating and focusing ideas before you begin to outline. However, outlining can be important for establishing a sense of order and level of importance among your ideas. This technique can also show you where gaps in understanding your topic remain.

You can write an informal (or scratch) outline that uses broad strokes to cover what you will be writing about, or you can use far greater detail in a formal outline. Either way, you will gain an understanding of what to include in your writing and in what order. An informal outline is best used for paragraphs or short essays. It includes a sentence that describes what the paragraph or essay is about, and then, using phrases, it lists only the major items to be discussed. Consider the following informal outline that one student, Carolyn, wrote:

Television has ruined professional sports.
— Too much money
— Emphasis on personalities, not team play
— Overexposure of teams and players

Such a brief outline may not appear to be helpful to you at first glance, but consider that it accomplishes three necessary things: (1) the introductory sentence shows the specific topic Carolyn is writing about, (2) Carolyn can see that each of the items she will address relates directly to that topic, and (3) Carolyn can arrange the items in a logical order.

If Carolyn wanted to develop her outline in greater detail, she could write a formal outline. A formal outline is generally more detailed and is usually written in complete sentences. It is often more suitable for long essays or term papers, but a writer may also use it to clarify the organization of a shorter essay. A formal outline is created by dividing the essay into major sections, which are indicated by capital roman numerals (I, II, III, . . .). Within each major section are the subsections, which are indicated by capital letters (A, B, C, . . .). Additional subsections within the higher sections are shown with arabic numerals (1, 2, 3, . . .) and subsections within an arabic numeral are indicated by lower-case letters (a, b, c, . . .). A formal outline for Carolyn's essay might look like this:

Television has ruined professional sports.

    I. *There is too much money in professional sports, thanks to the presence of television.*

       A. *Salaries and profits are astronomical.*

       B. *Players are more interested in playing easy and making money rather than playing hard and risking potential injury.*

       C. *Strikes have disrupted professional sports over the issue of money, alienating the fans.*

    II. *Television has created an emphasis on personalities, not team play.*

       A. *Close-ups and interview shows encourage "hot dogging" rather than solid play.*

       B. *Endorsements go to flashy players with catchy nicknames, leaving other players jealous and resentful.*

       C. *Players try to increase their individual performance statistics even when sacrificing themselves would be better for the team.*

III. Television has created pressure to market sports, leading to overexposure of certain teams and players.

A. Rather than trust the appeal of a sport, television now encourages the marketing of certain teams and players to maximize fan appeal.

B. Colorful uniforms and dramatic or unusual highlight sequences entice fans.

C. Championship teams get promoted throughout the country, leading to the decline of regional loyalties for struggling, hard-luck clubs.

This formal outline could be developed to another level of detail. Underneath each of the sentences that begins with a capital letter, you would use an arabic numeral (1, 2, 3, . . .) and write a complete sentence for each detail you wanted to include.

The informal outline is best suited for shorter works, whereas the formal outline can be reserved for longer works. Each item in the informal outline is only a brief description of what will eventually be included. The formal outline requires a great deal more precision, but you will find it quite helpful in developing your thoughts. Once you have completed an outline, you are truly ready to begin composing a paragraph or essay.

Don't forget that outlining is a prewriting tool, one to be used as a way of fleshing out your ideas. An outline does very little good if it is created after the final draft of a paragraph or essay has been written. Revising your outline during the writing of your draft, however, can be an excellent idea. Rewriting your outline to reflect the changes you make during the drafting process will give you a sense of how those changes affect the work, overall.

EXERCISE 2.6

Select one of the topics that you generated in Exercises 2.1 through 2.5 and write an informal or scratch outline.

Once you have completed that task, expand your informal outline into a formal outline.

Keeping a Journal

When you take a science or mathematics class, you may be asked to keep all your notes and homework in a binder. Your instructor might even require that you turn in your binder periodically so that your laboratory work or homework can be checked. The principle behind this practice is that such a record of your work will indicate how your knowledge and understanding in certain fundamentals of the field grow and how additional knowledge is built from those fundamentals.

Think of a journal as a laboratory book for English. A journal is a running record of personal experiments in your use of language and the development of your ideas. A journal, then, is not the place where you write about what you ate for lunch that day. A journal explores your own thoughts and reactions to your experiences. You have total freedom in your journal to express your sincere responses to your own emotions. Be sure, though, that you date each entry so that the journal is in chronological order.

If your instructor has asked you to keep a journal for your English class, remember that your writings should be focused on matters that concern the class. As your journal entries increase in number and variety, they can be a wellspring of information and inspiration. In addition to the journal exercises in this book, you should do *all* your prewriting assignments in your journal. That way, you have your prewriting materials together to help you with your writing assignments.

The journal-writing questions in this book are designed to help you generate ideas to use as you work through each chapter. Additionally, you may want to answer prereading questions in your journal before reading a professional writing sample. Such prereading questions are a way for you to think about the material before you begin the act of reading, and they can be useful in guiding you toward writing topics that you will find relevant and interesting.

JOURNAL EXERCISE

Spend five minutes writing down all the words you can think of that describe yourself. Then look at these words and ask yourself, Does my writing reflect these traits?

COMPUTER EXERCISE

Brainstorm or freewrite for five minutes on one of the topics from Exercises 2.1 through 2.3. Then select another student to be your writing partner and switch seats with or transfer your computer file to your partner. Examine your partner's brainstorming material briefly. Freewrite for five minutes again, this time using your partner's writing as the basis for your freewriting. After the second freewriting period is over, return to your seat or your computer file and read what your partner has written. Notice the different directions and perspectives on your own writing that your partner has taken. You may want to save *both* versions of your freewriting for future interest.

GRAMMAR INSTRUCTION AND EXERCISES:
Capitalization and End Punctuation

Read the following sentences:

> jason walked over to the doctor standing by the bedside, he asked, "will she live" the doctor shook her head "no" he cried and started sobbing.

Now read the sentences with capitalization and end punctuation added:

> Jason walked over to the doctor. Standing by the bedside, he asked, "Will she live?" The doctor shook her head. "No!" he cried and started sobbing.

Notice how much easier the second passage is to read. That is because the second passage uses capitalization and end punctuation, whereas the first does not. Capitalization indicates the beginning of every sentence, and end punctuation shows the end of each sentence. Additional questions and emotions are shown by using a question mark and an exclamation point.

Capitalization

You may find capitalization can be tricky because it is sometimes overused. Here are three simple rules to remember with capitalization:

1. Capitalize the first word in a sentence.
2. Capitalize the first word in a sentence that is a direct quote.
3. Capitalize all proper nouns, job titles, and titles of creative works.

The First Word in a Sentence

Capitalize the first word in a sentence. If the first word is a number, write the number out, unless the number represents a date.

The performance dragged on for over three hours.

Sixty-three people died in the plane crash.

1992 was an important year for women in national politics.

A Direct Quote

Capitalize the first word in a sentence that is quoted directly, even if it is not the beginning of the entire sentence.

One red rose held firmly in his hand, the young man asked, "**Will** you marry me tomorrow?"

Of course, a quotation that begins a sentence should be capitalized as well.

"**The** buck stops here" is a famous motto.

Proper Nouns

Be sure to capitalize all proper nouns, jobs titles, and titles of creative works.

Santa Barbara is a beautiful city on the coast north of **Los Angeles**.

The officials from the **American Medical Association** met with **Dr. Scott Puppo** to discuss charges of incompetence.

I read the book **The Invisible Man** by Ralph Ellison last year.

(See page 397 for a discussion of underlining. See pages 379–82 for a further discussion of capitalization.)

End Punctuation

The end of a sentence is marked with a period, a question mark, or an exclamation point.

The Period

The period is a neutral mark to be used at the end of a sentence. Use it if no particular emphasis is needed.

> There are currently nine judges on the Supreme Court, but originally there were only six.

> Please put that knife back where it belongs.

> The manager asked the umpire if he needed an appointment with an optometrist to correct his vision.

(See page 385 for further discussion of periods.)

The Question Mark

Use a question mark after a direct question is posed.

> Who is that masked man?

> May I please have a second helping?

Be sure to include a question mark when you quote a direct question.

> Freud asked, "What do women want?"

> "When do you think it will stop raining?" wondered Sally as she looked out the window.

(See pages 385–86 for further discussion of questions marks.)

The Exclamation Point

The exclamation point is used to express a strong feeling or emotion.

Stop! Thief!

Watch out!

Ed McMahon says I could win millions of dollars!

(See page 386 for further discussion of exclamation points.)

EXERCISES   Rewrite the following sentences using proper capitalization and end punctuation.

1. "the pie in the oven is ready," mike said

2. "ouch it's hot" he exclaimed, jumping away

3. sally rushed over and asked, "did you burn yourself"

4. mike answered, "boy, that sure hurts"

5. "let me look at it," said Sally "do you have some ice"

6. "that's what I get for being too anxious, I suppose," muttered mike under his breath

7. "Thanks," he said after sally put ice on his finger then he sat down at the table

8. "can you get the pie for me" asked mike

9. sally put on some mittens she reached into the oven and pulled out the pie then she set it carefully on a hot pad

10. "now," she said, "we can eat"

3 The Building Blocks

Basic Structures of the Paragraph

Ask yourself the following questions:

- *What is a paragraph?*
- *How is a paragraph different from an essay?*
- *What is the purpose of a paragraph?*
- *Do all paragraphs do the same things?*
- *What should I say in a paragraph?*
- *Can any sentence be in any paragraph?*
- *Are there parts to a paragraph?*
- *How can I make a paragraph coherent?*
- *What should I say in a paragraph?*
- *Can I end a paragraph whenever I want to?*
- *How should I end a paragraph?*

Learning to write paragraphs is an important first step because paragraphs are the basic building blocks of essays. In the same way that a combination of letters can create a word, and words come together to create a sentence, paragraphs are put together to form an article or essay. However, there are rules surrounding how letters shape words. Not all letters in any combination create a word in the English language. When you combine letters together such as *s - p - e - t - i - a - n,* you can consult a dictionary to see if you have formed a word. (You have not.) With paragraphs, however, there are no easy answers about what is acceptable and what is not. There is no dictionary of paragraphs. You have to judge the correctness or appropriateness of your paragraphs by some other means.

Another difficulty in determining paragraph correctness is that many people have been misled about the nature of paragraphs from reading newspapers and magazines. Because their readers may have trouble reading large blocks of dark print in narrow columns, newspaper editors take liberties with paragraphs. Seldom are newspaper paragraphs more than three sentences long, and many are only one or two. Numerous magazines also use shorter paragraphs as a way of making their printed pages more readable. For most of your assignments as a student, however, such brief paragraphs may be considered unacceptable by your instructor.

So, what is a paragraph and how long should it be? A **paragraph** is a group of sentences that discusses the same topic. All the sentences are relevant to the topic of the paragraph. In other words, there should be no sentence that discusses anything else. The paragraph should be as long as it needs to be to fully cover the topic presented. This means there is no set length for a paragraph; rather you should have a strong sense of when more needs to be said and when you have said enough. The topic of a paragraph is found in the topic sentence.

Topic Sentences

The smells of autumn in my childhood are still with me. Freshly cut grass reminds me of the first days of Youth League football practice. The smell of burning leaves brings back images of my father, rake in hand, making a pile of red and orange, a pile I would throw myself into many times before he told me to stand aside so he could burn it. Newly laid asphalt on the streets takes me back to when my school's playground would be resurfaced for the start of each school year. Even the smell of mothballs makes me think of sweaters my mother pulled out of stuffy closets as autumn began to give way to winter.

This paragraph's topic can be found in the very first sentence: *The smells of autumn in my childhood are still with me.* This sentence is the

topic sentence of the paragraph because it states the topic that the paragraph discusses: *the smells of autumn*. For the topic sentence to be effective, it must be specific and direct, and it must express a point of view or argument.

Being Specific

Look at the following topic sentence:

> Storms can be bad.

What does this sentence mean? The meaning is unclear because the term *bad* is vague. It may convey several meanings: being morally corrupt or evil, having a defect or flaw, or containing a measure of severity. If you are interested in writing about the dangers that storms can pose, another, more specific word should be found.

> Storms can be dangerous.

This sentence is better, but too many questions still remain unanswered: Dangerous to whom? And just what type of storms are you writing about?

> Storms off the north Atlantic coast can be dangerous to fishing
>
> boats that work far from shore.

Now the topic sentence is very specific, leaving little room for doubt. Not all your topic sentences will need this kind of detail, but all topic sentences need to be as specific as you can make them.

The Crystalline Word

One way to make sure your topic sentence is specific is to choose the **crystalline word,** which is a word that contains the main idea or attitude that you're expressing. Take a look at this topic sentence:

> Lonely people should adopt pets.

In the sentence, the crystalline word is *lonely*. Without that word, the sentence loses any kind of distinctive edge or attitude. Instead, the sentence would be bland, a virtual platitude that is too broad to be realistic:

People should adopt pets.

Be on the lookout for the crystalline word in a sentence, a paragraph, or an essay. Remember that the crystalline word encompasses the essence of what is being said. It best expresses the core ideas present in the writing, no matter what the length.

Being Direct

Don't back into your topic sentence by asking questions when you should be making statements. Although asking rhetorical questions of the reader can be effective in some situations, using a question as a topic sentence can create problems.

What makes a good marriage?

The answer to your question may not be immediately obvious to your reader. You put the burden on the reader to come up with the response that you want him or her to have, but many responses are possible for such a question. Indeed, the biggest weakness in asking a rhetorical question is that you assume your reader will come to the same answer that you do. Often, though, this is not the case.

A good marriage requires respect, trust, and good communication

between partners.

This topic sentence is much better since it now makes a statement rather than poses a question.

Your topic sentence should not try to tackle more than one topic, unless you're specifically comparing or contrasting two topics. Trying to tackle two topics in one paragraph can lead to serious problems with paragraph structure. Instead, different topics should be discussed in different paragraphs. Note the following sentence:

Carrie is a wonderful mother, and I think she needs to get

a new car.

This sentence seems nonsensical. Only if you can draw some connection between motherhood and cars can this topic sentence make any sense.

Carrie is usually a wonderful mother, but she endangers her child

by driving that old Pinto.

You can now proceed to describe the dangers of driving old Pintos with young children inside. The connection between motherhood and cars is now apparent. If no connection between topics exists, they should be split into separate topic sentences for separate paragraphs.

Expressing a Point of View or Argument

By giving your sentence a point of view about a topic, you are creating an **argument**. You may instinctively shy away from the word *argument* because it implies unpleasant confrontation and disruption. Indeed, some cultures encourage the avoidance of public confrontation and argument. But *argument* is used here to mean a point that you're trying to make. To argue, in this sense, means that you're attempting to advance some point of view by providing some basis of support. No sense of hostility need be implied. (This can occur, however—read the editorials and opinion pieces in your local newspaper to experience that.) In a classroom setting, however, you're expected to conduct your argument in an intelligent, reasoned fashion. Emotion can play a part, but it should not be overwhelming.

To understand argument, look at the following sentence:

There are seven distinct colors in a rainbow.

Such a topic sentence contains no strong sense of argument. The proof of how many colors are in a rainbow will be relatively simple. A similar problem exists in the following sentence:

There are seven distinct colors in a rainbow: red, orange, yellow, green, blue, indigo, and violet.

The trouble with this topic sentence is that now you have nowhere else to go. There is no logical next step, no room for development. Factual statements that are easily verified do not make good topic sentences. Either a statement is true or it is not. There is nothing else to say.

Some exceptions to this may be made for strictly expository writing, such as that found in science textbooks and encyclopedias. In expository writing, the writer attempts to avoid argument and instead presents a collection of facts without bias. Usually, topic sentences in expository prose are not expressing simple facts but are discussing complicated or sophisticated thinking that needs to be developed more fully.

Even in expository prose, there are **inferences,** which are interpretations based on the observation of fact. Since such statements are interpretations, they are arguable. For instance, different scientists can look at the same data about dinosaurs and infer different causes for dinosaur extinction. Even without explicit inferences, an undercurrent of argument always exists in expository prose because the authors hope and expect that their readers will find what they say to be true.

JOURNAL EXERCISE

What would you like to know more about? Spend ten minutes writing a list of things that stimulate your curiosity. Include subjects not only from your school work but also from your personal life. Then write about the steps you can take to learn more about each item on your list.

Using an Outline to Develop Your Argument

So, an argument is your main idea or opinion—one that you're choosing to prove as true. On the level of the paragraph, your topic sentence states that idea, and the rest of your paragraph works to show the reader that what you say is true. On the level of the essay, your thesis sentence states the idea, and the rest of your essay works to show the reader that what you say is true. (See Chapter 9 for instruction on the thesis sentence.) When you looked at the informal (scratch) outline in Chapter 2, under the heading Outlining, you saw a single sentence that expressed the main idea for a paragraph, followed by three words or phrases expressing points of discussion about the main idea. One sample outline looked like this:

> *Television has ruined professional sports.*
> *—— Too much money*
> *—— Emphasis on personalities, not team play*
> *—— Overexposure of certain teams and players*

In this example, the sentence *Television has ruined professional sports* is the topic sentence. If the writer wanted to develop a single paragraph with that as her topic sentence, she might have written something like this:

> *Television has ruined professional sports. For one thing, television has added so much revenue to sports that players' salaries have become too high. Television also rewards "hot dogs" who attract attention with their feats, not the dull, boring players whose sacrifices lead to winning games. Finally, certain teams and players—usually last year's champions—get shown on screens all around the country while local teams and players on lesser teams are ignored. So, television has basically enriched players and owners but left the fans impoverished.*

The argument is contained within a single paragraph, trying to prove to the reader that *Television has ruined professional sports.*

The crystalline word also helps you to identify the argument in your topic sentence. *Ruined* is the crystalline word in the topic sentence about television and professional sports. Indeed, if you substitute another verb for *ruined,* such as *hindered* or *hurt,* you substantially change the sense of the argument.

What, then, makes a good topic sentence? The topic sentence should be specific, addressing one topic only: the topic that will be discussed in the paragraph. Second, the topic sentence should be a direct statement, not a question or even a quotation. Questions tend to leave your reader hanging, not always sure what the answer is. Instead, statements should express your point of view exactly. Quotations from other writers usually are not a good idea because you should present your own point of view, not someone else's.

EXERCISE 3.1

Read the following sentences and indicate which ones would make effective topic sentences. Rewrite any that would not.

1. My classroom has thirty-three people in it.

2. The French are reputed to be the rudest people in the world, but my vote goes to the Swiss.

3. An airport can be an important civic asset or a liability.

4. Would you want a former hippie for a father?

5. Bring that cat here!

6. Gold is the best investment in uncertain times.

7. The bombing of the federal building in Oklahoma City shook many people's sense of safety in public places.

8. Mother/daughter relationships sometimes defy the expectations of even the closest observers.

9. Kay was born in Virginia in 1963.

10. The scandal rocked the small town.

EXERCISE 3.2

Write an effective topic sentence for each of the following topics:

the Monday blues   interviewing for a job
a holiday celebration   the view from my bedroom window
fads   night people
embarrassing moments   patriotism
car mechanics   boring people

Choosing Where to Place the Topic Sentence

Choosing the Topic Sentence as the First Sentence

In the sample paragraphs you have already seen, the topic sentence was the first sentence of each paragraph. This is often the case because the topic sentence is an effective introduction to the paragraph. When you choose to begin your paragraph with your topic sentence, you're giving yourself the luxury of having the topic sentence perform double duty: to state the topic of the paragraph and to introduce the reader to that paragraph. For this reason, you will discover that having the topic sentence be the first sentence of your essay is often your best choice. Examine the following paragraph written twice, first with the topic sentence at the end and then with the topic sentence at the start of the paragraph:

Amongst the light breeds can be found Arabians, thoroughbreds, Asians, Anglo-Arabs, and Americans. Heavy-breed horses include English Shires, Clydesdales, and Austrian Pinzgauers. Ponies include any horses other than Arabians that are relatively small, including Welsh, Shetland, and Argentine. **Horses can be divided into several different breeds, including light breeds, heavy breeds, and ponies.**

Horses can be divided into several different breeds, including light breeds, heavy breeds, and ponies. Amongst the light breeds can be found Arabians, thoroughbreds, Asians, Anglo-Arabs, and Americans. Heavy-breed horses include English Shires, Clydesdales, and Austrian Pinzgauers. Ponies include any horses other than Arabians that are relatively small, including Welsh, Shetland, and Argentine.

The first example is awkward because it starts off listing types of horses. The reader wonders why there is such a list, and it is not until the end of the paragraph that the reader understands the topic. In the second paragraph, the topic sentence introduces the subject of horses as well as details just what will be discussed—types of horses.

Choosing the Topic Sentence as the Last Sentence

You can choose to leave the topic sentence for the end of your paragraph. This technique is generally used when the ideas in the paragraph are all leading to some general conclusion, which is stated in the last sentence of the paragraph. If you decide to use this method, you must remember to give your paragraph some sort of introduction so that your reader doesn't struggle to understand your topic. Otherwise, a reader approaching your paragraph will be confused. Because of these constraints, you may find that you will be limited in how often you can effectively use the topic sentence as the last sentence of a paragraph. Examine the following paragraph:

> Before you begin to make the cake, be sure that you start with all your ingredients on hand and that you preheat the oven to 350 degrees. Mix one cup of sugar with a quarter cup of melted butter until the mixture is creamy. Slowly add one quarter cup of melted baking chocolate. Then add the baking soda, baking powder, and cake flour. Pour into two eight-inch cake pans and pop them into the oven for twenty-five minutes. **You have now created Mom's wonderful chocolate cake.**

The first sentence of the paragraph helps to acquaint the reader with the topic of the sentence with the phrase *Before you begin to make the cake.* It signals to the reader what to expect, but it does not constitute the topic sentence. The final sentence of the paragraph serves as the topic sentence because all the sentences lead up to the conclusion stated in it—that you have baked a wonderful chocolate cake.

Still, the same paragraph could easily be rewritten with the topic sentence at the start of the paragraph. Examine this paragraph:

> **In order to create Mom's wonderful chocolate cake, just follow these directions.** Start with all your ingredients on hand and preheat the oven to 350 degrees. Mix one cup of sugar with a quarter cup of melted butter until the mixture is creamy. Slowly add one quarter cup of melted baking chocolate. Then add the baking soda, baking powder, and cake flour. Pour into two eight-inch cake pans and pop them into the oven for twenty-five minutes.

As you can tell from a quick comparison of the two paragraphs, the first paragraph is not appreciably better than the second paragraph. However, the second paragraph, with the topic sentence as the first sentence, seems clearer since it indicates better to the reader what the paragraph is about and what the reader should expect to discover in the paragraph.

Choosing the Topic Sentence in the Middle of the Paragraph

Occasionally you will find a writer will not put the topic sentence at the beginning or the end of a paragraph but will choose to put it somewhere in between. The danger with this technique is that a reader can easily mistake a different sentence for the topic sentence, thereby coming away from the paragraph with a slightly different message. Note the following example:

> Oscar Wilde once wrote, "Democracy simply means the bludgeoning of the people by the people for the people." But how can this be? Most of us in America grow up with the idea that democracy is not only a good form of government; it is the best. **Still, we must admit that democracy has had its troubles.** Poverty, racism, and drug abuse plague our cities, the rich get richer and the poor get poorer, and democratic governments often only assist in that equation. In a democratic government, the majority rules, but the majority is not always right. In spite of that, we must conclude that, as Wilde's countryman Winston Churchill once noted, "Democracy is the worst form of government except all those other forms that have been tried from time to time."

Here, the boldfaced sentence serves as the topic sentence of the paragraph about the troubles with democracy. Generally, your instructor will prefer that you not place the topic sentence in the middle of the paragraph until you have demonstrated that you can avoid confusing the reader.

Here is the same paragraph rewritten with the topic sentence as the first sentence:

> **We must admit that democracy has had its troubles.** Poverty, racism, and drug abuse plague our cities, the rich get richer and the poor get poorer, and democratic governments often only assist in that equation. As Oscar Wilde once wrote, "Democracy simply means the bludgeoning of the people by the people for the people." But how can this be? Most of us in America grow up with the idea

that democracy is not only a good form of government; it is the best. After all, in a democratic government, the majority rules. However, the majority is not always right. Still, we must conclude that, as Wilde's countryman Winston Churchill once noted, "Democracy is the worst form of government except all those other forms that have been tried from time to time."

This paragraph, now rearranged, focuses the reader's attention more strongly on the issue of the troubles with democracy. It avoids the problem inherent in beginning a paragraph with a quote (the difficulty of determining the writer's point of view instead of the quoted person's point of view). The paragraph is now more direct in presenting the writer's own viewpoint.

EXERCISE 3.3

Circle the topic sentence in each of the following paragraphs.

1.   The Toyota truck is a fine vehicle, better than the new Nissan. Not only does it look great, but the cab space is quite charitable, especially compared to the tight fit of recent Nissans. Not only that, but the Toyota truck has actually managed to increase its pulling power while still maintaining roughly the same gas mileage. The same cannot be said for the Nissan.

2.   Undoubtedly there is freedom in the United States. But what kind of freedom is it? Certainly we are not free to murder, rape, and steal. In the long run, freedom really is not freedom at all, since it only leads to anarchy and, inevitably, to the imposition of the will of the stronger onto the weaker. Instead, freedom must be seen as a balance between the freedom of one individual versus the rights of another to also enjoy freedom. This has created a massive web of laws and litigation, which, to many people, appear to restrict our freedom. But that is the point: freedom must be the ability to act within a system of just and fair laws, not the ability to act willy-nilly on any emotion, desire, or drive one may experience.

3.   The advent of television has almost certainly brought with it effects its designers neither anticipated nor necessarily wanted. Families may stay together in the home more often, but it is to watch a program together, like zombies, not interacting. Graphic violence and suggested sex without consequences have proven to be a strong corrosive influence on American middle-class values. The network news broadcasts, which once seemed to be the epitome of somber reporting (compared to "yellow" print journalism) are now more concerned with shock and sleaze. Television quite simply has done to America in almost 40 years what it took the barbarians hundreds of years to do to Ancient Rome: destroy it.

4.   Traditionally, American workers have been grouped into two main categories: white-collar workers and blue-collar workers. The white-collar worker was the professional type who wore a suit to work each day. These workers would include doctors, lawyers, professors, executives, and middle-level managers. The blue-collar worker was the laborer and wore the uniform of his company, often in blue. These workers would include plumbers, truck drivers, electricians, factory workers, stevedores, and janitors. But as America approaches the twenty-first century, these easy distinctions have started to blur.

5.   Often people create their own failures, even if they do not realize it. For example, boyfriends or girlfriends do something— start an argument, become unfaithful, ignore the other—that creates a situation that forces the other to break off the relationship. This may happen because the person wanted to get out of the relationship to begin with but was too weak to confront the other and so created a destructive situation in which the relationship was bound to fail. Another situation can occur with students. Students claim they fail courses because of a teacher's unrealistic expectations or heavy workload, yet they consistently sabotage their own efforts by not turning in required work, failing to study or attend class, or developing a negative attitude.

6.   The most important thing to do with the cake is to be sure to let it cool down fully. Then, making sure you buy absolutely the best brand, open a can of ready-made icing. Take a spreading knife designed specifically for this purpose and gently smooth the icing on the tops of the cakes. Once you have done that, stack the two cakes and put icing on the sides. Buy several premanufactured figurines to decorate the top of the cake. Eat whatever icing is left in the can so that nothing goes to waste. Now you have successfully finished decorating your first homemade cake.

Coherence in Paragraphs

All other sentences in a paragraph spring from the topic sentence. Your topic sentence indicates what you choose to write about. Therefore, all the material you include in the paragraph must be relevant to the topic. In this sense, a topic sentence is like an umbrella—every sentence in the paragraph should fit underneath the topic sentence. As a writer, you need to look at every sentence in your paragraph and compare it to your topic sentence. Ask yourself: Does this sentence logically relate to the topic sentence? If the answer is no, take the sentence out.

For an example of incoherence in a paragraph, read the following:

Topic sentence   Clint Eastwood and Meryl Streep were both superb in <u>The Bridges of Madison County</u>. Eastwood's portrayal of Robert Kincaid seemed to bring this character to life, with a combination of strength and understanding. Streep's rendition of Francesca

Support   revealed why this Italian housewife in Iowa was so unhappy. The chemistry between the two was the best: realistic, strong, but without the excessive gestures and groping so often seen in movies today. Still, I think adultery under any circumstance is wrong.

Wrap-up sentence   Eastwood and Streep were in top form for this film, and the awards and acclaim they received for <u>Bridges</u> were well deserved.

The sentence *Still, I think adultery under any circumstance is wrong* is clearly out of place. Although it may represent the writer's heartfelt conviction, the sentence does not belong in a paragraph that is analyzing the performances of two actors in a movie. Remember, the topic sentence will determine what should be in a paragraph. In this case, only sentences that directly pertain to Eastwood's and Streep's performances are relevant.

Examine each of the following paragraphs for problems of coherence. Indicate which sentence in each paragraph does not belong.

1. Once a fashion model reaches superstardom, the next step seems to be acting. Cindy Crawford was one of the first, by moving from fashion pages to MTV. Then Elle MacPherson appeared with British star Hugh Grant in a popular movie called Sirens. Kate Moss, Claudia Schiffler, Naomi Campbell, and Elle MacPherson then worked together in the provocatively titled movie Unzipped. Male models never get any recognition. All count on their name recognition and looks more than their acting to draw in audiences.

2. The local zoo is often more than just a place to see animals. It's a place where endangered species are being saved. Watching animals live behind bars can be a depressing experience. Zoos care for the animals, observe their patterns of behavior, and encourage the animals to mate. Zoos also have to keep close track of family trees, so as to be careful not to inbreed a species. Thus, inter-zoo loans are sometimes necessary for successful breeding. The payoff, though, may be a resurgent species.

3. One of the most beautiful and important tourist attractions in France is the Palace of Versailles. A visitor coming upon the palace for the first time will be impressed by its enormous size. It is so big that the palace is capable of housing literally thousands of people. Visitors should be aware that nearby restaurants are overpriced. The Hall of Mirrors is perhaps its most famous attraction, but the gardens that surround the palace are equally impressive.

4.   Edgar Allan Poe was a great American writer. He is sometimes seen as the inventor of the modern short story and the modern detective story. Writing is hard. Most Americans know Poe through movies made of his stories and poems. The most famous of Poe's works, "The Raven," was made into a movie starring Vincent Price.

Choosing Support for Your Paragraph

Most of the sentences in your paragraphs will be support for the topic sentence. This is where the merits of your argument are played out: Your reader will be either convinced or unconvinced as to the truth of what you have to say based on the quality of the support you choose to provide.

Choosing Personal Experience

Often, your personal experience is a good source of information for your writing. For instance, if you want to warn a friend against flying without making prior seat reservations, you might choose to tell him or her about the time you lived in an airport for three days over a holiday weekend, trying to get a seat on a flight home. The moral to your story is clear: advance seat reservations on airlines are necessary, especially on holiday weekends. In this case, you have special experience that helps to illustrate a general problem.

However, sometimes using personal experience can create problems. Note the following example:

Topic sentence   Airplanes are a terrible way to travel to Europe. When I went to Europe last summer, my flight was delayed an hour on the ground before take-off, and that meant I missed my connecting flight in **Support** Frankfurt. I then wasted several valuable hours of my vacation sitting in the airport, trying to get on another flight to Stockholm, which was my ultimate destination. I had to switch airlines, and as a result, my luggage didn't make it until two days later. Until **Wrap-up sentence** airlines are more responsible, I'm going to travel to Europe by ship!

Of course, this writer's experience is the type of frustrating adventure that few people enjoy. Yet, the topic sentence, *Airplanes are a terrible way to travel,* cannot be fully justified with this personal experience alone. Thousands of people fly across the Atlantic each day, and sometimes mix-ups and delays occur. However, in general, most people would find themselves seriously inconvenienced if they had to take an ocean liner that would extend their travel time from several hours to as much as a few weeks.

One danger of relying solely on personal experience is that the experience itself can be too subjective—what you experience may not be the same as what someone else in the same situation has experienced. If that's the case, you wind up in a weak position: you argue that flying to Europe is a bad idea because of your terrible experience, but many thousands of people fly the same route with no special problems and would travel no other way.

Personal experience is most effective when you have something special to write about—something that can be particular to you or a fairly small number of people. In that case, your experience makes you something more of an expert. However, avoid using personal experience as the *only* basis of your support.

Choosing Examples and Statistics

You can use facts in your paragraphs to support your topic sentence. These facts will generally come in one of two forms: examples and statistics. *Examples* are specifics, such as particular names, places, or events. *Statistics* are generally numerical gatherings of bits of information.

When you choose to use an example of something, you are providing a specific detail. For instance, a recipe would not say "sprinkle with an herb"; rather, it would say "sprinkle with basil" (or with whatever appropriate herb). "War causes many bad things to happen" is greatly improved by being specific: "War causes death, injury, poverty, disease, and displacement."

When you make an assertion in your topic sentence, you can use examples or statistics to prove your assertion. If your topic sentence is *Automobile manufacturers have resisted attempts to revolutionize the combustion engine,* you must be able to tell about specific instances in which important new designs have been ignored or thwarted by automobile manufacturers. Don't assume the reader will believe your statement without such proof.

Using statistics to support your topic sentence can be tricky because facts presented in a numerical fashion are subject to interpretation. Mark Twain once quoted Benjamin Disraeli as saying, "There are three types of lies: lies, damned lies, and statistics." This distrust of statistics may have resulted from the abuse of one type of statistic: opinion polls. Opinion polls can be notoriously subjective since biased pollsters can manipulate or misrepresent the results they get. This is especially true in the hands of advertisers pushing products ("Four out of five doctors use . . .") or politicians promoting their agendas ("Sixty-eight percent of Americans agree with me . . ."). Unfortunately, how opinion polls are created determines their reliability. In the hands of experienced professionals, statistics can be created to support almost any point of view.

Fortunately, when you move away from opinion polls toward scientific data, you can find reasonably reliable statistics. Librarians can assist you in finding journals, encyclopedias, almanacs, and other sources that can provide you with objective information, such as how many soldiers died in World War II, the rate of decay of an uranium atom, or the amount of cheese produced in Wisconsin over the last decade.

Choosing Factual Evidence versus Opinion and Interpretation

You may have noticed how someone may make a statement such as "Mothers are a source of joy, inspiration, and love." This sounds like a fact and appears to be intended as a fact, but it is not a fact. Instead, the statement is only an opinion or interpretation of fact. Unfortunately, some mothers are abusive or neglectful of their children. Statements that cannot be objectively or rationally verified are not facts. Indeed, much of what you read or hear in the newspapers and on television is intended to be taken as fact by the speaker. However, you must be able to determine for yourself which statements constitute factual evidence and which do not. Read the following sentence from John L. O'Sullivan:

The best government is that which governs least.

O'Sullivan's statement may find many adherents, but he is clearly expressing only an opinion. There is no single objective way to prove this statement because it rests on certain assumptions about government that not everyone agrees with all the time. For instance, during the nineteenth century in the United States, government policy was to avoid regulating business as much as possible. This was called a laissez-faire (or hands-off) policy. There was only minimal government regulation. However, businesses in the nineteenth century routinely hired children as laborers, engaged in monopolistic business practices, and allowed employees to work under dangerous conditions. These practices eventually were ended, in part, by greater government regulation. Thus, some would argue, governments have an interest in regulating labor and business practices in order to protect workers and consumers. However, that statement, too, is only a statement of opinion, not a fact.

Opinion, however, is not bad. After all, facts do not do much on their own; they must be interpreted. Ultimately, your reader can be swayed to agree with your opinion if facts are presented in a logical and convincing fashion. That, of course, is your goal.

EXERCISE 3.5

Read each of the following statements and indicate which are statements of fact and which are statements of opinion.

1. Joe Montana led the San Francisco 49ers to four Super Bowl victories.

2. The sun is almost 93 million miles from the earth.

3. William Shakespeare is the greatest writer of all time.

4. Chiropractors are quacks who profit from people's fears of conventional medicine.

5. A teenage athlete's chances of getting a college degree and working as a doctor, lawyer, or business person are better than his chances of becoming a professional athlete.

6. Gardening is the best therapy for people with stress.

7. In all the stories about Sherlock Holmes by Sir Arthur Conan Doyle, Holmes never once utters, "Elementary, my dear Watson."

8. Single-parent families are bad for children.

9. Despite their high rate of infant mortality, the Aborigine population in Australia is increasing.

10. People who play golf are snobs.

Transitions

As you move within your paragraph from one idea to the next, you must remember to provide ways to help your reader follow along. One way to do this is through the use of **transitions.** Transitional words and phrases serve as guideposts, telling the reader where the ideas in the paragraph are headed. In Chapters 4 through 8, you will be introduced to the transitional words and phrases that are used for a variety of purposes.

Wrap-Up Sentences

The topic sentence is usually the beginning of your paragraph. The support is the middle. Now, you need an end. Your paragraph should have a wrap-up, or closing, sentence. Some instructors also call this the *secondary topic sentence.* Your wrap-up sentence should not repeat your topic sentence exactly, but it should repeat a key idea from the topic sentence or show how some idea has been advanced. In this way, your paragraph will have a sense of closure and finality. (Of course, if your topic sentence is the last sentence of your paragraph, it also serves as the wrap-up sentence.) Also, as you will see in Chapter 10, wrap-up sentences can be an effective way of providing transitions between paragraphs when you build your essay.

Examine the following paragraph:

> My grandfather's lemon farm was the most wonderful place I knew as a child. His farm spread out for acres, with rows upon rows of gnarled branches, green leaves, and yellow fruit. I loved harvest time when we would climb aboard trucks and venture down the narrow dirt paths to help collect the crates the day laborers had filled. I would watch these strange men, dark brown, sweaty from the heat, as they lugged what seemed to be impossibly heavy loads, lifting them into the truck with a certain ease. Then I would crawl back, pull out a lemon, and rub it under my nose. That smell still lives in my memory, a certain mark of my childhood.

The last sentence of the paragraph brings the reader back to the present, in which the speaker is recalling childhood, not actually experiencing it.

Titles for Paragraphs

If you are writing a paragraph-length assignment, your instructor may require that it have a title. A title serves as a description of what the paragraph is about. Don't simply describe the assignment (i.e., "Definition Paragraph") unless your instructor asks for that. The best title is a short, concise summary of the *content* of the paragraph. Think of your title as an introduction to the paragraph itself, something your reader encounters even before the topic sentence.

Student Writing Assignment: Paragraphs

Write a paragraph based on one of the topics that follow. Be sure that your paragraph includes a topic sentence, support, a wrap-up sentence, and a title of your own choosing. Follow the steps listed in the Start-Up Suggestions and Self-Revision Questions. Bring your paragraph to class for peer editing. Revise your paragraph and then complete the section labeled Your Choices to discuss the decisions you made during the composing and revising process.

second marriages	dorm food
conservation efforts	visiting the dentist
school prayer	hobbies
celebrity scandals	spending time alone

Start-Up Suggestions

Follow these steps before writing your first draft:

1. When you are considering a topic to write about, talk to your friends about some of the issues the topic raises. See which issues tend to get the most powerful or thoughtful reactions. Think about how your opinion compares to that of your friends.
2. Try to do some research on your topic. Has anything appeared lately on television or in the newspapers on your topic? What is being said?
3. Write in your journal for ten minutes about your topic. Try to explore what you know about the topic and what opinions you have about the topic.

4. Brainstorm or freewrite for ten minutes on an issue you have chosen. Then use the looping exercise described in Chapter 2 to brainstorm or freewrite on more specific topics.
5. Draft a topic sentence that clearly states the topic of the paragraph and your attitude or opinion about the topic.
6. Make a scratch, or informal, outline of the paragraph.

Self-Revision Questions

Answer these questions after writing your first draft and before rewriting the draft for submission to your peer-editing group.

1. Underline the topic sentence of your paragraph. Is it specific and direct? Does it express a point of view? Is it properly placed?
2. Do you have adequate support to prove your point of view? Is it based solely on personal experience, or do you have examples, facts, and expert opinions, as well?
3. What do you think is your crystalline word?
4. Did you remember to include a wrap-up sentence for your paragraph? Is there a sense of closure?
5. Did you remember to include a title of your own choosing? Is it descriptive and concise?

Revise your paragraph and submit it to your peer-editing group.

Peer-Editing Guidelines for Paragraphs

Answer these questions for each of the paragraphs written by other members of your peer-editing group.

1. Does the paragraph have a topic sentence? Where is the topic sentence? Write down the topic sentence.
2. Is the topic sentence clear about what topic the paragraph is addressing?
3. Does the topic sentence express an opinion about the topic?
4. What would you choose as the crystalline word of the paragraph?
5. Is the support relevant to the topic sentence?
6. Is the support sufficient to prove the assertion?
7. What type(s) of support does the author use?
8. Does the writer provide effective transitions within the paragraph?

9. Does the writer include a title that is descriptive and concise?

10. What *one* change would most improve the paragraph?

Prepare the final draft of your paragraph, taking the comments of your peer-editing group into account.

Your Choices: Paragraphs

Answer these questions after you have finished your final draft.

1. Why did you choose your topic?

2. What changes did you make to the topic sentence? Why?

3. Did your peer editors choose the same crystalline word that you chose? If not, what changes did you make to your topic sentence to emphasize that word?

4. Were all the sentences relevant to the topic?

5. What support did you use? Is your support as specific as it can be?

6. If you added extra material, was it necessary? Why or why not? Did you add enough material to strengthen any weaknesses in your support?

7. What changes to the support did you make from the rough draft to the final draft? Why?

8. What transitional words did you use? Why?

9. Did you have to change your wrap-up sentence from rough draft to final draft? Why or why not?

10. Did you remember to give your paragraph a title? Why did you choose that title?

COMPUTER EXERCISE

Here is an exercise you can complete either while in the prewriting phase of writing or after you have completed your first rough draft. Create a file containing only your topic sentence for the Student Writing Assignment. Send the file to your writing partner or another student in your class. Have that student write what he or she *expects* to see covered in the rest of your paragraph. Then have the other student return the file to you. Does your paragraph cover what the student expected it to cover? If there is a wide discrepancy, your topic sentence may need to be rewritten to more accurately reflect what your paragraph will be about (or you may wish to reconsider how you will develop your paragraph). Do the same for your partner.

THE REVISION PROCESS:
A Student Writing Sample

Eileen, a business major, decided that she wanted to write about conservation efforts for her first paragraph. In order to do this, she started by asking many of her friends what they thought of conservation efforts. She was a little surprised to find that there was quite a mix of opinions. Several of her business-major friends were hostile to many conservation efforts. They felt that the conservation movement had gone too far in trying to preserve the environment and that businesses were being hurt and potential jobs lost due to environmental rules and regulations. Some of Eileen's other friends were very much in favor of conservation, and they were worried about what the earth was going to look like in the future if current levels of pollution and consumption continued.

Once Eileen sat down to freewrite, she actually had already gathered a quite a bit of information on her subject. Her ten-minute freewrite went as follows:

Conservation really seems to be a big deal right now I'm kind of surprised how emotional everyone gets about it I guess some people really feel like it's cost them a lot of money and time and some people have even lost the land that they own because it turned out some endangered species or something was on it and I just don't think that's right but should we just go and develop everything I mean don't we need to be a little more humble about what we do as human beings I guess I think some things are worth saving but is everything worth saving I'm not so sure about that it does seem like if it's a little tiny insect or something it's asking an awful lot of have people give up everything for it maybe we could make some decisions about what should be saved and what shouldn't I don't think you can please everyone so some people are just going to be mad try to split the difference I suppose

At this point, Eileen read over her freewriting. She liked several points, especially the phrases *some things are worth saving but is everything worth saving* and *some people are just going to be mad.*

After Eileen's freewriting experience, she decided that she still wasn't sure how she felt about the topic of conservation efforts. She decided to make a list of questions she still had. Her questions were as follows:

Are all plants and animals worth saving?

How much are businesses hurt by conservation?

Can business be helped by conservation?

Who decides what stays and what goes?

Does conservation destroy jobs or create jobs?

What would happen if there were no conservation efforts?

Are we responsible for the earth?

After thinking about her list of questions, Eileen decided to go to the library. There, she found a magazine with a cover story addressing the conflict between environmentalists versus business leaders and owners of private property. This article led her to read several others.

After her trip to the library, Eileen felt ready to write a topic sentence. This was her first effort:

Conservation efforts are worthwhile sometimes.

This immediately led to a problem. What did she mean by *sometimes?* Eileen decided that she would have to define the term better. Instead, she wrote:

Conservation efforts are worthwhile when they do not hurt too many jobs or businesses.

At first, Eileen liked her new sentence, but when she showed it to one of her friends whom she had spoken to earlier, her friend said that all conservation efforts hurt some business somewhere. This sentence then would allow for virtually no conservation efforts, which was not what Eileen had intended.

Instead, Eileen tried a different tactic. This time, she rewrote her sentence to focus on what she already believed:

Conservation efforts must be balanced with the needs of businesses.

This topic sentence allowed Eileen to develop her ideas in the rest of the paragraph. Eileen built the rest of her paragraph on what she believed were common-sense arguments on how to balance the two competing desires of business people and conservationists.

The first draft of her paragraph looked like this:

> Conservation efforts must be balanced with the needs of businesses. We cannot act as though the earth can sustain any sort of punishment or pollution that we create. That behavior will get us into trouble since we must live on the earth, as well. But when we start worrying more about snail-darters than the jobs people need to make a living, then we've swung the pendulum too far in the wrong direction. Government agencies that protect the environment need to be sensitive to the needs of people. Businesses need to be sensitive to the idea that money isn't everything and that a good environment has no price.

Eileen felt very pleased with this draft when she took it to her peer-editing group. When her group answered the peer-editing guideline questions regarding the paragraph, however, they found some trouble spots. In response to the questions that concerned the topic sentence, the group generally responded favorably, but one person felt that the topic sentence was still a little vague because the word *balance* was not entirely clear. When the group considered the questions dealing with support, they agreed that the paragraph needed more details. They were also unable to agree on a crystalline word. Some felt the word was *balance,* but others chose *behavior* and *needs*. They all agreed that the best change for the paragraph would be to give some specifics.

Eileen reviewed their comments and rewrote her paragraph, trying to insert some specific details that would make her points stronger.

She also made sure to provide transitions when she did so. This was her final draft:

Conservation vs. Business

The government must balance conservation efforts with the needs of businesses. The earth will not be safe if toxic wastes pollute our water, if air pollution is allowed to spread, and if entire plant and animal species are destroyed. But when we start worrying more about snail-darters, spotted owls, and kit foxes than the jobs people need, then we have swung too far in the wrong direction. The government needs to be sensitive to the needs of people. However, businesses need to be sensitive to the idea that money isn't everything. After all, we need a clean, healthy environment to live in, and that has no price.

Once Eileen completed her final draft, she filled out the questions from the Your Choices list. In those questions, she commented, in general, that most of her rewriting involved becoming more specific about her topic. Her topic sentence itself was rewritten to make the relationship between businesses and conservationists clearer, and she chose examples of environmental situations she read about in the library. In response to the trouble her group had with the crystalline word, she tried to reemphasize the idea of *balance*. She also decided to rewrite her wrap-up sentence since it seemed too weak in the original draft.

GRAMMAR INSTRUCTION AND EXERCISES:
Simple, Compound, and Complex Sentences

A complete sentence is a complete thought. In order to form a complete sentence, you must have three things:

1. A subject
2. A verb
3. A complete thought

What is a subject? A **subject** is a word or phrase that the sentence is about. As such, the subject is usually a noun or a pronoun and all of its modifiers.

> **The baby** sat up in his crib and wailed.

> **Bob and Carol** entertained the visitors from Russia.

> **The can of pop** burst in the freezer.

A **verb** is word showing action or state of existence.

> The sun **rose** above the horizon.

> The tanker truck **exploded** in the movie's final scene.

> My brother-in-law **is** a computer systems analyst.

The **complete thought** is a more difficult concept because it rests on your ability to recognize when the logic introduced in the sentence is executed properly. However, you can look for certain clues. If your sentence begins with a conjunctive adverb, such as *since, when,* or *while,* you have created the expectation that something else must follow. The following sentence is incomplete because there is nothing following to complete the thought started with the word *while.*

> **While** Shaunna was walking down the street.

What's wrong? The reader is waiting for more—to learn what happened while Shaunna was walking down the street. The following sentence provides a complete thought.

> While Shaunna was walking down the street, fire trucks raced by,
> headed toward her apartment building.

(See pages 334–39 for further discussion of complete sentences.)

Simple Sentences

A **simple sentence** is made up of one independent clause. An **independent clause** has a subject, a verb, and a complete thought. Thus, an independent clause can be a complete sentence.

The American Revolution started with the fighting at Lexington and Concord.

Some universities and colleges make attempts to recruit foreign students.

Electric cars will become more popular in the next century.

(See page 336 for further discussion of simple sentences.)

Compound Sentences

A **compound sentence** is a sentence with two or more independent clauses. These clauses can be joined with a semicolon or with a comma and a coordinating conjunction.

Alex wanted to go to Harvard**, but** his grades were not strong enough.

My Russian history class is nearly empty**;** however, my art appreciation class is full.

The mail carrier may bring the package**, or** a private delivery service may have it.

I love spaghetti with meatballs**;** I can't stand fettucini alfredo.

(See page 336 for further discussion of compound sentences.)

Complex Sentences

A **complex sentence** has an independent clause and at least one dependent clause. A **dependent clause** has a subject and a verb but does not express a complete thought. Therefore, a dependent clause cannot stand on its own as a complete sentence.

Although I have traveled to Europe four times, I have never been to Ireland.

Gene went to see the doctor because his knee was bothering him.

Sarah, who is visiting Israel next summer, is taking classes in Hebrew.

(See pages 336–37 for further discussion of complex sentences.)

EXERCISES   Rewrite each sentence, underlining the subject(s) once and the verb(s) twice. Be aware that some sentences may have more than one of each. Then identify whether the sentence is simple, compound, or complex.

1. Saskatchewan is a lightly populated province in western Canada.

2. Seashells have been used as decorations by many people around the globe; in ancient times some seashells were used as money.

3. Babe Ruth is probably still the most famous person who ever played baseball.

4. Ms. Arreguin prefers her salads with Roquefort dressing, but Mr. Garnett likes Thousand Island.

5. Diane just loved the film <u>Treasure of Sierra Madre</u>; of course, she's always been a big Humphrey Bogart fan.

6. Last week Paulette went skiing for the first time since her automobile accident.

7. When Douglas was in the Boy Scouts, he learned to tie many knots, but now he can't remember any of them.

8. Jesse just finished his certification program; now he can work as an emergency medical technician.

9. Although the tribal language has been lost, their customs and dress have been preserved.

10. Smoking has been restricted in many places, but it is still legal.

4 Telling It Like It Is

Narration, Description, and Example in Paragraphs

JOURNAL EXERCISE

Write about a recent event or encounter that has had a strong impact on you. Use as many specific details as possible.

When you come together with your friends or family to talk, one of the things you probably do is tell stories. They might be tall tales that did not actually happen, or they might be reports of real-life happenings. No matter which, the most entertaining stories have a you-are-there feel.

You probably know people who are better storytellers than others, whether they are describing an eventful party, a trip abroad, or a particularly boring instructor. Why is that? Good storytellers fill their stories with vivid, striking details to create strong images in their listeners' imaginations. These details bring to life the characters, places, and events in the report, fictional or not.

In many ways, the uses of narration, description, and example in paragraphs are among the most fundamental techniques of writing. What you're going to learn in this chapter is no different from what you already do instinctively: tell stories.

Why Choose Narration?

Paragraphs based on **narration** answer the question What happened? As such, you may use narrative paragraphs to relate a personal experience to your reader. You may even think of the narrative paragraph as doing the same thing that a narrator does in a film documentary. The narrator guides the listener through the documentary, explaining important images or sequences. You, as the writer of a narrative paragraph, have the same role.

EXERCISE 4.1

Either brainstorm or freewrite for ten minutes on one of the following topics for narrative paragraphs. Try to develop as many specific details as possible to relate the story completely.

my first date	an unforgettable teacher
a rite of passage	a visit to the hospital
a traumatic childhood experience	my first ride on an airplane
the death of a pet	setting up my first home on my own

Topic Sentences

A topic sentence for a paragraph based on narration should make clear to the reader just what event is going to be related in the paragraph. The topic sentence should also suggest some sort of opinion or angle for the work. That is, there should be some point to telling the story, and the topic sentence is an effective place to make that point clear. Take a look at this example:

Last winter my family went to Arizona.

This sentence is a direct statement of fact, but it goes nowhere with the topic. Did anything interesting happen on the trip? Did you learn something? Did you have a good time or a bad time? This topic sentence does not encourage the reader to look forward to the rest of the paragraph. Instead, if an opinion or point of view is introduced in the topic sentence, there would be more room for development. Here is the sentence rewritten:

> Last winter my family had an interesting time when we went to Arizona.

The trouble with this sentence is that the phrase *an interesting time* is too vague. There is still no clue for the reader about what happened or what to expect. The word *interesting* can be used in both a positive and a negative way.

> Last winter my family experienced a new, wonderful lifestyle when we vacationed for a week in Arizona.

This topic sentence is more effective than the earlier ones because it contains an opinion and it directs the reader's attention to what may come later in the paragraph.

One thing to remember in order to develop an effective topic sentence for a paragraph based on narration is to focus your topic sentence on just one event or story. Any attempt to squeeze in two or more stories will only confuse your reader. Each story or event should be in its own paragraph.

EXERCISE 4.2

Read the following topic sentences and decide which ones would be effective topic sentences for narrative paragraphs. Rewrite any that are not.

1. The day I got my braces off was unforgettable.

2. The box was covered with gold leaf.

3. Louis L'Amour was a great writer of Westerns.

4. The kidnappers joked about how they would spend the ransom money, but they had not counted on the swift response of the FBI early that morning.

5. The day my daughter was born was one of the happiest days of my life.

6. Character names from Ancient Greek myths have found their way into everyday English.

7. Experimental psychologists are primarily interested in studying learning and memory.

8. My Volkswagen finally died on my last trip to Las Vegas.

9. The anti-vivisectionists' arguments range from the emotional to the spiritual.

10. Sally Ride was the first female American astronaut.

Support

When you choose narration, your support should be presented in **chronological order,** which means moving from the earliest point in time to the latest. In order to do this, you should have a good understanding of the sequence of events that you intend to include in your writing. This means you should do some prewriting exercises as a way to better remember and *order* the events. One way to accomplish this is to brainstorm a list of actions or ideas associated with the event.

A second consideration when writing narration is to decide what to include and what to leave out. If your paragraph is going to address the wonderful vacation you experienced in Arizona, you will probably not be able to tell your reader about each and every thing that occurred. You will need to stay focused on your story without being distracted by side issues.

Examine the following narrative paragraph:

Topic sentence   Last winter my family experienced a new, wonderful lifestyle when we vacationed for a week in Arizona. We left Michigan in

Support   April, when the weather was still quite cold and gloomy, and flew to Phoenix. Uncle Joseph met us at the airport, and the moment we walked outside, we felt like we were in another world. We gawked at the beautiful desert scenery and the modern, clean city. When we got to Uncle Joseph's Spanish-style villa, the first thing all of us did

Support   was switch to bathing suits and jump into his pool. After swimming in the pool, we went to a Mexican restaurant and had the most fantastic enchiladas. In the evening, we took a leisurely stroll around his neighborhood. For the next six days, we just repeated the activities of that first day, with an occasional round of golf

Wrap-up sentence   thrown in. Thanks to that week, I am seriously considering moving to Arizona after I finish college.

This paragraph works well because it is arranged in chronological order, which allows the reader to follow the events described easily. Also, there are not too many details in the paragraph—just enough to ensure that the reader can understand by the end of the paragraph why the writer wants to move to Arizona.

Transitions

When you move from one event to another in narration, you must be sure to provide transitional words or phrases to make the meaning clear to the reader. In narrative paragraphs, some of the transitional words you may find yourself using are *first, second, third, then, later, next, after, during, subsequently,* and *when.*

Read the following paragraph. Note the specific details that are used to tell a story. The transitional words and phrases are printed in bold type. Some verb tenses indicate different time sequences, so they are also bold.

One of the most traumatic experiences of the second grade was having my bike stolen. **I had gotten** the bike, a red Schwinn with white hand grips, for Christmas and begged my parents to let me ride it to school. **I had leaned** it up against the metal bike rack with the bigger kids' bikes, but **when** I got out of school **that afternoon**, it was gone. **At first**, I just couldn't believe someone would steal my pretty red bike. I actually waited for someone to come back with it, as though the bike had been taken by mistake. **When** it was clear no one was coming back, I walked home slowly. I cried **when** I told Mom, and **then** I cried again **when** Dad came home. He called the police, and **a few days later** the bike was located at the bottom of a creek, the front end bent beyond repair. **That first experience** started to teach me the lesson that not everyone is nice. **In fact**, some people steal.

In this paragraph, the author is looking back to an early childhood experience and recalling vividly the sequence of events surrounding the theft of his first bicycle. The first sentence serves to introduce the topic of the paragraph, and the details given relate the story in chronological order.

Be aware that sometimes the **verb tense** can be helpful in determining the chronological order. The verb tenses in the preceding paragraph move between the past tense and the past perfect tense, showing that one event in the past occurred before the other event in the past. Examples of shifting verb tense are found in the second and third sentences (*had gotten* and *begged; had leaned* and *was gone*).

Student Writing Assignment: Narration

Write a narrative paragraph based on one of the topics in Exercise 4.1. Follow the steps listed in the Start-Up Suggestions and the Self-Revision Questions. Then bring your paragraph to class for peer editing. Revise your paragraph and then complete the section labeled Your Choices: Narration to discuss the decisions you made during the composing and revising process.

Start-Up Suggestions

Follow these steps before writing your first draft.

1. Brainstorm or freewrite for ten minutes on your topic in your journal. Examine what you've written.
2. Write in your journal about your own storytelling abilities. Have you traditionally been a good storyteller? Who else in your family tells good stories? Why are their stories good?
3. Listen to how your friends tell stories. (Their stories can be as simple as to tell what they did last night.) What sort of tone do they use—humorous, serious, angry? What kinds of words do they use? Pay close attention to the details good storytellers include in their stories as well as those that are left out.
4. Create a list of specific examples of incidents that may relate to the topic you've chosen. When you're drafting your paragraph, see which ones will be helpful to you.

Self-Revision Questions

Answer these questions after writing your first draft and before rewriting the draft for submission to your peer-editing group.

1. Ask yourself: Does my topic sentence directly answer the question What happened?

2. Is the topic sentence the first sentence in the paragraph? If not, is there a good, logical reason for placing it elsewhere?
3. Does your paragraph create images by using vivid and appropriate details?
4. What appropriate, effective transitions have you used? (You may wish to review the list of transitional words and phrases under the heading Transitions.)
5. Does your paragraph have a reasonable and logical wrap-up sentence?

Revise your paragraph and submit it to your peer-editing group.

Peer-Editing Guidelines for Narration

Answer these questions for each of the paragraphs written by other members of your peer-editing group.

1. Does the paragraph have a topic sentence? Underline the topic sentence.
2. Is the topic sentence effective? Is it in response to one of the topics assigned?
3. Does the topic sentence clearly introduce the story developed within the paragraph?
4. Is the support relevant to the topic sentence?
5. Is the development of the paragraph sufficient to tell the story?
6. Are the details specific or does the paragraph just provide generalizations?
7. What visual images were created in your imagination?
8. Does the paragraph provide effective transitions? List the transitional words used.
9. What one change would most improve the paragraph?
10. What is the paragraph's crystalline word?

Prepare the final draft of your paragraph, taking the comments of your peer-editing group into account.

Your Choices: Narration

Answer these questions after you have finished your final draft.

1. How did you choose your topic?
2. How did you choose the title for your narrative paragraph?

3. Did you have to change your topic sentence as you moved through your drafts? Why or why not?
4. Did you need to revise your support to ensure that your story was told in chronological order? If you did not write your story in chronological order, how is it arranged and why did you choose to arrange it in that way?
5. Did your peer editors find that your details created images in their imaginations? Did you need to change or add more in your rewrite? Which ones?
6. What transitional words or phrases did you use? Why?
7. What other changes to the support did you make during the drafting process? Why?
8. If you added additional material, why was it necessary?
9. Did you have to change your wrap-up sentence? Why or why not?
10. Did you agree or disagree with your peer editors' choice for the crystalline word? If you disagreed, did you make any revisions to emphasize the word you wanted?

Why Choose Description?

A paragraph based on **description** depicts or illustrates a person, place, or thing. The descriptive paragraph may help show what something looks like or how it feels, tastes, sounds, or smells. The details in your descriptive paragraph need to be sharp and vivid to appeal to your reader's senses. You are trying to re-create in your reader's imagination something that exists in the physical world; therefore, you must supply your reader with details. They may be typical or essential to the topic being described, or the details may be unusual or outlandish qualities that set one thing apart from all the others.

EXERCISE 4.3

Either brainstorm or freewrite for ten minutes on one of the following topics for a descriptive paragraph. Try to develop as many specific details as possible to depict the image of the topic.

a person whom you admire   a local landmark
your favorite room   the inside of your car
tonight's sunset   a strange or unusual locale you
a gathering place for your   have visited
    friends   the view outside your window

Topic Sentences

A topic sentence for a paragraph based on description should indicate both the subject of the description and your attitude or opinion about the subject. In other words, the topic sentence prepares the reader for what will come in the rest of your paragraph: depiction and observation. If you think about these two words, they are not exact synonyms. *Depiction* implies that the characteristics of the object being described will be reproduced in the reader's imagination. *Observation,* though, suggests that the viewer—you, the writer—is active. Your duty is not simply to show the characteristics of an object but to show those characteristics in a certain light, with subjectivity. Examine the following sentence:

> Mount Rushmore has the faces of four U.S. presidents carved
> onto it.

There is very little here to grab a reader's attention. The sentence is factual, and one could imagine that the rest of the paragraph might go on to name the four presidents and even describe their faces. But the reader will learn little here. Look at a rewrite of the sentence:

> The dramatic presentation of four U.S. presidents on Mount
> Rushmore makes one proud and a little sad.

Now the writer is ready to develop a paragraph describing the physical characteristics of Mount Rushmore's famous faces. The paragraph will have some direction because it will reinforce the ideas expressed in the topic sentence about the emotional effect of seeing Mount Rushmore.

Remember, the descriptive paragraph is trying to answer the question How did it look (or taste, feel, smell, sound)? Your answer to that question must involve the physical senses, but it may also involve the many emotional associations you have with those senses.

EXERCISE 4.4

Examine the following topic sentences. Indicate which ones would be effective topic sentences for descriptive paragraphs. Rewrite any that are not.

1. The new downtown shopping center's architecture seems inspired by Alice's Adventures in Wonderland.

2. Trench warfare during World War I was a horrifying experience.

3. The result of the rise in air pollution has been a decrease in the ozone layer.

4. My used car finally died.

5. Two palm trees stand side by side in front of the archway.

6. Rosemarie seems very sweet.

7. Sleeping on an old couch can be difficult.

8. The castle's appearance suggested a quality of magic and romantic intrigue.

9. Walking is an excellent form of low-stress workout.

10. The criminal justice system needs to be changed so that more defendants are convicted.

Support

When you are writing a descriptive paragraph, you must choose which physical details are the most striking or important. You may be able to describe virtually every detail about some topics, but with most, you will have to choose which ones to include and which ones to exclude. For instance, if you want to describe the appearance of a young child's stuffed teddy bear, you might be able to include virtually every detail about the teddy bear that you can discover. However, if you want to describe the appearance of a big city's waterfront, your task would be much more difficult. You would have to choose which buildings to describe and which ones to overlook or which ships and docks to leave in and which ones to leave out.

Examine the following paragraph:

Topic sentence   The shopping mall is more than a place to shop; it's a place to see America. Outside of the mall is the parking lot. Is there a car for sale in this country that you cannot find parked in a mall lot on any

Support   given weekend? There's the black Mercedes, next to the pink Cadillac and the Ford truck. As you walk into the mall, you see people: young children running around screaming, studiously bored teenagers smoking and watching each other, harried parents juggling packages and baby bags, senior citizens sitting and watching. As you walk down one row of stores or another, you can find the same shops with the same products that appear in almost every corner of America today. The mall you are in may use a few

Wrap-up sentence superficial touches, such as pastel facades, to appear distinctive, but essentially all malls look, smell, and feel the same.

Transitions

Descriptive paragraphs are often presented in **spatial order,** in which you show how things are arranged in terms of their physical locations. In order to help the reader understand the spatial order described in a paragraph, the following transitional words and phrases can be helpful: *above, below, behind, on, along, along with, to the right, to the left, on top of, underneath, inside, outside, nearby, in the distance,* and other such words or phrases that indicate direction or location.

The following sample is from a student who was asked to describe her favorite room in her home. She wrote:

> My favorite room is my son's nursery. As soon as I walk **in the door,** I see his white crib, including a mobile with tiny, cute, stuffed bunnies hanging down. **On the wall behind** the crib is a picture from a Beatrix Potter story, with Peter Rabbit and Benjamin Bunny. **To the right** is the rocker, which sits **in the corner,** waiting for the early morning feedings. **Along the far wall** is his white changing table, which matches the crib. **To the right of that and next to the doorway I'm standing in** is his white dresser. **On the wall above the dresser** is the shelf where I pile his stuffed animals, toys, and picture books. The room is small but very cozy, and he and I both love it.

In this descriptive paragraph, the writer takes you around the room from a single vantage point, the doorway. In this way, she can point out all the prominent features of the room, and the reader is able to re-create the room in his or her imagination.

Student Writing Assignment: Description

Write a descriptive paragraph based on one of the topics in Exercise 4.3. Follow the steps listed in the Start-Up Suggestions and Self-Revision Questions. Then bring your paragraph to class for peer editing. Revise your paragraph and then complete the section labeled Your Choices: Description to discuss the decisions you made during the composing and revising process.

Start-Up Suggestions

Follow these steps before writing your first draft.

1. Brainstorm or freewrite for ten minutes on your topic in your journal. Examine what you've written.
2. Write in your journal about how you describe things to friends and family. Do you feel you have the kind of vocabulary that allows you to express yourself, or are you constantly searching for words that will say exactly what you mean?
3. Talk to your friends and listen to their vocabulary. Do they refer to the color of a car as *red,* or do they make distinctions such as *cherry, fire engine red,* or *cabernet?*
4. Create a list of specific details that illustrate the main idea of the topic you have chosen to describe. Be sure that your list includes details that appeal to several of your senses, *not* just to your sense of sight. Consult your list when you're drafting your paragraph.

Self-Revision Questions

Answer these questions after writing your first draft and before rewriting the draft for submission to your peer-editing group.

1. Ask yourself: Does my topic sentence directly introduce the topic that is described in the paragraph?
2. Is the topic sentence the first sentence in the paragraph? If not, is there a good, logical reason for placing it elsewhere?
3. Have you chosen strong, specific details to describe your topic? Have you made sure to maintain spatial order?
4. Have you remembered to appeal to the physical senses?

5. Have you used appropriate, effective transitions? (You may wish to review the list of transitional words and phrases under the heading Transitions.)
6. Does your paragraph have a reasonable and logical wrap-up sentence?

Revise your paragraph and submit it to your peer-editing group.

Peer-Editing Guidelines for Description

Answer these questions for each of the paragraphs written by other members of your peer-editing group.

1. Does the paragraph have a topic sentence? Underline the topic sentence.
2. Is the topic sentence at the start of the paragraph? If it is not, where is it? Is it an awkward placement?
3. Is the topic sentence effective? Does it present the item to be described?
4. Is the support sufficient?
5. Is the support relevant to the topic sentence?
6. For support, does the paragraph use details that appeal to the reader's physical senses? List the details used and to what senses they appeal.
7. Does the paragraph provide effective transitions? List the transitional words used.
8. What is your favorite thing about the paragraph?
9. What one change would most improve the paragraph?
10. What is the paragraph's crystalline word?

Prepare the final draft of your paragraph, taking the comments of your peer-editing group into account.

Your Choices: Description

Answer these questions after you have finished your final draft.

1. How did you choose your topic?
2. How did you choose the title for your descriptive paragraph?
3. Did you have to change your topic sentence as you moved through your drafts? Why or why not?

4. Did you need to revise your support to ensure that your story was told in spatial order? If you did not write your description in spatial order, how is it arranged and why did you choose to arrange it in that way?

5. Did your peer editors find all of your appeals to the physical senses? Did you need to add more in your rewrite? Which ones?

6. What transitional words or phrases did you use? Why?

7. What other changes to the support did you make during the drafting process? Why?

8. If you added additional material, why was it necessary?

9. Did you have to change your wrap-up sentence? Why or why not?

10. Did you agree or disagree with your peer editors' choice for the crystalline word? If you disagreed, did you make any revisions to emphasize the word you wanted?

Why Choose Example?

The paragraph based on **example** is one that illustrates a concept or event. You give your reader specific details to help depict or characterize a general idea. You may choose to write about a specific instance to show how a statement can be seen as true, or you may choose to write about a particular person who embodies a concept or idea. Just remember that your examples should clearly develop the idea presented in the topic sentence and that you should make clear just how the example is related. A paragraph based on example gives life to an idea.

EXERCISE 4.5

Either brainstorm or freewrite for ten minutes on one of the following topics for a paragraph based on example. Try to develop as many specific details as possible.

a heroic act	a true scholar
excessive materialism	a frightening event
foreign influences in American cooking	rude behavior
a role model for children	bad horror films

Topic Sentences

The topic sentence for a paragraph based on example needs to name the topic and identify the particular incident or person that illustrates the topic. The topic sentence must show that the ideas move from the general (the topic) to the specific (the incident or person illustrating the topic). Examine the following topic sentence:

A lot of people are incompetent.

This topic sentence suggests that *people who are incompetent* will be the topic of the paragraph, but the sentence lacks any specific incident or person. Indeed, the wording of the sentence is too vague at this point to know if the writer intends to address how people are incompetent at performing their jobs or in how they live their daily lives. The topic sentence needs to be rewritten.

A lot of workers are incompetent.

This topic sentence is better because it has narrowed the focus of the paragraph. Nevertheless, the sentence could be improved. Examine the sentence after another rewrite:

American workers at all levels of employment are too often grossly incompetent.

This topic sentence is more focused and directed. The writer clearly has a direction in which to head for the rest of the paragraph, by looking at examples of incompetence at several different levels of employment.

EXERCISE 4.6

Examine the following topic sentences. Indicate which ones would be effective topic sentences for example paragraphs. Rewrite any that are not.

1. Ross Perot is a real American success story.

2. The effects of the AIDS epidemic still do not rival the damage that the plague inflicted during the fourteenth century.

3. Many books on childrearing are geared toward mothers, and most only barely mention fathers at all.

4. Of the great nineteenth-century English novelists, Jane Austen stands out as the best woman writer.

5. Memphis, New York, and Chicago all had legitimate claims to be the home of the Rock and Roll Hall of Fame, but Cleveland eventually won out.

6. Late-night television hosts such as David Letterman use off-the-wall humor in their shows.

7. <u>Bazaar</u> is a word from Farsi that has been adopted into English.

8. Only a few professional sports are played without a time clock.

9. Stories about being stranded on a desert island are still popular.

10. Unfortunately, acts of prejudice and hatred against homosexuals still occur in the United States.

Support

When you are writing a paragraph based on example, you should be aware that you have two possible ways of supporting your topic sentence. One way is to find a single example of your topic and develop that thoroughly in your paragraph. The other way is to have several different examples of the topic in each paragraph.

The following illustrates a paragraph based on example. This paragraph was developed by finding one example and developing it fully.

Topic sentence   Sometimes the brightest people can start off poorly in school, and the support of the family can make the difference. For example, **Example** Albert Einstein showed little promise as a scholar when he was a child. He was subjected to a very regimented and strict program of study, and in return, he achieved poor grades. If left solely to the German educational system of his time, Einstein would probably never have amounted to much. However, two uncles cultivated an interest in mathematics and science in Einstein. Eventually, he did do well in school and, of course, went on to become one of the greatest scientists of the twentieth century. If those uncles had not taken an interest in young Albert's education, the world today might **Wrap-up sentence** be a very different place.

This paragraph uses the example of Albert Einstein to illustrate the point of the topic sentence: poor students can eventually turn out well if they have family support.

Another type of paragraph based on example provides several specific instances of a concept, not just one. In such a paragraph, you must choose clear examples that don't need extended explanations. Note how the examples in the following paragraph are elaborated upon only enough to show how they relate to the topic sentence:

Topic sentence	Public television has a good range of educational shows that appeal to the subtle but different needs of young children between
Example 1	the ages of two and six. <u>Barney</u>, which features a wholesome purple dinosaur and a band of squeaky-clean elementary school-aged children, appeals to the youngest age group. <u>Barney</u> employs simple ideas and lots of repetitive phrases, songs, and characters so that young children feel comfortable with the familiarity of each
Example 2	episode. <u>Mr. Rogers' Neighborhood</u> appeals to slightly older children, with its gentle adult male host and magical kingdom. Here, children three or four years old learn more about vocabulary and appropriate social behavior. The use of film clips and a busy
Example 3	urban environment on <u>Sesame Street</u> can be too chaotic for very young children, but children in the four- to six-year range will love it. <u>Sesame Street</u> excites the imaginations of the children who have probably become bored by the slower-paced <u>Barney</u> and <u>Mr. Rogers' Neighborhood</u>.

Transitions

Paragraphs based on examples can employ transitional words and phrases such as *for example, for instance, specifically, in this case, as an illustration, namely,* and *one situation.* Paragraphs based on example may also use other sorts of transitional words and phrases as needed, including those associated with narration and description.

American workers at all levels of employment are too often grossly incompetent. At the lowest levels of employment, **for example**, are the young people who work in fast-food restaurants.

As long as you order a predetermined combination, they can do the job, but if you ask them to hold the mayonnaise or add extra tomato to a hamburger, they fail. You wind up with extra mayonnaise and no tomato. Higher up the ladder, you find, **for instance**, managers who do not know how to schedule staff. **Specifically**, managers in service and retail industries often have too little staff on duty. In **one situation**, there was a theater manager running an eight-movie screen complex while using only three tired teenagers to sell popcorn, sodas, and candy on a Saturday night. Also not immune from such incompetence are lawyers, doctors, engineers, and teachers. **In these cases**, they usually hide their incompetence better, but the people they work for eventually figure it out. Indeed, this is part of the problem: if a teacher or doctor can be incompetent and still work, why not kids flipping burgers?

Student Writing Assignment: Example

Using the topic you selected for your prewriting in Exercise 4.5, write a paragraph based on example. Follow the steps listed in the Start-Up Suggestions and Self-Revision Questions. Then bring your paragraph to class for peer editing. Revise your paragraph and then complete the section labeled Your Choices: Example to discuss the decisions you made during the composing and revising process.

Start-Up Suggestions

Follow these steps before writing your first draft.

1. Brainstorm or freewrite for ten minutes on your topic in your journal. Examine what you've written.
2. Write in your journal about your topic. Don't worry if at first you don't come up with many examples. Just try to write about how you feel about the topic. These feelings may jog your memory so that you *can* remember some interesting examples.

3. Talk to your friends or classmates. If, for instance, you're writing about foreign influences in American food, ask them what their favorite foods are and why. Take note of the different varieties of cuisine and determine where they came from.

4. Create a list of specific examples that illustrate the main idea of the question you have chosen to answer. Consult your list when you're drafting your paragraph.

Self-Revision Questions

Answer these questions after writing your first draft and before rewriting the draft for submission to your peer-editing group.

1. Ask yourself: Does my topic sentence effectively introduce the topic for which I am providing examples?

2. Is the topic sentence the first sentence in the paragraph? If not, is there a good, logical reason for placing it elsewhere?

3. Have you chosen strong, specific examples to illustrate your point? If you are using one extended example, is it compelling enough? If you are using multiple examples, do you have at least three strong examples that all logically relate to the topic sentence?

4. Have you used appropriate, effective transitions? (You may wish to review the list of transitional words and phrases under the heading Transitions.)

5. Does your paragraph have a reasonable and logical wrap-up sentence?

Revise your paragraph and submit it to your peer-editing group.

Peer-Editing Guidelines for Example

Answer these questions for each of the paragraphs written by other members of your peer-editing group.

1. Does the paragraph have a topic sentence? Underline the topic sentence.

2. Is the topic sentence effective? Does it indicate that examples will be provided for one of the assigned topics?

3. Does the topic sentence clearly take a stance about the topic?

4. Is the support sufficient?
5. Is the support relevant to the topic sentence?
6. For support, does the paragraph use one extended example, or does it use several examples? List the example or examples used.
7. Does the paragraph provide effective transitions within the paragraph? List the transitional words used.
8. Are the examples specific, or are they generalizations?
9. What one change would most improve the paragraph?
10. What is the paragraph's crystalline word?

Prepare the final draft of your paragraph, taking the comments of your peer-editing group into account.

Your Choices: Example

Answer these questions after you have finished your final draft.

1. Why did you choose your topic?
2. How did you choose the title for your example paragraph?
3. Did you have to change your topic sentence as you moved through your drafts? Why or why not?
4. Did you need to revise your support to ensure that your examples sufficiently proved the point of your topic sentence?
5. Did your peer editors find your examples interesting and convincing? Did you need to add more in your rewrite? Which ones?
6. What transitional words or phrases did you use? Why?
7. What other changes to the support did you make during the drafting process? Why?
8. If you added additional material, why was it necessary?
9. Did you have to change your wrap-up sentence? Why or why not?
10. Did you agree or disagree with your peer editors' choice for the crystalline word? If you disagreed, did you make any revisions to emphasize the word you wanted?

EXERCISE 4.7

Determine whether each of the following paragraphs is based on the use of narration, description, or example. Evaluate how the support in each paragraph reveals the rhetorical mode of the paragraph.

1.   The concert hall is truly beautiful and inspiring. To start at the top, the ceiling itself is handpainted with scenes of angels, all apparently hearing the music as it ascends heavenward. The walls are painted in an Italianate fresco, the bottom portion of which resembles a scene in an outdoor courtyard cafe. Painted on the walls are patrons in the finest clothing of the late-nineteenth-century fashions. However, the historical theme is disrupted once one looks to the floor, which is carpeted, and to the seats, which are comfortably upholstered. In the front is a large proscenium, with massive red velvet curtains that open up onto the wooden stage. The overall effect is to capture the quaintness of a historical period while providing modern comfort and conveniences.

2.   I knew we had to score a touchdown or the game was lost. As I sprinted out to my position as wide receiver, I noticed their safety was trying to inch up closer to the line. I figured he would blitz, so I looked at our quarterback and twisted my wrist when he looked at me, a signal that meant I suspected a blitz by the defense. He stomped his heel, which was his confirmation signal. I ran the slant inside, right behind the blitz. The ball hit me in the hands; I tucked it in and ran as fast as I could. No one was going to catch me, and no one did.

3.   The grotesque nature of the monster was obvious from its physical appearance. Misshapen, armored, and oozing puss from the wound, it had an aura of the primeval past, a creature at home in the steamy jungles of mystical and lethal wonders. Its very presence seemed to compact time, to take Jordan to an era when human beings had not evolved, and her closest ancestor would have been an afterthought, at best, in the battle for supremacy.

4.   What many people fail to recognize is that there are many ways of being supportive of a spouse. For instance, many spouses do not say enough encouraging things to each other on a daily basis. Comments such as "I'm sure you'll get the promotion. You're very good at your job" or "I'm impressed with how you handled that trouble with the children" can boost a partner's self-confidence. Also, actions are another way to be supportive. Saying that one will help out around the house is only supportive if one actually does do more housework. Spouses can also support each other in social situations. Listening to stories that may be old to a spouse but new to others or simply touching or holding hands when others are around is a nice way to say "I'm thinking of you."

5.   The ferry ride across the bay was nearing its completion when Donald noticed that his luggage was missing. First, he looked under his seat. Then, he left his seat and walked down the aisle, inspecting each row to see if he could find his bag among the luggage, parcels, and legs of the other passengers. Then, feeling more panicked, he strode around the perimeter of the ferry, searching everywhere without luck. As the ferry docked, Donald stood at the exit and watched as each passenger left. None had his luggage. Explaining his dilemma to a member of the crew, he was allowed to stay on board a few extra minutes. After another exhaustive but fruitless search, Donald knew his luggage was gone for good.

COMPUTER EXERCISE

If your classroom network has a universal access or common area, either you or your instructor may choose a topic for brainstorming and place it into the area. Type in specific details or examples that fit the topic. This classroom computer brainstorming session should be done with a time limit of either five or ten minutes. If you do not have universal access, brainstorm individually and then send the file to your instructor.

Once the five or ten minutes is over, examine all the examples as a class and discuss the merits of each. You may wish to move some of the examples into your own journal file for future use.

This exercise can be used for any of the rhetorical modes in this or a later chapter.

THE REVISION PROCESS:
A Student Writing Sample

Assigned to write a paragraph based on example, Deanetta, a returning student and mother of two, began by choosing the topic *rude behavior.* Her return to school had placed her in a class where students were behaving badly, she felt. This inspired Deanetta to write about the class for her assignment.

For her prewriting, Deanetta decided to brainstorm a list of examples of rude behavior she had seen exhibited in her class. Here is her list:

Examples of Rude Behavior

— *interrupted in class*
— *comments out loud*
— *personal business expressed during class time*
— *childlike behavior*
— *walking in late and slamming the door*
— *talking out loud while instruction is going on*
— *changing the subject after the fact*
— *popping gum in class*
— *student behind me taps my shoulder all the time*
— *not considering office hours*

Deanetta looked over her list. She had to decide if she could get all of these examples into one paragraph or if she would have to trim her list. She noticed that even in the list some items, such as *childlike behavior,* were not specific. Other items, such as *popping gum in class,* were specific. Still other items might seem unclear to a reader, such as the brief *not considering office hours.* She knew some of these items would have to be explained in greater detail in her paragraph.

Her next step was to form a topic sentence. To begin her paragraph, Deanetta chose the following sentence:

I have a class with some of the rudest people.

That seemed unsatisfactory since she had not said which class. So she rewrote:

I have a math class with some of the rudest people.

Finally, she decided to make her topic sentence even more specific by stating:

In my morning math class, there is a group of people that exhibits the rudest behavior I've seen in a long time.

Deanetta was not entirely comfortable with this sentence, but she was impatient to write the rest of her paragraph, so she kept it for her rough draft.

For her paragraph, Deanetta knew that she would be presenting not just one but several examples of rude behavior. Therefore, she had to make sure her transitions were strong and her examples were presented in a logical order. This was her first paragraph:

Rude Behavior

In my morning math class, there is a group of people that exhibits the rudest behavior I've seen in a long time. As soon as the instructor gets into his lecture or a formula, someone will interrupt him with a comment that doesn't even pertain to what he's talking about. For example: "Ah, somebody moved the fan, do you think we can get it back?" Another student is making loud outbursts, while yet another student is arguing with the instructor about her test grade during class time, not considering using the instructors office hours for personal matters. While the side show is going on the person behind me is tapping (wrong word) hitting my shoulder asking "What did they say?" every ten minutes. Sometimes it's hard

to hear because of the gum popping. We all know that the door
slams really hard. Do you think that the half dozen people that
makes their late entrance remembers that the door slams? No.
There are so many distractions because of rudeness. I hope I can
make it through this semester.

When Deanetta took this to her peer-editing group, they had high
praise for how interesting the paragraph was but pointed out a number
of problems. To begin, they did not like the wording of her topic sentence. Although she had the basic information, the sentence seemed
long and there was an error in one of the verbs (*exhibits*). There was an
awkward phrase (*is making loud outbursts*), and they did not like the
parenthetical remark and the change of verbs (*tapping (wrong word)
hitting*). There was a major transition problem beginning with the
sentence *We all know* . . . Other spelling and grammar errors were
pointed out, as well.

When Deanetta rewrote her paragraph, she considered these issues and made some additional changes of her own, most involving cutting unnecessary words. Indeed, her final draft, reproduced here, is actually seventeen words shorter.

Rude Behavior

A group of people in my morning math class exhibit rude
behavior. As soon as the instructor gets into his lecture or formula,
someone will interrupt him with a comment that doesn't pertain to
what he's talking about. For example, someone will ask,
"Somebody moved the fan. Do you think we could get it back?"
Another student makes loud outbursts while yet another student is
arguing with the instructor about her test grade during class time,
not considering using the instructor's office hours for her personal
matters. While this sideshow is going on, the person behind me is
hitting my shoulder every ten minutes, asking, "What did they say?"
After all, sometimes it's hard to hear the instructor because of all
the gum popping. Although the door slams hard, the half dozen
people who arrive late always forget and let it slam. There are so
many distractions because of rudeness that I only hope I can make
it through this semester.

When Deanetta completed her Your Choices: Example worksheet, her comments mostly focused on her need to tighten up her language and provide effective transitions within the paragraph. She noted that her topic sentence had to be rewritten, not because she had left anything out but because her wordiness had been a problem.

GRAMMAR INSTRUCTION AND EXERCISES:
Verbals

You may have noticed that when you form sentences, you sometimes use a verb as the subject or object in a sentence. Examine the following sentence:

> She enjoyed **hearing** the sound of her own voice.

In this sentence, *hearing* is not a verb; rather, it functions as the object of the verb *enjoyed.* This means that *hearing* is a verbal. **Verbals** are verb forms that function as other parts of speech, such as nouns, adjectives, or adverbs. Verbals come in three forms: participles, gerunds, and infinitives.

Participles

A **participle** may be either past or present, depending on its ending. **Past participles** are marked by the *-ed* ending (except for irregular verbs, in which the form varies), and **present participles** end with *-ing.* Participles function as adjectives within sentences.

> **Terrified**, the child ran to his mother.   *Terrified* modifies *child.*

> The **chanting** monks managed to get their CD on the best-seller list.   *Chanting* modifies *monks.*

> *Note:*   When used with helping verbs, such as any form of the verbs *to be* or *to have,* participles form verb phrases.

Bruce **is running** from Maine to California to promote the benefits of exercise.   *Running* is the main verb of the verb phrase.

Candy **has worked** at this service station for five years now.

Worked is the main verb of the verb phrase.

Gerunds

Gerunds are verb forms that act like nouns. The gerund appears in the *-ing* form, so it is identical to the present participle. However, its function is different.

Swimming is a terrific form of exercise.

Swimming is a noun functioning as the subject of the sentence.

My wife and I enjoy **walking** in the evening.

Walking is a noun functioning as the object of the verb *enjoy*.

To see the difference between participles and gerunds, look at the following sentences:

Carla woke her **sleeping** roommate when she dropped her books to the floor.   *Sleeping* is a participle since it modifies *roommate*.

Sleeping is a wonderful way to spend an early Saturday morning.

Sleeping is a gerund since it functions as the subject of the sentence.

Infinitives

The **infinitive** is the "to" form of a verb: *to watch, to listen, to understand*. Infinitives can act as nouns, adjectives, and adverbs.

Congress decided **to cut** the budget for the arts and humanities.

To cut is a noun acting as the object of the verb *decided*.

The man **to sharpen** your knives works in a culinary shop at the mall.   *To sharpen* is an adjective describing *the man*.

The audience clapped **to show** its appreciation.   *To show* is an adverb describing *clapped*.

(See pages 352–54 for further discussion of verbals.)

Identify the participles, gerunds, and infinitives in the following sentences and describe whether they function as nouns, adjectives, or adverbs.

1. Many Americans, even those without Irish heritage, enjoy celebrating St. Patrick's Day.

2. The dog wanted to come into the house, but we would not let him.

3. Shouting, the ruffian was taken away by the police.

4. Cover your mouth when you expect to cough.

5. Marcia endured the boring lecture by jotting notes to her friends.

6. The workers tried to build a brace to support the falling structure.

7. Reading silently, Sergei knew the letter must have been painful to write.

8. Understanding your role in the company will protect your job in the long run.

9. The ambassador to Sri Lanka tried to convey the president's disappointment with the progress of the latest trade talks.

10. The new members of the marching band have many new formations to learn.

5 The Thing Itself

Definition and Classification Paragraphs

JOURNAL EXERCISE

Are you the kind of person who has trouble remembering people's names? Are you always wondering what to call something? Write in your journal about the importance of names of people, places, or things. What sorts of connections do you see between the names and the things named?

Think about names. Have you ever heard people say something like "He looks like a Jack" or "Her name is Tiffany but she doesn't look at all like one." What do people mean by that? They mean that those names contain some associations, often of physical traits, that the people may or may not live up to. Generally, there are ideas behind names. Some people, for example, will hold off on naming a baby until the child is born, so they can be sure to give the baby the "right" name.

What's in a name? Juliet, in William Shakespeare's *Romeo and Juliet,* says, "That which we call a rose by any other name would smell as sweet." But advertisers and business people recognize just how important a name is. If a product lacks a good, appealing name, it may not sell. Names are sometimes test marketed, with small, representative groups responding to a given name while other groups respond to other names. Even existing companies change their names. Datsun became Nissan to reflect the company's growing emphasis on selling quality cars that the former name did not convey, International Harvester became Navistar to modernize their image in the face of falling sales, and Federal Express shortened their name to FedEx to reflect its efficient, speedy service.

Choosing Words

How about words that are not names? A name for a product or even a person can be created by one person; however, other words have meanings only by the implicit agreement among speakers of a language. In other words, only one person is needed to create a name, but many people are needed to give meaning to a word. The word *rose* can refer to a type of flower because speakers of English agree that it is one meaning of *rose.*

The meanings of words used by speakers of a language can be found in a **dictionary.** There are, of course, many different dictionaries, and they can vary in terms of their length, complexity, number of words defined, and supplementary materials. Small pocket dictionaries give simple definitions to the most common words. Paperback dictionaries, often quite popular with students for carrying to class, cover approximately 50,000 to 60,000 words. A hardcover desktop dictionary, an important reference text for every serious college student, may have over 75,000 words. An unabridged dictionary, meaning that no words have been left out, will run over 450,000 words. Nevertheless, most all dictionaries have to supply similar or identical definitions of words; otherwise, communication would be impossible.

Take, for instance, the word *ladder. Merriam-Webster's Collegiate Dictionary,* Tenth Edition, defines *ladder* as "a structure for climbing up or down that consists essentially of two long sidepieces joined at intervals by crosspieces on which one may step." *The American Heritage Dictionary of the English Language* defines *ladder* as "a device consisting of two long structural members crossed by parallel rungs, used to climb or descend." As you can see, the two definitions are quite similar.

The differences between the two are not substantial; they are different ways of describing the same thing.

Concrete Words

Ladder is a fairly simple term because, as a noun, it is **concrete,** which means that the word represents something physical. A ladder can be seen and touched. A ladder has material reality. The other senses—hearing, tasting, and smelling—may also be used to detect or describe something that is concrete.

Abstract Words

Some words that are used in everyday language have no material reality; rather, they represent ideas, emotions, or concepts, such as *justice, love,* and *democracy.* These words are called **abstract.** You cannot hear justice; you cannot see love; you cannot touch democracy. Instead, you can sense symptoms of abstract words: you listen to a trial; you see a couple holding hands; you hold an election ballot in your hands. The symptoms can describe the word, but they are not the word itself.

Why Choose Definition?

Definition paragraphs usually concern themselves with exploring the meanings of abstract words. Occasionally, they may also be used to describe unusual and rare concrete words. The definition paragraph is different from the descriptive paragraph. The definition paragraph develops an understanding of what a concept or idea means, whereas the descriptive paragraph is usually focused on reproducing in the reader's imagination a person, place, or thing.

EXERCISE 5.1

Without using a dictionary, write, in your own words, a brief definition of each of the following terms.

love	charisma
justice	discipline
success	peace
intelligence	evil

Topic Sentences

The topic sentence you write for a definition paragraph should lay the groundwork for the rest of the paragraph. The definition topic sentence will introduce your reader to the main concept you choose to develop for the paragraph, but, by its very nature, it will not be able to totally cover everything. That is what the rest of the paragraph will do. Look at these topic sentences:

> When your gas gauge reads "Empty," or "E," that means you are out of gas.

> The dictionary says that <u>counterfeit</u> means that something is fake or a forgery of the original.

Neither one of these sentences is very satisfactory as a topic sentence for a definition paragraph. The first sentence simply does not lead the reader anywhere. The meaning of "Empty," or "E," on a gas gauge is well understood. There is nowhere to go because, in this context, "Empty" needs no further definition. The second topic sentence does not give the writer's point of view about the word, only the dictionary's. There is no direction for the paragraph to take and no sense of dissatisfaction with the dictionary's definition. The definition given seems to be accepted; as such, there is no paragraph to write.

A better, more effective topic sentence will take a stance or present an attitude about the word being defined. As a writer, you should make sure that the reader has a strong sense of where you will head in the rest of the paragraph. Examine these two topic sentences:

> Many people feel that to be truly "educated" in today's world, one must have at least a passing acquaintance with computers and how to use them.

> The standard of living deemed "poor" in the United States rests upon an unfavorable comparison to other social classes within this country, not with the rest of the world.

The first topic sentence takes a well-known word and essentially adds a quality to its expected meanings. The writer acknowledges that a great deal of debate occurs over what should constitute a truly educated person and that such a definition is always open for debate and change. At one time, knowledge of Latin and Ancient Greek were considered the hallmarks of an educated person. Today, those subjects are studied only by a relatively few students and are not considered by most educators to be mandatory for a good education. Thus, a topic sentence like the first would be another voice in the debate about education and, more particularly, the importance of computers in education.

The second topic sentence involves stipulating a new way of looking at the word *poor.* That is, the writer is supplying a new meaning for the word. The author recognizes that *poor* is a relative term. However, the questions is, Relative to what? If people with low incomes in the United States are compared to people with high incomes, they can be considered poor. If those people are compared with the average person in a nation where standards of living are extremely low, then those poor people in the United States would suddenly look reasonably well off. Such an argument might be useful in discussing the problems of international economics or the devastating effects of starvation, war, or disease in many foreign countries.

EXERCISE 5.2

Examine each of the following topic sentences and determine whether it is an effective topic sentence for a definition paragraph. Indicate each correct sentence with the letter *C* and rewrite the others.

1. I think fatherhood is more than what television commercials say it is.

2. True intelligence is a function of emotional maturity as well as comprehension and computation skills.

3. Isn't it true that trust is something that cannot be regained?

4. Feminism is not man hating.

5. A tourist visits foreign places; a traveler experiences them.

6. I'd say Paradise is a cooler of soda, a bag of chips, and six straight hours of televised football games.

7. Addiction is not simply a physical phenomenon but a psychological one, as well.

8. My dictionary says that <u>freedom</u> means release from bondage.

9. Death is not an end but a new beginning.

10. If the children of the sixties are the Me Generation and the children of the nineties are Generation X, who are the people in between?

Support

When your instructor asks you to write a paragraph based on definition, you will need to determine what strategy or strategies you will use to define the word. An obvious place to begin, of course, is your college dictionary. However, dictionaries can be notoriously unsatisfactory for defining some abstract words. Instead, attempt to write your own definition of the word as best you understand it *before* you check with a dictionary. Take, for instance, the following definition of the word *clean* developed by Gloria, a community college student:

> <u>Clean</u> means more than the absence of dirt; it means that the thing or person is neat, straight, and put together properly.

However, when Gloria looked up *clean* in a dictionary, she found the following definition: "1. free from dirt or filth. 2. free from defect or blemish. 3. pure or not adulterated." Although her definition contained elements similar to the dictionary's definition, she felt her definition went further. What Gloria has discovered is a good way to develop the rest of her paragraph: that clean is more than the absence of something (such as dirt); it is also the presence of something else (neatness), which may also need explaining. After all, *dirt* is a concrete term that needs little explanation, but *neatness* is an abstract term that will need to be explained.

EXERCISE 5.3

Referring to the same term you defined in Exercise 5.1, consult a dictionary and write down the definition you find there. Note where your definition from Exercise 5.1 substantially differs from the dictionary's. Consider whether your definition is simply expanding on the ideas more concisely stated in the dictionary or whether you're considering areas beyond what are covered in the dictionary.

Gloria's prewriting on *clean* is a good start. She may wish to shape up her own definition in light of the dictionary's definition and come up with a topic sentence. Thus, her revised topic sentence might read:

<u>Clean</u> means more than being free from dirt or filth but also being

neat and orderly.

Now Gloria needs to build support for her topic sentence. She can do so by deciding among the following strategies:

■ ***Stipulation.*** A definition that is stipulated is one in which the writer supplies his or her own meaning for the term. Clearly, the stipulated meaning cannot be grossly different from the accepted dictionary definition (also known as the **denotation**), but it can add to or break up the definition. In the earlier topic sentence about the standard of living, the writer attempted to stipulate the meaning of the word *poor*.

■ ***Negation.*** Negation is a way of defining something by saying what it is not. It can be an effective means of stripping away mistaken assumptions or **connotations** from a word. For instance, saying, "A good marriage is not simply a partnership based on convenience" is negation. However, negation alone is seldom enough. You cannot define something entirely by saying what it is not; you must eventually say what it is.

■ ***Synonym/Antonym.*** Can you find other words that mean the same thing? Those are called **synonyms.** Sometimes presenting a synonym for a word can enlighten a reader who is unfamiliar with the original term. A reader unfamiliar with the word *futilitarianism,* for example, might better understand the word *pessimism.* Be aware, however, that synonyms rarely have the exact same meaning. Different words for the same thing can have different connotations, such as the words *friend* and *pal.* Both refer to a close, personal acquaintance, but *pal* contains a familiarity that goes further than *friend*. *Pal* also is used more often to describe the friendship between two men than two women. On the other hand, **antonyms** are opposites. If your reader understands the opposite of something, then that may make the original term easier to understand. A reader looking to understand the term *propriety* can contrast it to antonyms such as *improperness* or *obscenity.*

■ ***Example.*** The technique of example (discussed in Chapter 4) is a means of illustrating or giving specific instances of an abstract concept. In other words, you define the word by showing events, persons, or places that seem to embody the meaning of the word. You could define the word *silence* by giving examples of different types of silences, such as showing how the silence of a room full of people who all suddenly stop speaking at the same time is different from the silence of a room in which only one person is present.

You can use one, two, three, or all four of these writing strategies when you are developing a definition paragraph.

Transitions

When you're writing a definition paragraph, be sure to provide good, logical transitions, especially when you move from one definition strategy to another. The transitional words and phrases will signal to the reader which strategy you're using. If you're stipulating meaning, use words and phrases such as *that is, this means, consider,* and *if.* Negation involves transitional words and phrases such as *this does not mean, is not,* and *no.* The example strategy employ words and phrases such as *specifically, in this case, for example, for instance, namely,* and *one situation.*

Look at the following passage written by Gloria. As she defines the word *clean,* she employs three writing strategies. The transitional words and phrases are printed in bold type.

> <u>Clean</u> means more than being free from dirt or filth but also being neat and orderly. **That is**, there is more to being clean than just not being dirty. A kitchen that is clean, **for instance**, has a certain shine to it. **It's not** that there are **no** coffee grounds in the sink or that there is **no** empty milk carton on the counter. <u>Clean</u> means that all the kitchen items have been put back where they belong, the food is in the cupboard or refrigerator, and nothing is lying around collecting dust. <u>Clean</u> is pleasing, an emotional quality beyond the physical requirements of sanitation. **If** looking at the kitchen doesn't make you smile, it's not clean.

Student Writing Assignment: Definition

Write a definition paragraph based on the topic you chose for Exercise 5.1 and Exercise 5.3. Be sure to use the strategies of stipulation, negation, synonym/antonym, and example in your paragraph. Follow the steps listed in the Start-Up Suggestions and Self-Revision Questions. Then bring your paragraph to class for peer editing. Revise your paragraph and then complete the section labeled Your Choices: Definition to discuss the decisions you made during the composing and revising process.

Start-Up Suggestions

Follow these steps before writing your first draft.

1. Look up your word in at least two different dictionaries. See if one definition appears better or more complete than the other.
2. Brainstorm or freewrite for ten minutes on your topic. Examine what you've written for examples, synonyms, or antonyms.
3. Write in your journal about your personal attitudes toward the concepts involved with the word you chose.
4. Write a list of examples that you think fit the word you chose. Then write a list of examples that suggest the opposite of your word.
5. Draft a topic sentence for your definition paragraph.
6. Draft a scratch, or informal, outline for your paragraph based on your topic sentence.

Self-Revision Questions

Answer these questions after writing your first draft and before rewriting the draft for submission to your peer-editing group.

1. Underline your topic sentence. Is it the first sentence in your paragraph?
2. Does your topic sentence provide a definition for the word that can be expanded on later?
3. Does your paragraph support your topic sentence through the use of specific details rather than generalizations? Have you supplied sufficient examples to explain your meaning?

4. Have you used appropriate, effective transitions? (You might want to review the list of transitional words and phrases under the heading Transitions.)
5. Do you have a wrap-up sentence?

Revise your paragraph and submit it to your peer-editing group.

Peer-Editing Guidelines for Definition

Answer these questions for each of the paragraphs written by other members of your peer-editing group.

1. What is the paragraph's topic sentence?
2. Does the topic sentence introduce one of the topics assigned?
3. Does the topic sentence reveal the author's opinion about the topic?
4. Is the support sufficient and logical?
5. Is the support relevant to the topic sentence?
6. Does the author use stipulation, negation, synonym/antonym, and example? Describe the instances of each.
7. What transitional words and phrases does the author use? Are they sufficient?
8. What was your favorite part of the paragraph?
9. What one change would most improve the paragraph?
10. What is the crystalline word of the paragraph?

Prepare the final draft of your paragraph, taking the comments of your peer-editing group into account.

Your Choices: Definition

Answer these questions after you have prepared your final draft.

1. Why did you choose your topic?
2. Why did you choose your title? Did you have to revise it after the first draft? If so, explain why.
3. Did your topic sentence need revising? How?
4. Which dictionary's definition of your word did you use to start your paragraph? Why?

5. Which of the definition strategies (stipulation, negation, synonym/antonym, example) did you use? Why?
6. What specific details did you add to the final draft?
7. What did you change in your support? Why?
8. What did you leave unchanged? Why?
9. Did your wrap-up sentence need revising? Why?
10. Did you agree or disagree with your peer editors' choice for the crystalline word? If you disagreed, did you make any revisions to emphasize the word you wanted?

Why Choose Classification?

When biologists examine specimens, one thing they must know is how to identify the individual specimens. Specimens are identified by putting them into **classifications.** These classifications start out at the most general level—determining what kingdom it is a part of, animal or plant. The levels of classification become increasingly narrow until the specimen can be defined at the level of genus, species, and even subspecies.

When you classify an item, you are saying that it is one type within an array of several possible types. In order for you to classify, you must have a complete set of possible classifications or categories, and the item examined must fit into one of those classifications. You might say something like, "The students in my class are nerds, preps, jocks, bubbleheads, or wannabes." In that case, each student (including yourself) must be placed into one of those five categories.

Of course, you also can categorize items in more than one way. Think of automobiles. They may be categorized by price level (cheap, moderate, expensive, superexpensive), maker (Ford, Toyota, Nissan, Chevrolet, and so forth), type (subcompact, economy, midsize, luxury), country of origin (American, German, Japanese, Korean, British, Italian), purpose (family car, racing car, all-terrain sports vehicle, heavy-duty hauling truck), or any number of other ways. The same can be said for other items that you may wish to classify.

What is important is that the classifications be logically consistent or have some unifying idea. For instance, you would not mix categories, such as starting a classification of automobiles, by describing countries of origin and then adding *luxury cars* as another category. That would make no sense, since luxury cars are made in many countries. It is not the same type of category as *American, German, Japanese,* and so forth. *Luxury cars* would be more suited to classification based on size or type of vehicle.

When you examine something for the purposes of classification, you must think about what type of categories you will be using. Your decision on how to categorize items may well depend on the point you're trying to make. For instance, if you want to describe the general population of students on your campus, you may choose to divide by race or ethnic background, or perhaps you're interested in the breakdown of students by major, age, or nation of origin. Since all students have ethnicity, majors (including "undeclared"), age, and nation of origin, these are legitimate categories. You may not, however, break down a population of students by an array of categories that are too narrow to encompass all the students. For example, the sentence mentioned earlier about all students in the class being *nerds, preps, jocks, bubbleheads, and wannabes* is a greatly restricted list of possibilities (not to mention offensive to anyone placed in an unflattering category!) that would be inadequate for describing a large student population.

EXERCISE 5.4

Using classification, place the following items into categories or logical groups. Be ready to explain the bases of your classifications. You should discover at least three different ways to categorize the items.

spaghetti with meat sauce	szechwan beef
bagels	eggplant parmesan
egg rolls	won-ton soup
bacon and eggs	corn on the cob
chips and salsa	refried beans
steamed rice	garlic bread
hot dogs	menudo soup
minestrone	bean burrito

Topic Sentences

The topic sentence for a classification paragraph must state the general subject that is being examined and the categories into which it is being divided. The categories must be sufficient to include all items within the subject in one of the categories. Examine this topic sentence:

Eggs can be cooked by two methods: hard boiled and fried.

If this were your topic sentence, you would have missed soft-boiled eggs, poached eggs, scrambled eggs, even omelettes and soufflés. Remember that your topic sentence must be able to cover all of the possibilities.

Make sure that the categories do not overlap, either. Such a situation creates inaccuracies because one item should not belong to more than one category at a time. For example, dividing a choir into *men, women, and tenors* is a mistake since tenors are men, as well. Another way to categorize the choir would be into *basses, tenors, altos, and sopranos* or, more simply, *men and women*.

EXERCISE 5.5

Examine each of the following topic sentences and determine whether it is an effective topic sentence for a classification paragraph. Indicate each correct sentence with the letter *C* and rewrite the others.

1. Colleges and universities come in three types: public, private secular, and private religious.

2. There are many types of pollution, including air and water.

3. Republicans can generally be divided as follows: country club or Wall Street Republicans, western state Republicans, and socially conservative Republicans.

4. People are basically winners or losers.

5. Immigrants to America can be broken down by the region of origin: Europe, Asia, Africa, the Pacific Islands, and Latin America.

6. Films are romances, comedies, mysteries, or R-rated.

7. Films can be grouped together by their ratings: G, PG, PG-13, R, and NC-17.

8. Workers in industrial societies are broken down into two categories: white-collar workers and blue-collar workers.

9. Several different types of sandwich breads include white, whole wheat, sour dough, and bread that is made fresh daily.

10. Popular magazines include weekly news magazines, hobby-oriented magazines, and <u>People</u>.

Support

When you are faced with writing a paragraph based on classification, you must determine what your principle of classification will be. Will you be grouping cars together by their type? Cost? Purpose? Once that decision has been made, your topic sentence will include the various categories. The rest of the paragraph, your support, should expand on each of the categories, usually giving examples for each one. Examine the following paragraph:

Topic sentence   While to most people, all surfers look alike, they actually come in three types: the kook, the soul surfer, and the pro. The kook is a

Type 1   new surfer, a novice. The kook is actually the most dangerous surfer because he doesn't know what he's doing on the waves. The kook

Type 2   has no control of his board. **Another** type is the soul surfer. The soul surfer has made surfing a lifestyle and probably holds a low-wage, low-responsibility job that allows him to surf whenever he can. **On**

Type 3   **the other hand**, the pro is the expert. The pro is athletic, agile, and daring, and other surfers can only hold him in awe. His gear is in better shape than the soul surfer's, sometimes because he has a sponsor but also because he knows he needs the finest gear to surf his best.

Notice that Jake devoted several sentences to each type of surfer, trying to show the reader how to recognize each type of surfer. The examples include information about the dress and behavior of the surfers that distinguishes what type of surfer is riding the waves.

Transitions

The transitional words and phrases in a classification paragraph will include *also, additionally, another, on the other hand, however, in addition, first, second,* and *last.* In Jake's paragraph and in the following paragraph, the transitional words are printed in bold type.

The federal government is divided into three branches: the executive, the legislative, and the judicial. **First**, the executive branch includes the office of the president, the president's cabinet, and a wide array of agencies that also fall under the president's control. The president has a wide range of responsibilities, but, most basically, the president operates the federal government and enforces its laws. **On the other hand**, the legislative branch, made up of two houses of Congress, must write the laws in the form of bills. The federal government cannot spend money without the authorization of Congress. **Last**, the judicial branch, made up of the Supreme Court and federal appellate courts, is in charge of interpreting the law and determining whether laws are constitutional. This approach to government has been effective at preventing any one branch from becoming too strong.

Student Writing Assignment: Classification

Write a paragraph based on classification using one of the following subjects. Make certain that you explain to your reader your basis or unifying principle for classification. Follow the steps listed in the Start-Up Suggestions and Self-Revision Questions. Then bring your paragraph to class for peer editing. Revise your paragraph and then complete the section labeled Your Choices: Classification to discuss the decisions you made during the composing and revising process.

methods of child rearing	governments
part-time jobs	methods of studying
roommates	newspapers
religions	athletes
computers	desserts

Start-Up Suggestions

Follow these steps before writing your first draft.

1. Find research materials, either at home or at the library, concerning your topic. Can you discover any unifying principles that can group together categories within your topic?
2. Do a clustering exercise (described in Chapter 2), in which you place your topic at the center and the types of your topic around the center. Can you expand your cluster to another level, finding examples of each type?

3. Write in your journal about any personal experiences you may have related to your topic. Try to examine your personal attitudes toward the different types within your topic.
4. Draft a topic sentence that not only clearly states the unifying principle of your classification but also reflects in some way your attitude or opinion about the topic.
5. Form a scratch, or informal, outline based on your topic sentence.

Self-Revision Questions

Answer these questions after writing your first draft and before rewriting the draft for submission to your peer-editing group.

1. Underline your topic sentence. Is it the first sentence in your paragraph?
2. Does your topic sentence directly answer the topic assigned?
3. Does your paragraph support your topic sentence through the use of specific details rather than generalizations? Have you supplied sufficient examples to explain your meaning?
4. Have you used appropriate, effective transitions? (You might want to review the list of transitional words and phrases under the heading Transitions.)
5. Do you have a wrap-up sentence?

Revise your paragraph and submit it to your peer-editing group.

Peer-Editing Guidelines for Classification

Answer these questions for each of the paragraphs written by other members of your peer-editing group.

1. What is the paragraph's topic sentence?
2. Is the categorization in the topic sentence based on a detectable unifying principle? What is that principle?
3. Does the topic sentence include all the possible categories based on the unifying principle?
4. Is the support sufficient and logical? Do any of the categories overlap?
5. Is the support relevant to the topic sentence?
6. Do all the items discussed fit into one of the defined categories? Are any items left out?

7. What transitional words and phrases does the author use? Are they sufficient?
8. What was your favorite part of the paragraph?
9. What one change would most improve the paragraph?
10. What is the crystalline word of the paragraph?

Prepare the final draft of your paragraph, taking the comments of your peer-editing group into account.

Your Choices: Classification

Answer these questions after you have finished your final draft.

1. Why did you choose your topic?
2. Why did you choose your title? Did you have to revise it after the first draft? If so, explain why.
3. Did your topic sentence need revising? How?
4. Did you change the unifying principle of your classification?
5. Did you need to add or delete any categories? Why or why not?
6. What specific details did you add to the final draft?
7. What did you change in your support? Why?
8. What did you leave unchanged? Why?
9. Did your wrap-up sentence need revising? Why?
10. Did you agree or disagree with your peer editors' choice for the crystalline word? If you disagreed, did you make any revisions to emphasize the word you wanted?

COMPUTER EXERCISE

Type your paragraph for the last student writing assignment onto your computer if you have not done so already. Then underline all of the important words that you believe appear in your paragraph. Pass your paragraph to your writing partner and receive his or her paragraph. Examine the words that your partner has underlined, and determine if you agree that those are, indeed, important words. If you have any additional words to suggest or would like to suggest that some of the words have only minor importance, use brackets [ ] to make comments in your partner's text. Then exchange the paragraphs again and see what your partner has done with your paragraph.

You should find that the underlined words contain the paragraph's main message. They should be the words that are distinctive, reflecting the overall tone of the writing.

THE REVISION PROCESS:
A Student Writing Sample

Jocelyn was faced with her definition assignment. She decided to write on the topic *love*. She knew this word was going to be popular among her classmates, so she wanted to make sure that she wrote about the word in a way that would stand out. She decided to begin by examining her own ideas about love with a five-minute freewrite. She wrote:

> *love does seem to be such an easy word in some ways love means that you like someone a lot well, more than just like my mother used to tell me that you don't love things you only love people I wonder if that's true I guess it's really what you mean love could mean a lot of different things to different people I guess my mom thought love always had to be the same is it? I know love can't always be the same because I love my boyfriend and I love my mom and those aren't the same things of course and I love some food too even though I know mom said I'm not supposed to*

When Jocelyn had finished, she looked over her freewrite and decided that she liked the idea of looking at different types of love.

She looked in a dictionary and discovered that the definition of *love* was "affection for another arising out of kinship or personal ties." That seemed to include the idea of both her boyfriend and her mother. She read another: "warm attachment, enthusiasm or devotion." That seemed to tie in with what Jocelyn felt was a love of objects.

Finally, Jocelyn made a list of things that she felt she loved. The list read as follows:

—   *Mom and Dad*
—   *Simon*
—   *summer days*
—   *chocolate*
—   *kittens*

—   *my sister (usually)*
—   *Italian food!*
—   *sleeping in late*

Jocelyn decided that her list covered people, things, and circumstances. With that in mind, she decided to write her topic sentence.

For her first topic sentence, she just decided to write a definition of *love*. She wrote:

Love is an intense feeling of affection.

That did not, however, seem adequate. Not only was this definition quite broad, but it lacked any of Jocelyn's opinion about love. Instead, she tried the following:

The word love is more than an intense affection for another person.

Last, Jocelyn decided that the word *affection* could be misleading, suggesting more of a romantic relationship than she intended to mean. So, she rewrote the topic sentence again:

The word love means more than an intense affectionate concern for another person.

From this topic sentence, she was ready to build her paragraph. It is reproduced here:

The Different Forms of Love

The word <u>love</u> means more than an intense affectionate concern for another person. That is to say, there are also emotions and feelings involved for things other than people. A child, for instance, has a certain attachment for a favorite toy or blankey. They associate this with a form of love. Consider the love of a cool breeze on a hot day or the feeling of the warm sunshine on your face. You have people who have a favorite television show and you may have heard them comment on how they just love this or that show. Then you will have people who love certain types of food, drink, cars, or even music. Of course that is not the same type of love one feels for a soft cuddly kitten or a warm playful puppy, but it is love all the same. Love does not have to be an intense sexual drive for another person. For example, the deep love and caring feeling that a parent has for a child is not sexual nor is the loving bond between siblings. Therefore we can see that love is not limited to the affection from one person to another. It seems apparent that love is also emotional and involves mixed feelings that can be applied to an inanimate as well as animate thing or object.

This rough draft was submitted to Jocelyn's peer-editing group. Although they generally approved of the paragraph, they wanted Jocelyn to tighten up her use of language and be as specific as possible. They noticed that she did use stipulation in her definition of *love,* and that negation appeared, especially to counter the argument that love can only be felt between two people. Synonyms were used as part of the stipulation, but Jocelyn did not employ any antonyms. The group liked her use of examples and felt that they were a strong aspect of the paragraph.

In her movement from the rough to final draft, Jocelyn worked to improve her language skills, cutting any unnecessary words and trying to keep the attention on the specific examples of things that can be loved.

The Different Forms of Love

The word <u>love</u> means more than an intense, affectionate concern for another person; it includes affection, emotion, and feelings involving things as well as people. For instance, a child has an endearing attachment for a favorite toy or "blankey." To that child, the attachment is a form of love. Close your eyes and consider the sensation you feel on a hot day, as a cool and gentle breeze graces your skin or you experience the feeling of the warm sunshine on your face. Do you not love it? Take the love people have for certain foods, drinks, cars, or forms of art or music. No, it may not be the same type of love one feels for a soft, cuddly kitten or a frisky, warm puppy. Yet it is love, all the same. Love does not have to be an intense sexual drive for another person. Look at the deep love that a parent has for a child; it is not sexual love, nor is the loving bond between siblings. Therefore, we can see that love is not limited to the affection just between two people. It is apparent that love is not only emotionally intense but also involves deep concern and strong feelings that can be applied to animate as well as inanimate objects.

GRAMMAR INSTRUCTION AND EXERCISES:
Parallel Structure

Look at the following flawed sentences:

Jon likes swimming, running, and to hike.

The boxer was a brute in private but projecting a genteel public image.

The crafts were all made from natural products, not products derived from artificial substances.

Parallel structure requires that you use the same word constructions for each part of a list or for comparisons and contrasts.

Items in a list

Lists of items require parallel structure, whether written in sentence form, as a vertical list, or in an outline.

Original:

Jon likes swimming, running, and to hike.

Corrected:

Jon likes swimming, running, and hiking.

Note: The repetition of a group of words in a list should include the same types of words in each group.

Original:

Cindy looked for her ring under her bed, checked her dresser top, and her closet was examined, as well.

Corrected:

Cindy looked for her ring under her bed, on top of her dresser, and inside her closet.

A vertical list uses a few words for each item.

Original:

Items required for my backpacking trip:

-- sleeping bag

-- tent

-- mess kit

-- buy some trail food for snacking along the way

-- get some bandages in case of an emergency

Corrected:

Items required for my backpacking trip:

-- sleeping bag

-- tent

-- mess kit

-- trail food

-- bandages

Outlines can use either phrases or complete sentences for each division or category. Stay consistent with your use of either one.

Original:

<u>Title</u>: Animal Rights Means No Rights for Human Patients

      A. The importance of human life

      B. Seeking to protect animals

      C. Medicine and morality

      D. There's no way medicine can totally replace animal research

Corrected:

<u>Title</u>: Animal Rights Means No Rights for Human Patients

    A. The importance of human life

    B. The protection of animals

    C. Medicine and morality

    D. No substitution for animal research

Comparisons and Contrasts

Sentences that make comparisons and/or contrasts between items, either directly or indirectly, must use parallel structure. Indirect or suggested comparisons use conjunctions such as *but* and *and*.

Original:

The boxer was a brute in private but projecting a genteel public image.

Corrected:

The boxer was brutish in private but genteel in public.

Parallel structure is also required for direct comparisons or contrasts.

Original:

The crafts were made from natural products, not products derived from artificial substances.

Corrected:

The crafts were made from natural products, not artificial ones.

(See pages 364–67 for further discussion of parallel structure.)

EXERCISES   Fix the faulty parallel structure in each of the following sentences.

    1. Columbus sailed to the New World in the Nina, the Pinta, and another boat that was known as the Santa Maria.

    2. The problem was difficult, complicated, and it did not lend itself to negotiations.

3. Marianne walked into the session anxious; when she left, she felt revived.

4. The musical was exciting, new, and it was appealing.

5. The jury decided that the witness was either lying or she had been confused.

6. Richard's tour took him to the cathedral, the museum, and then he visited a little cafe.

7. Many Hollywood actors have created scandals by their involvement with drugs, lavish spending, or by becoming involved romantically with married co-stars.

8. Because the weather was horrible and also because we had run out of money, we decided it was time to return home.

9. Ann played tennis, cleaned out the garage, and then the kitchen was repainted by her, as well.

10. The box contained marbles, jacks, and also in there were some old baseball cards.

6 Similarities and Differences

Comparison and Contrast Paragraphs

JOURNAL EXERCISE

Write about the last major purchase you made: a car, a computer, or maybe even a new pair of shoes. Did you look at more than one brand or model before buying? Did you investigate the similarities and differences in terms of the cost? Appearance? Performance? Reputation of the manufacturer? When you had to decide which of two items to buy, how did you make your choice?

Can you remember a time when you were confronted with a difficult decision, one that would have a major impact on your future? Before making that decision, you probably thought about the benefits and drawbacks of each option. Perhaps you even drew up a list. Eventually, however, you had to make a choice. If you made a good decision, the chances are you made that choice based on looking at all the possible outcomes and choosing the option that gave you the best hope for success and happiness.

For many people, the decision to attend college can be difficult. They have to compare what life in and beyond college might be like to life without college. Some see college as a way to meet new people, hear new ideas, and gain greater personal and professional satisfaction. Others, however, may not attend college because they prefer to earn money immediately, live off their wits, or develop skills only work experience can provide.

The choices you make in life are not always dramatic. Do you buy the Chevy Blazer or the Toyota 4×4? Your decision may be based on cost, availability, and reliability. Do you listen to jazz or rock? Your choice of radio station will reflect your current mood and setting. Should you take a chemistry course to fulfill your general requirement in science, or should you try biology? Your choice may be based on your past academic or personal experience with these fields or simply on which course is available at the time you need it.

Why Choose Comparison and Contrast?

Comparison means looking at the similarities between two things, people, places, or ideas. **Contrast** means looking at the differences between two things, people, places, or ideas. Usually, the subjects are of the same type: Republican and Democratic parties (U.S. political parties), Chinese and Thai food (cuisines of Asia), Elvis Presley and Bruce Springsteen (rock icons), or Cadillacs and Lincolns (luxury automobiles). Imagine you wish to compare and contrast the Republican and Democratic parties. When you *compare* the two U.S. political parties, you can look at how both parties work within the established political system rather than outside of it, how both have ties to special interests, how both use similar techniques in campaigning, and how both have their own heroes from the past whose ideals are still respected today. When you *contrast* the two parties, you can look at how they differ in terms of their approaches to social issues, their vision of America's place in the world community, and their preferences regarding the relationship of government and business.

EXERCISE 6.1

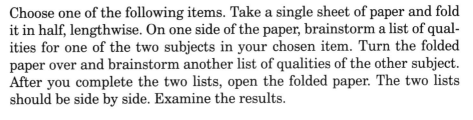

Choose one of the following items. Take a single sheet of paper and fold it in half, lengthwise. On one side of the paper, brainstorm a list of qualities for one of the two subjects in your chosen item. Turn the folded paper over and brainstorm another list of qualities of the other subject. After you complete the two lists, open the folded paper. The two lists should be side by side. Examine the results.

two restaurants you enjoy
two TV shows you watch regularly
two cars you have driven
two schools you have attended
two friends

Topic Sentences

A comparison and contrast paragraph must have a topic sentence that presents your idea, attitude, or view about both subjects. If your topic sentence covers only one subject, the reader will be surprised when a second subject appears. If there is no idea, attitude, or view expressed, the topic sentence could be meaningless. Look at these two examples:

Coffee houses are a wonderful place to meet people.

Coffee houses and diners have many similarities and differences.

The first sentence discusses coffee houses only, so the reader will expect to read only about coffee houses. If the paragraph then discusses diners, the reader will be confused.

The second sentence mentions both coffee houses and diners but says little about them. As a result, the sentence is meaningless. To test this, substitute any two items for *coffee houses* and *diners*. The sentence says the same thing, no matter what subjects are used. The problem is that this topic sentence expresses no view or attitude about the subject.

A better topic sentence may result by combining the two topic sentences:

Although both diners and coffee houses provide food and drink, coffee houses allow for greater socializing among the patrons.

EXERCISE 6.2

Examine each of the following topic sentences below and determine whether it is a good topic sentence for a comparison and contrast paragraph. Indicate each correct sentence with the letter *C* and rewrite the others.

1. There are many similarities and differences between tea drinkers and coffee drinkers.

2. Although both Los Angeles and New York are important media centers, only in New York can one find so many magazine and book publishers.

3. Toddlers are more difficult to care for.

4. Computers today can be compared to automobiles at the turn of the century.

5. Texas barbecue is different from Kansas City barbecue.

6. My cousin Rusty is like my Uncle Ray.

7. Whales in captivity are less likely to bear cubs.

8. Despite the fact that both countries are considered democracies, the United States and Canada actually have different forms of government.

9. High school and college are alike in some ways and not alike in other ways.

10. Romance among seniors and among the young is similar and different.

Support

When your instructor asks you to write a paragraph using comparison and contrast, you need to determine the points of similarity and difference of the subjects. If the points of one subject have nothing in common with the points of the other, your paragraph will fail to make reasonable sense, and no valid conclusion about the two subjects can be reached. For example, look at this passage from a student named Richard:

> My father asked me to decide whether I wanted to attend State University or go away to Cobble College. State U. has great sports teams and lots of my friends will be going there. Cobble College costs $15,000 a year and is supposed to have some of the best dorm food in the country. I haven't decided where to go yet.

Richard's indecision is hardly a surprise. He needs to discover some points in common between the schools and determine which of these are most important in making his choice. One way to do this would be to use a prewriting technique, such as listing. Richard could make two parallel lists, one for each school, and brainstorm a list of the qualities of each school. The lists might look something like the following:

State U.	Cobble College
public	private
graduate programs	no graduate school
great sports teams	great dorm food
large, mostly local student population	highly acclaimed school of architecture
friends from high school will go there	expensive—$15,000
inexpensive	requires that I live on campus my first year
urban setting	far from home
over 30,000 students	national student population
lacks prestige	influential alumni, including two Nobel Prize winners
	rural setting

After brainstorming, Richard should consult the two lists and see which points in common could be discussed. If he were to draw lines from one point to the point in common from the other list, his lists would look something like this:

State U.   *Cobble College*
public ———————————— *private*
graduate programs ———— *no graduate school*
great sports teams   *great dorm food*
large, mostly local   *highly acclaimed school of*
   student population   *architecture*
friends from high   *expensive—$15,000*
   school will go there   *requires that I live on*
inexpensive   *campus my first year*
urban setting   *far from home*
over 30,000 students   *national student population*
lacks prestige   *influential alumni, including*
                        two Nobel Prize winners
                        rural setting

Then Richard needs to decide which of the points are most important. If he is interested in becoming an architect, then Cobble's prestigious reputation in that field may be important. If he is on a limited budget, State's affordability will be very important. Essentially, for each point discussed for one school, a corresponding point from the other list needs to be included.

EXERCISE 6.3

Using your brainstorming list from Exercise 6.1, draw lines to connect the corresponding points of one list to the other.

Once you have reviewed your lists, you are then free to formulate your topic sentence. Remember that the topic sentence must contain both subjects and a view or attitude about those subjects. When Richard tried his hand at a topic sentence, he wrote the following:

Cobble College and State University have a lot in common and a lot that is different.

This topic sentence failed to express any particular view about his subjects. Richard tried again with a new topic sentence:

Cobble College and State University both have strong points to me.

This still seemed unsatisfactory because a reader would be unable to distinguish between one school and the other. Richard revised his topic sentence a third time and came up with the following:

Although both schools have their advantages, Cobble College is a better choice for me than State University.

This topic sentence satisfies the requirements that both subjects be listed and that a view or attitude about the subjects be expressed.

At this point, Richard was ready to write the body of his paragraph. He decided to write about the corresponding points from his brainstorming lists, moving back and forth between colleges.

Topic sentence   Although both schools have their advantages, Cobble College is a better choice for me than State University. Cobble College is a

Point 1   small, rural private school, which I like, but it is quite expensive at $15,000 a year. State is a large, urban, public institution but costs

Point 2   less than half of what Cobble does. However, Cobble has a great school of architecture, which is my major, while State's is not well regarded. I know I'll miss my friends if I go to Cobble because

Point 3   they'll all be at State, but I cannot pass up this opportunity to create a great future for myself.

The technique used to organize the support in this paragraph is known as a *point-by-point* pattern. The paragraph is organized around a series of points and discusses the qualities of Cobble College and State University in relation to those points: characteristics and costs of each institution, reputations of the schools, Richard's friends, and Richard's hopes for the future. Note that points such as sports teams and dorm food were not included since they were not as important to this student.

A different technique for organizing support is the *subject-by-subject* pattern. In this pattern, the student discusses all the points that relate to one subject and then discusses all the points that relate to the other subject. The technique can work well when the text involved is not too long and the subjects contain implied similarities. If Richard's paragraph were rewritten in the subject-by-subject pattern, it might look something like this:

Topic sentence   Although both schools have their advantages, Cobble College
                     is a better choice for me than State University. Even though I dislike

Subject 1   large, urban environments such as State's, it is a public institution,
                     so it is very affordable. Many of my friends will be going to State,
                     as well, and I know if I don't go there, I will miss them. However,
                     State's architecture program is not well regarded, and Cobble

Subject 2   College's is considered one of the best. Cobble, located in a
                     beautiful, rural setting that I find very appealing, is quite expensive
                     at $15,000 a year. Still, I cannot pass up this opportunity to create a
                     great future for myself at Cobble.

Transitions

Transitional words or phrases will help you move from the discussion of one subject to another or from one point to another. Transitions are important because they give the reader a sign or indicator as to where your writing is headed. Transitions also show whether you're discussing the similarities between two subjects or the differences. The following is a list of words and phrases typically used as transitions in paragraphs that compare and contrast:

Comparison	Contrast
also	however
moreover	nevertheless
similarly	on the other hand
in addition	on the contrary
in comparison	in contrast
another	still
in the same fashion (way)	but
too	yet
as well as	unlike
in like manner	conversely
likewise	at the same time

The transitions you employ depend on the type of paragraph you are writing, the method of development you use, and how emphatic you want the transition to be. Here is one example of using a transition in a subject-by-subject paragraph:

> Many weight lifters use free weights to achieve their desired results, but Nautilus machines may, in fact, be better. Free weights are a big favorite but mostly from tradition and machismo. After all, a central part of working out in a gym is lifting bar bells and grunting loudly. **In contrast**, Nautilus machines lack the image associated with free weights but are actually better for weight lifters. Recent studies have shown that Nautilus-style machines work out the muscles more efficiently and cause fewer injuries. Since a weight lifter's muscles are not twisted or turned during a workout, the amount of tension on the muscles and joints is constant. The muscles do no unnecessary labor. Workouts are safer and more productive.

A paragraph written in the point-by-point style requires more frequent transitions between subjects. You will need to keep careful track of exactly what is being talked about when. Notice how the author handled transitions in this paragraph:

> Old-time movies handled sex more subtly than today's movies do. In older movies, everything was implied; **on the other hand**, movies today show too much. Older movies never showed a couple in bed together, **but** now, a sex scene or "peekaboo" shot in every movie seems mandatory, no matter how irrelevant to the story. **Yet**, while the older movies didn't show explicit sex, the stars had sex appeal. People like Rita Hayworth, Cary Grant, and Katherine Hepburn were able to express their desires with a glance or a wink, **unlike** today's stars, who need to show skin to communicate desire. **However**, when they take off their clothes, they also remove their mystique. They're just not as sexy as their fully dressed predecessors.

Choosing Comparison Only

A comparison-only paragraph examines the similarities of two subjects. This type of paragraph draws connections between two subjects that do not appear to have much in common initially. A student named Colette wrote this comparison-only paragraph:

> Japan and Great Britain serve roughly analogous roles in Asia and Europe. Both countries are island nations and, as such, have had to learn how to marshall their resources. Both countries have rigid social structures, an elaborate sense of propriety and etiquette, and histories as imperialistic powers. At times, both the British and the Japanese have been guilty of ethnocentrism, as well.

Colette created her paragraph by first prewriting on the subjects of Great Britain and Japan. Her brainstorming list looked liked this:

Great Britain	*Japan*
island nation	imperialism (WWII)
class structure	technology—cars, phones, cameras
ethnocentric	
strong sense of etiquette and propriety	emperor plus parliament rule
sparsely populated in north, heavily in south	samurai warrior tradition
	island nation
colonialism/imperialism (17th-20th cent.)	class structure
	dense cities
trade is important	ethnocentrism
democracy with monarchy	trade—heavily dependent on exports
	strong sense of etiquette and propriety

As you can see, the paragraph did not attempt to incorporate all of the ideas on the list but only those that Colette felt were most helpful in making her point.

When forming a topic sentence for a comparison-only paragraph, you should have two topics and a statement about how the two are similar. For instance, in the paragraph on Japan and England, the notion that these two countries are analogous, or comparable, in the roles in their respective regions forms the central idea around which the paragraph is developed.

EXERCISE 6.4

Examine each of the following topic sentences and determine whether it is a good topic sentence for a comparison-only paragraph. Mark each correct sentence *C* and fix the others.

1. Both the hand-held calculator and the abacus have places in the modern world.

2. Everyone knows Jamaica is a great vacation spot, but Alaska is also a wonderful place to go on a holiday.

3. Soy bean futures are a better investment than stocks.

4. Manual dexterity is required to play the piano or the violin.

5. Global warming gets more media coverage than other pollution problems.

6. IBM and Apple together can lay claim to popularizing an entire industry: the home computer.

7. The Chicago Cubs have a record for futility that is rivaled only by the Boston Red Sox.

8. Samson let his hair grow, but I prefer to keep mine cut short.

9. Although the turquoise necklace is beautiful, a simple diamond pendant would be better for formal occasions.

10. American football players serve the same role as ancient Roman gladiators.

From one of the following pairs of subjects, make a brainstorming list for each subject, just as you did in Exercise 6.1. Then write a comparison-only paragraph.

> liberals and conservatives
> kindergarten and the adult world
> a horse and a car
> a shed and a mansion
> wood and plastic
> people and animals

Choosing Contrast Only

A contrast-only paragraph is designed to examine the differences between two subjects, particularly those that initially appear to have much in common. Wayne, a student who has traveled a lot, wrote this:

> While the average American tends to blur the distinction between Mexican and Spanish foods, the foods actually have little in common. Take the tortilla, for example. Most Americans think of tortillas as thin, flat, corn- or flour-based wafers that can be used to make burritos, tacos, enchiladas, and tostadas. Tortillas can also be cut, fried, and served as chips with salsa. However, an American ordering a tortilla in Madrid had better not expect that. In Spain, a tortilla is a thick, round cake made of potatoes, eggs, and onions fried in olive oil, sometimes with thin strips of serrano ham or green pepper. A Spanish tortilla is served as either a <u>tapa</u>, or appetizer, or is a meal by itself, served either hot or cold. While in Mexico the tortilla is a means to an end, the building block of many foods, in Spain the tortilla is an end unto itself.

In this case, Wayne began with a brainstorming list on the subject of *food:*

Spanish food   *Mexican food*
Paella   *tamales*
sangria   *tequila*
serrano ham   *tortillas*
tortillas   *corn*
garbanzo beans   *mole*

Wayne noticed that two of the items had the same name yet were not the same food. Using that as a starting point, Wayne formulated his paragraph to point out the differences between the two cuisines.

When forming a topic sentence for a contrast-only paragraph, you should have two topics and a statement about how the two are different. For instance, in the paragraph on Spanish and Mexican food, the notion that Spain and Mexico have quite different cuisines forms the central idea around which the paragraph is developed.

EXERCISE 6.6

Examine each of the following topic sentences and determine whether it is a good topic sentence for a contrast-only paragraph. Mark each correct sentence *C* and fix the others.

1. People's attitudes at end of the twentieth century are less optimistic than they were the end of the nineteenth century.

2. Painting and music are both forms of art.

3. Broadway productions lack the originality of regional theater productions.

4. San Francisco reminds one of the grand cities of Europe.

5. Joggers run for their health; runners do it for the competition.

6. Alligators and crocodiles have distinct physical differences.

7. The breakup of AT&T was similar to the breakup of the great railroads of the last century.

8. The flying skills of commercial pilots are just as good as those of military pilots.

9. Japanese-manufactured semiconductors are virtually indistinguishable from those made in the United States.

10. Children and their parents approach violence on television with different assumptions about reality.

EXERCISE 6.7

From one of the following pairs of subjects, make a brainstorming list for each subject, just as you did in Exercise 6.1. Then write a contrast-only paragraph.

> sports fans and theater fans
> running and jogging
> daydreams and sleeping dreams
> boats and ships
> butterflies and moths

Student Writing Assignment: Comparison and Contrast

Write a paragraph based on comparison and contrast using one of the topics listed in Exercise 6.1. Follow the steps listed in the Start-Up Suggestions and Questions for Self-Revision. Then bring your paragraph to your class for peer editing. Revise your paragraph and then complete the section labeled Your Choices: Comparison and Contrast to discuss the decisions you made during the composing and revising process.

Start-Up Suggestions

Follow these steps before writing your first draft.

1. Check newsstands and magazine racks for recent articles on your topic. Consult a librarian on how to find older articles in your library. Read as much material as you can on the subject.

2. Write in a journal for ten minutes about any personal experiences you have had with your topic, particularly at school or work. How did you respond to those experiences?
3. Freewrite for ten minutes on your topic. Then use the looping exercise (described in Chapter 2) to freewrite on more specific topics. Try to discover a new angle on or aspect of the topic, especially if it has been in the public consciousness for a long time.

Self-Revision Questions

Answer these questions after writing your first draft and before rewriting the draft for submission to your peer-editing group.

1. Underline the topic sentence of your paragraph. Ask yourself: Is it clear that I am comparing, contrasting, or both?
2. Are the topics you have chosen of the same type?
3. Does your development follow the point-by-point or the subject-by-subject method?
4. Do you include plenty of specific details to support your topics?

Revise your paragraph and submit it to your peer-editing group.

Peer-Editing Guidelines for Comparison and Contrast

Answer these questions for each of the paragraphs written by other members of your peer-editing group.

1. Underline the topic sentence of the paper. Ask yourself: Is it clear that the paragraph is comparing, contrasting, or both?
2. Does the paragraph clearly indicate what two subjects are being compared or contrasted?
3. Are the topics of the same type?
4. Does the paragraphs's development follow the point-by-point or subject-by-subject method?
5. Is the paragraph's pattern of development effective for the topic?
6. Does the paragraph provide good transitions between topics?
7. Does the paragraph include plenty of specific details to support the topics?
8. Is all the support relevant to the topic sentence?

9. Does the paragraph end abruptly or does it have a sense of closure?
10. Does the paragraph accomplish the purpose laid out in its topic sentence?

Prepare the final draft of your paragraph, taking the comments of your peer-editing group into account.

Your Choices: Comparison and Contrast

Answer these questions after you have finished your revision.

1. Why did you choose your topic?
2. Why did you choose your title? Did you have to revise it after the first draft? If so, explain why.
3. Did your topic sentence need revising? How? If you placed your topic sentence some place other than as the first sentence of the paragraph, why did you do so?
4. What changes to the support did you make? Why?
5. What did you leave unchanged? Why?
6. What transitional words or phrases did you choose? Why?
7. Which comparison/contrast pattern did you choose? Why?
8. What specific examples or illustrations did you include?
9. What technical problems did you need to resolve?
10. Did you agree or disagree with your peer editor's choice for the crystalline word? If you disagreed, did you make any revisions to emphasize the word you wanted?

COMPUTER EXERCISE

Select two subjects for comparison and contrast, perhaps from the list in Exercise 6.1. Divide the subjects so you are assigned one and your writing partner, the other. Spend ten minutes brainstorming a list of qualities for your subject. Then send a copy of your list in a file to your writing partner and receive one in return. Examine your lists and determine which points you found in common and not in common. Write a paragraph showing comparison and contrast based on the points in common. Then look at the paragraph your partner wrote, and discuss the similarities and differences between your paragraphs.

THE REVISION PROCESS:
A Student Writing Sample

Anthony, a thirty-year-old community college student, decided to write a paragraph showing comparison and contrast of his experiences living on the East Coast and on the West Coast. He began the writing process by freewriting:

When I lived on the East Coast I really enjoyed all the changes of seasons and autumn with the way the leaves seemed to turn red and green you don't see that out here too much but winter is not something that I really miss it just goes on too long by February each winter I was sick of snow the food back East was a lot better in a lot of ways the Italian definitely can't be matched out here in the same way they don't do Mexican too well back there I was shocked the first time I walked in a supermarket in California I had never seen so many different types of vegetables and fruits warm weather does have its advantages but I do think people on the West Coast are more superficial I know its a stereotype but its true because people act so friendly but then they don't remember you or say hi unless there is something they want back home people are more real if they don't like you they'll let you know but friends are friends for life I think that's the trouble everyone here moves around so much there's just so much to do flowers in January is hard to get used still most of the time I notice that people have a lot more in common than they realize— everyone is looking for a good school, a good job, a person to love, and a house to own except here its more likely to be a condo.

After the freewriting period was over, Anthony looked over his writing and decided to make two lists of attributes he found on the East Coast and the West Coast.

East Coast	West Coast
change of seasons	no change of seasons
nice autumns	great Mexican food
winters too long	incredible variety of
better food—great Italian	vegetables in the
people are more real	markets
people become lifelong	superficial people
friends	people lack commitment
people aren't phony nice	people lack sincerity
people are more stable	people move around a lot
school, job, love, and home	school, job, love, and home

When Anthony looked at the two columns, he thought he had enough material to create a comparison and contrast paragraph. His next step was to develop a topic sentence. His first choice was the following:

There are many similarities and differences between living on the East Coast and living on the West Coast.

Upon review, however, Anthony considered the phrase *many similarities and differences* too vague since it gave little indication of what lay ahead. Instead, he chose to be more specific with his next try:

The differences between the East Coast and West Coast deal with weather, food, and people's attitudes, but people on both coasts share many of the same values.

This attempt appeared to be too wordy. Anthony tried again:

Although people living on the East Coast and West Coast experience differences in their weather, food, and social interaction, people on both coasts ultimately seek the same things out of life.

Anthony kept this topic sentence, as it seemed to say best what points he was going to discuss in the paragraph. Next, Anthony had to decide on whether to do a subject-by-subject organization or a point-by-point organization. Since his paragraph seemed to contain a variety of points that were appropriate to each subject, he decided to use the point-by-point paragraph pattern. His first draft read like this:

> Although people living on the East Coast and West Coast experience differences in their weather, food, and social interaction, people on both coasts ultimately seek the same things out of life. The weather on the East Coast changes so people get to experience the joy and beauty of spring and autumn, and the heat of summer and the freezing cold of winter. West Coasters only experience sunny and warm weather interrupted by two weeks of rain each year. On the East Coast, food is valued highly, and in the big cities, the Italian food is not to be beaten. On the West Coast, the approach to food is more casual, and the height of good taste is authentic Mexican cuisine. On the East Coast, people do seem more real--that is, they act how they feel. If they don't like you, they don't act friendly like they do here. West Coasters think that's being rude, but I think it's being honest. Still, I know that deep down everyone is searching for the same things: a good education, a good school, someone to love, and a nice home to live in. Only in California, that home will be a condo, not a brownstone.

When he was finished writing, Anthony was slightly surprised at the size of his paragraph. Nevertheless, he took this draft to his peer group for review. They came back with some of the following comments:

- Too long
- Too superficial—not enough examples
- Needs to maintain a consistent tone
- Not everything seems to go together—What does weather have to do with people's personal attitudes?
- Aren't there any great Italian restaurants on the West Coast? Why not?

Anthony realized that he had to cut the amount of material that he was writing about. Instead of trying to include everything from his prewriting in his paragraph, he decided to cut the material on the weather and food and focus just on the similarities and differences of the people on both coasts. That led him to the following draft:

Although people living on the East Coast and West Coast differ in their approaches to friendship, people on both coasts ultimately seek the same things out of life. On the East Coast, people do seem to act on how they feel. If they don't like a person, they don't pretend to be friendly like many people on the West Coast. West Coasters think that's being rude, but actually it is a sign of the East Coaster's honesty. On the other hand, friendships made among East Coasters are strong and usually last a lifetime; friendships on the West Coast are more casual and superficial because the people themselves move around more often. West Coasters don't stay in one place long enough to establish the close personal bonds necessary for a deep friendship. Still, deep down, people on both coasts are searching for the same things: a good education, a good school, someone to love, and a nice home to live in. Only on the West Coast, that home is likely to be a newly built condo, not a hundred-year-old brownstone.

Finally, Anthony decided to trim his paragraph and use as much specific language as possible. He liked his opening and closing, but the middle part of his paragraph still seemed wordy. He also wanted to avoid the awkwardness of the phrases *East Coasters* and *West Coasters*. Here was his final draft:

Although people living on the East Coast and West Coast differ in their approaches to friendship, people on both coasts ultimately seek the same things out of life. On the East Coast, people act on how they feel. If they don't like a person, they don't pretend to be friendly. People on the West Coast think that's rude, but actually it is a sign of a person's honesty. Friendships made among East Coast people are strong and usually last a lifetime; friendships on the West Coast are more casual and superficial because people don't stay in one place long enough to establish close personal bonds. Still, deep down, people on both coasts are searching for the same things: a good education, a good school, someone to love, and a nice home to live in. However, on the West Coast, that home is likely to be a newly built condo, not a hundred-year-old brownstone.

GRAMMAR INSTRUCTION AND EXERCISES:
Run-Ons and Comma Splices

Run-ons and comma splices are two similar sentence problems: they both occur when a sentence continues beyond its natural conclusion. Instead of ending the sentence, the writer joins or splices two or more sentences together either without any punctuation (*run-on*) or with only a comma (*comma splice*). Look at the following sentences:

Russ decided not to return home for the holidays, he cashed in his plane ticket.

The field behind the barn had been neglected there really seemed to be no practical use for it.

The brothers joined the army at the same time they were sent to different training centers.

Angelica studied agriculture, she wanted to help increase crop productivity through better research into fertilizers.

The mud was preventing Kris from getting her truck out, she was lucky she had a cellular phone with her.

All of these sentences are either run-on or comma-spliced sentences. In each one, there are actually two independent clauses expressing two complete thoughts.

To fix the problem, you have four choices: use a period, use a coordinating conjunction with a comma, use a semicolon, or make one independent clause dependent. You must choose which solution will make the best sentence.

Use a Period

Use a period to separate two independent clauses. This way, each independent clause becomes its own sentence. This works best when the sentences are logically sequential and need no additional modifications.

Comma Splice:

The mud was preventing Kris from getting her truck out, she was lucky she had a cellular phone with her.

Corrected:

The mud was preventing Kris from getting her truck out. She was lucky she had a cellular phone with her.

Use a Coordinating Conjunction with a Comma

Sometimes when you wish to tie two independent clauses together, you may choose to do so with a coordinating conjunction and a comma. The coordinating conjunction will give the meaning necessary to show the relationship between the two independent clauses. The seven coordinating conjunctions are *and, but, or, so, for, yet,* and *nor.* Learning to use them properly will help you to create meaning. Remember that this option is available to you when you have a run-on as well as when you have a comma splice.

Comma Splice:

Russ decided not to return home for the holidays, he cashed in his plane ticket.

Corrected:

Russ decided not to return home for the holidays, so he cashed in his plane ticket.

Run-On:

The brothers joined the army at the same time they were sent to different training centers.

Corrected:

The brothers joined the army at the same time, but they were sent to different training centers.

Use a Semicolon

You can use a semicolon to link two independent clauses together. This will pull the two clauses together, suggesting a stronger relationship than indicated by a period.

Comma Splice:

Angelica studied agriculture, she wanted to help increase crop productivity through better research into fertilizers.

Corrected:

Angelica studied agriculture; she wanted to help increase crop productivity through better research into fertilizers.

You can also add a conjunctive adverb after the semicolon if additional help is needed in making the relationship clear. If you do so, be sure to use a comma after the conjunctive adverb. Conjunctive adverbs include words such as *however, moreover, therefore, consequently,* and *hence.*

Run-On:

The brothers joined the army at the same time they were sent to different training centers.

Corrected:

The brothers joined the army at the same time; however, they were sent to different training centers.

Make One Independent Clause Dependent

You can avoid the problem of having two independent clauses joined improperly by changing one of the clauses into a dependent clause. This will require you to add a subordinating conjunction or a relative pronoun. Subordinating conjunctions include words such as *because, since, while, after,* and *if.* Relative pronouns include words such as *who, whose, which, that,* and *what.*

> Original:
>
> Angelica studied agriculture, she wanted to help increase crop productivity through better research into fertilizers.
>
> Corrected:
>
> Angelica, who studied agriculture, wanted to help increase crop productivity through better research into fertilizers.
>
> *or*
>
> Angelica, who wanted to help increase crop productivity through better research into fertilizers, studied agriculture.

Be aware that the meaning of your sentence may change slightly depending on which clause you keep independent and which one you make dependent.

> Original:
>
> The field behind the barn had been neglected there seemed to be no practical use for it.
>
> Corrected:
>
> The field behind the barn had been neglected because there seemed to be no practical use for it.
>
> *or*
>
> Because the field behind the barn had been neglected, there seemed to be no practical use for it.
>
> ***Note:*** When the dependent clause follows the independent clause, no comma is used. When the dependent clause comes before the independent clause, use a comma to separate the two clauses.

(See pages 342–46 for further discussion of run-ons and comma splices.)

EXERCISES   Examine the following items for run-on and comma-spliced sentences. Rewrite each run-on or comma-spliced sentence. If an item is correct, indicate it with the letter *C*.

1. Thomas wasn't able to see for long distances, he had to go to the optometrist to be fitted for glasses.

2. I cracked a mirror seven years of bad luck await me.

3. In the fall when the days start to get shorter I find that putting my baby down to sleep is a lot easier, in the summer it's a lot harder.

4. Jerry saw a flock of canvasback ducks when he was hunting up in Canada, he didn't get any though.

5. Daffodils are an ideal flower in a wooded setting they require little care.

6. The human digestive system is quite intricate, my cousin Brad, who is in medicial school, was telling me about it the other day.

7. The decorator was fond of using tapestry pillows as accents, however, the cost of the pillows was quite high.

8. The island of New Guinea is actually divided into two halves, to the west is Indonesia and to the east is Papua New Guinea.

9. Sir Walter Raleigh was the favorite of England's Queen Elizabeth I, the next monarch, King James I, had him put to death.

10. The message was left for Sophia to make sure that she finished her homework she had already left to go to a party with some friends.

7 Reasons and Results

Cause and Effect Paragraphs

Consult a newspaper or TV news program. Watch for any particular event or incident. Ask yourself: What caused that event or incident? What is likely to result from this incident?

Asking the question Why? is a vital part of human experience. We want to know what led up to a certain incident or event and what was the reason or reasons behind it. For instance, in a history class, you might examine the reason the United States became involved in the Vietnam War. In an economics class, you might analyze what factors led to the Great Depression. In a chemistry class, you might try to discover what reactions led a solution's color to change. In a marketing class, you might examine why customers become attracted to or repulsed by certain types of advertising.

Another recurring question is What's next? What happened because the United States refused to join the League of Nations? What will occur if income taxes are cut? What results from mixing an acid with an alkaline? How will consumers react differently if a TV commercial's background music is changed from classical to urban hip-hop?

Choosing Cause and Effect

The questions Why did that happen? and What will happen next? have everything to do with examining causes and effects. A **cause** is the reason or reasons an event or condition happened, and an **effect** is the result or results of an event or condition. Any event or condition can be analyzed for either its causes or its effects. You can look at the same thing from essentially two different sides. You are just asking a different question. For instance, the event could be that your friend Rosa went bankrupt. You could ask two questions:

Why did Rosa go bankrupt?   Cause

What will happen because Rosa went bankrupt?   Effect

The event or condition in each of the questions is the same. The difference is that in the first question, you want to look at the *reasons* behind the event or condition, and in the second question, you want to look at the *results* of the event or condition.

When you write about cause and effect, you will usually have to emphasize one or the other, depending on your purpose. For instance, you might write:

Rosa's overindulgence with credit cards led to her bankruptcy.
Emphasizing the *cause,* her overindulgence

Rosa's bankruptcy will keep her from purchasing a new

condominium for at least seven years.
Emphasizing the *effect,* her inability to buy a condominium

As you might already imagine, writing about causes and effects can be complicated by the fact that often you find several causes for an event or condition or you find several results of an event or condition. This is especially true for complex or wide-ranging issues. For instance, to say *The Vietnam War was started by the North Vietnamese shooting at U.S. destroyers in the Gulf of Tonkin in 1964* almost implies that North Vietnam and the United States enjoyed a normal state of relations until the unprovoked incident. In fact, however, relations between the United States and North Vietnam had never been good since the split of Vietnam into communist north and democratically aligned south.

Another possibility is that causes or effects can happen in a **series**, in which one cause came from another cause that came from another cause or one effect led to another effect that led to another effect.

FIGURE 7.1

Events in a
Series

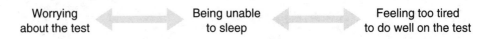

Worrying about the test ⟷ Being unable to sleep ⟷ Feeling too tired to do well on the test

For example, if you are too worried about an upcoming test, you may not get enough sleep the night before, and this sleeplessness could lead to your not doing well on the test. Figure 7.1 shows how this series might be expressed.

If you read Figure 7.1 from the left to the right, you are reading to emphasize effect: your worrying about the test led to your inability to sleep, which led to doing poorly on the test. If you read from right to left, you are reading to emphasize cause: you did poorly on the test because you did not get enough sleep, and you did not get enough sleep because you were too worried about the test.

Ask yourself these generic questions, filling in each blank space with the event or condition in which you are interested:

What was the reason that _____ happened?

This question will lead you to an examination of causes.

What will result because _____ happened?

This question will lead you to an examination of results.

When you examine causes, you are answering the question Why? You are looking at the reasons that led to an event or situation. Fill in the blanks of the following sentence:

(The event or condition occurred) because (of the cause).

Event or Situation		Cause
you bounced a check	because	you failed to pay attention to your checking account balance
you slept through your morning class	because	you failed to set your alarm clock
you won first prize in an air-band contest	because	you spent hours practicing and working on your costume

Although these examples show a simple one-cause-to-one-event relationship, most events or situations are created by multiple causes. Consider the following event:

You change your major from business to English.

This event can be caused by several factors:

1. You realize that your personal interests lie more in English than in business.
2. You discover that, in the long run, English may be a more versatile degree than business.
3. You are considering law school and find that English is a superior undergraduate degree for that field.
4. You decide that you value your intellectual growth more than making a great deal of money.

In this case, no single sentence can adequately describe the relationship between the event or condition and its causes.

EXERCISE 7.1

Select three of the following topics. Then list as many causes as you can think of for the events or conditions described. Here is an example:

Topic: Juvenile delinquency

Causes:
poor parental oversight
lack of positive role models
peer pressure
pessimistic view of the future
lack of respect for authority figures
feeling left out of society
violence seen as an effective solution to problems
lure of the drug culture
no fear of punishment, expulsion, or incarceration

Topics:
1. Americans' love affair with professional sports
2. The divorce rate
3. The popularity of R-rated movies
4. Immigration to the United States
5. Generation X's slacker image
6. Domestic violence
7. Drunk driving
8. Homophobia
9. The population exodus to the coasts
10. Two-income families

Why Choose Cause?

When you write about cause, you are answering the question Why did that happen? Often, there is more than one cause for a situation or event. Your task as a writer is to make that relationship clear.

Topic Sentences

The topic sentence for a paragraph based on *cause* must state the event or situation being looked at and the primary reasons behind it. The topic sentence must clearly state that the relationship between the two is *causal*. This can, however, be difficult or confusing. For instance, here is a topic sentence that appears to present a causal topic but actually does not:

> The baseball strike of 1994 caused many fans to turn away from the game permanently.

Even though this topic sentence includes the word *caused,* the emphasis in this sentence is actually on the *result* of the strike: turning fans away from the game. As such, this sentence is more suited to a paragraph developed by effect, answering the question What happened next? Since the subject of the sentence is the strike, a cause paragraph would examine the causes of the strike. Instead, the sentence actually is looking at the effect.

If you choose to examine not the baseball strike but the turning away of fans from major league baseball, then you must rewrite the sentence. Examine this sentence:

> Sports fans have turned away from major league baseball because of bitterness over the strike of 1994.

This sentence answers the question Why did fan interest in major league baseball decrease? The topic sentence answers the question by stating that there is lingering bitterness over the last baseball strike. Thus, this topic sentence examines cause.

Here is another topic sentence for a paragraph based on cause:

> The baseball union went on strike because management demanded it agree to a salary cap.

This sentence makes clear that the *reason* the baseball union went on strike was its rejection of the management's latest offer. This topic sentence is suitable for a paragraph developed by cause because it answers the question Why did the baseball union go on strike?

EXERCISE 7.2

Examine each of the following topic sentences and determine whether it is an effective topic sentence for a paragraph developed by cause. Indicate each correct sentence with a letter *C* and rewrite the others.

1. Excessive television watching causes impressionable teenagers to act out violent fantasies.

2. Cars can last a long time if maintained properly.

3. Many species are endangered due to the encroachment of civilization.

4. Spiders spin webs to catch their prey.

5. The result of the latest congressional elections will not be felt for years.

6. Many diseases are caused by bad lifestyle habits.

7. An apple a day helps keep the doctor away.

8. A supportive home environment can help children to succeed in school.

9. Illegal immigrants come to the United States to escape poverty and oppression.

10. Illegal immigration has placed tremendous burdens on the public health systems in America's border states.

Support

When you are faced with writing a paragraph developed by cause, you must determine what the cause or causes are and in what order you will present them. Is there just one cause that you will develop? Or are there several causes? How much weight will you give to each? You must answer these questions in order to write an effective paragraph based on cause. Your support will generally include examples and statistical information. Examine the following paragraph:

Topic sentence   The Spanish-American War of 1898 was caused by an increasingly aggressive American government spoiling for an easy fight. For most of the nineteenth century, the United States

Support   had tried to stay away from world affairs, but toward the end of the century, America began to look for opportunities to flex its growing muscle. It found an easy target in Spain, a decaying European power that still held sway in a few colonies left over from its long rule in Latin America. Since Americans were sympathetic to Cuba's fight for independence and U.S. newspapers vigorously reported Spain's brutal repression of the independence movement, public sympathy began to run hot against the Spanish. The mysterious sinking of the <u>USS Maine</u> gave the United States the excuse it needed to intercede on Cuba's behalf; soon, the United States

Wrap-up sentence   was at war. When the war was over a few months later, Spain had lost Cuba, Guam, Puerto Rico, and the Philippines, and the United States was set to become a major world power in the twentieth century.

Notice that the topic sentence notifies the reader that the causes of the Spanish-American War will be developed in the paragraph. The support relies on some general background information, such as Spain's weakened position, and some specific information, such as Cuba's independence movement and the sinking of the *Maine*. The wrap-up sentence suggests effects because it addresses what followed the war, but it also ties in with the topic sentence since the paragraph is developed around the idea that America went to war to enhance its own power.

Transitions

The transitional words and phrases used in a paragraph developed by cause will include words such as *cause, result, because, since, for,* and the pair *if . . . then.* In the following paragraph developed by cause, the transitional words and phrases are printed in bold type:

Society's obsession with tabloid journalism, both in print and on TV, is caused by our desire to feel superior. **Since** celebrities have status that the general public does not, celebrities can be intimidating. **Therefore**, when a scandal involving a celebrity hits the pages or screen, the average person can actually feel uplifted. After all, **if** this movie star has an alcohol problem, or a member of royalty is getting a divorce, or that fashion model is having an affair, **then** the reader is not only titillated and entertained but is also morally uplifted. "I may not have fame, fortune, or looks," the reader reasons, "but at least I've got my dignity." **Because** tabloids expose the underside of fame, celebrities are no longer intimidating. The average person can even feel sorry for the wealthy and famous.

Student Writing Assignment: Cause

Using one of the following subjects, write a paragraph based on cause. Be certain that you make clear to your reader what the cause or causes behind your topic are. Follow the steps listed in the Start-Up Suggestions and Self-Revision Questions. Then bring your paragraph to class for peer editing. Revise your paragraph and then complete the section labeled Your Choices: Cause to discuss the decisions you made during the composing and revising process.

adult illiteracy
concern about physical appearances
popularity of private schools
child abuse
noise pollution

sexism
professional success
love of pets
obesity
technophobia (fear of technology)

Start-Up Suggestions

Follow these steps before writing your first draft.

1. Ask yourself: Why does _____ happen? (Fill in the blank with your chosen topic.)

2. Write a list of possible causes that you think of when you answer the question in Suggestion 1.
3. Do a clustering exercise (described in Chapter 2), in which you place your topic at the center and the causes you have listed around that topic. Can you expand your cluster to another level, finding causes for the causes?
4. Draft a topic sentence that states clearly the relationship between your topic and the cause or causes.
5. Form a rough, or informal, outline that lists the basis of support for what caused the event or situation to occur.

Self-Revision Questions

Answer these questions after writing your first draft and before rewriting the draft for submission to your peer-editing group.

1. Does the topic sentence clearly show the relationship between your topic and the cause or causes?
2. Is the topic sentence the first sentence in the paragraph? If not, is there a good, logical reason for placing it elsewhere?
3. Does your paragraph indicate whether there is a single cause, multiple causes, or a series of causes?
4. Do you have sufficient support in the paragraph?
5. Have you used appropriate, effective transitions? (You may wish to review the list of transitional words and phrases under the heading Transitions.)
6. Does your paragraph have a reasonable and logical wrap-up sentence?

Revise your paragraph and submit it to your peer-editing group.

Peer-Editing Guidelines for Cause

Answer these questions for each of the paragraphs written by other members of your peer-editing group.

1. Does the paragraph have a topic sentence? Underline the topic sentence.
2. Is the topic sentence effective? Does it introduce one of the topics assigned?

3. Does the topic sentence clearly show the relationship between the topic and its cause or causes?
4. Is the support relevant to the topic sentence?
5. Does the paragraph sufficiently develop the causal relationships?
6. Does the paragraph avoid discussion of effect and remain focused on discussion of cause?
7. Does the paragraph use specific evidence to support its points?
8. Does the paragraph have effective transitions between ideas? List some of the transitional words and phrases used.
9. What is the crystalline word of the paragraph?
10. What one change would most improve the paragraph?

Prepare the final draft of your paragraph, taking the comments of your peer-editing group into account.

Your Choices: Cause

Answer these questions after you have finished your final draft.

1. How did you choose your topic?
2. How did you choose the title for your paragraph based on cause?
3. Did you have to change your topic sentence as you moved through your drafts? Why or why not?
4. Did you need to revise your support to ensure that the causal relationships were clear?
5. Did your peer editors have difficulty following the relationship between your topic and its cause or causes?
6. What transitional words or phrases did you use? Why?
7. What other changes to the support did you make during the drafting process? Why?
8. If you added additional material, why was it necessary?
9. Did you have to change your wrap-up sentence? Why or why not?
10. Did you agree or disagree with your peer editors' choice for the crystalline word? If you disagreed, did you make any revisions to emphasize the word you wanted?

Why Choose Effect?

When you examine effects, you are looking to answer the question *What happened next?* or *What will happen next?* (depending on whether you are looking at a current event or situation or one in the past). In either case, a paragraph based on effect analyzes the result or results of a situation or event. Examine this list of possible events or situations and the resulting effects:

Event or Situation	Effect
you were promoted at work	now you have more responsibility and more money
donations to charities decrease	less food and medicine are available for the needy
the price of coffee goes up	more people switch to tea

As you can see from these examples, sometimes you can find a simple one-effect-for-one-event relationship, but usually events or situations lead to multiple effects. Consider the same statement we looked at earlier for causes:

You change your major from business to English.

This event can have several effects:

1. Your entire course of study has changed.
2. Some of the classes you took for your business degree may not count toward your English degree.
3. Your earning potential may drop.
4. You may find school more intellectually stimulating.
5. You have an entirely new circle of friends and associates related to your new major.
6. You start to save your books rather than sell them back at the end of the semester.

EXERCISE 7.3

Select three of the following topics. Then list as many effects as you can think of for the events or conditions described. Here is an example:

Topic: Juvenile delinquency

Effects:
graffiti and other acts of vandalism
higher crime rates
high dropout rates

illiteracy

older people fear the young

the justice system begins treating juvenile offenders as adults

drug abuse

lost futures, lost hopes

Topics:

1. Americans' love affair with professional sports
2. The divorce rate
3. The popularity of R-rated movies
4. Immigration to the United States
5. Generation X's slacker image
6. Domestic violence
7. Drunk driving
8. Homophobia
9. The population exodus to the coasts
10. Two-income families

Topic Sentences

The topic sentence for a paragraph based on *effect* must state the event or situation being looked at and the primary results of it. The topic sentence must make clear that the relationship between the two is one of effect. Just as with the paragraph based on cause, there can be some confusion with paragraphs based on effect. For instance, the following topic sentence may appear to describe an effect but it is actually describing a cause:

Many people immigrate to the United States because of its

economic opportunities.

This sentence emphasizes a cause by answering the question *Why* do people immigrate to the United States? However, the sentence can be rewritten to emphasize effect:

One effect of having numerous economic opportunities in the

United States is to attract many immigrants.

In the rewritten topic sentence, the emphasis is on the result of economic opportunities, the attraction of immigrants. As you can see, with the same topic you can choose either to emphasize cause or to emphasize effect. Here is another topic sentence:

> An effect of economic opportunities in the United States is to draw many immigrants to its shores.

This sentence makes clear that the *result* of the United States economy is the attraction of immigrants. By including the word *effect*, the writer creates the emphasis in the paragraph as one based on effect.

EXERCISE 7.4

Examine each of the following topic sentences and determine whether it is an effective topic sentence for a paragraph based on effect. Indicate each correct sentence with a letter *C* and rewrite the others.

1. Snowfall creates a wonderland for children but pesky annoyances for adults.

2. Cooking is an art form because everyone can make dishes that express their personalities.

3. The increase in the nation's speed limit was a response to the near-total neglect of the 55 miles-per-hour limit.

4. The fall of the Soviet Union has led to a complicated series of foreign-policy problems.

5. Since math is my hardest course, I am hiring a tutor to help me learn enough to pass.

6. The crime rate has dropped because of stiffer sentencing laws.

7. Fire departments are seeing their budgets cut as a result of lower tax revenues.

8. The effect of bottle-return laws has been disappointing.

9. Teenager curfew laws do little to stop criminal activity but do impose unreasonable burdens on all teenagers.

10. Mandatory general education courses cause students to take classes in which they have no interest.

Support

When you're faced with writing a paragraph based on effect, you must determine what the effect or effects are and in what order you will present them. Is there just one effect you will examine? Or are there multiple effects? Is there a series of effects? How much weight will you give to each? These questions must be answered in order to write an effective paragraph based on effect. Examine the following paragraph:

Topic sentence

Support

Wrap-up sentence

A recent discovery in the Gobi Desert has resulted in many scientists' concluding that dinosaurs are closely related to modern-day birds. The fossilized remains of an oviraptor--a small, meat-eating dinosaur--were discovered sitting on top of a nest of eggs, just as any bird today might do. The discovery of the apparent behavioral similarities between dinosaurs and birds will have the effect of reinforcing a previously held belief based on the skeletal similarities of dinosaurs and birds. This discovery may well be the first step toward a greater understanding of how a <u>Tyrannosaurus rex</u> is related to a backyard blackbird.

Notice that the topic sentence emphasizes the effect of the discovery in the Gobi Desert—that a strong conclusion can be drawn from the discovery about the relationship between dinosaurs and birds. The support relies on specific information about the discovery, including what was discovered, and the conclusion that was based on the behavioral similarity to birds. The wrap-up sentence also suggests another, longer-range effect: charting a greater understanding of the relationship between dinosaurs and birds. The wrap-up sentence also ties in with the topic sentence since it reflects the topic of the paragraph.

Transitions

The transitional words and phrases used in a paragraph based on effect include words such as *effect, consequently, result, as a result, thus, hence, therefore, thereby, due to this,* and *so.* In the following paragraph based on effect, the transitional words and phrases are printed in bold type:

On-line computer services are having the **effect** of changing how the world communicates. No longer do people have to go to their local libraries to find reading materials; on-line services can connect users to a blinding array of reading possibilities. One

result is that people can now peek into library holdings all around the world. Encyclopedias need not take up shelf space: they can be found on-line, just like newspapers and magazine articles. The abbreviated language that has developed around e-mail is changing language itself, **thereby** making the information superhighway an entirely separate method of communicating, different from standard talking or writing. **Consequently**, new standards of literacy are popping up, as well: Can you read what's on the Internet?

Student Writing Assignment: Effect

Using one of the following subjects, write a paragraph based on effect. Be certain that you make clear to your reader what the effect or effects of your topic are. Follow the steps listed in the Start-Up Suggestions and Self-Revision Questions. Then bring your paragraph to class for peer editing. Revise your paragraph and then complete the section labeled Your Choices: Effect to discuss the decisions you made during the composing and revising process.

adult illiteracy
concern over physical appearances
popularity of private schools
child abuse
noise pollution

sexism
professional success
love of pets
obesity
technophobia (fear of
    technology)

Start-Up Suggestions

Follow these steps before writing your first draft.

1. Ask yourself: What happens (or has happened or will happen) because of _____? (Fill in the blank with your chosen topic.)
2. Write a list of possible effects that you think of when you answer the question in Suggestion 1.
3. Do a clustering exercise (described in Chapter 2), in which you place your topic at the center and the effects you have listed around that topic. Can you expand your cluster to another level, finding effects of the effects?

4. Draft a topic sentence that states clearly the relationship between your topic and the effect or effects.
5. Draft a rough, or informal, outline that lists the bases of support for what the effects of the event or situation have been or will be.

Self-Revision Questions

Answer these questions after writing your first draft and before rewriting the draft for submission to your peer-editing group.

1. Does the topic sentence clearly show the relationship between your topic and the effect or effects?
2. Is the topic sentence the first sentence in the paragraph? If not, is there a good, logical reason for placing it elsewhere?
3. Does your paragraph indicate whether there is a single effect, multiple effects, or a series of effects?
4. Do you have sufficient support in the paragraph?
5. Have you used appropriate, effective transitions? (You may wish to review the list of transitional words and phrases under the heading Transitions.)
6. Does your paragraph have a reasonable and logical wrap-up sentence?

Revise your paragraph and submit it to your peer-editing group.

Peer-Editing Guidelines for Effect

Answer these questions for each of the paragraphs written by other members of your peer-editing group.

1. Does the paragraph have a topic sentence? Underline the topic sentence.
2. Is the topic sentence effective? Does it introduce one of the topics assigned?
3. Does the topic sentence clearly show the relationship between the topic and its effect or effects?
4. Is the support relevant to the topic sentence?
5. Does the paragraph sufficiently develop the relationship based on effect?
6. Does the paragraph avoid discussion of cause and remain focused on discussion of effect?

7. Does the paragraph use specific evidence to support its points?
8. Does the paragraph provide effective transitions between ideas? List some of the transitional words and phrases used.
9. What is the crystalline word of the paragraph?
10. What one change would most improve the paragraph?

Prepare the final draft of your paragraph, taking the comments of your peer-editing group into account.

Your Choices: Effect

Answer these questions after you have finished your final draft.

1. How did you choose your topic?
2. How did you choose the title for your paragraph based on effect?
3. Did you have to change your topic sentence as you moved through your drafts? Why or why not?
4. Did you need to revise your support to ensure that the relationships based on effect were clear?
5. Did your peer editors have difficulty following the relationship between your topic and its effect or effects?
6. What other changes to the support did you make during the drafting process? Why?
7. What transitional words or phrases did you use? Why?
8. If you added additional material, why was it necessary?
9. Did you have to change your wrap-up sentence? Why or why not?
10. Did you agree or disagree with your peer editors' choice for the crystalline word? If you disagreed, did you make any revisions to emphasize the word you wanted?

COMPUTER EXERCISE

With your writing partner, choose a writing topic, possibly from Exercise 7.1 or Exercise 7.3. Decide who will write on *cause* and who will write on *effect*. Then, working separately, brainstorm on the computer a list of the causes or effects related to your topic. After ten minutes, show your screens to each other. Together, you should have both sides of the topic—the causes for the topic as well as the effects. Discuss between yourselves the relationships between the causes and the effects that you find.

Once you have done that, complete the following two sentences:

_____ are the primary causes of <u>(your topic here)</u>.

_____ are the primary effects of <u>(your topic here)</u>.

You can now share your sentences with the rest of your class.

THE REVISION PROCESS:
A Student Writing Sample

Mai was faced with writing a paragraph based on effect. She decided to write on the topic of *people's concerns over physical appearance* since she felt she already knew a lot about the topic, both from her own experience and from observing her friends. She wrote out this sentence:

What happens because of people's concerns over physical appearance?

Based on this question, she made the following list:

— *trying to date the nicest-looking person*
— *shunning ugly people*
— *trying to improve your own appearance*
— *watching the fashions*
— *spending a lot of money on your appearance*
— *working out to keep in shape*
— *dieting, even anorexia or bulimia*
— *life is easier if you're good looking*

Mai realized that she had a lot of effects—more than she could cover in just a single paragraph. She examined the list and decided to pick what seemed to be the most important effect: *trying to improve your own appearance*. She decided that some of the effects on her list were effects of this effect. Mai then wrote the cluster in Figure 7.2.

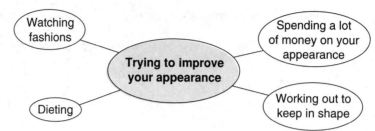

FIGURE 7.2
Mai's Clustering
for Her Effect
Paragraph

When she finished, she saw that she would be able to include a lot more items from her list than she initially thought.

Mai put together her topic sentence based on her single first effect. Her first topic sentence ran as follows:

> *Because of people's concerns over physical appearance, people spend a lot of time and effort with their own physical appearance.*

Mai found this sentence to be too bulky, and she didn't like the repetition of the words *physical appearance* and *people*. She worked at it again:

> *People's concerns for physical appearance often lead them to spend a lot of time working on their own.*

Mai liked this topic sentence better. She was ready to start her own draft. Here is the draft she submitted to her peer-editing group:

Physical Appearance

People's concerns for physical appearance often lead them to spend a lot of time working on their own. Since people care about how other people look, it's only logical for them to know that other people care about how they look, and if they want to go out with someone, they have to look good. You look good for the other person. The down side is that some good-looking people are not very nice. Also, some people are very nice who are not good looking and they get left out, like my friend Kahn, who is a little overweight and no guy will pay attention to her. If Kahn had some money, she could work out and lose some weight, but she really doesn't right now. People spend a great deal of money on beauty products, work out gyms, and new clothes, and then they can look very good.

Despite her topic sentence, which they all liked, Mai's peer-editing group had a lot of trouble with the rest of her draft. They felt that she did not stay focused on her topic—that her support was not always relevant. They thought that the story of her friend Kahn should be made a stronger part or dropped completely. The narrowness of the development, dating, bothered one of the group members, but others thought that since the assignment was for a single paragraph, Mai was wise to limit what she addressed. They also wanted her to eliminate the use of the word *you*, which seemed awkward.

Mai decided that when she rewrote the paragraph her friend would play an even stronger part. This led her to revise her topic sentence, as well, away from the more neutral tone that it had to one that more expressed her own opinion. Here is Mai's final draft:

Physical Appearance

People's concerns for physical appearance often lead them to ignore the many good qualities that people have. People care about how other people look, and it's only logical for them to care about how they look. If they want to go out with someone, they have to look good, but this is wrong because many people who don't look as good as others might be better people. My friend Kahn is a little overweight and no guy will pay attention to her. If Kahn had some money, she could work out and lose some weight and buy nice clothes, but she doesn't right now. The people who have money can buy beauty products, work out at gyms, and get new clothes, and then they can look very good. Those who don't have that get overlooked.

When Mai completed her Your Choices questions, she noted that she had had to change her topic sentence in order to fit what she actually had wanted to say. Her writing led her to a different idea than the one she had started with, but her paragraph, she felt, was stronger. She also improved some of her sentences and tried to eliminate her inappropriate use of the word *you*.

GRAMMAR INSTRUCTION AND EXERCISES:
Sentence Fragments

What's wrong with the following sentences?

> The heart-shaped mirror in the bathroom.

> Until the conference in Boston has time to digest all of the new data regarding the outbreak of tuberculosis.

> Even though the winning ticket has not yet been claimed by some lucky contest entrant.

> Amy Tan, author of <u>The Joy Luck Club</u> and <u>The Kitchen God's Wife</u>.

> Paulette, making her first communion at the age of eight.

You probably felt that each of these sentences left something out, that some part of the meaning was missing. In fact, none of these is a complete sentence. They are *sentence fragments*.

A sentence fragment occurs when a group of words fails to express a complete thought. This can happen for three reasons. The fragment may:

1. Lack a subject
2. Lack a verb or verb phrase
3. Contain only a dependent clause and therefore fail to express a complete thought

To fix a sentence fragment, you must first understand what is missing.

Lacking a Subject

Sentences that lack a subject fail to answer the question Who or What is doing the action in the sentence? Examine the following fragment:

> Tasted so good, so sweet.

What tasted so good, so sweet? Because this is unknown, the sentence is a fragment. Corrected, the sentence might read:

> The plump, red apples tasted so good, so sweet.

Lacking a Verb or Verb Phrase

Groups of words that lack a verb or verb phrase fail to describe the action or state of being in the sentence. Examine the following fragment:

A person who has turned against his own country.

What about the person? The fragment lacks a verb that tells the reader more about the person. (Note that the verb phrase *has turned* refers to the subject *who,* not the *person.*) Corrected, the sentence might read:

A person who has turned against his own country is no better than
a foreign enemy.

Another type of sentence may appear to contain a verb but actually contains only part of a verb phrase. Examine this sentence:

The horses running on the sand.

The word *running* is not sufficient to create a complete sentence because it requires a helping verb. To correct the error, either add a helping verb or change the verb form:

The horses are running on the sand.

or

The horses run on the sand.

Dependent Clause Only

A group of words that forms only a dependent clause fails to express a complete thought. A dependent clause must be combined with an independent clause in order to form a complete sentence. Consider this example:

While Jerry was walking down the street.

This fragment does not finish the thought. What happened while Jerry was walking?

While Jerry was walking down the street, he saw a '57 Thunderbird
parked against the curb.

(See pages 339–42 for further discussion of sentence fragments.)

Examine the following items for sentence fragments. Rewrite each sentence fragment so that it is a complete sentence. If an item is a complete sentence, indicate it with the letter *C*.

1. I always start my day with the same breakfast. Orange juice, toast, and coffee.

2. Eddie Matthews, one of the best third basemen ever, who played for the Milwaukee Braves.

3. Although the guard had seen the truck stop at the gate just a few moments earlier. She could no longer see the vehicle or its occupants.

4. The shutdown of the Giganto Company factory, which manufactured rubber goods such as tires, sneakers, and rain gear.

5. Inside the power plant undergoing repairs to replace obsolete equipment.

6. Jake worried about an infestation of insects even though the crops were growing well in the fields.

7. Bonnie seen the advertisement for the cruise, and she wants to make her reservations now.

8. Seeing Manny in this new light, she decided that perhaps she had judged him too harshly.

9. The total lack of cooperation, the incessant lying, and the consistent denials creating a sense of distrust between the management and the labor union.

10. Because the car parked behind the shed is starting to rust.

8 How Things Work

Process Paragraphs

JOURNAL EXERCISE

What do you know how to do? Write a list of activities you know how to perform or things you know how to make or construct.

Have you ever taken something apart, like a radio or a clock, to see how it works? You may have found circuits or tubes, gears or gadgets, and if you experimented with the thing long enough, you might have figured out how everything fit together. Writing process paragraphs involves the same idea. In a **process** paragraph, you are looking for a way to discover the steps by which something is done or how something operates or is put together.

Processes are an essential part of life. Consider the human body: How many different processes are occurring at any one time? There are the processes that convert food into usable energy, the processes of inhaling and exhaling in order to take in oxygen and release carbon dioxide, and the processes that allow movement, speech, hearing, and thought itself.

Outside of our own bodies is the natural world, filled with innumerable processes. Indeed, the development of life on this planet begins with the sun, which shines as a result of a process called *nuclear fusion*. Scientists and environmentalists analyze the earth's processes to better understand them and the ways humankind's actions influence those processes.

Simpler than the human body or the earth are machines. How does a household vacuum cleaner work? What about a computer? Machines are created by processes in a factory and operated by processes in the home or workplace. In fact, sometimes you buy things that require assembly, such as a child's bicycle or a stereo cabinet. The instructions that accompany the bicycle or stereo cabinet are examples of process writing.

When you write about process for an audience, however, you don't simply want to show the steps of a process; that would be as boring as an instruction manual. Instead, you want to say something about the process, the result of your analysis. You need to have an opinion or point about what you are presenting.

Why Choose Process?

Process paragraphs answer the question How do you do this? or How was that made? One of the most commonly used forms of process papers is a recipe because it shows the reader how to create a food dish. Any sort of repair manual or how-to self-help book uses a form of process writing. Take a look at the following list of things:

an automobile	a wedding cake
a ship in a bottle	a Stradivarius violin
a microchip	a bow tie
a constitutional amendment	a Polish sausage

How are any of these things made? The answer is that a process was followed. You, as a writer, must be able to describe that process as clearly and logically as possible.

When a process paragraph tries to answer the question How do you do this? the best way to write about process is to present the events or steps in **chronological order.** Every step or event follows another step or event. You may recall that chronological order was discussed in

Chapter 4, in the discussion about narration. However, unlike the narrative paragraph, the process paragraph is not telling a story as much as it is describing a procedure or protocol. A discussion of what happened the night the electricity went out is *narration,* but the procedure or protocol of how to restore electricity to the home is a *process.*

Process paragraphs also ask the question How was that made? In a sense, process covers both sides of the same coin: a process paragraph may show the steps involved in creating something, or it may begin with the something and try to break it down into parts to see how those parts work together to create the whole. Thus, the process paragraph is often a way of discovering or learning how something is formed or how it operates. A process paragraph might ask How was the Great Wall of China built? or How did General Motors decide to begin marketing electric cars?

Process paragraphs that emphasize how something was made or done are, in some ways, working backward from the finished whole and discovering how to put it together. For example, instead of beginning with a bunch of parts, such as the ingredients for salsa, and then showing the steps used to create the salsa, you begin with the salsa and work backward, uncovering the tomato, cilantro, onion, garlic, and chilies.

Not all items or situations that are examined in process paragraphs can be constructed in a household kitchen or garage workshop. Some suitable topics include:

the sun	the income tax code
your personal budget	the make-up of your family
the history of racism in the United States	the elements of a successful party
	traffic flow in your city or town
reproduction in ferns	

When you write a process paragraph about such a topic, you are actually discussing its parts and the way they work together. Sometimes these parts are best described as **stages.** For example, a topic such as *the history of racism in the United States* is likely to be best understood if it is broken down into various stages, such as the stages covering the era of slavery, the period of Reconstruction, the period of legal segregation, the birth and growth of the Civil Rights Movement, and the contemporary era. Indeed, no writing that traces history creates a finished product; instead, it explains how a situation developed over time and it may speculate on where events will lead in the future.

EXERCISE 8.1

Brainstorm or freewrite on one of the following topics that emphasize how to do something. Choose a topic with which you are already familiar.

making your favorite sandwich   washing a dog
organizing a birthday party   painting a still life
winning at poker   changing a tire on a car
sewing a button on a shirt or blouse bathing an infant
packing for a weekend trip   planting a bush or shrub

Topic Sentences

The topic sentence of a process paragraph must make clear what the topic of the paragraph will be and how that topic will be addressed. For instance, consider the following topic sentence:

It is not hard to frame a picture.

Aside from informing the reader that the topic of the paragraph will be *how to frame a picture,* very little is presented or known at this time. A better way to address this same topic would be to include some sort of reasons for learning the process.

The successful framing of a picture is not hard so long as one has the right materials.

This topic sentence is stronger than the first one because it introduces another element besides the topic: the idea that one must have the right materials. If the reader knows what the materials are, then the reader will be able to construct a good picture frame with the guidance the rest of the paragraph will supply. In other words, the reader is being supplied with a motivation or reason to read the paragraph. However, what are the materials needed for picture framing? Some readers will find the preceding topic sentence too vague because this question remains unanswered. An even stronger topic sentence might be written:

The making of a picture frame is not difficult so long as one has the proper wood or metal to make the sides of the frame, glass to make the cover, and fastening pieces to secure the picture in the frame.

This topic sentence presents much better—more specific—reasons for reading for the paragraph.

Your topic sentence for your process paragraph does not always have to mention all the parts or pieces involved in the process. Sometimes that is simply not practical or desirable. Your topic sentence should, however, be as specific as possible. For example:

> Crude oil must be processed in several stages to refine it for use as gasoline in cars.

To detail in the topic sentence each stage that crude oil must pass through would make the topic sentence too wordy. Those details are better left for the rest of the paragraph.

EXERCISE 8.2

Examine each of the following topic sentences and determine whether it is an effective topic sentence for a process paragraph. Indicate each correct sentence with a letter *C* and rewrite the others.

1. There are several steps to changing a light bulb.

2. Driving in a foreign country can be made easier if a few simple precautions are followed.

3. The art of book binding can be learned by knowing where to buy the materials, how to operate the machinery, and how to add finishing touches.

4. I know how to plant a hibiscus bush properly.

5. Passing exams without studying can be accomplished easily.

6. Preparing for your own funeral can be a great deal of fun.

7. When you know how to surf the Internet, a whole new world opens up.

8. To become a great basketball player, you had first better be able to meet some physical ability requirements.

9. The age of a tree can be learned without cutting it down.

10. When you prepare a formal dinner party, you must plan the menu, decorate your home, and pick the right music.

Support

There are several important factors to consider when writing the process paragraph. One requirement is that all the steps or stages need to be presented in the correct order. Imagine the difficulty your reader would face if you decided to show how to wrap a birthday present by beginning with the stage of attaching the bow to the already wrapped present, then jumping to a discussion about taping technique, and then discussing how to cut the wrapping paper. After reading your paragraph, your reader should be able to duplicate or at least understand how to duplicate the process. Examine the following paragraph:

Topic sentence   Anyone who drives should know how to change a flat tire. First, before you drive, you must make sure that you have an inflated

Support   spare tire, a jack that works, and a crowbar. If you are driving and have a tire go flat, be certain to choose a safe place to pull off the road. You don't want to take a chance of getting hit by another car while you're working on your own. Get out the crowbar, jack, and tire. Use the sharp end of the crowbar to remove the hub cap from the tire. Use the other end of the crowbar, which has a socket in the same shape as the wheel's lug nuts, to loosen the lug nuts. Next, attach the jack and lift the car so that the wheel comes off the ground. Now, spin the wheel clockwise with one hand, and apply the socket end of the crowbar to each lug nut. Turning the wheel will loosen each lug nut. Remove all of the lug nuts, and then take the wheel off the car. Put the flat tire in the trunk of your car and put the spare on. Place the lug nuts back on, first by hand, and then with the crowbar, spinning the wheel counterclockwise. Once all lug nuts are on tight, lower the wheel to the ground and remove the jack. Finally, tighten the lug nuts even more with the crowbar, reattach the hub cap, and put everything away in the trunk of your car. You are now

Wrap-up sentence   ready to drive to an auto shop to get your flat tire repaired.

Notice that the topic sentence not only introduces the topic of the paragraph; it also includes a reason for reading the paragraph: anyone who drives should know how to change a flat tire. The support is presented in chronological order or time sequence. The specific actions of each step of the process are clear. The equipment needed and parts involved are all included: spare tire, jack, crowbar, wheel, hub cap, and lug nuts.

Sometimes parts or pieces of equipment are not as commonly known as the jacks and crowbars. You may have to define for your reader any unusual terms or items involved in your process. For instance, if you were to describe the process of photosynthesis to a reader, you might have to define terms such as *chloroplast* and *lipids* that would appear in any discussion of the process.

In some process paragraphs, you may also want to mention what should *not* be done. This is especially true if some action or step would be dangerous or could cause the entire process to fail. Examine this paragraph:

> Preparing for your first driver's test can be a nerve-wracking experience, but you can be successful if you follow a few steps. First, be sure to arrive for your test five to ten minutes ahead of schedule, just to be sure you are not late. **Don't try to be overly friendly with the examiner; he or she may regard your friendliness as a mask to cover an inability to drive.** Instead, be polite, but do not talk, except to respond to the examiner's questions. . . .

EXERCISE 8.3

Refer to the topic that you selected in Exercise 8.1 and write a list of the steps involved in the making of the item. Use complete sentences to describe each step, and be as specific as possible. Order the steps chronologically.

Transitions

The transitions used in a process paragraph are much the same as the ones used in a narration paragraph. They include such words as *again, also, finally, first, second, third, meanwhile, next, last, later, then,* and *while.* In the following process paragraph, the transitional words and phrases are printed in bold type:

> Breaking up a relationship is always difficult, but if you follow a few simple steps, you can avoid a lot of unnecessary pain. **First,** do not delay. If you're ready to leave, hanging on just to avoid the inevitable will only make things worse. **Second,** when you tell the person, be honest. If you cared enough about the person to go out

with him or her, you should care enough to be honest. That does not, however, mean delving into aspects of your life that are off limits. If, for instance, you have a new love interest, your old boyfriend or girlfriend does not need to know the details of this new relationship. **Third**, be respectful of the person. Avoid name-calling or assigning blame for the failed relationship. **Finally**, do not give false hope. If it's over, it's over. And don't use the line "We can still be friends." Only time will tell if that is true or not.

Student Writing Assignment: Process

Write a process paragraph using one of the following topics or one of the topics in Exercise 8.1. Make clear to your reader how each stage or step of the process leads to the next stage or step. Follow the steps listed in the Start-Up Suggestions and Self-Revision Questions. Then bring your paragraph to class for peer editing. Revise your paragraph and then complete the section labeled Your Choices: Process to discuss the decisions you made during the composing and revising process.

how to write a holiday season
   letter or a round-robin letter

how to watch TV

how to flatter effectively

how to ask for money from
   your parents

how to control your night dreams

how to meet someone you
   would like to date

how to act like a child

how to use a camera

how to ride a bus

how to offer constructive
   criticism

Start-Up Suggestions

Follow these steps before writing your first draft.

1. Brainstorm or freewrite for ten minutes on your chosen topic.
2. Examine the results of your prewriting and underline all the steps that you discover.
3. Number the steps chronologically as they would happen in the process. Note that they may not appear in order in your prewriting.
4. Make a list of the steps for the process based on your prewriting. Then ask yourself: Have I left anything out?
5. Draft a topic sentence that states clearly the process to be discussed and includes a reason for knowing about that process.
6. Draft a scratch, or informal, outline of your paragraph.

Self-Revision Questions

Answer these questions after writing your first draft and before rewriting the draft for submission to your peer-editing group.

1. Does the topic sentence clearly show what process is being explained?
2. Is the topic sentence the first sentence of the paragraph? If not, is there a good, logical reason for placing it elsewhere?
3. Does your paragraph indicate the order of the steps or the stages of the process?
4. Do you have sufficient support in the paragraph?
5. Do you stay focused on your topic throughout the paragraph?
6. Do you mention anything important that should not be done or should be avoided?
7. Have you used appropriate, effective transitions? (You may wish to review the list of transitional words and phrases under the heading Transitions.)
8. Does your paragraph have a reasonable and logical wrap-up sentence?

Revise your paragraph and submit it to your peer-editing group.

Peer-Editing Guidelines for Process

Answer these questions for each of the paragraphs written by the other members of your peer-editing group.

1. Does the paragraph have a topic sentence? Underline the topic sentence.
2. Is the topic sentence effective? Does it introduce one of the topics assigned?
3. Does the topic sentence provide an argument or opinion about the process to be described?
4. Is the support relevant to the topic sentence?
5. Does the paragraph sufficiently describe each step or stage of the process?
6. Does the paragraph maintain chronological order throughout the discussion of the process?
7. Does the paragraph mention anything that should be avoided or not done?

8. Does the paragraph provide effective transitions between ideas? List some of the transitional words and phrases used.
9. Having read the paragraph, do you now think you could duplicate the process described? Why or why not?
10. What is the crystalline word of the paragraph?

Prepare the final draft of your paragraph, taking the comments of your peer-editing group into account.

Your Choices: Process

Answer these questions after you have finished your final draft.

1. How did you choose your topic?
2. How did you choose your title for your process paragraph?
3. Did you have to change your topic sentence as you moved from draft to draft? Why or why not?
4. Did you need to revise your support to ensure that each step or stage of the process was clear?
5. Did your peer editors have difficulty following the steps or stages of the process?
6. What transitional words or phrases did you use? Why?
7. What other changes to the support did you make during the drafting process? Why?
8. If you added additional material, why was it necessary?
9. Did you have to change your wrap-up sentence? Why or why not?
10. Did you agree or disagree with your peer editors' choice for the crystalline word? If you disagreed, did you make any revisions to emphasize the word you wanted?

COMPUTER EXERCISE

Exchange with your writing partner either your paragraphs from the Student Writing Assignment or ones written on a topic in Exercise 8.1. Read your partner's paragraph. Break the paragraph into a list of steps and enumerate each of the steps. Examine the list. Do any steps appear to be left out? Are any unclear? Are any out of order? If so, mark them and pass your paragraph back to your partner. When you receive your paragraph, check your partner's comments. How well did you do?

THE REVISION PROCESS:
A Student Writing Sample

The following sample was written by Michael for a process paragraph assignment. Since he rode the bus to school daily, Michael chose the topic *how to ride a bus*. He began by freewriting on the topic.

How to ride the bus? I ride the bus every day I know a lot about the bus system here it actually isn't too bad but you do have to get used to a few things like how they won't give change I found its a lot easier just to have a bus pass but even that keeps going up all the time you'd think that since most people who ride the bus don't have much money they'd keep the fares down but really it seems if you look at the people on the bus you wouldn't believe they had the money for a fare much less a bus pass you have to be smart on the bus don't sit near any freaks or anyone who looks drunk I try to find an empty seat near the front not that anything bad has ever happened to me but you need to be smart one time these guys got in a huge argument in the back and the driver pulled over and the cops even had to come and I thought there was going to be some real trouble but actually everyone calmed down a few guys got off and then it was ok but really it's not too bad but to be honest I am hoping to buy a car soon because having your own car is definitely better

When Michael was done with his freewriting, he found that he had gone off track quite a bit, but he actually liked where he was headed. Rather than talk about monthly fares or daily fares, Michael decided that he would take a look at the people on the bus.

He decided to do a looping exercise by starting with *You have to be smart on the bus.* He wrote that sentence as the start of a second freewriting session.

> *You have to be smart on the bus* I guess I'm an expert by now with all the bus riding I've done I have a regular route and regular times but I still try to stick to myself, get a seat near the front and keep my eyes open its not all that bad actually sometimes I read the whole way to school but let me tell you at night on the bus if I read I only read with one eye because things can get a little wild no one has ever hassled me but I've seen really tough looking guys probably gang-bangers get on a bus and I tell you I was nervous I couldn't wait to get off the bus lets you see that not everyone is a yuppie with a Benz or whatever frankly you can find a whole lot of world on a bus I have seen guys in suits, businessmen and gangsters so I suppose eventually everyone rides a bus

At this point, Michael decided he would format a topic sentence based on how to cope with riding the bus. Here was Michael's first topic sentence:

> *There are several important steps to riding on a bus.*

That was quickly thrown out. The phrase *There are several important steps* was vague, and there was no reason given for a reader to want to know about the process. It contained nothing of what he really wanted to say. The next try was better:

> *Riding on a bus requires that you know several things.*

Michael was not pleased with the *you know several things* part of this sentence, so he decided to rewrite it again.

> *A smart person knows several important keys to riding on a bus successfully.*

Michael felt that this topic sentence was good because the word *successfully* supplied the reader with a reason for wanting to read the paragraph. The phrase *several important keys* was a little stronger than *several things*, although he felt it was still vague. However, he thought there would be so many ideas in the paragraph that including them in the topic sentence would be awkward.

Michael decided that the entire paragraph itself should focus on the major aspects of what he had learned about riding on a bus. He knew also that he should write in chronological order. That meant that he would have to follow a time sequence. He decided to show what he personally did when he got on a bus.

> A smart person knows several important keys to riding on a bus successfully. First, before the person ever boards the bus, he or she must know what the bus number is, what time the bus arrives, and where it's going. You don't want to be standing alone at a bus stop too long. Second, have a monthly pass or have the exact change ready. Don't open your wallet or fiddle with a purse. That might tempt bad guys to think you've got a lot of money. Next, find an open seat near the front. The backs of buses are uncomfortable and sometimes disruptive people sit there. Finally, keep an eye open for trouble, especially at night. Most of the time nothing will happen, but you want to be aware if it does.

When Michael checked with his Self-Revision Questions, he realized that he had made bus riding sound like a near-death experience. He knew the bus system was not as bad as the paragraph made it sound. He had never been hassled, robbed, or hurt; he just wanted to point out how to avoid trouble. When Michael rewrote the paragraph for submitting to his peer group, he decided to soften the impact of the warnings and to talk about the variety of people who travel on the bus.

> A smart person knows several important keys to having a good ride on a bus. First, before the person ever boards the bus, he or she should know what the bus number is, what time the bus arrives, and where it's going. Second, have a monthly pass or have

the exact change ready, which will be faster and wiser than
fumbling with money in front of people. Next, find an open seat
near the front. Disruptive people sometimes sit in the back.
However, once you're on a bus, usually nothing bad will happen
and actually you can learn a lot about people and life if you keep
an eye open. Everyone from business men to gang members rides
the bus eventually, so what you see on a bus is slice of life. Don't
miss it--that's part of the fun of taking the bus.

When Michael's peer-editing group answered the questionnaire, one
thing they noted was that the paragraph seemed to be about two different things: steps about how to be careful and people-watching on the
bus.

The peer group wanted a more positive paragraph. Although they
thought that the assignment may have said "How to ride a bus," they
encouraged Michael to focus more on people-watching on the bus,
which they argued was a part of riding the bus. Michael checked with
his instructor just to be certain, and the instructor gave Michael en-
thusiastic approval for the new direction of his paragraph. Here is
Michael's final draft:

The Fun of Riding a Bus

By following a few simple steps, a smart and observant person
can have a good time riding on a bus. First, everyone should know
a few basic things before riding the bus, such as knowing what bus
to take, when it arrives, and where it's going. Second, a person
should have a monthly pass or exact change so there is no
fumbling with money in front of people. Once on the bus, a person
should find a seat where he or she will not only feel safe should any
trouble arise but can also people-watch. Don't be afraid to look
around--a person can see much of America not _from_ the bus
but _in_ the bus. Don't stare at anyone, of course, and always
have something to read in case no one interesting is on the bus.
However, since everyone, from business people to gang members,
rides the bus eventually, what one sees on a bus is a slice of life.
Finally, a person should not get so involved in people-watching that

he or she forgets to get off at the right stop! Bus riding can be fun if one knows how.

When Michael filled out his Your Choices questionnaire, he realized just how much he had done in creating his paragraph. He had changed his topic, his topic sentence, a lot of his support, his wrap-up sentence, and the whole general "feel," or tone, of the paragraph. Although he enjoyed the final paragraph a lot more than he had his previous drafts, he wasn't totally pleased with the final results. He wished he had conveyed the idea of how much fun people-watching on the bus can be, and that he had spent less time on the mechanics of actually riding on the bus.

GRAMMAR INSTRUCTION AND EXERCISES:
Subject-Verb Agreement

Subjects and verbs should agree with each other in person and in number. Examine the following sentences:

> The team are going to St. Louis for the regional championships.

> Dr. Lollard and Father Berger volunteers at the homeless shelter every month.

> Either the driver or the mechanics is responsible for the accident on the speedway.

> The problem are the broken timing belts.

The trouble with each of these sentences is the failure of the subject and the verb to agree in terms of number. That is, if the subject is plural, the verb should be in the plural form; if the subject is singular, the verb should be in the singular form. Here are the revised sentences:

> The team **is** going to St. Louis for the regional championships.

> Dr. Lollard and Father Berger **volunteer** at the homeless shelter every month.

> Either the driver or the mechanics **are** responsible for the accident on the Speedway.

> The problem **is** the broken timing belts.

Part of the difficulty can come when there is confusion about the nature of the subject. This can come in the following forms:

1. *A collective noun as subject.* A **collective noun** is a noun that signifies a group, such as *team, family, class,* or *flock.* Collective nouns are singular in form.

> The family is waiting for the train inside the station.

> This class performs better on the test than the last one did.

> A flock of seagulls follows the fishing boats out to the open ocean waters.

2. *A compound subject.* A **compound subject** consists of more than one subject. A compound subject that is joined by *and* or a comma signifying the same takes the plural form of the verb.

> Billy, Bobby, and Ben race toward the goal.

> The phonograph and the harpsichord were both put up for auction.

> Jeannine and her sisters sew all their own clothes.

When a compound subject is joined by *or* or *nor,* the form of the subject closest to the verb determines whether the verb will be singular or plural.

> Neither the president nor the members of Congress have the authority to make such a personal decision for me.

> Either the coach or the players have to come out to speak to the media after this evening's defeat.

> ***Note:*** In *either/or* and *neither/nor* subject constructions, placing the singular noun in the first position and the plural noun second is generally preferred.

Awkward:

Neither the tenants nor the landlord wishes for the dispute to end up in court.

Neither the landlord nor the tenants wish for the dispute to end up in court.

3. *Subject and subject complement.* A **subject complement** follows a linking verb and is usually a noun, pronoun, adjective, or group of words that functions as a noun or adjective. For instance, in the sentence *The problem is the broken timing belts,* the word *belts* is the subject complement. Remember, however, the subject determines whether a verb is singular or plural in a sentence, not the subject complement. Therefore, the subject and subject complement do not have to agree in number; only the subject and verb must agree.

Larry and Dennis form the best two-man volleyball team in the tournament.

The **record is** 755 home runs by Hank Aaron.

The **ships are** the best the navy can afford.

4. *Subject not at the start of the sentence.* Subjects in sentences that begin with phrases such as *There are* or *Here is* follow these phrases and determine whether the verb is singular or plural.

There **are** eight **exits** to the movie theater.

Here **is** the new **key** to the bolt lock.

5. *A phrase or clause separating subject and verb.* Do not be confused by any phrase or clause that comes between the subject and its verb.

The **reasons** for the fund-raising drive **are** not difficult to understand.

The **lions** in the pride that lives on the plains that extend south beyond the border **have** all been tagged to help researchers track them.

One of the members **finds** herself in a rather difficult position due to a conflict of interest.

(See pages 354–57 for further discussion of subject-verb agreement.)

Examine the following sentences for subject-verb agreement errors. Rewrite each sentence that has an error. If a sentence is correct, indicate it with the letter *C*.

1. Two mechanics who work at the dealership in Lubbock was found to have been stealing automobile parts.

2. Neither the doctors nor the hospital staff knows what problems the blood shortage will bring.

3. Big Lou as well as the other dogs eat raw ground beef.

4. The jury have arrived at a verdict.

5. Margaret and Theresa are riding to school together in the truck.

6. There are, to be certain, no single understanding or explanation that can fully encompass the chaos of that tragedy.

7. The police accost anybody they suspect are carrying illegal firearms.

8. The central problem with the heater are the broken coils.

9. A system of checks and balances is one of the hallmarks of this nation's government.

10. Each of the parties agree that peace is the desired outcome of the negotiations.

9 What's Your Point?

Creating the Thesis Sentence

JOURNAL EXERCISE

Locate a recent copy of your local newspaper and read the editorials section. Respond in your journal to something that interests you, whether you agree with the point expressed or disagree. Can you determine why you respond that way?

When you write, how often do you write only one paragraph? On some written examinations, short answers that run only one paragraph may be required, but more typically, you will be required to write longer works. Naturally, this experience probably corresponds to what you see in your own reading, as well: most written works are often at least several paragraphs long. You have been studying how to write single paragraphs for different purposes, but ultimately, you will need to be able to join those paragraphs together to form essays.

An **essay** is a written work at least several paragraphs in length on a single subject. An essay is a way to explore your own ideas about a subject and present to your reader your personal opinions or ideas about that subject. This main opinion or idea about a subject is called a **thesis** and is presented in a **thesis sentence.** Some essays never have a thesis sentence; the reader must derive the thesis from a careful understanding of the text. In an academic writing situation, however, a thesis sentence is usually required.

Since the essay exists to prove the thesis sentence, the thesis sentence is the most important sentence of your essay. That is, your thesis sentence is the main idea or opinion that the essay is attempting to develop or prove true.

What Does a Thesis Sentence Look Like?

A thesis sentence must be a declarative statement, which means that it must assert or state something. In this respect, the thesis sentence sounds a lot like a topic sentence. Just as a topic sentence tells the reader the main idea of a paragraph, so, too, does a thesis sentence tell the reader the main idea of an essay. The thesis sentence is broader than the topic sentence since the thesis sentence covers the entire essay rather than just one paragraph. Examine these two sentences:

> Cats make good house pets because they clean themselves, they don't need to be walked, and their waste is confined to a kitty litter box.

> Cats make good house pets because they don't need to be walked.

Which of the two makes the better thesis sentence and which makes the better topic sentence? The first sentence is broader than the second, covering three different reasons why cats make good house pets; the second sentence states only one aspect of why cats make good house pets. The first sentence is less likely to make a good topic sentence because it introduces too many ideas for a single paragraph. For many writers, the first sentence would make the better thesis sentence. The second sentence, because it examines a more limited aspect of cats, is more suitable for a topic sentence. Many writers would be better able to cover in just one paragraph the material suggested by the second sentence.

Shaping the Thesis Sentence

When you write to present information more than to persuade or convey an opinion, you are engaged in **expository writing.** In expository writing, most of the text is factual information, such as examples or statistical information. Expository writing is found most often in matters in which the author's opinions can be pushed aside in favor of simply showing the facts, particularly in science or social studies.

Traditionally, instructors view expository writing as different from **persuasive** or **argumentative writing,** in which an author is explicitly attempting to sway the reader to a certain point of view or to prove some point of debate. This type of writing is most openly **subjective,** which means a writer shows bias in his or her treatment of a subject. Some hold that expository writing is **objective** writing, which means a writer holds back his or her opinion about the subject. However, such a claim can be limited and misleading, since almost all writing reflects the opinions of the writer. Even if no obvious bias is present, the issue of which details to include and which to leave out and other such choices reveal a subjective quality to expository writing. Only the most scientifically rigorous writing can be called objective, and even scientific writing can be subjective if the writer is biased in how the scientific information is presented.

In some forms of expository writing, such as with personal narratives, you may not be expressing an opinion that is debatable. Examine the following:

> My grandparents helped teach me the value of respect for one's
>
> elders.

Since you know what your grandparents did or did not do, the thesis sentence is not debatable, unless you are not telling the truth. However, the thesis sentence does have an angle or opinion; it shows your personal attitude toward your grandparents.

With thesis sentences based on the rhetorical modes traditionally labeled as expository, there is often considerable room for debate. Examine the following thesis statements:

> The continent of Australia contains the most magnificent natural
>
> wonders in the world.   Description

> The destruction of the Aztecs by the Spanish explorer Cortez is an
>
> example of how unbridled greed and ethnocentrism contributed to
>
> the annihilation of the native cultures of the New World.   Example

True charity involves giving of yourself, not just your money.
Definition

People who go to coffee houses on a regular basis are either caffeine addicts, art world "wannabes," or lonely losers.
Classification

Community colleges are better places to go for the first two years of school than traditional four-year institutions.   Compare/contrast

Many fans have turned away from major league baseball because of repeated strikes by players.   Cause

An increase in the gasoline tax will encourage greater fuel conservation and will fund more badly needed road repairs.
Effect

Studying for final exams should be done in three steps.   Process

All of these thesis sentences are debatable. Therefore, none can be seen as strictly expository.

As a student, you will most often be asked to write an essay that fulfills one of the purposes of writing that we have already discussed in Chapters 4 through 8. You will need to have a thesis sentence and, except in some scientific courses, that thesis usually will require that you present some opinion or interpretation of information. In order to do this properly, you should be sure that your thesis sentence has an argument.

Argument-Based Thesis Sentences

An **argument** in the academic world does not convey the same feeling that the word *argument* may in your daily life. The emotions of hostility and anger are not necessarily present. What is present in the idea of argument is opinion—something that can be debated. If a statement is not debatable but is easily provable by rational means, you do not have an argument, and consequently, you do not have a thesis sentence. Examine the following statement:

The United States has fifty states.

This sentence is a declarative statement because it presents information, but there is no argument. This is a statement of fact that is commonly known and easily verified if it is unknown. There is no opinion, nothing debatable, in the sentence. Examine this sentence:

Puerto Rico should become the fifty-first state in the United States.

This is a thesis sentence. The statement is clearly debatable, since there are many reasonable people who oppose the idea of Puerto Rico becoming an official state. Others can be found who support this statement. Thus, there is argument.

Fact-Based Thesis Sentences

One requirement of a thesis sentence, then, is that it must not be an easily verifiable fact. Some thesis sentences do concern themselves with questions of fact, but these are facts that are derived from considerable research. Such a sample thesis might be:

Secondhand smoke is a factor in lung disease among nonsmokers who live with smokers.

This thesis sentence would require factual information or research. Even then, some researchers might disagree with this statement, feeling that the effects of secondhand smoke have been overstated. They might say something like:

The dangers of secondhand smoke have been overstated by antismoking advocates.

You can see how, even in matters that appear factual, debate and argument can occur.

How Is the Thesis Sentence Put Together?

There is no one single right way to create your thesis sentence, but generally speaking, it should present a claim about a subject. Also, some instructors require that you include the controlling ideas for that claim.

The Claim

Recall from Chapter 1 that the **subject** is the general area of your investigation, and the **topic** is the specific aspect on which you focus. The **claim** is what you have to say about that topic; it is your main idea or opinion. All thesis sentences must have a claim that states the point or argument of the essay; indeed, many times, the claim is *all* the thesis sentence contains. Notice that in the following examples, the claim alone serves as a thesis sentence:

Subject: American high schools

Topic: Social events at American high schools

Claim: American high schools put too much emphasis on social events.

Subject: Pets

Topic: Cats as pets

Claim: Cats make better pets than dogs do.

Subject: Travel

Topic: Student travel in Europe

Claim: The only things a student needs to travel through Europe are a backpack, a Eurail pass, and a credit card.

Subject: Movies

Topic: Special effects in the movies

Claim: Special effects have overwhelmed most science fiction movies.

EXERCISE 9.1

Write a claim for each of the following subjects.

fashion	families
boats	ways to relax
volunteer work	role models
television	food
hobbies	nature

Controlling Ideas

Sometimes your thesis sentence may consist only of the claim, but other times the thesis sentence also includes the controlling ideas. The **controlling ideas** of a thesis sentence, also termed the **points of support,** are the specific concepts that will prove that the thesis sentence is true. The concepts are the rational support for the thesis. The controlling ideas can provide a quick outline of what you will later discuss about the thesis sentence. For example, consider the following thesis sentence:

> Learning a second language is valuable because in doing so you will open your mind to a new culture, you will be able to communicate with new people, and you will be able to travel freely in countries that speak that language.

This thesis sentence can be broken down into two principal parts: the claim and the controlling ideas.

Claim:

Learning a second language is valuable.

Controlling Ideas:

1. You will open your mind to a new culture.
2. You will be able to communicate with new people.
3. You will be able to travel freely in countries that speak that language.

Each of these controlling ideas demonstrates a **rational basis** for why the claim is true. The rational basis provides the reasoning by which your essay will be proven true.

Other thesis sentences with controlling ideas may not be as long or bulky. Sometimes each of the controlling ideas is one part of the whole argument.

> The three most important locations for socializing in my high school were the cafeteria, the locker room, and the hallways.

This thesis, based on analysis, contains the claim within the controlling ideas. That is, since the claim states that there are three important locations, we must know those specific locations to get the full claim. There is overlap here between the claim and the controlling ideas.

EXERCISE 9.2

Rewrite each of the following thesis sentences by adding or completing the controlling ideas.

1. Old architecture can inspire people to imagine the past.

2. The city is a terrible place to live because of the noise.

3. Showing a movie is one way that a dorm can raise money.

4. He deserved the promotion because he worked hard.

5. America's fear of communism was a cause of the war in Vietnam.

6. The workers decided to strike due to their unsafe working conditions.

7. She decided to attend business school.

8. Success in life requires timing.

9. Students who spend their time going to athletic events should be studying instead.

10. The crime rate has decreased because the population is getting older.

EXERCISE 9.3

Add three controlling ideas to the claims you wrote for Exercise 9.1. Try to keep your thesis sentences from becoming too wordy.

What Can Go Wrong with a Thesis Sentence?

As you saw in Chapter 5, sometimes negation is a good way to help define a term. So, to help you focus on what makes a good thesis sentence, the following sections discuss the types of things that do *not* make for good thesis sentences.

Rhetorical Questions

A thesis sentence is not a question. Even if you believe the expected answer to your question is obvious, you should not put your reader in the position of having to supply the answer. Sometimes your reader will simply be put off; other times he or she may respond to your question in a different way than you intended. Examine this example:

Do you have trouble managing your money?

This would not be a good thesis sentence for an essay on the importance of good money management. Some readers will simply answer no. At that point, you have offered them no reason to go on reading your essay. Instead, you should make sure your thesis sentence is a declarative statement.

Having a budget is the best way to manage your money.

Unrealistic or Absolutist Thesis Sentences

Just because a thesis sentence can be a statement of opinion does not mean that you can say *anything*. Remember, you have to be able to *prove* your thesis sentence. Thesis sentences that are unrealistic either involve subjects for which sufficient or credible research does not exist or are stated in ways that make the claims impossible to prove. Such a thesis sentence might look like the following:

Since the universe is so vast, life forms must exist on other planets.

This statement, although it contains some logic, cannot ultimately be proven. It rests entirely on conjecture and speculation. Indeed, a whole range of subjects—such as unidentified flying objects, extrasensory perception, and astrology—can be problematic for students because the claims of their advocates seldom are believed by the scientific community. This puts you, as a writer, in the awkward position of believing information from these sources simply because you believe it (perhaps based on your subjective personal experience), not because there is a rational basis for believing it. Instructors seldom feel comfortable assessing or grading work based solely on students' beliefs.

Absolutist thesis sentences give no ground. They make claims that are all one way or the other, and that tends to lead to overgeneralization. Consider these examples:

All politicians are corrupt.

There is no way that the Dallas Cowboys cannot win the Super Bowl.

People in fraternities and sororities are not serious about their education.

These thesis sentences admit no possibility of exception or error. As a result, they will be impossible to prove because there are some politicians who are not corrupt, the Cowboys do not win the Super Bowl every year, and there are many people in fraternities and sororities who are deeply committed to their education.

Instead, these thesis sentences need to be softened with the use of qualifiers. **Qualifiers** are words that provide reservations about what is said. A short list of qualifiers includes:

almost	some	sometimes
most	often	oftentimes
many	may be	maybe
in some cases	usually	should
seem(s) to have		

Revised, the thesis sentences could read:

Too many politicians are corrupt.

The Dallas Cowboys should win the Super Bowl this year.

Some people in fraternities and sororities are not serious about their education.

Overuse of Qualifiers

One danger of qualifiers is that if you use too many of them in a sentence, you have couched your claim in terms that ultimately lead to nothing.

It may be possible that the Dallas Cowboys might win the Super Bowl some time.

Such a thesis sentence has overused the qualifiers *may be possible, might,* and *some time* to the point that the sentence actually asserts nothing. You need to be assertive in your thesis sentences, just not extreme.

Phrases such as *I think, I believe,* and *I feel* are also qualifiers and generally should be avoided in your thesis sentences. Some student writers use these phrases on the assumption that they add emphasis and credibility to their thesis sentences. Usually, however, the phrases have the opposite effect. Consider the following:

I feel that computer technology has done more harm than good.

Why should your reader be persuaded that the fact that you *feel* this makes the point any more true? You should avoid the phrase altogether:

Computer technology has done more harm than good.

Too Broad Thesis Sentences

Your thesis sentence must fit the length of your essay. In college, you will often be asked to write essays that are relatively short, such as 500 words in length. Although 500 words may sound like a lot to you right now, you can actually run out of space quickly if you are trying to tackle too much in your thesis sentence. Imagine trying to develop one of the following thesis sentences in a 500-word essay:

School is important in one's life.

Today's young people hold a variety of goals and aspirations.

The threat of nuclear terrorism in the post-Cold War world is growing.

Any attempt to handle one of these subjects in 500 words will lead only to a very superficial treatment. Instead, you need to focus on a particular aspect of your subject, so that you discuss, in depth, a small part of it. Remember, that is your topic. For instance, you might rewrite one of the preceding sentences as follows:

Many young people today are interested in preserving the environment.

Similarly, you don't want topics that are too narrow or brief. Often these topics are not truly topics but rather statements of fact.

Interest rates have held steady for the past six months.

The ratio of students to teachers at this school is 36 to 1.

A computer that cost $2,000 five years ago can be had for under $500 today.

Obvious Thesis Sentences

An obvious thesis sentence is one that makes a claim over which there is little debate or perhaps even interest. Sometimes these thesis sentences may be trite expressions or observations that have been made many times before. As a writer, you want to find subjects and topics that are interesting. Finding unique ideas is not always realistic, but giving an old idea a new twist is. Examine the following sentences:

Corner grocers are becoming a thing of the past.

The president of the United States has an important job.

Materialism has destroyed the true meaning of Christmas.

These thesis sentences go over well-trod ground. Your reader will probably already be familiar with the arguments or observations that you might bring to bear on any one of them, and your essay would run the danger of being boring to both you and your reader.

Instead, find the new idea, new attitude, or new angle that can make each of these thesis sentences fresh. Consider these revisions:

The rise of supermarkets, at the expense of the corner grocer, has been beneficial for the modern American family.

The president of the United States does not have an important job because the decisions that most affect people's lives are made by business and banking executives.

Materialism helps ring in Christmas cheer for everyone.

Confusing Thesis Sentences

Confusing thesis sentences usually try to take on too much. Remember that a thesis sentence should be about the main idea or opinion in an essay; if you have more than one main idea, your essay will be chaotic. You don't want contradictory ideas or unrelated ideas present in a thesis sentence. Reflect on these examples:

Welfare should be abolished, but the government must still supply aid to the needy.   Government aid to the needy *is* welfare.

I want to join the military, but I also want to form my own punk rock band and tour the country.   Which will it be?

There are advantages to living at home while you go to college, and there are advantages to living on your own.
No specific point of view or argument is stated.

Signposts

A **signpost** announces to your reader what he or she should expect to happen next. This is a weak technique, for it suggests that you do not trust that your reader will be able to follow along.

In this essay I will discuss how the rain forest is vital to the earth's oxygen supply.

I want to talk about how important early detection of breast cancer is for women.

The thesis of this essay is that divorce is often harmful to children.

Instead, simply remove the signposts and your thesis sentences will be much stronger.

The rain forest is vital to the earth's oxygen supply.

Early detection of breast cancer is important for women.

Divorce is often harmful to children.

A Few Simple Dos and Don'ts of Thesis Sentences

1. **Do** have a thesis sentence that is appropriate for the length of your assignment.

2. **Do** have a thesis sentence that states what the topic of the essay is.

3. **Do** have a thesis sentence that states an argument.

4. **Do** have a thesis sentence that is supported by a rational basis.

5. **Don't** have a thesis sentence that asks a question.

6. **Don't** have a thesis sentence that is absolutist or unrealistic.

7. **Don't** have a thesis sentence that uses too many qualifiers.

8. **Don't** have a thesis sentence that is too broad.

9. **Don't** have a thesis sentence that is obvious to the point where few people would take issue with it.

10. **Don't** have a thesis sentence that states a fact that cannot be argued.

11. **Don't** have a thesis sentence that is confusing.

12. **Don't** have a thesis sentence that includes a signpost or announcement.

EXERCISE 9.4

Revise the following thesis sentences, making them more effective.

1. There are eight types of salad dressing in the cafeteria.

2. When Bill Clinton was sworn in as the forty-second president of the United States, he became the first president to serve who was born after World War II.

3. Can you imagine life without plastic?

4. Chocolate ice cream after dinner is better than vanilla.

5. Going to school while living at home with my parents has been good and bad.

6. I believe that it is possible that air pollution could be harmful to infants' lungs under some conditions.

7. This paper is going to be on the subject of offensive television advertising.

8. The death penalty has some good points and some bad points.

9. Virgos make good accountants.

10. If the Chicago Cubs ever win a pennant, we will know that hell has finally frozen over.

11. Immigrants are in America to take advantage of the welfare system.

12. If everyone were more courteous, the world would be a better place.

13. My history class has twenty-six students.

14. Mothers are beautiful people.

15. People who watch soap operas are morally corrupt and intellectually barren.

16. Who wants to live in a society in which the rich get richer and the poor get poorer?

17. The subject of this short essay will be the 3,000-year history of discrimination against the Jewish people.

18. Parents can be influential in their children's lives.

19. Americans are in love with their cars.

20. Golf is a popular sport.

COMPUTER EXERCISE

Put your list of ten thesis sentences from Exercise 9.1 onto a computer file if you have not done so already. Exchange lists with your writing partner. Read and make careful comments about whether the thesis sentences are effective before returning the lists to each other.

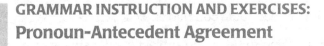

GRAMMAR INSTRUCTION AND EXERCISES:
Pronoun-Antecedent Agreement

Examine the following flawed sentences:

> The members of the guild will hold its annual meeting next Tuesday.
>
> A student who wishes to receive their grades must turn in a self-addressed, stamped envelope to the registrar.
>
> Neither of the sisters wants their own phone line.
>
> Every parent has to think of their child's future.
>
> Anyone applying for the scholarship needs to send their transcript to the foundation.

The problem in each of these sentences is the failure of the pronoun to agree with its antecedent. The **antecedent** is the word or group of words for which the pronoun is substituting. If the antecedent is plural, then the pronoun should be plural; if the antecedent is singular, then the pronoun should be singular. Consider the rewritten sentences:

> The **members** of the guild will hold **their** annual meeting next Tuesday.
>
> A **student** who wishes to receive **his** or **her** grades must turn in a self-addressed, stamped envelope to the registrar.
>
> **Neither** of the sisters wants **her** own phone line.
>
> **Every parent** has to think of **his** or **her** child's future.
>
> **Anyone** applying for the scholarship needs to send **his** or **her** transcript to the foundation.

Part of the difficulty comes when there is confusion about the number of the noun or in identifying the correct noun as the antecedent. Here are some keys:

1. Usually a singular pronoun is used when the antecedent is an **indefinite pronoun** such as *anybody, anyone, each, every, everybody, everything, many a, neither, nobody, no one, one, somebody,* and *something.*

Many a hockey player has lost **his** teeth during practice or games.

Each of the women in the contest has agreed to allow **her** name to be used in advertisements.

Neither of the planes has returned to **its** base.

2. A few indefinite pronouns are always plural: *both, few, many, others, and several.*

Both of the students admitted that **they** had plagiarized **their** last assignment.

The **others** are waiting with **their** skis at the top of the slope.

Several of the farm animals have **their** likenesses printed on a billboard.

3. A few indefinite pronouns can be singular or plural depending on the noun for which they are substituting: *all, any, more, most, none,* and *some.*

Most of the **water** finds **its** way to the ocean.

None of the **soldiers** survived to see **their** loved ones.

Some of the **fathers** have **their** sons learn to play sports at too young an age.

4. Nouns joined by *and* usually take a plural pronoun, except when both nouns refer to the same person or thing.

Sal and Ben hope to take **their** act on the road.

Anwar Sadat and Itzhak Rabin will always be remembered for **their** efforts to create peace in the Middle East.

The former star football player and Supreme Court justice was able to speak with authority on **his** experience with prejudice against the intellectual abilities of athletes.

Remember, following rules of subject-verb agreement, as discussed in Chapter 8, can be a good guide for determining pronoun-antecedent agreement if your antecedent is also the subject of the sentence. Look at this sentence:

> The members of the guild will hold its annual meeting next
> Tuesday.

You can avoid confusion about the proper antecedent by being careful not to be tricked by the presence of phrases or clauses between the antecedent and the pronoun. The correct antecedent here is *members,* not *guild.*

> The members of the guild will hold their annual meeting next
> Tuesday.

(See pages 357–59 for further discussion of pronoun-antecedent agreement.)

EXERCISES

Examine the following sentences for pronoun-antecedent agreement errors. Rewrite each sentence that has an error. If a sentence is correct, indicate it with the letter *C.*

1. Every videotape is labeled according to their contents.

2. Some of the surfers are taking his or her boards down to the southern end of the beach.

3. Either the director or her actors will have to find new jobs if she cannot make a more entertaining movie than this!

4. Each male poet included in this anthology was educated at Harvard.

5. The U.S. soccer team surprised the world with their victory over Colombia in the 1994 World Cup.

6. An employee who wants their dental plan changed can do so during the month of November.

7. Neither the panda bears nor the hippopotamus named Heidi was able get much sleep in their new pens.

8. The faculty is known for their dedication to instruction.

9. All of the sandwiches must be covered or they will go stale.

10. Each of the tables has had their surfaces refinished.

10 Building from Within

Moving from Thesis to Essay

Write about your past experience with essay writing. Consider how frequently you have been asked in school to write essays. Recount one or two specific essays you have written. How well did you do on those essays? Do you find yourself dreading an essay assignment, or do you feel confident when faced with one?

Now that you have learned to develop an effective thesis sentence, you're ready to start your essay. How do you begin an writing an essay? The answer is right in front of you: with your thesis sentence.

Your thesis sentence can be the basis of a topic sentence outline for your essay. In Chapter 2, we discussed writing outlines. The scratch, or informal, outline contains only broad generalities, mentioning in two or three words each of the topics to be discussed. The formal outline involves writing complete sentences and providing several different levels of detail. However, you can choose to write a briefer version of the formal outline, called the *topic sentence outline,* in which you list the thesis sentence and the topic sentences that you develop for the essay. These topic sentences are created from the controlling ideas found in the thesis sentence. Examine the following thesis sentence from Chapter 9:

> Puerto Rico should become the fifty-first state in the United States.

By adding three controlling ideas to the thesis, you can create a larger sentence:

> Puerto Rico should become the fifty-first state in the United States because it already receives U.S. government aid, its people are already taxpaying U.S. citizens, and its economy will grow only when the island is guaranteed the security of statehood.

The thesis sentence now has two parts: the claim (from the beginning of the sentence until the word *state*) and the controlling ideas (the rest of the sentence after *because*). You can then create your topic sentences from the controlling ideas.

Thesis Sentence:

Puerto Rico should become the fifty-first state in the United States because it already receives U.S. government aid, its people are already taxpaying U.S. citizens, and its economy will grow only when the island is guaranteed the security of statehood.

Topic Sentence 1:

Puerto Rico already receives a large amount of U.S. government aid, so statehood would merely make legal the relationship that exists in fact.

Topic Sentence 2:

Like the American colonists two hundred years ago, Puerto Ricans should not suffer taxation without representation.

Topic Sentence 3:

Making Puerto Rico part of the United States would encourage the corporate and business world to invest in Puerto Rico, thereby improving its economy.

Each of these topic sentences is now ready to begin a good, solid paragraph. If you look at each topic sentence individually, you can see that the idea expressed in that sentence is relevant to the thesis sentence. Taken together, the topic sentences help prove the thesis sentence. That, of course, is your ultimate goal.

Why Does an Essay Have to Have Structure?

Many students find essay writing to be a hit-or-miss affair. They know that an essay consists of a thesis sentence and several paragraphs to support the thesis sentence, but beyond that, the essay is a mystery. They don't know when they've written a good essay or a bad one because they have no consistency in their writing, and they are unaware of what elements are needed to create a good essay.

Part of the trouble begins with structure. Sometimes students avoid the idea of structure because they associate having *structure* with being *rigid, unimaginative,* or *dull.* Many students feel that structure inhibits their ability to express themselves or binds them to a predetermined formula for presenting their ideas. Truthfully, structure, when handled poorly, *can* do these things.

Structure, however, helps you to develop your ideas logically. Structure can assist your thinking process and can aid your reader in following your thinking. Structure actually is a neutral term, not good or bad. In the wrong hands, an essay that follows a formula *does* seem rigid, unimaginative, and dull. With an understanding of the elements of essay writing, however, you can use structure to present even the most complicated arguments clearly, logically, and convincingly.

What Are the Parts of an Essay?

Just like a paragraph, an essay can be broken down into parts. These parts are the introduction, the main body, and the conclusion. They correspond with the idea of having a beginning, a middle, and an end. Within each of these parts are other parts, each of which has a function or purpose.

The Introduction

The introduction is the start of your essay. For a shorter essay, the introduction is usually only one paragraph long. Only if you have a lengthy essay (over ten pages, for instance) will you write an introduction of more than one paragraph. Your introductory paragraph must accomplish at least three basic tasks: catch the reader's interest, introduce the subject matter of the essay, and present the thesis sentence.

Catch the Reader's Interest

Imagine yourself waiting in a dentist's or doctor's lounge, passing the time until your appointment. What do you do? Perhaps you grab a magazine from a nearby table. You flip through the magazine, looking for something to read. Perhaps you start reading one article but quickly lose interest and turn the page to find another. Why?

What has happened is the writer has failed to catch your attention. Aside from the title and any accompanying photographs or illustrations, only the initial words of the article can "sell" you on reading it. If you are not sold, you will not read.

As a writer, you must try to catch the reader's attention from the very first sentence of your essay. This is accomplished by choosing a **hook,** or **lead-in,** that will capture the reader's interest and attention. There are a number of ways to do this:

■ *Provide personal anecdotes.* Tell a story about something that happened to you. Obviously, the content of the story must be relevant to your topic. Instructors who prefer that you rely strictly on research will, of course, not prefer this technique.

■ *Ask a question.* Although questions do not make good thesis sentences, they can make good hooks. They set the reader up for the thesis sentence.

■ *Give examples.* Cite a real-life incident that illustrates some problem or situation that concerns your subject. The more dramatic the example, the better.

■ *Use statistics.* Presenting shocking or disturbing information in the form of statistics can lend credibility and urgency to your thesis sentence.

■ *Use a hypothetical situation.* Present a "what-if" scenario in which you ask the reader to imagine a possible event, process, or scene.

■ *Give a surprising fact.* Find material that illustrates that some generally acknowledged fact about your subject is wrong.

■ *Use a quotation.* A quotation from a famous person can be a good way to catch your reader's attention. The quotation should, of course, be relevant to your subject.

■ *Define a term.* You should not begin your essay with a stock phrase (see the next section on hooks to be avoided), but you can lead in to your essay with the definition of a key word or phrase.

There are certain types of hooks, or lead-ins, that should be avoided.

- Don't use hooks or lead-ins that sound like apologies, such as "I didn't have the time to think about this as much as I would have liked . . ."
- Don't begin with gross overstatements, such as "Since the beginning of time . . ."
- Don't begin with a well-worn opening, such as "According to *Webster's Dictionary* . . ."
- Don't use a signpost, such as "In this essay I will discuss . . ."
- Don't begin by referring to your title. For instance, if your title is *Skiing in Colorado,* don't begin by writing "I like going there because . . ."

Introduce the Subject Matter

Your essay must be about something, and you cannot assume that your reader knows what that something is. Even after the title and the hook, you must explain to the reader what your subject is and what your particular focus (or topic) within that subject will be. Remember, the term *subject* refers to a broad field of investigation; a *topic* is a specific aspect of that field. For instance, if your subject is *life in the military,* you need to inform your reader about what aspect of life in the military you are going to discuss. That will be your topic. Will your essay be only about the man or woman in the service, or will it also address the family of the serviceman or servicewoman? Will the essay talk about the stress of long absences from family, or the frequent moves, or the economics of military life? Obviously, you will not be addressing all of these issues; they would be too much to cover in an essay. Your reader needs to know what the particular focus within your subject will be.

As you introduce the subject and topic of your essay, you are narrowing the scope of what you will write about in the essay. This is important because it will lead you logically to the presentation of the thesis sentence.

Present the Thesis Sentence

When should you present your thesis sentence? Many of your writing instructors will suggest that you place your thesis sentence as the last sentence of your introductory paragraph. Although this may seem restrictive, there are logical reasons for placing the thesis sentence in that spot.

When you make your thesis sentence the last sentence of your introductory paragraph, you are bringing to a close the logic of the paragraph. That is, you started your paragraph with a hook, or lead-in, and then you introduced your subject and your focus within that subject. To present your thesis at that point brings to conclusion the logical narrowing that has occurred. Examine the following introductory paragraph:

Hook At one time, over 60 million bison, also known as the plains buffalo, roamed the American continent before European settlers arrived. Within the space of a few hundred years, concentrated mostly within a few decades, this animal was hunted to near extinction. Now, however, the bison has made a comeback. This is just one example of how conservationists have helped preserve an important part of America's native environment and history. Nowadays, however, conservationists face hostility not only from those who do not value nature but also from those who say conservation efforts have failed. **Conservation efforts can be**

Thesis **successful, but efforts must be judged over the span of decades, not just a few years.**

The thesis statement is a logical conclusion to the ideas developed in the introduction.

Still, there are alternatives to placing the thesis sentence at the end of the introduction. In order to choose where you ought to place your thesis sentence, you should consider not only your instructor's requirements but also how different placements affect your essay. Consider these alternatives:

■ ***Begin your essay with your thesis sentence.*** In this technique, the hook is also the thesis sentence. This has the advantage of informing your reader right from the start just what your focus is. The drawback is that the rest of your introduction may be difficult or problematic to write. After all, what do you talk about in the introduction after you've presented your thesis? A certain amount of backtracking and confusion may result from starting your essay with your thesis sentence.

■ ***Place your thesis sentence somewhere in the middle of your introduction.*** Just as with placing your topic sentence somewhere in the middle of your paragraph, this technique is fraught with danger. The advantage of this technique is that it allows you maximum flexibility in your introduction. The disadvantage is that your reader may entirely miss your thesis sentence or take another sentence to be your thesis sentence.

■ *Place your thesis sentence as the first sentence of your second introductory paragraph.* This technique is used most often when your introductory paragraph consists entirely of an extended example or hypothetical situation. In this case, you basically use the entire paragraph to set up the thesis sentence. Again, the drawback is the potential for your reader to miss the thesis sentence entirely, perhaps mistaking it for a topic sentence.

■ *Place your thesis sentence in the conclusion only.* In this technique, you do not present a thesis until the concluding paragraph of the essay. This may serve to your advantage if you're trying to develop a sense of suspense about your thesis or if your thesis is so controversial that you don't want to present it to the reader until he or she has been first exposed to the support for the thesis. This technique also contains great potential to confuse the reader, and for many readers, the delaying of the thesis may be more irritating than intriguing.

The Main Body Paragraphs

The middle of the essay is where you present your support for your thesis. In Chapter 9, you learned to develop controlling ideas for your thesis. Those controlling ideas are developed in separate paragraphs in the main body. Together, they form the bulk of your essay.

Patterns of Support

A key issue is how to arrange the paragraphs in the main body. Generally speaking, you want to choose the paragraph pattern that will be most logical and appropriate for your subject. The following are four common patterns:

■ *Strongest to weakest.* In this pattern, you present what you feel is your strongest argument first, then your next strongest, and then your weakest. To determine the strongest point, you should know which of your ideas is most convincing or has the best evidence. The advantage of this pattern is that you can sway the reader more easily from the beginning with your powerful points. The first paragraph of the main body is already in an inherently strong position in the sense that the reader's attention may be greater there than later on. The disadvantage is that if you don't sway your reader with your strongest point first, the likelihood of doing so with your weaker ones later is less.

■ *Weakest to strongest.* This pattern takes advantage of the strength of the position of the first main body paragraph to bolster the content of the weakest paragraph. You can then gradually build your argument. The advantage to this pattern is that your reader gets a sense of a crescendo, the growing strength of your points. The disadvantage is that the strongest paragraph is in one of the weaker positions in the essay, right before the conclusion, where it may get overlooked.

■ *Chronological.* The paragraphs are arranged by the time elements, usually from the past to the most recent. This pattern is often used with essays that are based on narration or process/analysis.

■ *Spatial.* Paragraphs are arranged in the order in which things are physically located in space. This pattern is most often used with essays that are based on description.

The Conclusion

The conclusion is the end of your essay. You may find yourself wondering what to write in a conclusion, especially when you feel you have already said everything you want to say. But a conclusion can reinforce your thesis, help your reader better understand what he or she has already read, and provide a sense of closure or ending.

Restate Your Thesis

Just as your introduction narrowed from a broad look at your subject to finish with your thesis sentence, your conclusion should work in reverse. Your conclusion should begin with a restatement of your thesis and move toward broader issues.

When you restate your thesis, what you're actually doing is fulfilling the old maxim of many speech classes: Tell them what you're going to tell them, tell them, and then tell them what you told them. This is helpful to your reader so that there is no misunderstanding about what the main idea or opinion of your essay is.

Do not just retype the thesis sentence exactly as it appeared in the introduction. To restate the thesis sentence, it is best to juggle your words around, but the meaning, of course, should be the same.

Summarize Your Main Points

Your instructor may like you to summarize the points of your essay, so that your reader can see the logical unity of the main body. This has the advantage of keeping those points fresh in the reader's mind. Unfortunately, the disadvantage is that a summary of one's own essay can seem redundant, and the reader may not wish to read a conclusion that offers nothing new. Short essays rarely need to be summarized.

Answer the Question *So What?*

Imagine your reader asking, at the conclusion of the essay, So what? To answer, you need to give a sales pitch: explain the relevance or importance of the thesis sentence that you have been discussing throughout the essay.

End with a Bang

End your essay with a bang, not a whimper. Bring your conclusion to a resolute close, so that the reader feels satisfied that all important ground has been covered. One way to do this is to return to ideas mentioned in the introduction. See how this concluding paragraph relates its ending with the introductory paragraph presented earlier:

Restatement of thesis sentence

Anwers the question *So what?*

Clincher

> Despite the criticism that exists of today's conservationists, they have been and can continue to be successful in their quest to repair the damage human progress has done to the natural world, if only they are given the time and money to do so. Surely, it is not too much to ask of people to be concerned for their world, to be responsible for the actions taken in the name of civilization. After all, we are not separate from the natural world; we live as a part of that world. Hopefully, we can hand to our children an Earth that looks a little bit more like its natural self--bison included.

Be sure to avoid some of the following errors made with conclusions:

■ ***Don't apologize.*** Never try to explain to your reader that you could have done a better job if only you had had more time, or your typewriter ribbon hadn't gone dry, or your computer printer hadn't needed the toner changed.

■ ***Don't introduce new evidence or a new argument in your conclusion.*** The conclusion is not the place for giving new information or presenting a new argument; that is what the main body is for. Otherwise, you will leave your reader with a sense that more discussion is needed.

■ ***Don't end too quickly.*** Never write a one-sentence conclusion. Your reader may well feel abandoned or shorted. Your essay should end smoothly.

■ ***Don't contradict your thesis.*** Don't finish off an essay about the abuse of animals in research laboratories by telling how your mother's life was saved by medical technology developed with the help of animal research.

■ ***Don't get off track.*** Stick to your subject and your thesis. Your conclusion is not the place for entering into new areas of interest not addressed in your essay.

Transitions

Just as in paragraphs, transitions are an important part of essays. The first major transition occurs when you move from the introduction to the main body. One way to evaluate the need for transitions is to see how closely connected your thesis sentence is to your topic sentences.

Introduction to Main Body

Consult your thesis and topic sentence outline. Make sure that each of the topic sentences relates back to the thesis sentence in some way, by repeating either some key word or idea within the claim. If your thesis sentence includes both the claim and the controlling ideas, then you have already made the task of providing transitions simple. The repetition of key words from the thesis sentence in the topic sentences of each of the main body paragraphs will logically connect the two and thus provide the transitions needed.

Between Main Body Paragraphs

In Chapters 3 through 8, you learned about making transitions within paragraphs. However, you should be aware that you will also need to provide transitions as you move from one paragraph to another within the main body of your essay. If your thesis sentence includes the controlling ideas, then all your topic sentences must relate to the thesis sentence. Even if this is so, and especially when you do not explicitly state the controlling ideas in the thesis sentence, you need to provide transitions.

One way to do this is to use words such as *first, second,* and *finally.* The trouble is these words function as signposts, are artificial guides rather than real ones, and attract undue attention to themselves. There is a certain stiffness in writing that has to employ signposts in order to be coherent.

Instead, try to string your paragraphs together by connecting a key word in the wrap-up sentence of the previous paragraph with a key word in the topic sentence of the next paragraph. Be careful not to fall into the trap of introducing a new topic in the previous paragraph: that leads to writing that is stilted and illogical. Examine the following passage, which begins with the last sentence of one paragraph:

> . . . After a firm foundation of concrete has been laid, you are ready to begin the next phase of building a house with a new material: wood.
>
>> Wood is the next item that you will use to build a house. . . .

Such exchanges are mechanical and distracting. If the topic of *wood* has nothing to do with the first paragraph, then it should not be mentioned until the second paragraph. The following passage is more effective in using transition between paragraphs:

> . . . After a firm foundation of concrete has been laid, you are ready to begin the next phase.
>
>> In the next phase of building a house, you will use wood. . . .

Main Body to Conclusion

The final transition occurs between the conclusion and the main body. Again, like the transition from the introduction to the main body, the important idea is that there must be a logical connection. This should be the repetition of a key word or idea. Since your conclusion will start with a restatement of the thesis, this is made easier for you.

Avoid using signposts such as *Concluding . . . , In conclusion . . . , To wrap up this essay, I wish to say . . .* , and so on. Again, these signposts might give your reader the sense that you must rely on such artificial techniques to maintain the structural integrity of your essay.

Student Writing Assignment: Essay

Write a five-paragraph essay on one of the following subjects or on a subject of your own choosing. The subjects listed here are rather broad; as part of your assignment you will need to narrow your focus to create a thesis sentence appropriate to the length of this assignment. Follow the steps listed in the Start-Up Suggestions and Self-Revision Questions. Then bring your paragraph to class for peer editing. Revise your paragraph and then complete the section labeled Your Choices: Essay to discuss the decisions you made during the composing and revising process.

computer technology	drinking in college
immigration	art in America
the importance of rituals	the cosmetics industry
role models for children	space exploration
the environment	advances in medicine

Remember that what you have learned about the rhetorical modes in the previous chapters should be applied in your essay. Your thesis sentence may lead to you analyze a cause or an effect, you may need to define an important term, or you may present the stages of a process. Be aware that your thesis sentence will determine what tasks your essay must complete.

Start-Up Suggestions

Follow these steps before writing your first draft.

1. Try adding words to the subject as a way to narrow down your subject to a manageable topic. For instance, with the subject of *television,* you could add *children* or *commercials,* or with *immigration,* you could add *illegal* or *history of.* This may give you insight into the variety of topics available for investigation within your general subject.
2. Go to your local or college library and look up *The Library of Congress Subject Headings.* This reference book lists many subheadings for subjects as officially defined by the Library of Congress. You may even wish to consult with your librarian about how to find books or magazine articles on your subject.
3. After you have investigated your subject and developed some ideas you are interested in exploring, brainstorm or freewrite for ten minutes. Look over your writing and see if you've discovered some new directions to pursue or are reinforcing old ones.
4. Try to develop a thesis sentence with a claim and three controlling ideas. Don't worry at this stage if your thesis sentence seems a little long or unwieldy; it can always be trimmed later.
5. Form a thesis and topic sentence outline. You are now ready to begin drafting your essay.

Self-Revision Questions

Answer these questions after writing your first draft and before rewriting the draft for submission to your peer-editing group.

1. Underline the thesis sentence of your essay. Where is the sentence located? If it is not the last sentence of your introduction, is there good reason for that?
2. Does your thesis sentence include both the claim and three controlling ideas? If you left off the controlling ideas in order to keep your thesis sentence briefer, did you mention them earlier in your introduction?
3. Did you remember to give your essay a title? Is the title reflective of the content of the essay?
4. Does your essay have a hook to grab the reader's interest? What type of hook did you use? (Consult the heading Catch the Reader's Interest in this chapter to check the types available.)
5. Is the main body of your essay divided into three paragraphs, each clearly about a different controlling idea in the thesis sentence?
6. Do each of the main body paragraphs have a topic sentence that reflects the content of the paragraph and ties the topic back to the thesis sentence?
7. Does each paragraph of your main body have sufficient support?
8. Do you have transitions between one paragraph and the next throughout the essay?
9. Does the conclusion restate the thesis sentence and answer the question *So what?*
10. Did you make sure that the last sentence of the essay provides closure?

Revise your essay and submit it to your peer-editing group.

Peer-Editing Guidelines for the Essay

Answer these questions for each of the essays written by other members of your peer-editing group.

1. Does the hook grab your interest? Why or why not?
2. Underline the thesis sentence, including the claim and the three controlling ideas.
3. Are the three controlling ideas logical and convincing?
4. Is the thesis sentence appropriate for the length of the essay assigned?
5. Does each paragraph of the main body have a topic sentence that reflects the content of the paragraph and ties the topic back to the thesis sentence?

6. What type of support does the author use?
7. Is the transition between each of the paragraphs effective?
8. Does the conclusion restate the thesis sentence and answer the question *So what?*
9. What is the crystalline word in the essay?
10. What one piece of advice would most improve the essay?

Prepare the final draft of your essay, taking the comments of your peer-editing group into account.

Your Choices: Essay

Answer these questions after you have finished your final draft.

1. How did you choose your thesis sentence?
2. Did you have to revise your thesis sentence? Why or why not?
3. Did you have to change any of your controlling ideas? Why or why not?
4. Why did you choose the hook that you used?
5. Did you change any of your topic sentences to ensure that they reflected the topics of their respective paragraphs?
6. What transitional words did you use?
7. Did you make sure that each paragraph had a good wrap-up sentence?
8. How did you reword the thesis sentence in the conclusion?
9. Was your conclusion fully developed, or did you need to expand it in order to answer the question *So what?*
10. Did you agree or disagree with your peer editors' choice for the crystalline word? If you disagreed, did you make any revisions to emphasize the word you wanted?

COMPUTER EXERCISE

Exchange a draft of your essay with your writing partner. Using either parentheses ( ) or all capital letters to distinguish your comments from your partner's writing, peer edit your partner's essay. You may use the Peer-Editing Guidelines supplied in this chapter, or you may develop your own.

THE REVISION PROCESS:
A Student Writing Sample

As you may recall from Chapter 2, Carolyn, a student, wrote the following informal outline:

> *Television has ruined professional sports.*
> *— Too much money*
> *— Emphasis on personalities, not team play*
> *— Overexposure of teams and players*

From her informal outline, Carolyn was able to construct a thesis sentence that included both her claim and the controlling ideas:

> *Television has ruined professional sports by providing too much money, emphasizing personalities instead of team play, and overexposing certain teams and players.*

Carolyn's claim is the first part of her thesis, ending with the word *sports,* and her controlling ideas begin with the word *by* and continue to the end of the sentence. From her thesis sentence, she was then able to form her thesis topic sentence outline:

> *Thesis Sentence:*
> *Television has ruined professional sports by providing too much money, emphasizing personalities instead of team play, and overexposing certain teams and players.*
>
> *Topic Sentence 1:*
> *There is too much money in professional sports thanks to the presence of television.*
>
> *Topic Sentence 2:*
> *Television has created an emphasis on personalities, not team play.*
>
> *Topic Sentence 3:*
> *Television has created pressure to market sports, leading to overexposure of certain teams and players.*

Once Carolyn had her thesis topic sentence outline, she was able to decide on how she wanted to develop the points within each of her main body paragraphs. What she included in each paragraph was determined by her own knowledge and any research that she had to do.

With her additional points, Carolyn expanded her outline, creating what is essentially a formal outline:

<u>Thesis</u>: Television has ruined professional sports.

   I. There is too much money in professional sports thanks to the presence of television.

     A. Salaries and profits are astronomical.

     B. Players are more interested in playing easy to keep making money than in playing hard and risking potential injury.

     C. Strikes have disrupted professional sports over the issue of money, alienating the fans.

  II. Television has created an emphasis on personalities, not team play.

     A. Close-ups and interview shows encourage "hot dogging" rather than solid play.

     B. Endorsements go to flashy players with catchy nicknames, leaving other players jealous and resentful.

     C. Players try to increase their individual performance statistics even when sacrificing themselves would be better for the team.

 III. Television has created pressure to market sports, leading to overexposure of certain teams and players.

     A. Rather than trust the appeal of a sport, television now encourages the marketing of certain teams and players to maximize fan appeal.

     B. Colorful uniforms and dramatic or unusual highlight sequences entice fans.

     C. Championship teams get promoted throughout the country, leading to the decline of regional loyalties for struggling, hard-luck clubs.

Notice that Carolyn decided to trim down her thesis sentence to just her claim, rather than include the controlling ideas for the claim. She chose to do this because her thesis sentence seemed too long when weighed down by the controlling ideas.

Next Carolyn was ready to begin drafting her essay. Carolyn knew that one of her first tasks was to find a hook to grab the reader's attention. Looking over recent newspaper clippings and magazine articles, she found what she was looking for: a football player had signed a contract worth $35 million. She was ready to begin her first draft:

Too Much Money

In 1995, Deion Sanders signed a contract with the Dallas Cowboys to play football for $35 million. This outrageous sum of money was made possible mostly because of one simple reason: television. Football owners get a big chunk of their money from television. While owners earn money from tickets, hot dogs, or even baseball caps with team logos, television money is what really matters. It's made player salaries to high, it's changed the emphasis from teams to individuals, and it's lead to the creation of national sports loyalties instead of local ones. Television has ruined professional sports.

There is too much money in professional sports thanks to the presence of television. As can be seen with the Deion Sanders contract, salaries and profits are astronomical. The money puts players into bad spot because then the players are more interested playing easy to keep making money rather than playing hard and risking potential injury. Diving for a fly ball, reaching for that extra yard, or trying to stop an opponents slam could cause a career ending injury, so why bother? Give up the hit, the yard, or the points and keep collecting the paychecks. And as if that wasn't enough. Players feel like they have to strike if anyone threatens that. The owners are just as bad too. The rest is that strikes have disrupted professional sports, alienating the fans who just want to see a good game.

Television has created an emphasis on personalities, not team play. It's no accident that multimillionaire Sanders is also known as one of the biggest show-offs in football. Television shows close-ups of spectacular plays, and interview shows encourage "hot dogging" rather an solid play. After all, doesn't everyone want to see flashy highlights? The endorsements, which bring in a lot of money, go to flashy players with catchy nicknames. Other players are left out, and may feel jealous and resentful. The result is that today's players only care about the individual performance and statistics. Sacrificing for the team is an old idea for athletes who haven't figured out how to make the really big money.

Television has created pressure to market sports, leading to overexposure of certain teams and players. Rather than trust the appeal of a sport, television now encourages the marketing of certain teams and players to maximize fan appeal. Thus, when you see ads for merchandise, they always have the models wearing Dallas Cowboy or San Francisco 49er gear. Colorful uniforms and dramatic or unusual highlight sequences entice fans—teams even change their colors to get more merchandise money, like the New England Patriots or the San Diego Padres. Finally, championship teams get promoted throughout the country, leading to the decline of regional loyalties for struggling, hard-luck clubs. Teams without winning records wind up getting left off of television, and even in their own local areas, they are less publicized than the glamorous, successful teams.

Television money has been very bad for sports. Some money is fine; the players deserve to be paid, and the owners should make money too. But there's been far too much money, and it's started a money-first mentality in sports. What needs to be done is remember the fans, and return the television money to them by lowering ticket prices at the gate so regular people can afford to come see the games in person.

When Carolyn brought this essay to her group, her peer-editing group had one universal comment: too long. They believed Carolyn had a good idea, but they felt that to talk about all sports was too much. They noticed that most of her comments and examples applied to professional football, so they suggested that she restrict her comments to just football, as the addition of other sports was just confusing. Within the main body paragraphs, there was too much going on. The first topic sentence needed to be stronger, set apart from the actual thesis sentence. The group wanted Carolyn to cover fewer ideas overall, but they also wanted more concrete proof rather than just general statements. They did like the example of Deion Sanders and how Carolyn used it again in the main body. The peer editors felt she should repeat the example in her conclusion to provide some closure to the essay, as well. They pointed out some spelling and usage errors (such as *player salaries to high* instead of *players' salaries too high*).

With those thoughts in mind, Carolyn produced her final draft:

Too Much Money

In 1995, Deion Sanders signed a contract with the Dallas Cowboys to play football for $35 million. This outrageous sum of money was made possible because of one simple reason: television. Football owners get a big chunk of their money from television. While they earn money from tickets, hot dogs, and even baseball caps with team logos, television money is what really matters. It has made players' salaries too high, it has changed the emphasis from teams to individuals, and it has led to the creation of national loyalties instead of local ones. Television has ruined professional football.

Too much money in professional football has ruined the quality of play on the field. As can be seen with the Deion Sanders contract, salaries and profits are astronomical. The money puts players into a position where they are more interested in playing safe to keep making money rather than playing hard and risking potential injury. Diving for a catch, reaching for that extra yard, or trying to stop an opponent's touchdown could cause a career-ending injury, so why bother? Give up the catch, the yard, or the seven points and keep collecting the paychecks.

Television has created an emphasis on personalities, not team play. It is no accident that multimillionaire Sanders is also known as one of the biggest show-offs in football. Television encourages "hot dogging" rather than solid play by repeatedly showing footage of eye-catching plays. After all, doesn't everyone want to see flashy highlights? Flashy players with catchy nicknames—like Neon Deion—also get all the endorsement money while other players are left out and may feel jealous and resentful. The result is that today's players only care about individual performance and statistics, since that is what will make them money. Sacrificing for the team is an old idea for athletes who have not yet figured out how to be "hot dogs."

Television has created pressure to market sports, leading to overexposure of certain teams and players. Rather than trust the appeal of a sport, television now encourages the marketing of certain teams and players to maximize fan appeal. Thus, when you see ads for merchandise, they always have the models wearing Dallas Cowboy or San Francisco 49er gear. Championship teams get promoted throughout the country, leading to the decline of regional loyalties for struggling, hard-luck clubs. Teams without winning records wind up getting left off of television, and even in their own local areas, they are less publicized than the glamorous, successful teams.

Television money has been very bad for pro football. Some money is fine; the players deserve to be paid, and the owners should make money, too. But there has been far too much money, and it has started a money-first mentality in sports. What needs to be done is to remember the fans and to return the television money to them by lowering ticket prices at the gate so regular people can afford to come see the games in person. Deion Sanders and all the others would still be making an awful lot of money even if they made just half of what they do now. After all, $17.5 million would be nothing to sneeze at!

Verb Tense Agreement

Choosing the correct verb seems so simple: present, past, or future. With only three time frames, how could one get confused? Try these sentences:

> Shelley described the painting. She says it has lots of reds and oranges against a white background.

> Francisco enjoyed the movie. He especially likes the opening scene with Michael Douglas.

> Mia was always late for class when it rained. Today she is late again, and it's raining.

> The president is speaking to reporters as the story of the disaster broke in the news.

Verb tenses need to agree with each other. You must keep the time relationships between two events clear. Verb tenses indicate whether two events occurred simultaneously (or nearly so) or if one event occurred before the other. They signal to the reader when an event occurred or will occur: in the present, the past, or the future.

The Present Tense

The **present tense** is used for events that are either occurring now or occur on a regular basis. Also, in writing about literature, the present tense is used even though the author may have died a long time ago.

> Today the price of ground beef is $1.99 a pound.

> I set my alarm clock for 5:30 a.m. every night.

> Shakespeare uses the character of Polonius to make fun of long-winded politicians.

The Past Tense

The **past tense** is used for events that have already occurred. If two or more events in the past occur at close to the same time, use the past tense for both events.

Last week, the movie <u>Waiting to Exhale</u> opened.

My uncle mowed the front lawn but forgot to mow the back lawn.

The restaurant closed after it failed an inspection by the Health Department.

The Future Tense

The **future tense** is used for events that will happen at some later time.

I will complete my degree by the end of next spring.

The new lights will save the company thousands of dollars in electric bills in just one year.

The Perfect Tenses

All three time frames—present, past, and future—can be described using the **perfect tenses: present perfect, past perfect,** and **future perfect.** The perfect tenses allow you to distinguish the time relationship between two or more events. The perfect tenses are formed by using the verb *to have* as a helping verb with the past participle form of the main verb (the *-ed* form in regular verbs).

I **have found** that until I know what is going on in a given situation, I fare better if I keep my mouth shut.   Present perfect

Joan **had worked** hard to be promoted, and last January she became the newest partner in the firm.   Past perfect

After this semester, Marisa **will have completed** eighty-six undergraduate units, but she still does not know what field she wants to major in.   Future perfect

Verb Tense Disagreement

Much of the trouble students experience with verb tense agreement occurs when two or more events occur at different times.

The police found the killer who escaped.

This sentence is confusing. Did the killer escape from the police or did the police find the killer after he escaped? The sentence needs to reflect the fact that both events are in the past and that one event occurred before the other.

> The police found the killer who had escaped.

In this corrected sentence, the past tense verb *escaped* was changed to the past perfect *had escaped.* The use of the *past perfect,* which indicates an action completed at an indefinite time in the past, allows for the distinction in time to be made between the actions of the killer and those of the police.

Using a Consistent Tense

Another problem for many students is that they move back and forth between time periods, usually the past and present, within a single piece of writing. Generally speaking, you need to stay consistent: if you are writing in the present tense, stay with the present tense throughout, and do the same if you are using the past tense. (See pages 346–48 for further discussion of verb tenses.)

EXERCISE　　The following paragraph has inconsistent use of verb tenses. Rewrite the paragraph, making the necessary corrections.

> Since I lived now in Miami, I will not have a cold yet. I thought this is because the weather is always nice, even in the winter. Before, when I live in upstate New York, there is snow on the ground for five months of the year. You cannot go outside without five layers of clothes worn on your body. Now, in Miami, I will have worn only one layer of clothes at a time, except sometimes I did need a sweater in the evening. I do plan to visit some friends of mine in Syracuse, but I thought I would wait until the summer. Still, I will need to bring extra clothes so I am sure I am not cold. Miami is definitely healthier than upstate New York was because I had not had a cold in Miami in the last two years that I live here.

11 Adapting the Essay to Your Purpose

Using and Combining Rhetorical Modes

In Chapters 4 through 8, you learned how to use different rhetorical modes. You also discovered that each mode has its own purpose. For instance, you learned that comparison and contrast involves examining the similarities and differences between two people, things, or ideas. When you write an essay, however, you may well find yourself confronted with more than one purpose at a time. Which rhetorical mode should you use?

The simple answers are that you must choose the rhetorical mode that you need for your purpose and that often you will choose *more than one in an essay*. Indeed, it is rare to find an extended piece of writing that uses only one rhetorical mode. More typically, essays combine the rhetorical modes to accomplish the goals of the writing task.

How to Use Rhetorical Modes in an Essay

When you first examined the rhetorical modes, you looked at their applications at the paragraph level. This enabled you to develop more easily your skills at writing each mode. However, instructors rarely ask you to write only one paragraph for an assignment. More frequently, they will require you to write essays. Thus, you will need to be able to use rhetorical modes at the level of the essay.

Adapting what you have learned at the paragraph level to the essay is not difficult. After all, the principles are still the same. The differences arise in how you outline your work, the amount of space available, and the level of detail to which you can develop your ideas.

In order to understand best which rhetorical modes to use, the following is a review the purpose of each:

- **Narration** is the telling of a story with some central idea or message (Chapter 4).
- **Description** portrays something or someone by appealing to the reader's physical senses (Chapter 4).
- **Example** illustrates a concept or event (Chapter 4).
- **Definition** explains the meaning of a term, often an abstract concept (Chapter 5).
- **Classification** groups things into categories based on a single unifying principle (Chapter 5).
- **Comparison/contrast** discusses the similarities and differences between two people, things, or ideas (Chapter 6).
- **Cause** shows the reasons or motivations that make something happen (Chapter 7).
- **Effect** shows the results or consequences of an event or action (Chapter 7).
- **Process** discusses the steps by which something is created or accomplished, or it discusses how the parts of something fit together to form the whole (Chapter 8).

When you learned to use each of these modes at the level of the paragraph, you learned the importance of the topic sentence. Remember, the topic sentence shows what the entire paragraph is about. Topic sentences for all of the rhetorical modes look different. For example, the types of key words that might appear in a classification topic sentence should not be expected in a process topic sentence.

Recall what you learned in Chapter 9: thesis sentences are broader than topic sentences. Thus, you can look at a topic sentence and expand the central idea into a thesis sentence. Remember the example from Chapter 9:

Cats make good house pets because they clean themselves, they

don't need to be walked, and their waste is confined to a kitty

litter box.

Cats make good house pets because they don't need to be walked.

When you examined these two sentences in Chapter 9, you saw that the first sentence was much broader than the second sentence. The first contains three controlling ideas; the second supplies only one reason why cats are good house pets. Therefore, the first sentence makes the better thesis sentence and the second sentence makes the better topic sentence.

EXERCISE 11.1 ───

Write a thesis sentence for each of the following subjects in the given rhetorical mode.

1. a shocking event   Narration
2. a landmark, park, or wilderness area   Description
3. sexism   Example
4. power   Definition
5. types of friends   Classification
6. high school and college   Comparison/Contrast
7. obesity   Cause
8. free speech   Effect
9. falling in love   Process
10. the contents of your junk drawer or closet   Process

Why Combine Rhetorical Modes?

One thing you may have already noticed, either in your own writing or in readings by other authors, is that not all pieces of writing follow one rhetorical mode without venturing into another. Indeed, the division of writing into separate and distinct rhetorical modes is admittedly artificial because most essays will use different rhetorical modes at different points. They do this in order to accomplish their purpose: to prove that the thesis is valid.

At the back of this book is a section containing articles and essays written by professional writers. One of the articles is titled "Action as the Antidote for Boredom." The article contains several different rhetorical modes: cause (Why are people bored?), effect (What happens when people are bored?), example (Who are the people who are bored?), definition ("Boredom is a form of anger without enthusiasm.") and process (What are the mechanics of boredom?). Indeed, a careful analysis of almost any essay will uncover more than one rhetorical mode.

Why is this so? Writing can take the author in many different directions. Within a single essay, the writer may choose many different purposes in order to achieve the main purpose of proving his or her thesis sentence to be true. Look at the following student-written paragraph about child care:

A caregiver's main goal is to keep children involved with their bodies and the world around them. A caregiver needs to make sure that the child is involved with whatever the caregiver is doing, whether that be diapering, feeding, washing, or dressing. Involved means keeping the baby physically in tune with what is going on. This way, the child can learn. For example, when a caregiver changes a baby's diaper, the baby learns about cooperation and body awareness. A caregiver should not simply ignore the baby and "just get this smelly thing changed." Attention needs to be paid to the baby, including touching and verbally addressing the baby. As another example, when a toddler initiates play time, the caregiver should not just leave the child alone; rather, the caregiver should become involved. This does not mean taking control; it just means participating in the toddler's games.

Examine the paragraph. How many different rhetorical modes are there? The entire paragraph could be considered a process paragraph. However, the paragraph contains the following rhetorical modes:

Definition	<u>Involved</u> means keeping the baby physically in tune with what is going on.
Example	For example, when a caregiver changes a baby's diaper, the baby learns about cooperation and body awareness.
	As another example, when a toddler initiates play time, the caregiver should not just leave the child alone; rather, the caregiver should become involved.
Comparison/ contrast	A caregiver should not simply ignore the baby and "just get this smelly thing changed." Attention needs to be paid to the baby, including touching and verbally addressing the baby.
	This does not mean taking control; it just means participating in the toddler's games.

EXERCISE 11.2

Write one paragraph on one of the following subjects using, at a minimum, the rhetorical modes listed.

1. caring for the elderly   Definition, comparison/contrast, process
2. selecting a college   Description, classification, process
3. the impact of music on teenagers   Narrative, definition, cause and effect
4. jobs that require manual labor   Example, classification, process
5. unusual pets   Example, description, comparison/contrast

EXERCISE 11.3

Analyze each of the following paragraphs and identify which parts illustrate which rhetorical modes.

1.   More people are beginning to use computers to communicate. For instance, electronic mail, or e-mail, is very popular. A computer user can send e-mail virtually anywhere around the world. Some people believe e-mail may eventually make the ordinary paper letter obsolete; however, paper will always have the advantage of being tangible. Another type of communication is the on-line talk room, which anyone can enter and have a conversation with anyone else. Undoubtedly, the future holds the possibility of even more types of communication.

2.   Community colleges and night-time business colleges are very different. Business colleges are private schools that cater to working adults. They usually offer only a few majors, such as administration, accounting, and systems management. Business colleges can be very expensive--as much as $10,000 for just seven months. Since their courses are all accelerated, business colleges can be very difficult. Students have little time to study the material. On the other hand, community colleges usually offer many majors and are not expensive. Because community colleges offer semester-length courses, students have more time to study. Most people, if they have the time, should attend a community college for their education.

3.   Car repairs are best when done at home. First, working on your car at home is less expensive than taking it to a garage. Some places charge over $60 an hour just for labor alone. Also, you can be sure that your car will get all the proper attention; you will give the car all the attention it needs. No mechanic will be distracted, thinking about the weekend while fixing your brakes. Such behavior does happen, and at best, it could cause you to bring your car back in, and at worst, it could cause an accident. When you work on your car yourself, you know the job will be done right.

4.   Learning can build a person's self-esteem. When I was in high school, I was in a drafting class that helped me gain self-esteem. This drafting class was my favorite class in school. I was very interested in what I was doing, and as a result, I earned a good grade. In all my other classes, I did not do so well, but that was because I wasn't as interested. Compared to my other classes, drafting just seemed a lot more important. That is the reason why I am now thinking about becoming an architect. I think I would never have considered such a career if I hadn't felt so good about my drafting abilities.

5.   There are three types of students here at Omigosh College: those who are majoring in the sciences, those who are majoring in the humanities, and those who are majoring in partying. Science majors are easy to detect: they look like nerds with calculators and pocket pencil holders, and they generally reveal a high level of stress. They either have nervous tics or they strum their fingers on chairs and tables, murmuring, "I've got to get back to the lab" to themselves. Humanities majors dress a lot more casually. Their dress suggests that they are preparing themselves for a life without money or careers. They're less stressed than science majors, and all they can talk about is how they have truly "meaningful" majors. The party majors are rarely seen in classrooms, but they're at the Commons and other local pubs. They profess to have no worries since they have little concern or regard for their futures as well as their present. Unlike the humanities or science majors, they will not earn a degree, but at least they're having fun. The motto of the party major is "Let's destroy our bodies and minds while we can!"

On the level of the essay, you will find that you employ different rhetorical modes besides the one on which your thesis sentence focuses. Take a look at the following student essay. Adam chose several different modes even though his thesis sentence involves comparison/contrast: *Cats make better pets than dogs.*

Cats over Dogs

Hook

Narration

Thesis sentence:
Comparison/contrast

After the Northridge earthquake in Los Angeles a few years ago, I discovered something interesting about my pets. My cats took care of themselves by hiding in places where things could not fall on them, and they ate whatever food they could find. On the other hand, my dog was crying and needed to be taken care of. He still needed me to feed him and take him for a walk. From my experience, I saw that indoor cats make better pets than indoor dogs because cats do not need to be exercised, they clean themselves, and they are born potty-trained.

Topic sentence 1

Comparison/contrast

Examples

Indoor cats do not need a person to exercise them but dogs do. Dogs need to be walked every day so that they can be healthy and more calm. Cats do not depend on a person for exercise because cats exercise on their own. Although both pets need their exercise, cats manage on their own. Therefore, cats need less attention than dogs.

Topic sentence 2

Comparison/contrast

Indoor cats are easier to keep clean than dogs. For instance, when dogs are taken for a walk, they usually do not come back as clean as when they left. Dogs will get dirty by walking through mud puddles and rolling around on people's lawns. Cats do not need to be taken on walks, so they are not as dirty as dogs. When dogs get dirty, they need to be given a bath, and when cats get dirty, they clean themselves. Therefore, cats have a better sense of hygiene than dogs do.

Topic sentence 3

Comparison/contrast

Cause and effect

Finally, cats are easier to potty-train than dogs. Dogs are unpredictable about when they need to go to the bathroom, so they need to be taken outside on a regular basis. Cats do not have this problem because they are born potty-trained. All you have to do is place kittens into a litter box, and when the time comes, they will continue to use the litter box virtually without help. Cats are simply more independent than dogs.

Restatement of
thesis sentence

Indoor cats make better pets than indoor dogs because cats don't need to be exercised, they clean themselves, and they're born potty-trained. Think about these things the next time you're

Answers the
question *So what?* considering owning a pet. Unless you don't have enough to do in your life already, a cat should be your choice.

What Rhetorical Modes Can You Find?

The hook, or lead-in, of the essay is a brief anecdote or narrative of the author's experience after the Northridge earthquake in California in 1994. The narration flows into the author's thesis sentence:

> From my experience, I saw that indoor cats make better pets than indoor dogs because cats do not need to be exercised, they clean themselves, and they are born potty-trained.

The main body paragraphs help prove the comparison/contrast thesis sentence. Note, however, that the author uses examples to develop his ideas. For instance, the second paragraph provides examples of both dogs' and cats' exercise requirements. The third paragraph, on cleaning, also includes some description of the animals' behaviors. The fourth paragraph includes cause and effect regarding the potty-training of dogs and cats, including a brief passage of process (showing how to potty-train kittens).

The conclusion restates the thesis sentence:

> Indoor cats make better pets than indoor dogs because cats don't need to be exercised, they clean themselves, and they're born potty-trained.

Adam then answers the question *So what?* by encouraging the reader to get a cat as a pet, rather than a dog.

Student Writing Assignment: Combining Rhetorical Modes

Write a five-paragraph, 500- to 600-word essay on one of the following subjects or on a subject of your instructor's choosing. Use at least four of the rhetorical modes during the course of your essay. Your instructor may ask that you indicate in your margins where the rhetorical modes are being used. Follow the steps listed in the Start-Up Suggestions and Self-Revision Questions. Then bring your essay to class for peer editing. Revise your essay and then complete the section labeled Your Choices:

Combining Rhetorical Modes to discuss the decisions you made during the composing and revising process.

1. bad role models
2. the paperless office of the future
3. coping with a death in the family
4. the importance of physical appearance
5. alternative medicine

Start-Up Suggestions

Follow these steps before writing your first draft.

1. Brainstorm or freewrite for ten minutes on your topic. See which rhetorical modes are already appearing in your writing. Ask yourself: Do I find comparison/contrast? Process? Classification? Any other mode?
2. Go to your library and find materials on your topic. Take note of which rhetorical modes the authors use in the materials you find.
3. Make a list of possible topics for your essay. Match your ideas with rhetorical modes for expressing those ideas.
4. Create your thesis sentence, including three controlling ideas. In what rhetorical mode is the thesis sentence itself?

Self-Revision Questions

Answer these questions after writing your first draft and before rewriting the draft for submission to your peer-editing group.

1. Review your thesis sentence. Is it too long? Can you say the same thing in fewer words?
2. Are your three controlling ideas logical and related to the claim of the thesis sentence?
3. Do you have a strong topic sentence for each main body paragraph, or do you jump straight into presenting specific evidence to support your viewpoint?
4. Have you been able to use several of the rhetorical modes to make your case? Which ones? Where?

Revise your essay and submit it to your peer-editing group.

Peer-Editing Guidelines for Essays with Combined Rhetorical Modes

Answer these questions for each of the essays written by other members of your peer-editing group.

1. Does the author have a good title? What is it?
2. What is the thesis sentence?
3. Which rhetorical mode does the thesis reflect?
4. Are the three controlling ideas logical and convincing? What are they?
5. Do each of the main body paragraphs have a topic sentence that reflects the content of the paragraph and ties the topic back to the thesis sentence?
6. Which rhetorical modes appear in the essay? Where?
7. Are any rhetorical modes not used that should have been used? Where? Why?
8. Is the essay dull or interesting? Why?
9. Does the essay provide adequate transitions between paragraphs as well as within paragraphs?
10. What is the crystalline word in the essay?

Prepare the final draft of your paragraph, taking the comments of your peer-editing group into account.

Your Choices: Combining Rhetorical Modes

Answer these questions after you have finished your final draft.

1. How did you choose your thesis sentence?
2. Did you have to revise your thesis sentence? Why or why not?
3. Did you have to change any of your controlling ideas? Why or why not?
4. Did your peer-editing group find all the rhetorical modes you thought you had used?
5. Did your peer-editing group discover any rhetorical modes that you were unaware that you had used?
6. What transitional words did you use?
7. Did you make sure that each of your paragraphs had a good wrap-up sentence?
8. Did you have to add any additional evidence to support your topic sentences?

9. Was your conclusion fully developed, or did you need to expand it to answer the question *So what?*
10. Did you agree or disagree with your peer editors' choice for the crystalline word? If you disagreed, did you make any revisions to emphasize the word you wanted?

COMPUTER EXERCISE

Decide on a subject and two or three rhetorical modes. Write them in a file and pass that file to your writing partner. Have your partner do the same for you. Then write a paragraph on the subject, using the rhetorical modes given. Compare your results. Do you find that you can use any rhetorical mode your partner gives you? Can your partner?

THE REVISION PROCESS:
A Student Writing Sample

Susan, a returning student, decided to write her essay on a particular interest of hers: organic gardening. She knew a lot about organic gardening because she had been doing it herself for several years. So, when she decided to freewrite for her essay, many ideas came to her quickly:

> organic gardening is definitely a good idea I've been gardening for years and I would never use pesticides I just don't understand how people with children keep those poisons around don't they know what that stuff can do? my kids love to watch me work in the garden I remember that time when we bought the praying mantis eggs they were thrilled about that other kinds of insects also help including lady bugs although they are frustrating they fly away so easily well there isn't anything to be done about that but it's so much better and safer than using pesticides and the vegetables I think are better if not at least I feel good about what we're eating I'm always worried about store bought food

that's why we buy at the organic grocery store although it is a bit of a drive from our house it just seems like a better idea all around

Susan then decided to formulate a thesis sentence. She wrote: *Organic gardening is the best way to garden.* Next, she had to decide on her three controlling ideas. She looked over her freewriting and saw *I don't understand how people with children keep poisons around* and *safer than using pesticides. Safety,* then, would be one of her ideas. That quickly led to *healthier,* since the two ideas seemed related. The third controlling idea came only after she thought some more about the time that she spent in her garden with her children. She thought about the praying mantis eggs and another incident she had not mentioned in her freewriting in which she bought some decolette snails. With that, she generalized that organic gardening was *a great science project for children.* Susan then formulated her thesis:

Organic gardening is the best way to garden because it is safer, healthier, and makes for a great science project for kids.

Susan made her thesis topic sentence outline, rewriting the thesis sentence so that it would have parallel structure:

Thesis Sentence:
Organic gardening is the best way to garden because it is safer, healthier, and a better way to teach science to kids.

Topic Sentence 1:
Organic gardening is safer than using insecticides for pest control.

Topic Sentence 2:
Gardening the organic way is also healthier for you.

Topic Sentence 3:
Organic gardening can be a great science project for kids.

Now Susan was ready for her first draft.

The Benefits of Organic Gardening

I think we all, at some time or another, have read in the paper about accidental poisonings, residual amounts of pesticides in our food, and of the scientific use of beneficial insects to keep levels of garden pests down. Organic gardening avoids using pesticides and employs nature's own techniques to keep pests away. Organic gardening is the best way to garden because it's safer, healthier, and a better way to teach science to kids.

Organic gardening is safer than using insecticides for pest control. When you use insecticides in your garden, you must have a safe place to store them. It comes in handy to have the poison control number by the phone just in case a poisoning does occur. When it comes to gardening, it is a lot safer to simply pick the bugs off the plants than to spray with poison which you might inadvertently inhale.

Gardening the organic way is also healthier for you. Since there is no need for the use of insecticides, you know exactly what your eating, you don't have to worry about residual pesticides that are still left on your food, even after you've washed it. Insecticides of any kind when sprayed can be harmful to people with upper resperatory problems. These people can have an asthma attack if they breath it in because (there lungs can't handle the poison,) it interfers with their ability to breath. Many of these people have to leave the property for a few hours or more while spraying is being done.

Organic gardening can be a great science project for children. It can teach them which insects are benificial to the garden and which are not. Many plant nurseries sell insects which feed and lay eggs on garden pests. You could buy decolette snails to eat the common garden variety, or you could buy lady bugs for a problem with aphids. My kids like the praying mantis egg cases, it's fun to see them hatch, grow and gobble up many varieties of insects.

These types of insects are great at ridding the garden of pests, making the use of insecticides not needed.

No one wants to have to hide poison from their kids and hope they can't reach it, worry about just how much insecticides their families are really consuming, or have to breath in insecticides while spraying the garden for pests, but that's exactly what you do if you don't grow or buy organic foods. It's just that simple.

When Susan went to her peer group, she found that they liked a great deal of her essay. When they looked for rhetorical modes, they discovered definition (what organic gardening is), comparison/contrast (with use of pesticides), cause and effect (dangers pesticides pose), process (how to do organic gardening), and examples (the list of bugs for the garden).

A few things bothered them, however. The introduction was fine except for a problem in the thesis sentence. The peer-editing group objected to the word *kids* as being too informal; they preferred the use of the word *children*.

In the first main body paragraph, they noted a transition problem after the sentence ending . . . *safe place to store them*. In the second main body paragraph, they felt some of the wording could be changed, and they noted that *respiratory* was misspelled. They felt that the parenthetical remark (*there lungs can't handle the poison,*) seemed awkward and unnecessary and contained the misspelled word *there* for *their*. They also felt it needed a wrap-up sentence. The third main body paragraph seemed to be good, with sufficient examples.

The conclusion came in for criticism because it did not begin with a restatement of the thesis sentence and, given the tone of the rest of the essay, it seemed a bit too negative overall. As a final matter, the peer editors suggested that Susan cut down on the use of the word *you* and move toward the third-person pronoun.

After consideration of her peer group's comments and her rewriting of other passages, Susan produced the following final draft:

The Benefits of Organic Gardening

I think everyone at some time or another has read in the paper about accidental poisonings, pesticides in our food, and the scientific use of beneficial insects to keep levels of garden pests down. Organic gardening avoids using pesticides and employs nature's own techniques to keep pests away. Organic gardening is the best way to garden because it is safer, healthier, and a better way to teach science to children.

Gardening the organic way is safer than using pesticides for pest control. When people use pesticides in their gardens, they must have safe places to store them. The accidental poisoning of a child is something no one wants to think about, but you better if you keep poison on your property. When it comes to gardening, picking the bugs off the plants rather than spraying with poison that you might inadvertently inhale is a lot easier.

Gardening the organic way is also healthier for you since there is no need for pesticides. People do not have to guess about what may still be on their foods, even after they have washed them. Insecticides of any kind, when sprayed, can be harmful to people with upper-respiratory problems. These people can have an asthma attack just by breathing in the fumes, which interferes with their ability to breathe. Many of these people have to leave their property while spraying is being done. If only they would throw out the pesticides, they would never have to put up with those troubles again.

Organic gardening can be a great science project for children. They can learn which insects are beneficial to the garden and which ones are not. Many plant nurseries sell insects that feed and lay eggs on garden pests. You could buy decollete snails to eat the common garden variety or you could buy ladybugs for a problem with aphids. My children like the praying mantis egg cases. It is fun to see them hatch, grow, and gobble up many varieties of insects. These types of insects are great at ridding the garden of pests, making the use of insecticides not needed.

Organic gardening can be a healthier way to garden, safer, and a better learning experience for children in the area of science. People owe it to themselves and their families to try the organic way just once. Who knows, maybe you, too, will become hooked on the organic way.

GRAMMAR INSTRUCTION AND EXERCISES:
Adjectives and Adverbs

Think of how dull the world would be without adjectives and adverbs! Cars would have no color, speed could not be described, and police sirens would all blare the same way.

Adjectives are words that modify nouns and pronouns, and **adverbs** are words that modify verbs, adjectives, and other adverbs. As a writer, you should recognize that adjectives and adverbs can be single words, phrases, and even clauses.

You should be able to determine whether a word is an adjective or adverb by how it is used in a sentence. An adjective, for instance, answers the questions Which? What kind? and How many?

> The **morning** traffic is congested.   Which?
>
> My **leather** jacket was stolen last night.   What kind?
>
> The **three** parties signed the peace agreement.   How many?

Adverbs, on the other hand, answer the questions When? How? How often? Where? and To what extent?

> The baby woke up **early**.   When?
>
> The detective decided to shoot **quickly** before there were more deaths.   How?
>
> The car makes a rumbling sound **intermittently**.   How often?
>
> The children belong **here** with their family.   Where?
>
> The cook **thoroughly** mixed the eggs, flour, baking powder, and vanilla extract.   To what extent?

Adverbs can also modify adjectives and other adverbs.

> Since her job would pay her more if she had a diploma, her graduation was **especially** important.
> Modifying the adjective *important*
>
> He decided **quite** quickly to choose the easier option.
> Modifying the adverb *quickly*

One danger you must beware of is confusing adjectives with adverbs. Be sure not to use adjectives to modify verbs or verbals.

Original:

If you don't measure close, you may not cut the fabric accurate.

Corrected:

If you don't measure closely, you may not cut the fabric accurately.

Original:

If you laugh too loud, you will distract everyone around you.

Corrected:

If you laugh too loudly, you will distract everyone around you.

One particularly tough set of adjectives and adverbs is *good* and *well*. *Good* is an adjective but often is misused as an adverb when the word *well* should be employed.

Original:

I didn't do very **good** on my English grammar test.

Corrected:

I didn't do very **well** on my English grammar test.

Good is used after a linking verb (a verb that shows state of existence).

The spaghetti sauce smells **good**.   *Good* modifies the sauce's scent.

Dad looks **good** in his tuxedo.   *Good* modifies Dad's appearance.

This soft carpet feels **good** under my feet.   *Good* describes the touch of the carpet.

Well is used as an adverb and an adjective. When *well* is used as an adjective, it means "in a state of good health."

Mary runs **well** when she remembers to do her stretching

exercises first.   *Well* describes how Mary runs.

Norm slept **well** into the morning.   *Well* describes how long Norm slept.

Mrs. Dunlap is finally feeling **well** this morning after having been ill

for two days.   *Well* describes Mrs. Dunlap's state of good health.

(See pages 367–70 for further discussion about adjectives and adverbs.)

Rewrite the following sentences so that the adjectives and adverbs are used correctly. Indicate each correct sentence with the letter *C*.

1. The senior citizens are picketing too close to the doorway of the disco.

2. Brad feels good now that the medicine has finally started to have an effect.

3. The steaks smell well.

4. The bank processed my paycheck too slow.

5. Fernando went over the engine thorough before giving the car his approval.

6. His portrait was painted rather bad.

7. The scientific determined figures had everyone shocked.

8. Most all dogs smell good, but only a few breeds can have their tracking abilities accepted in a court of law.

9. The helicopter appears to be handling bad.

10. The intricate detailed engraving is worth over $15,000.

12 Arguing Your Point

Logical Support and Logical Fallacies

As a young child, you often accepted what your parents told you as true, but as you grew older, you learned to judge for yourself what is true and what is not. Write about how you know what you know. Ask yourself: What is the basis for my understanding of what is believable and accurate?

Initially, you might think that knowing what is true and accurate should be fairly simple: you may rely on your common sense to tell you when something sounds too good to be true or "smells fishy," for example. But if you put your common sense to the test, what seems apparent and obvious to you may not be so to others. For instance, in some cultures, a person's responsibility lies first with the family and community, and a person's pursuit of happiness is limited within those confines. Many people in the United States, however, believe that the individual person is most important and that individuals should pursue happiness even at the expense of family or community. That is one reason why many immigrants to the United States are appalled by U.S. values; such values contradict those of their native cultures.

Your values may influence how you think about your world, and this thinking will be evident in your writing. Often, this thinking reflects hidden or false assumptions. When you write as though your reader shares your assumptions, you may be taking a large risk. Read the following brief story:

> A father and his child are riding in a car when they are
>
> involved in a horrible accident. The father is killed instantly, and
>
> the child suffers a severe injury and must be rushed to a nearby
>
> hospital. The child is taken to the emergency room, where it is
>
> determined that he needs surgery. The best surgeon on duty is
>
> called to save the boy's life. But the surgeon, upon entering the
>
> operating room and seeing the boy on the table, exclaims, "I
>
> can't operate on this boy. He's my son."

How can this be? If you assume that only men are surgeons, you have to develop an answer that questions who the boy's real father is. If you recognize that women are surgeons, too, you arrive at the correct answer: the surgeon is the boy's mother.

Naturally, people make assumptions in life all the time. In fact, people could scarcely move without assumptions, such as the assumption that the laws of gravity will not fail. Even in the preceding story, one can make assumptions about the surgeon—that the surgeon is a well-trained, well-educated medical doctor, for instance. However, the flaw comes when one assumes that the surgeon must be of a certain gender.

What Is Logical?

Your instructors ask that your writing be logical. What does this mean? What is logical, and how can you detect logic in your own writing? How can you tell when it is absent?

Fortunately, there are ways to examine logic. *Logic* is the means by which you know things. There are two principal paths to logical knowledge: induction and deduction.

Induction

Induction is a method of logic that arrives at a general conclusion based on the observation of specific incidents or examples. As such, a conclusion reached by induction is a generalization, which means it is subject to error. Thus, inductive reasoning provides us with *probability,* not *certainty*. For instance, if all of the surgeons you know are male, then in the story of the young boy in the accident, you may have guessed that the surgeon is more likely to be male than female. However, you cannot know with certainty which gender the surgeon is. Consider the following statement:

> I spoke to three people who had organic chemistry last term. They
>
> all said it was a very tough course. I expect organic chemistry to be
>
> a tough course when I take it this semester.

The conclusion is based on the observation that three students who took organic chemistry found the course very difficult. The chances are good that the writer of the statement will also find the course difficult. There is no certainty of this, however. If the three people are not representative of the general student population or are not as adept in chemistry as the writer, no adequate conclusion can be drawn. For instance, perhaps the writer has special abilities in chemistry or the three students she spoke to all have difficulty with the sciences or school in general.

The biggest trouble with inductive reasoning usually occurs when the sample incidents or examples are too small compared to the overall possible number. Consider the following:

> Since Seve ate seafood once and fell ill, seafood will always make
>
> Seve ill.

The conclusion is illogical because eating seafood once is probably not a sufficient number of experiences on which to base the conclusion. Too many other variables are left out: the food may be been poorly prepared, Seve may have been feeling ill before eating, and there are many types of seafood besides what Seve ate that may not make him ill.

Although inductive reasoning supplies only probability and not certainty, do not get the impression that we can do without it. Inductive reasoning is the basis for much of what people take for granted. For instance, we could hardly climb in our cars and drive down the road without using inductive reasoning. Our experience tells us what we can expect from other drivers on the road, how our cars will operate under the present circumstances, and that we should drive defensively because someone else on the road is likely to behave erratically. All such concepts are actually generalizations based on experience. However, our experience does not guarantee that every time we drive we will find drivers behaving as we expect them to.

Deduction

Deduction is a method of logic in which a conclusion is drawn from two premises, one major and the other minor. A **premise** is a statement or assertion that you are already certain is true. When used properly, deductive reasoning can supply *certainty*. This formula of argument containing three propositions is called a **syllogism.**

Major premise: Each person who works for TechnoTech must have a security clearance.

Minor premise: Beth works for TechnoTech.

Conclusion: Beth has a security clearance.

The major premise is a general statement. The minor premise is a specific instance or example. The conclusion applies the minor premise to the major premise. Sometimes the process can be flawed. Look at the following:

Major premise: The French love wine.

Minor premise: Giselle is French.

Conclusion: Giselle loves wine.

In this instance, the trouble is with the major premise. Many French people love wine, but it is a mistake to imply that *all* French people love wine, as the major premise does. Indeed, there are some French people who do not enjoy wine, and Giselle may be one of them.

Major premises that are arrived at based on induction, such as *The French love wine,* are subject to error because induction can only provide probability. A better major premise might read: *Many French people love wine*. This, of course, would lead to the conclusion that *Giselle is likely to love wine*. This statement is less absolute, but for that very reason, it is more accurate.

Another problem that can occur with deduction develops when the premises are applied improperly. Even though both statements may be true individually, the conclusion can be invalid.

Major premise: Enlisting in the military is an act of patriotism.

Minor premise: Bruce is patriotic.

Conclusion: Bruce is enlisting in the military.

Although the major premise is true and the minor premise is true, the conclusion is not valid because there are other ways to be patriotic besides enlisting in the military, such as dedicating oneself to public service programs or being politically involved.

EXERCISE 12.1

Examine each of the following syllogisms. If the syllogism is valid, indicate that with the letter *C*. If the syllogism is invalid, write the reason the syllogism does not work.

1. Major premise: Welfare recipients are lazy freeloaders.

   Minor premise: Caitlyn is on welfare.

   Conclusion: Caitlyn is a lazy freeloader.

2. Major premise: Killing is wrong.

   Minor premise: Soldiers are trained to be killers.

   Conclusion: It is wrong to be a soldier.

3. Major premise: Healthy people eat lots of fruits and vegetables.

   Minor premise: Benjamin eats lots of fruits and vegetables.

   Conclusion: Benjamin is a healthy person.

4. Major premise: Anyone enrolled at Brenner College is allowed to use its computer lab.

   Minor premise: Jamal is enrolled at Brenner College.

   Conclusion: Jamal is allowed to use Brenner College's computer lab.

5. Major premise: Many American Catholics have traveled to Vatican City in Rome.

 Minor premise: Betty Lou has traveled to Vatican City in Rome.

 Conclusion: Betty Lou is an American Catholic.

Some Logical Fallacies to Avoid

One of the biggest pitfalls for writers to avoid is using logical fallacies in the development of an argument. A **logical fallacy** is a breakdown of the logical thinking process that can cause the writer to draw incorrect conclusions. There are many types of logical fallacies; only some of them are presented here.

Hasty Generalization

A **hasty generalization** occurs when a conclusion is based on a sampling that is too small.

> Religious people are so stiff and unfriendly. I remember at the church my parents went to, no one even said "Good morning" to me.

In this example, the speaker has experienced only one church. If he examined more examples, he might have found a great variety of styles and manners among religious people and churches.

> Professional athletes are a bunch of greedy, spoiled brats who don't care about anyone except themselves.

Although the sports pages indeed seem filled with stories of professional athletes acting this way, many athletes devote significant time, energy, and money to charities in their local communities. Stating that all athletes are greedy and spoiled is a hasty generalization.

In darker form, hasty generalizations are often the backbone of stereotypes and racist or sexist statements. Statements such as "Asians are bad drivers" or "Blondes are dumb" are often based more on accepting stereotypes than analyzing real-life experience. Any contradictory evidence is tossed out (e.g., "Oh, she's an exception") while examples that confirm the stereotype are highlighted. These types of stereotypical statements have no place in student essays.

Faulty Authority

Look at who is talking about what. Everyone has opinions, but not everyone is equally qualified or knowledgeable about a subject. This is known as **faulty authority.** As a reader, you should pay attention not only to what is being said but also to who is saying it. Ask yourself questions such as: What is this person's educational background, training, or experience? Does it relate to what he or she is speaking about? Examine the following:

> My English professor stated, "The teaching of history in this country has reached such low ebb that students don't have the minimum understanding of America's past."

An English professor, while certain to have an opinion, is not as qualified to assess the teaching of history as a history professor is.

As a student writer, you are unlikely to be an expert on many of the subjects that you come across, so you will have to learn to use a library to gather evidence. Don't make the mistake of guessing at numbers, making up statistics, or trying to recall statistics from memory without looking for the original source. Look for your evidence in reputable newspapers, news magazines, and journals.

Another issue is the age of the evidence. How old is your information? On some issues, materials that are just a few years old may be out of date. For instance, arguments about levels of pollution in the environment require as much current information as possible. Conclusions drawn from older information may be unjustified. Take a look at this example:

> In 1993, levels of air pollution reached hazardous levels on 23 days. No doubt the figure is higher today.

The conclusion is unjustified. No evidence is presented to show that air pollution has gotten worse; the writer merely assumes that it has. Circumstances may have changed for the better, not the worse. New research must be done to discover the current figures.

Questionable Cause and Effect

What caused what to happen can create many debates. The danger is found in oversimplifying complex issues, assuming that simply because two events happened close to each other in time, one caused the other to happen.

> Ever since the Supreme Court outlawed school prayer, national test
>
> scores have been dropping. The solution to our education problems
>
> is to bring back prayer in schools.

Of course, many people believe strongly in returning prayer to schools, but the implication presented here is overly simple: a return to prayer will mean better test scores. Other possible causes—such as the prevalence of television watching, the influence of broken and dysfunctional homes, the breakdown of authority, the effects of lazy teaching and overcrowded classrooms, and society's quest for instant gratification at the expense of long-term goals—are ignored in this argument.

A special type of questionable cause and effect argument often leaves the connection unstated.

> John F. Kennedy was considering abolishing the Federal Reserve
>
> Board, but he was murdered before he could take action.

This statement implies that Kennedy was assassinated *because* he considered abolishing the Federal Reserve Board. This statement can also be seen as an **innuendo,** in which a cause or effect connection is implied but not explicitly stated.

Emotional Blackmail

Advertisers and politicians are the masters of **emotional blackmail.** They prey on our fears, needs, pity, and joy. Arguments that rely on emotional blackmail hope to avoid rational scrutiny. If people are too angry or afraid, they will not look past the emotion to see more reasonable arguments.

> Do you want your home to be robbed, your family's possessions
>
> stolen, your hard-earned money taken? If not, buy Protect-U Home
>
> Security Service.

Who would want to be robbed? There is nothing in this ad to suggest that the Protect-U Home Security Service has the experience or ability to protect your home or that it is substantially better or more affordable than other home security services.

False Analogy

Is one thing like another? An **analogy** is a comparison between two otherwise unlike or unrelated people, objects, processes, or events. When used properly, an analogy helps a person understand difficult concepts, events, or processes. A **false analogy** can confuse or mislead. Read this ad:

> Would you keep a tree that had only forty or fifty leaves? Then why
>
> keep a cable service that offers only forty or fifty channels?

Is a television cable service like a tree? Some trees have over a thousand leaves. Is that what people require on their television screens—a thousand channels? The two compared objects, television cable service and trees, are too different to justify the analogy.

Begging the Question

When someone is **begging the question,** he or she assumes something that has not yet been proven in a statement. The statement seems logical on the surface, but not so after closer examination. Look at this example:

> The labor union has rejected management's fair and reasonable
>
> offer.

How does this writer know that the offer was fair and reasonable? Apparently, the labor union did not believe the offer was fair and reasonable. If the writer is a spokesperson for management, you can guess that the intention of this statement is to present the labor union as unfair and unreasonable. Here, the writer simply *assumes* that the offer is fair and reasonable. A better statement would be:

> The labor union has rejected management's offer of a 2.71% pay
>
> increase.

This statement presents the facts of the situation and does not assume anything.

Attacking the Messenger

A favorite technique for many debaters, on both public and private levels, is to ignore the substance of what is said and instead **attack the messenger** saying it. This is also referred to as *ad hominem*, meaning in Latin "against the man." Such an argument is designed to avoid the real issues at hand.

> Because Woody Allen left Mia Farrow and started a relationship with her adopted daughter, I don't think he should win an Oscar for his movie.

Whatever the circumstances in people's personal lives, their creative works should be judged on their own merits. Indeed, many of the world's greatest artists, writers, musicians, composers, dancers, directors, and intellectuals have behaved reprehensibly in their personal lives.

Some people do make the argument that political, religious, and military leaders need to be held to a higher standard of ethical and moral behavior. This debate often swirls on the front pages of newspapers when some leader is caught in an embarrassing scandal. This issue has much to do with how people see their leaders not only as policy makers but also as role models. Often, there is no specific consensus about a leader's activities but rather just a general feeling that people want their leaders to behave better than most other people.

Slippery Slope

Slippery slope is the argument that predicts that since one step or action was taken, a later event or action is inevitable and unavoidable. The fallacy occurs because the arguer assumes the second event *because of* the first event. For instance, part of the rationale for the U.S. involvement in Vietnam was the Domino Theory. This theory held that if one country in the region fell to the communist forces, all other countries would eventually fall, like a row of dominoes. However, although South Vietnam, Cambodia, and Laos all did fall, the predicted advance of communism did not occur.

EXERCISE 12.2

Identify or explain the logical error in each of the following statements.

1. We have grown up living around construction. How can something be wrong if you see it every day?

2. If the trees are gone, then where will the baby birds live while their mothers are off finding food for them? Where are the deer going to live? We need the natural habitat.

3. Those who can, do; those who can't, teach.

4. When the professional football player admitted that he had been unable to read while in college, it once again showed that major college football is corrupt.

5. Because that actress has been married and divorced eight different times, I don't think she's a very good actress.

6. According to a weekly tabloid, Elvis Presley never died but is traveling with extraterrestrials, bringing rock and roll music to other parts of the galaxy.

7. How can you say that astrology is bunk? I'm a Virgo and I've got a very orderly mind. I have a friend who is an Aries with a very bad temper. And I have another friend, a Taurus, who is as stubborn as a bull.

8. So many of the great industrialists started off poor, but through diligence and hard work, they rose to great wealth. Therefore, the key to becoming rich is to start off poor.

9. If we allow handgun registration, the next step will be handgun confiscation.

10. Are you a coward? Don't you love your country? Then join the army or people will think you're a yellow-bellied traitor.

Building Logical Arguments: Persuasion

The key to building a logical argument is to remember that you have a reader. Don't forget that your reader must be able to follow and be convinced by your arguments. What is difficult is that you are already convinced—after all, you chose your thesis—so you must put yourself into the shoes of someone who does not necessarily share your opinion or even assumptions about any given topic.

Keep in mind that persuasion is an important aspect of arguing an essay. **Persuasion** is the attempt to change your reader's views about something or to motivate your reader to take a course of action. Persuasive writing tries to sway a reader's opinion either by presenting convincing evidence or by appealing to the reader's values, needs, or emotions. However, when you are writing to persuade a reader, you must do more than present information: you must arrange that evidence so that a reader will be motivated to change his or her own opinion about the topic.

In many ways, you can compare your role as a writer to that of an attorney at a criminal trial. Another name for such a lawyer is *advocate* because the lawyer is trying to persuade the jury that the defendant is either guilty or innocent. The prosecutor is the advocate of the people, presenting the case and hoping to lead the jury to the conclusion of guilty. The defense attorney is the advocate for the accused, trying to show the jury that the prosecutor's case is not convincing and that the defendant is not guilty. Both advocates are trying to persuade the jury to agree with them.

Think of yourself as an advocate for your thesis. The reader is your jury; you take your case in front of your reader and present the evidence in such a way that he or she must conclude that your thesis is true. Examine the following essay from a student named Keith:

The Gun Control Myth

Hook   Recent polls show that people still consider crime to be one of their top concerns in life, ahead of world affairs or even the environment. This is no surprise since each day newspapers and television report on crime, and usually the crimes are violent.

Example   Often, the crimes involve the use of guns, and when this happens, people say, "If we just got rid of guns, this wouldn't have happened." This is absurd. The intentions of most people who want **Thesis sentence** gun control may be good, but the results will not work. Gun control is a bad idea based on myths, not facts.

Topic sentence 1   The first myth is that guns are responsible for crime, but this is absurd. Most people who own guns are not criminals but people who fear criminals and want to protect themselves, or they are hunters or gun collectors. Crime has been around a lot longer than **Cause and effect** guns, and simple logic tells us that when you have people who are addicted to drugs, people who see violence as a means to an end, and people who lack respect for other people's lives and property, then you will have crime. If somehow all guns disappeared overnight, crime would still occur.

Topic sentence 2

The second myth is that regular citizens with guns do not help keep people secure, police do. Of course, the police are important, but as the saying goes, "There's never a cop around when you need one." You can be attacked and robbed or murdered in a matter of seconds; there would be virtually no chance for help from the police. The police will arrive later, after the crime has occurred. It is better to prevent the crime altogether. Every day in America, crimes are prevented or stopped by regular citizens who are armed.

Narration

Topic sentence 3

The third myth is that a complete ban on types of weapons will stop violence. If this were true, Washington, D.C., would be the safest town in America because it has a ban on handguns. However, sadly, our nation's capital is a violent, unsafe place. The ban simply doesn't work, and it would not work anywhere else. After all, criminals are criminals because they do not obey the law. There is no reason to suspect they would obey a handgun ban.

Example

Restatement of thesis sentence

Gun control will just remove the guns from regular, law-abiding citizens while keeping them in the hands of criminals and the police. That gives too much power to both groups. There is nothing wrong with private gun ownership; there is something wrong with criminal acts being committed with guns. So, punish the criminals severely, and leave the good guys alone.

Answers the question
So what?

The thesis of Keith's essay is simple: *Gun control is a bad idea based on myths, not facts.* Keith's task is to persuade the reader to his point of view. He, of course, faces several difficulties in doing so since gun control is often an emotionally charged issue. Emotion tends to inhibit or short-circuit rational thought.

One of the important techniques in this essay is that Keith is directly confronting what he calls "myths." These myths are statements Keith believes gun control advocates use to advance their point of view. Keith attempts to expose three myths in his essay.

The first myth is one that Keith sees as being built on a faulty syllogism. The syllogism would run something like this:

Major premise: The commission of crime is bad.

Minor premise: Guns are used to commit crimes.

Conclusion: Guns are bad.

This conclusion is a result of the idea that anything that helps in the commission of crime is a bad thing. However, Keith sees that this syllogism is invalid because guns have other, legitimate purposes besides being used to commit crimes. An extension of the same logic is that the responsibility for the crime is shifted away from the criminal to the instrument of the crime. A careful reader might point out that although the gun is not responsible for the crime, the presence of a gun can make the situation more dangerous for victims of the crime.

The second myth Keith examines is based on induction. That is, the personal experience of many people is that the police, not ordinary citizens, are responsible for dealing with crime. However, Keith suggests that this is a dangerous and hasty generalization. Although most people do not experience crime on a regular basis, when a crime does occur, people need to have protection, and a gun can be that protection. A careful reader might point out that Keith himself is relying on a hasty generalization: that the police are never around when a crime is committed and that they cannot respond quickly enough to stop a crime from occurring.

The third myth is also based on a syllogism. This syllogism may be stated as follows:

Major premise: Many crimes are committed with handguns.

Minor premise: Handguns can be banned.

Conclusion: Fewer crimes will be committed if handguns are banned.

The trouble here lies with the minor premise: *handguns can be banned.* A governing body can pass a law banning handguns, but effectively administering that law can be difficult or even impossible. Thus, in theory the banning of handguns may lower crime rates, but in truth it is very difficult for the police to stop the sale and possession of handguns.

However, Keith's criticism is based on induction—the Washington, D.C., example is only one case—which could lead a careful reader to question whether a nationwide handgun ban might be more effective than a localized one. Comparisons to other countries' experiences with handgun bans might prove useful, but they would be limited, too, since other countries do not all share the size, circumstance, and history of the United States.

One of the commendable keys to Keith's essay is his tone. He manages to avoid excessive emotional appeals. He does not engage in name calling or end-of-the-world predictions; he even admits gun control advocates have good intentions. Still, there is no doubt where Keith stands on the issue.

Concessions

When Keith presented the arguments of gun control advocates, he was making a concession. A **concession** is a way to acknowledge the existence of points of view that differ from the one expressed in your thesis sentence. At first, you may think that telling the other side's points is a bad idea: Why give them time and space? Will it make your own argument less effective?

Why Choose to Use a Concession?

Whether you acknowledge the existence of competing ideas or not, the ideas are there already, floating through the air of public discussion. If you are dealing with a controversial topic, by its very definition there are competing ideas, and your reader is likely to be aware of at least one of them. If you write your essay with only your thesis in mind, you may appear unreasonable or hasty, as though you had not considered alternative arguments or points of view.

Therefore, you make your own argument stronger by admitting that other arguments exist. You show your reader that you are aware of competing arguments and that you have considered them and rejected them. You can even show your reader why you have rejected them. That will bring your reader along with your own thought processes, leading him or her to your own argument.

Choosing Your Concession Strategy

You may choose one of three ways to handle your concession argument.

1. *Admit that the other side has some valid points.* For instance, if you are arguing in favor of the death penalty, you can acknowledge that, indeed, innocent people have been executed in the past. Then, you must show how the benefit of the death penalty outweighs this potential drawback. In another case, if you are supporting a local highway-building project, you can admit that the environment will be harmed. However, you must then show that increases in the population and in traffic congestion make building the highway more important than preserving the environment.

2. *Show that the other side's arguments are based on inaccurate information.* You must establish that the evidence the other side presents is faulty, inflated, or out of date. For instance, if you are arguing in favor of establishing a local park and the other side is arguing that the project is too expensive, you must find evidence that shows the other side has inflated the costs of the project or that the other side has not taken into account private donations that will lower the cost to the public. In another argument, you may argue that the threat of global warming is not real and that the other side's dire predictions are based on insufficient scientific evidence or that the evidence has been misinterpreted. This type of concession implies that *if* the information were accurate, the argument might be right.

3. *Show that the other side's arguments are invalid or irrelevant.* If you want to argue that car pool lanes are an ineffective means of lessening traffic congestion and the other side argues that they will work if given enough time, you can point out that if the car pool lanes have not worked by now, they are not likely to work better in the future. If you want to argue that cameras should not be allowed in courtrooms and the other side argues that cameras help the public better understand courtroom proceedings, you can argue that courtrooms are not classrooms and that what matters most is that fair and impartial proceedings are held, not that cameras teach law to the public. In other words, you concede that the other side has made a point (e.g., educating the public about courtroom proceedings is a worthwhile goal), but you show that the point is not relevant (e.g., educating the public about law is not relevant to the purpose of a courtroom).

Choosing How to Present the Concession

You must choose how and when to present the concession arguments. Generally speaking, there are two methods:

1. *Devote an entire paragraph to concession arguments.* With this method, you bundle together the opposing arguments and then either negate them or dismiss them. This paragraph can be placed early in your essay (right after your introduction) for maximum effect. This allows the weight of your entire main body to overcome the concession arguments. You may choose to place your concession paragraph just before your conclusion, but doing so may leave the reader with a stronger impression of the opposing arguments than your own.

2. *Integrate the concession arguments into your main body paragraphs.* Using this technique will require you to match up concession arguments with your own controlling ideas and then present them in the main body. This technique works best when there is a clear correspondence between your arguments and the opposing viewpoints.

Transitions

You help your reader along when you have concession points in your essay. You do not want your reader to become lost or confused, and you especially do not want your reader to believe that you favor opinions you actually oppose. You should use words that *alert* the reader that concession points are coming. The following are a few transitional words and phrases that prepare readers for concession arguments:

of course	to be sure
certainly	granted
some people argue	another opinion is
while	however
opponents believe	a counterargument states
on the other hand	the opposition to this says
a different viewpoint holds	even though

Student Writing Assignment: Argument

Write a 500- to 600-word essay on one of the following topics. Be sure to include concession arguments.

astrology	gun control
obesity	overpopulation
illegal immigration	the importance of a college degree
second marriages	homelessness
multiculturalism	saving the environment

Follow the steps listed in the Start-Up Suggestions and Self-Revision Questions. Then bring your essay to class for peer editing. Revise your essay and then complete the section labeled Your Choices: Argument to discuss the decisions you made during the composing and revising process.

Start-Up Suggestions

Follow these steps before writing your first draft.

1. Since you may be unfamiliar with your topic, go to a library and scan the bookshelves or magazine racks for articles on your topic. Be sure to ask a librarian for help if you have difficulty finding materials.
2. When you are doing your research, read materials from more than one point of view. For instance, if you are writing about saving the environment, find articles that favor growth and construction at the expense of the environment as signs of human progress. This way, you will have a more rounded view of your topic.
3. Discover where opinions differ regarding your topic and determine why that is so. Then consult the list of logical fallacies and see if any of them apply to the reasoning that you find.
4. Make a list for each side of the topic and write down the arguments or supporting ideas behind each side. Some issues may have more than two sides, so you may need to make more than two lists. Which list of arguments do you find most convincing? Why?
5. Formulate a thesis sentence based on the argument about your topic that you find most convincing.
6. Draft an informal outline for your essay.

Self-Revision Questions

Answer these questions after writing your first draft and before rewriting the draft for submission to your peer-editing group.

1. Underline your thesis sentence. Can you identify the claim and three controlling ideas?
2. Check your topic sentences. Does each of them relate directly to the thesis?
3. Examine your evidence. Does the evidence logically support the topic sentence of the paragraph?
4. How have you handled the concession arguments?

Revise your essay and submit it to your peer-editing group.

Peer-Editing Guidelines for Argument

Answer these questions for each of the essays written by other members of your peer-editing group.

1. Does the essay have a good title? What is it?
2. What is the essay's thesis sentence?
3. Are the three controlling ideas logical and convincing?
4. What are the concession arguments?
5. How does the essay oppose the concession arguments?
6. How are concession arguments presented? If they are presented in a concession paragraph, where is the paragraph located?
7. Are there any obvious or important concession arguments that have not been presented?
8. Does the essay have effective transitions, particularly between the concession arguments and the essay's own arguments?
9. What is the crystalline word?
10. How is the grammar, spelling, and punctuation?

Prepare the final draft of your essay, taking the comments of your peer-editing group into account.

Your Choices: Argument

Answer these questions after you have finished your final draft.

1. How did you choose your topic?
2. How did you choose your thesis?
3. How did you choose your controlling ideas? Were there other ideas that you left out? Why did you reject them?
4. How did you discover the concession arguments?
5. What logical fallacies or problems did you find with the concession arguments?
6. Were any of the concession arguments so strong that you felt they might sway your reader away from your argument? If so, how did you compensate for that?
7. Did you feel compelled at any point to change your thesis sentence? Did you make such a change? Why or why not?

8. Did you have to change the structure of your essay from rough draft to final draft, particularly to address any problems with the concession arguments?
9. What technical errors did you have to fix?
10. Did you agree or disagree with your peer editors' choice for the crystalline word? If you disagreed, did you make any revisions to emphasize the word you wanted?

COMPUTER EXERCISE

Write a concession paragraph for one of the following thesis sentences. Then, either share your paragraph with your writing partner or with your whole class for the purpose of identifying the concession strategies that were used. (Remember, your concession paragraph will contain the arguments opposed to the argument in the thesis sentence.)

1. Parents should be the only ones responsible for educating their children on sexual matters.
2. Stricter gun control laws will help control violent crime.
3. Television networks should be prohibited from broadcasting from midnight to 6 a.m.
4. The best vacations are the ones spent at home.

When you are sharing concession paragraphs, use either brackets or all capital letters to identify what type or types of concessions are being used. This way, you can determine easily what is original to the paragraph and what is analysis.

THE REVISION PROCESS:
A Student Writing Sample

A young student, Nikki, decided to write her essay on second marriages because she was living with her mother, who was married for the second time. Nikki also had several friends whose parents had divorced and remarried. She began her prewriting by listing good and bad points about second marriages. Here are her lists:

Good	Bad
second chance	confuses children
new relationship	stepparents are problems
starting over/find nicer person	new husband may be no better than first one
better than being a single parent	blending families is hard
everyone needs love	commitment?
monetary benefits	

Nikki decided that she was in favor of second marriages even though she had some strong reservations. She decided that she could acknowledge these reservations in a concession. She did not quite know how she would handle the reservations, but she knew some of them would have to be included.

At this point, Nikki tried to create her thesis sentence. Her first draft was this:

> Second marriages are a good idea for women who are lonely and need love or money.

She knew this would not work too well since it referred only to women, and the reasoning was simplistic and almost insulting. She reshaped it:

> Second marriages are a good idea for people because second marriages can provide companionship, love, and money.

Nikki then reworked her sentence one more time:

> Second marriages can be a good idea if they provide love, companionship, and financial security.

Now Nikki was ready for her first draft. She knew what her three controlling ideas were going to be, but she was uncertain about her concession. She decided to create a concession paragraph and put all her concession points there, since that seemed the most effective way to present and dismiss the opposing arguments.

Second Marriages

Most people who get married want it to be for life, but sometimes it doesn't work out that way. And that can be tough, especially when there are kids involved. So, most people are looking to get married again. Second marriages can be a good idea if they provide love, companionship, and financial security.

There are problems with second marriages, mostly for the kids. When my mother got remarried, I was only 9 years old. I was angry with my mother for a long time, and I didn't let my stepfather do much of anything for me. But later things worked out, and I have a good relationship with my stepfather as well as with my father.

Second marriages are good for providing love. After all, shouldn't that be why everyone gets married? Just because one marriage didn't work out, no one should have to spend the rest of their life without love. I know my mother is a lot happier with her second marriage than she was being alone. Love is what makes everything worth it.

Companionship is also part of second marriages. Sometimes people just want someone there. If you're divorced, sometimes you can get real lonely, even if you have kids. People need other people to share their lives with. A husband or a wife is that person. Husbands and wives do things together that interest them both, and that can be a lot of fun.

People find financial security in second marriages. Times are tough, and nowadays people need two incomes just to have what people used to have with one. Divorced women usually are hit the hardest too. They often have kids to take care of, they have to get a job, and often the ex-husband doesn't give all the support he's supposed to give. So, getting married again can be a big help financially. That's important too since money determines what you can do so often.

Usually second marriages are good because they give the person someone to love, to do things with, and to help pay the bills.

Sometimes it will be a problem for the children, but they usually get over it. A lot of second marriages are much better than first marriages!

When Nikki took this draft to her peer-editing group, she was told that although her thesis sentence was good and her controlling ideas were fine, her concession was a problem. The group felt that she had not addressed the problems for children very well and that she had left out other major problems, such as the issue of commitment. The peer editors did not like Nikki's tone, saying it seemed too casual, too personal. For the crystalline word, they chose *second* because it was repeated many times in the essay, and it also seemed to encapsulate the notion that everything in a second marriage was an attempt to improve on the first one.

When Nikki rewrote her draft, she chose to keep the structure of her essay the same, including her concession paragraph. She decided to add more issues to the concession paragraph and remove some of her very personal observations, in hopes of reaching a more general audience. Someone also commented that her title was too broad, giving no indication about how she felt about second marriages. Here is Nikki's final draft:

The Benefits of Second Marriages

Most people who get married want it to be for life, but sometimes it does not work out that way. Divorce is difficult, especially when there are children involved. Living alone can be lonely, and it can be tough financially. So, most people who get divorced want to get married again. Second marriages can be a good idea if they provide love, companionship, and financial security.

There are problems with second marriages, mostly for the children. Often, children do not respond well to stepparents, although that can change with time and effort. Another problem could be the commitment factor: if someone is divorced once, maybe he or she will not try hard enough to save a second marriage once it hits trouble. Still, every marriage is different, so people have to hope for the best.

Second marriages should be all about love, just like first marriages are supposed to be. Having one marriage not work out should not mean a person has to spend the rest of his or her life without love. My mother is a lot happier with her second marriage than she was being alone. Love is what makes everything worthwhile.

Companionship is also part of second marriages. Sometimes people just want someone there. Divorced people often feel lonely even if they have children. Everyone wants someone to share his or her life with. A husband or a wife is that person. Husbands and wives do things together that interest them both. That is part of the fun of marriage.

People find financial security in second marriages. Nowadays, people need two incomes just to have what people used to have with one. Divorced women usually are hit the hardest, too. They often have children to take care of, they have to get jobs, and sometimes their ex-husbands do not give the financial support they are supposed to give. So, getting married again can be a big help financially. That is important, too, since money so often determines what a person can do.

Usually, second marriages are good because they give the person someone to love, to do things with, and to help pay the bills. Second marriages can be a problem for the children, but they usually get over it. Also, people fear that second marriages will end up like the first, but a lot of second marriages are much better than first marriages. There just needs to be a lot of love.

When Nikki finished her final draft, she completed the Your Choices: Argument questionnaire. She realized that her biggest frustration was that she wanted to say more. In some ways, she realized that her topic was very powerful, and she had a lot to say about it—perhaps too much, given the limitations of her assignment. She liked her controlling ideas, but she saw that she could have developed each one further by providing more specific examples. She did not find any logical fallacies in her essay, and she did not feel that any of the concession arguments were so strong that they overpowered her own. The crystalline word *second* had not pleased Nikki because she felt it was too negative, so she tried to emphasize the positive aspects of second marriages. She corrected several technical problems for her final draft, including recognizing that *everyone* required a singular possessive pronoun (she chose *his or her*) and eliminating the use of *you* in her essay.

GRAMMAR INSTRUCTION AND EXERCISES:
Using Commas Correctly

One of the most misleading myths that many people have learned over the years is to place commas where you pause in a sentence. The trouble is that people actually pause between *every* word in a sentence. Only the length of time differs.

A more reliable way of learning how to use commas is to master a few simple rules for the most frequent uses of commas. Keep your handbook nearby for rarer, more exotic situations. Here are ten rules:

1. *Use a comma to separate independent clauses joined by a coordinating conjunction.*

   People should take their right to vote seriously, but statistics show that a large number of Americans fail to vote year after year.

   Anaka failed her algebra final, so she has to take the class again.

2. *Use a comma to set off an introductory dependent clause.*

   Although my cousins live just across town, I see them only on holidays.

   Since the snow had not let up, Sheila canceled her plans to attend the pro wrestling match.

3. *Use a comma after a transitional word or phrase at the start of a sentence.*

   However, the importance of that development cannot be underestimated.

   In conclusion, the Norman Conquest remains the defining event of Britain.

4. ***Use a comma after an introductory request or command.***

Remember, there will be no dessert if you don't eat your peas.

See, I didn't forget to bring your CD back.

5. ***Use commas to separate three or more items in a series.***

The police hauled in the butcher, the baker, and the electrician.

Bobbee planted roses, petunias, and azaleas.

Note: Some writers prefer that the final comma be omitted. Check with your instructor to see if he or she has a preference.

Bobbee planted roses, petunias and azaleas.

6. ***Use commas to set off an interrupting element.***

Jennifer, not Kim, was named the valedictorian.

Al can, if you like, deliver the package tomorrow.

7. ***Use a comma to set off a direct address or a word such as* please, yes, *or* no.**

Mark, you had better get to school before it's too late.

Please, we only want to help!

8. ***Use commas to set off a nonessential element in a sentence.***

Mr. Hall, the portly gentleman in the tuxedo, made over three million dollars last year in the stock market.

The director, whose last three movies had bombed, nervously waited for a phone call from the studio.

9. ***Use a comma to set off an element that qualifies, contrasts, or takes exception with the rest of the sentence.***

What we need are results, not promises.

Manuel worked long hours at the office, often alone.

10. *Use a comma to separate coordinate adjectives.*

The crude, vulgar behavior of the fans was condemned by the players and the media.

The green, scaly dragon from the movie haunted Sean's dreams.

(See pages 387–91 for further discussion about commas.)

EXERCISES

Rewrite the following sentences, adding commas wherever needed. If no comma is needed, indicate that with the letter *C*.

1. One of my neighbors Mr. Jones died last night and I sure will miss him.

2. Mr. Saunders who made his money speculating in land owns the house with the red tile roof.

3. One day last week my employer Ms. Conway a jolly peculiar woman raised my salary first telling me I was about to be fired and laughing at me when I looked so surprised.

4. Although the report of your financial standing is still pending we feel that our companies based on our previous negotiations should have a very profitable relationship.

5. I went downtown and saw a man standing in the middle of the street with his shirt off in freezing weather.

6. Even though prices have remained steady for years my grandmother worries about inflation eating away her savings.

7. No I don't want to eat my radishes.

8. The trick of course is to know when enough is enough.

9. Besides kidnapping and murder the suspect was accused of robbery battery and transportation of illegal goods across state lines.

10. The man who gave the speech turned out to be none other than my father-in-law.

13 How to Say It

Style

JOURNAL EXERCISE

What does the word <u>style</u> mean to you? Give specific examples of style in fashion, music, or the movies. Then explain why you chose those examples and what they mean to you as examples of style.

Consider for a moment how you use language. Perhaps, on the surface, language seems fairly straightforward. It has words, and the words have meanings. If you don't know what a word means, you can look it up in a dictionary. However, words can have several meanings, and phrases, clauses, and sentences can become intricate constructions of meaning, like an erector set or the frame of a house. Language is multilayered and three dimensional.

The Expressive Power of Language

Have you ever wondered why, when we all have the same words in the English language, we sound so different from each other, not simply in terms of vocal tones but in the words and phrases we use? Expressions such as "Oh, that sounds just like her" exist because of these differences. You may have an unconscious knowledge when you prepare to listen to a parent, a friend, or an instructor about what kind of language you expect to hear. If your parent, friend, or instructor speaks differently than usual, you might respond by wondering if something is wrong ("Boy, Mr. McLaughlin doesn't sound like himself today!").

Thus, language is able to provide a tremendous variety of expression. This variety comes not solely from vocabulary, although that is a part, but also from the way or manner in which words are used. Indeed, a writer's choice of words, word order, phrases, sentence length, and patterns all create the writer's style.

Style is how language is used. You already have a style; you just may not be conscious of it. You also may not have an *effective* style. As a writer, you must be aware of each word you use to create a style that is clear, interesting, and persuasive. You can change your style, adapting to different circumstances, such as purpose and audience. You have already seen how purpose is handled with different rhetorical modes.

Choosing the Level of Language

Who is your audience? Your answer will determine, to a great extent, what you write and how you write it. As you saw in Chapter 1, you use different words depending on who you expect to read what you are writing. Indeed, language can be seen as existing on a continuum, with levels ranging from very strict, formal, public language to slang that is incomprehensible to people outside the writer's social sphere.

Because language exists on this continuum, the categories of language discussed next are only rough approximations. Some blending or blurring of the distinctions between the categories is, at times, inevitable. Often, informal English is spotted with slang expressions, and formal phrases or expressions may find their way into some people's colloquial language.

Formal Language

The most formal language is that usually found in many textbooks, government publications, and other public communications or documents. Formal English is often required in college classrooms, as well. It is the most widely accepted and understood form of English.

Formal English is characterized more by what is missing than what is present. What is missing are words and phrases that require inside or special knowledge to understand. Slang, technical language, jargon, and regionalisms limit your audience and are therefore generally considered unacceptable in formal English.

Colloquial Language

Colloquial English is the language of everyday use. It is informal and includes figurative language and expressions that are unacceptable in formal English. Figurative language includes metaphors and similes, such as *the dead of night* and *cool as a cucumber.* Yet, colloquial English is not restricted, generally, in its ability to reach audiences, except perhaps for those just learning to speak English.

Technical Language

Technical language is specific to a field of study or a profession, such as medicine, law, science, business, or education. A part of technical language is **jargon,** the language restricted to members of a specific field or profession. Jargon can be a necessary part of communicating between professionals or researchers, but it means little or nothing to outsiders. In the military, for instance, jargon often comes in the form of **acronyms,** which are abbreviations of long terms. A few acronyms have reached public consciousness, such as *snafu* ("situation normal—all fouled up") or *awol* ("absent without leave"), but most have not.

Slang Language

Slang is the most restrictive form of language. Only people within a certain group are initiated to the meanings of slang terms. Of course, this makes slang unacceptable as a form of communicating to anyone outside of the group because no one else will understand.

The use of slang can create a strong sense of solidarity within a group, which is part of the appeal of slang. If you are a teenager, for instance, you may enjoy using words or phrases your parents do not understand or use themselves, such as *dis* or *homeboy.* You can exclude from conversation anyone who is not like you by using slang.

Slang is very fluid. Different words and meanings appear and disappear with tremendous speed, and a word that marks a person as a member of a group one day will mark a person as out the next. Other words, such as *cool,* have stayed around so long that their meanings are well known and they have become part of colloquial language, no longer just slang. Instead of *cool,* for instance, teenagers may use the slang word *phat.*

Choosing Formal English

When you are writing in college, your audience will usually expect you to write in formal English. In classroom situations, of course, your real audience is often only the instructor, but remember that you are learning to write so that you can communciate with a broad range of people.

You may resist writing in formal English because you find it awkward or unusual; your preference may be to write in the language that you use with your peers, either slang or colloquial language. Although this desire is understandable, it limits your audience. You need to be able to adapt your writing to the appropriate situation.

Here are some general rules to follow when writing your papers in formal English. Your instructor may have some additional suggestions, too.

1. Avoid the use of first- and second-person pronouns such as *I, we,* and *you.* Stick to using third-person pronouns such as *he, she,* and *they.*

> Original:
>
> When you are trying to buy a car, a lot of times the salesmen will
>
> not even talk to you if you are a woman but will talk to your
>
> husband or boyfriend instead.
>
> Rewritten:
>
> When women try to buy cars, they often find that salesmen will
>
> not talk to them but will talk to their husbands or boyfriends
>
> instead.

2. Avoid expressions such as *I believe, I think,* and *I feel.* They do not add to the strength of your statements. Since you are writing the paper, the reader knows that it reflects your beliefs, thoughts, and feelings. If anything, such expressions detract from your arguments by making them appear overly personal.

> Original:
>
> I believe that the administration's current policy on gays in the
>
> military is unacceptable.
>
> Rewritten:
>
> The administration's current policy on gays in the military is
>
> unacceptable.

3. In order to keep the tone of the writing consistent, avoid nonstandard expressions or idioms such as *pave the way* and *down and out,* even if they are easily understood by English speakers.

Original:

Joel thought the math course would be a cinch, but instead it was a back-breaker.

Rewritten:

Joel thought the math course would be easy, but instead it was difficult.

4. Avoid slanted language, which is designed to convey an opinion or impression about the subject.

Original:

The girls were whining about so-called sexual harassment in the office.

Rewritten:

The women were complaining about the presence of sexual harassment in the office.

5. Avoid clichés or worn-out expressions such as *cold as ice* and *green with envy*. Also avoid mixing metaphors.

Original:

Adam wanted to climb the ladder of success at work, but he soon found that Celia had beaten him to the punch.

Rewritten:

Adam was trying to get a promotion, but Celia had already gotten the job.

6. Minimize or eliminate the use of contractions.

Original:

Parker should've watched the time because it's a shame he won't make it home for Xmas now.

Rewritten:

Parker should have watched the time because it is a shame he will not make it home for Christmas now.

7. Avoid using parentheses. A pair of commas will usually do the job.

Original:

Patti (the woman who lives next door) is going to have her second child soon.

Rewritten:

Patti, the woman who lives next door, is going to have her second child soon.

8. Avoid gross abstractions such as *the reality of life* and *the view of the world.*

Original:

Since the beginning of time, people have probably worried about money.

Rewritten:

People have probably worried about money since it was first invented.

9. Avoid sounding too opinionated because it detracts from your credibility.

Original:

The only interpretation an intelligent person can come to is that the profit motive does not dominate human behavior.

Rewritten:

One interpretation is that the profit motive does not dominate human behavior.

10. Avoid using too many qualifiers because you will seem uncertain about what you are saying.

Original:

It may be possible under certain circumstances that such a thing as nuclear fusion might be controllable.

Rewritten:

Nuclear fusion may be controllable.

11. Avoid using signposts. Do not tell the reader what you are going to do; just do it.

> **Original:**
>
> In this essay I will show how the dangers of secondhand smoke have been overplayed in the media.
>
> **Rewritten:**
>
> The dangers of secondhand smoke have been overplayed in the media.

12. Avoid using the passive voice. The active voice is better.

> **Original:**
>
> The river was crossed by the troops from NATO.
>
> **Rewritten:**
>
> The NATO troops crossed the river.

13. Avoid using the word *it* whenever reasonably possible. This pronoun has no meaning; the meaning must be supplied, thus creating more work for the reader.

> **Original:**
>
> Diane was hoping to avoid it, but now that it was here, she had to deal with it.
>
> **Rewritten:**
>
> Diane was hoping to avoid doing her taxes, but now that April 15 was here, she had to complete them.
>
> ***Note:*** In certain passive constructions, the word *it* has no meaning at all.
>
> **Original:**
>
> It is clear that John Wayne is a better movie cowboy than Clint Eastwood.
>
> **Rewritten:**
>
> Clearly, John Wayne is a better movie cowboy than Clint Eastwood.

14. Avoid overused modifiers such as *very, really,* and *so.* Find more descriptive nouns, verbs, adjectives, and adverbs instead.

Original:

The very red car was ticketed for going really fast.

Rewritten:

The bright red car was ticketed for traveling at high speeds.

15. Do not ask too many rhetorical questions. Make statements instead.

Original:

Who wants to pay higher taxes? Who wants to have their income lowered?

Rewritten:

No one wants to pay higher taxes or have his or her income lowered.

16. Know how to spell all proper names, terms, and words in your paper. Check the spellings of any words with which you may have difficulty.

Original:

Earnest Hemmingway is one of the most important American wrighters of the 20th Century.

Rewritten:

Ernest Hemingway is one of the most important American writers of the twentieth century.

17. Proofread everything.

Original:

The speci8al holiday event, spensoered by trhe Hospital Auxilary will be ;held in November at the Island Hotel.

Rewritten:

The special holiday event, sponsored by the Hospital Auxiliary, will be held in November at the Island Hotel.

Exercise 13.1

Find a paragraph in a newspaper or magazine that is written in formal English. Then rewrite the paragraph in colloquial English and then in slang English. (You may try technical English, as well, if you have enough knowledge of the jargon in the sciences, law, or military.) Be sure to label each level of English.

Sexism in Language

Sensitivity toward sexism in language is not merely an exercise in political correctness but an important part of reaching your audience and establishing your credibility. If you show no awareness of how sexism has permeated the English language, you risk offending an audience that knows that many newspapermen, policemen, and firemen are, in fact, women. Gender-neutral terms such as *journalist, police officer,* and *firefighter* have achieved public acceptance because they reflect more accurately the true circumstances of the workplace. As a writer, you should strive to avoid gender-specific terms whenever possible, especially when they are inaccurate.

Another difficulty is with the use of third-person pronouns. Traditionally, the third-person singular masculine pronoun, *he,* has been used to denote a person of either gender. Nowadays, though, many readers will chafe at such a sentence. You have several choices in how to cope with this difficulty.

1. *Use plural forms, making sure that the subject and verb agree in number.* With this method, you avoid the singular forms of nouns whenever possible. This allows you to use the gender-neutral third-person plural forms.

Original:

Any student hoping to graduate must meet with his counselor.

Rewritten:

All students hoping to graduate must meet with their counselors.

2. *Alternate between using the masculine and feminine forms of pronouns.* For instance, in one paragraph you use the masculine forms; in the next, the feminine. Many textbooks, including this one, use this technique.

Rewritten:

Any student hoping to graduate must meet with her counselor.

3. *Supply both forms of the pronoun, showing explicitly that the referent, the word the pronoun refers to, applies to both genders.* Many writers try to avoid this form because, when used frequently, it can make the writing awkward.

Rewritten:

Any student hoping to graduate must meet with his or her [or his/her] counselor.

EXERCISE 13.2

Rewrite the following sentences by removing the sexist language. If a sentence has no sexist language, indicate that with the letter *C*.

1. If someone wants to work as a fireman, policeman, or newspaperman, he should make sure that he learns what kind of qualifications he must have.

2. If you are going to see a new doctor, make sure you find out where he went to college.

3. All men are created equal.

4. If anyone has seen my glasses, could he please return them to me?

5. The congressmen voted to cut the pay of retiring veterans.

6. When you get to the gate, tell the guard he needs to issue you a parking permit.

7. Each flight attendant should have her flight bag ready.

8. Any person seeking to apply for a job as a nurse should include her résumé and letters of reference with the application form.

9. I would never vote for a politician if he did not agree with my opinion on abortion.

10. Each new student must have his or her photo taken for a student identification card.

Trimming the Excess Fat

One common misconception among students is that formal English is long-winded English. In an attempt to sound sophisticated, many try to stick as many large words as they can into their papers, usually with the assistance of a thesaurus. Remember, though, that thoughts can be sophisticated even if the words are relatively simple.

Cut Extra Words

Remember this one simple guideline: if a word can be cut, then cut it. Every word counts, and excess words only create problems. Extra words can distort your meaning, or worse, they can bore your reader. If a reader has to wade through too many words to find the meaning, you, as a writer, will be in trouble. Look at this example:

Original:

It was evident that the leader of the Chinese communists, who was, of course, Mao, had given up control of the day-to-day running of the government's functions.

Rewritten:

Evidently, Mao had relinquished control of the Chinese government's daily functions.

Choose Short Words

There is nothing implicitly evil about a thesaurus except how some students use it. These students feel too uncertain about their selections of words and choose to spruce up their work with synonyms gleaned from the pages of a thesaurus. The danger is twofold: a synonym may have a different connotation than the original word, and a synonym may distance the reader if its meaning is vague or obscure.

Original:

The sleuth apprised his patron that her lucre was circumspectly secluded.

Rewritten:

The detective told his client that her money was safely hidden.

Keeping It Simple

Simple does not mean simplistic, nor does it not mean using only one-syllable words. *Simple* means trying to communicate in a way that makes understanding easy. In fact, trying to express complicated ideas in a simple and clear fashion can be difficult. Most professional writers work hard to reach the largest possible audience, and that means trying to keep their writing as simple as possible. *Simple* means conveying the exact meaning intended, uncluttered by needless words and expressions. The vocabulary should be only as difficult as necessary to communicate effectively.

Simple also means trying to avoid excessive subordination or coordination. Clearly, you do not want all of your sentences to consist of just one independent clause, but if you string together too many complex or compound sentences, you are likely to confuse your reader.

Original:

Even though national parks and monuments were shut down and even though government workers were furloughed over Christmas with no paychecks, Congress still was unable to agree with the White House on a budget deal because of the partisan bickering and because of posturing toward the 1996 elections, which caused politicians to be more unwilling to compromise with each other than ever before.

Rewritten:

Even though national parks and monuments were shut down and government workers were furloughed over Christmas with no paychecks, Congress was still unable to agree with the White House on a budget deal. Partisan bickering and posturing for the 1996 elections caused politicians to be more unwilling to compromise than ever before.

The Physical Presentation

One aspect of writing that many students overlook is the physical presentation of their final drafts. Whether you turn in a final draft that is clean, legible, and bound or one that is messy, hard to read, and scattered among loose sheets of paper says a lot about how much you value what you have produced.

Guidelines for Typed or Printed Materials

As a rule of thumb, any paper produced outside of class time should be typed or printed on a computer. The following are some general guidelines for the proper presentation of typed or printed papers. Be aware that your instructor may have different or additional requirements.

- Use 8½- × 11-inch white paper. Colored sheets are only a distraction.

- Use medium or thick bond paper. Do not use erasable paper because the ink will smear when touched.

- If you are printing out your essay on a computer printer, be sure that the final product is easily readable. That means that the print is dark and at least near-letter quality. Don't forget to remove the tractor-feed strips!

- Keep wide margins on all sides. A good rule of thumb is one inch all around.

- Double-space your entire work.

- Indent the first word of each paragraph five spaces or half an inch.

- Do not use a title page for a short work.

- Your name, your instructor's name, class number, and the due date of the assignment should be typed on separate lines in the upper-left corner of the first page of your paper.

- The title should appear double-spaced after the due date on the first page of your paper. It should be centered, not underlined, and not placed in quotation marks. Capitalize the first word of the title and each significant word.

■ Begin your text double-spaced below the title.

■ Number each page by including your last name and the page number in the upper-right corner of your paper.

■ Use only one side of the paper unless you are using a thick bond of paper *and* you have your instructor's approval.

■ Even if you have run your essay through a spell-check program, proofread the final copy. Most spell-check programs are not able to detect usage errors, such as mistaking *then* for *than*.

■ Bind your paper using either a staple or a paper clip. Plastic folders may also be acceptable, although many instructors do not like them. Do not simply turn in loose sheets or try to fold the pages together in a corner. Such a presentation shows a lack of foresight or concern about the paper's physical appearance.

■ Keep a copy of your paper. If you type it, make a photocopy before you turn your paper in. If your paper is stored in a computer file, keep a copy of the file on a back-up disk. This copy will be helpful should your paper ever be lost or damaged.

Figure 13.1 shows an example of the first page of an essay.

Guidelines for Handwritten Materials

Occasionally, you may find yourself doing handwritten work in class, or your instructor may accept handwritten out-of-class work. Most of the guidelines—such as margins, headings, title, and pagination—should still be followed. Here are a few additional notes:

■ Use black or blue ink. Other colors are more difficult to read and can be distracting.

■ Write as legibly as possible. If your instructor cannot read your handwriting, your grade will likely suffer. If your cursive letters are difficult to read, then print.

■ Use only one side of the paper. Ink from the other side will be visible through the paper.

■ Neatness counts. If you must scratch words out, do so with a single line running horizontally through the middle of the letters.

```
                                                    Yarber 1

        Bobby Yarber
        Professor Hoffman
        English 100
        23 July 1997

                     The Well-Typed Manuscript
              As you can see, the well-typed manuscript
        follows a simple standard format. The margins are
        set at one inch all around the page. In the upper-
        right margin, you can find the student's last name
        and the page number. This should appear on every
        page of the paper. All type is double-spaced. In
        the upper-left corner, on separate lines, are the
        student's name, the instructor's name, the class
        name, and the due date. The title is centered on
        the page, and it is not underlined, put in quotation
        marks, bolded, oversized, or otherwise distinguished
        from the rest of the type.
              Use a standard character size for your type.
        Something close to 10 characters per inch (10 cpi)
        is good. Many instructors will have a hard time
        reading anything smaller. Do not use too large a
        type size because it will look as if you are merely
        padding your paper, making it appear longer than it
        actually is. Indent each paragraph half an inch or 5
        characters of 10 cpi type. Check your spelling by
        hand, even if you use a spell-checker, since most
        software programs still do not detect usage errors.
```

FIGURE 13.1
Sample
First Page of
an Essay

Student Writing Assignment: Style

Write a 500- to 600-word essay in which you analyze the differences between the style of language used in a college essay and one of the following:

a personal letter

a conversation between friends

a popular novel

a diary

a conversation with your
grandparents

a specialty or hobby-oriented
magazine

Be sure to use specific examples in your essay. Address the issues of tone, vocabulary, sentence length and complexity, and point of view.

Follow the steps listed in the Start-Up Suggestions and Self-Revision Questions. Then bring your essay to class for peer editing. Revise your essay and then complete the section labeled Your Choices: Style to discuss the decisions you made during the composing and revising process.

Start-Up Suggestions

Follow these steps before writing your first draft.

1. Search for good examples of college essays, either ones written by yourself or by peers. Examine them to see their characteristics, keeping in mind the issues discussed in this chapter.
2. Before you determine which item will serve as your second topic, you should look at several different ones. You may choose to scan the periodicals section of your library for hobby magazines or to examine some personal letters that you own. Remember, you want to find examples that will illustrate your ideas best.
3. Once you decide which item will be your second topic, find several good examples of it. Don't limit yourself to just one.
4. Make a list of the characteristics you find in both your college essays and your second topic.
5. Underline or mark in the margins of the works specific examples of those characteristics.
6. Formulate your thesis and topic sentence outline along the lines of a comparison/contrast essay.

Self-Revision Questions

Answer these questions after writing your first draft and before rewriting the draft for submission to your peer-editing group.

1. Review your thesis sentence. Is it in proper comparsion/contrast format? Does it address both similarities and differences?

2. Which method of development have you chosen: point by point or subject by subject?
3. Check your topic sentences. Does each one relate back to the thesis sentence?
4. Have you included specific examples of every characteristic?
5. Does your essay express a central opinion, or is it merely a compilation of observations?

Revise you essay and submit it to your peer-editing group.

Peer-Editing Guidelines for Style

Answer these questions for each of the essays written by the other members of your peer-editing group.

1. Does the essay have a good title? What is it?
2. What is the thesis sentence?
3. Is it an adequate thesis sentence for a comparison/contrast essay?
4. Are the points of support logical and convincing?
5. Which method of development did the essay use: point by point or subject by subject?
6. Is specific evidence presented? Of what type?
7. Does the essay make clear the connection between the evidence and the general observations made?
8. Does the essay have effective transitions between ideas and betweeen paragraphs?
9. What is the crystalline word?
10. What one change would most improve the essay?

Prepare the final draft of your essay, taking the comments of your peer-editing group into account.

Your Choices: Style

Answer these questions after you have finished your final draft.

1. How did you choose your second topic?
2. How did you come to your thesis sentence?
3. How did you choose your topic sentences?

4. How did you choose what evidence to include?
5. Did you leave out any evidence you now feel should have been included?
6. Why did you choose the method of development that you used?
7. Did you feel compelled at any point to change your thesis or to change your second topic? Why?
8. How did you choose which writing samples to use?
9. How did you choose which characteristics of the writing samples on which to focus?
10. Did you agree or disagree with your peer editors' choice for the crystalline word? If you disagreed, did you make any revisions to emphasize the word you wanted?

COMPUTER EXERCISE

Take an old essay or paragraph that you wrote for an earlier assignment. With your writing partner or a writing group, rewrite your old essay or paragraph for matters of style. When you rewrite a passage, use all capital letters so that you can easily distinguish the rewritten passage from the original. Then you can rewrite your partner's essay or paragraph.

Once you are done, compare the new version of the essay or paragraph to the older one. Is it easier to read? It should be. Save both versions and share them with the rest of your class. You may even want to label the versions "Before" and "After" just to emphasize the difference.

THE REVISION PROCESS:
A Student Writing Sample

Tom, an older student, decided to write his essay comparing college essays to personal letters that he had received over the years, mostly from his own grown children. He used his own college essays, all of which he had written for English classes.

As part of the prewriting process, Tom made two lists of characteristics that he found in the two writing situations. Here are the lists:

Letters	*Essays*
personal	*impersonal*
assumes you know people	*no previous knowledge*
age of writer shows	*no age shows*
bad grammar and spelling	*attempts good grammar*
very personal tone	* and spelling*
uses I and You a lot	*impersonal*
not very complicated	*avoids I and you*
* sentences*	*some complicated*
personal subjects	* sentences*
	not very personal subjects

After examining his list, Tom decided that he had found many more differences than similarities. He knew that there were obvious similarities—both were written in English, for instance. This did not seem too promising, though. He tried his first thesis sentence:

Although both personal letters and college essays are written in English, letters are more personal and less formal than essays.

This thesis sentence seemed too repetitious, and the similarity of being written in English was too broad. So, Tom decided to do another prewriting technique. This time, he chose to freewrite on the two topics. This is what he came up with:

Personal letters and college essays are both forms of writing and in my life they're both written in English what do they have in common? well, sometimes both try to tell me something, whether its Tanya telling me about her children or Jason talking about his job in either case they write very well actually although not like they're writing an essay I mean they don't expect me to grade their letters of course I do remember when Jason was in college he wrote asking me for money so he could go to Europe with his fraternity buddies so I guess that's like an essay because he was trying to argue his point he was pretty good too because I did send some money even though it didn't turn out to be a very good trip my college essays I don't like how they look now but even then at least you could see I was trying to be serious and get the point across

When Tom stopped writing and examined his focus freewriting, he knew he had found the key: *the purposes of letter writing and college essays sometimes were the same.* Some letters were trying to inform him and other letters were arguing a point to him. This led to Tom's new thesis:

Letters and college essays sometimes have the same purposes, but letters are more personal than essays.

With this new thesis sentence, Tom was ready to put together a thesis and topic sentence outline. He decided to use a point-by-point format to draw out the differences more.

Thesis: Letters and college essays sometimes have the same purposes, but letters are more personal than essays.

TS1: Letters are often used to inform and argue.

TS2: College essays are often used to inform and argue.

TS3: Letters use a personal style.

TS4: College essays are more formal and should be grammatically correct.

Tom was now ready for his first draft. To prepare, he gathered his letters and essays and marked them ahead of time so that he knew which sentences or phrases from each he would quote. That made it easier for him when he actually sat down to write the essay.

Letters vs. Essays

Style is an important part of how people write. If everyone had the same style, writing would be quite boring. But writers have different styles because they are different people, and people are also writing for different reasons. Two things that people write are personal letters and essays in college. Letters and college essays sometimes have the same purposes, but letters are more personal than essays.

Letters are often used to inform and argue. Sometimes letters write to inform, such as telling the reader about the latest developments in the writer's life. For example, my daughter wrote me recently to tell me that her children, my grandchildren, have been accepted into a special program for gifted children at school. My son once wrote me to argue that I should give him money to go to Europe on vacation. His argument was so good I gave him the money.

College essays also inform and argue. One essay I wrote told about an important event in my life, which was for me coping with the death of my wife. One argument I made in a college essay was in favor of providing school vouchers so that parents could better afford to send their children to private schools and get a better education.

Letters use a personal style. Most of the personal letters I receive are from my children and are addressed, "Dear Dad." They also assume that I know the people they're talking about (I usually do), such as when my son wrote, "Dave left General Motors to take a job in Portland." I knew that Dave was a friend of his. Letters from

my children use familiar slang expressions, contractions, and lots
of I and you.

College essays use a formal style with correct grammar and
punctuation. In college essays, one is not supposed to use the
first or second person pronouns, and one is not supposed to use
contractions. College essays assume no previous knowledge and
are written as though anyone might read them. Take this sentence
for example: "One can see that the causes that led to the American
involvement in Viet Nam were noble, but the method was flawed."

College essays and letters are very different in how they're
written, but sometimes they reasons they're written are similar. They
can be both written to argue points or to inform a reader. Just make
sure you never get the two mixed up!

Tom's peer group had a lot to say about this essay. Two members
of the group felt that the similarities he found were off the assignment
and that he should deal with language only and not purpose. A third
member disagreed and thought that purpose was a part of language
and style. They all agreed that they wanted more examples. They also
felt that Tom undercut his own points when he used first- and second-
person pronouns in one part of his essay and later said that college essays weren't supposed to have them. The hook in the introduction
seemed uninspired. No one liked the conclusion very much since it
seemed repetitive. One peer editor said the last sentence was silly,
which was a turn-off.

Tom put a lot of work into his rewrite. He wasn't convinced that
purpose was not an important part of style, so he decided to keep that
part over the objections of two of his peer editors. Still, he decided he
needed to be more specific throughout and to remove the first- and second-person pronouns except in the quotations. Here is Tom's final
draft:

Letters vs. Essays

Writing styles are as different as writers themselves. Style is
an important part of how people write because if everyone had the
same style, writing would be quite boring. Styles can also change,

depending on the situation. Personal letters and college essays are two different writing situations. Letters and college essays both have similar purposes, but letters are more personal than essays in their approaches to those purposes.

Letters are often used to inform and argue. Sometimes, letters write to inform, such as telling the reader about the latest developments in the writer's life. For example, letters can inform grandparents about their grandchildren's progress in school. Letters can also argue certain points, such as when a college student successfully argues to a parent why he should be given a loan to go to Europe on vacation. Letters, in fact, may be written for a wide variety of purposes.

College essays are also written for a wide variety of purposes, including to inform and argue. An essay can inform the reader about an important event in a writer's life, such as the death of a spouse. College essays can argue a point. One college essay argued in favor of providing school vouchers so that parents could better afford to send their children to private schools and get a better education. College essays generally inform or argue a central idea or thesis.

Letters accomplish their purposes using a personal style of language. Most of the personal letters use familar forms of addressing the reader, such as "Dear Dad." The personal letter writer also assumes that the reader knows the people mentioned in the letter or knows if the reader is not acquainted with that person. For instance, in the sentence "Dave left General Motors to take a job in Portland," the reader knew that Dave was a friend of the letter writer. Letters use familiar slang expressions, contractions, and lots of I and you. None of this offends the reader because the letter writer knows the reader well enough that the style of language they communicate in is shared.

College essays use a formal style with correct grammar and punctuation. In college essays, one is not supposed to use first-

or second-person pronouns and one is not supposed to use contractions. College essays assume no previous knowledge and are written as though anyone might read them. Take this sentence for example: "One can see that the causes that led to the American involvement in Vietnam were noble, but the method was flawed." The writer of college essays cannot assume anything about the reader, except that the reader speaks English. That means the writing will be impersonal and distant.

College essays and letters have different styles. Writers of college essays assume nothing about their reader; personal letter writers know their reader. Both are forms of communication, though, that try to achieve similar purposes.

When Tom filled out his Your Choices questionnaire, he remarked that he had chosen to write about personal letters because of the pleasure he had received from them over the years. He felt generally pleased with his rewrite. He was confident that he had made the right decisions about the issue of purpose and style that had been raised by his peer-editing group. Still, overall, he felt that the assignment had constrained him a bit; since the assignment was an essay *about* language, he had to conform to the expectations of the essay format. He would have liked to have been a little freer with the structure and a little more personal in his writing style.

GRAMMAR INSTRUCTION AND EXERCISES:
Colons and Semicolons

Colons and semicolons are among the most misunderstood forms of punctuation. The rules of each are simple, however, and with sufficient practice, you should be able to master both.

Colons

Colons have several possible uses but are most commonly used in three ways:

1. *To introduce a list or quotation.*

Three conspirators attended the meeting: Professor Gregg, Anna Torres, and Claude "The Tiger" Magnussen.

The steps to complete the shutdown of the hardware are as follows:
1. Inform all area managers of the impending shutdown at least twenty minutes prior.
2. Ensure that two backup disks have been properly made, labeled, and stored.
3. Place protective lids or coverings over all equipment.
4. Power down.

Socrates, as written down by Plato, spoke these words near the end of his life:

But already it is time to depart, for me to die, for you to go on living; which of us takes the better course is concealed from anyone except God.

2. *To set off a phrase, summary, or explanation.*

The performance would have been a success except for one minor flaw: the lead actor never showed up.

The radio volume was raised, but the static still drowned out the music: they could not hear the broadcast at all.

3. *To announce an important statement or question.*

The results of the latest AIDS research has left researchers more puzzled and concerned than ever: Will the virus continue to mutate? Will they ever be able to stop its destructive behavior?

The winner of the National League Cy Young Award has been announced: Greg Maddux has won once again.

Note: Do not place a colon between a verb and its objects or a preposition and its objects.

Original:

The two countries I want to see on my honeymoon are: Spain and France.

Rewritten:

The two countries I want to see on my honeymoon are Spain and France.

(See pages 391–93 for further discussion of colons.)

Semicolons

There are two principal uses of semicolons:

1. ***To join two independent clauses, especially to show a close relationship between the clauses.***

   You do not have to go to college to be a success professionally; the ability to work hard and learn on the job can make you a success, as well.

   The old woman used to be a leading movie actress; however, she had fallen on hard times before she died.

2. ***To separate items in a series when the items contain commas or are unusually long.***

   The members of the committee were Rosa Sanchez, public relations officer; Mark Ellis, vice president for internal affairs; Dick Nizet, chief of personnel; and Pam Engel, assistant executive officer.

   The following teams are synonymous with success on the playing field or court: the New York Yankees, who call on such great names as Babe Ruth, Lou Gehrig, Joe Dimaggio, and Mickey Mantle; the Boston Celtics, with stars such as Bob Cousy, Bill Russell, and Larry Bird; and the Dallas Cowboys, with legendary players such as Bob Lilly, Roger Staubach, Tony Dorsett, Emmitt Smith, and Troy Aikman.

(See pages 393–95 for further discussion of semicolons.)

Rewrite the following sentences, adding any missing colons or semi-colons as required. Remove any incorrect punctuation or unnecessary words. If a sentence is already correct, mark it with a *C*.

1. The parts of a Cross pen are: first, the silver point and second, the gold body.

2. I always knew there was one friend I could count on, Rick.

3. The worst part about the experience was: the nausea.

4. In our court system, no one is concerned with what is right or wrong, the only thing that matters is the law.

5. The express train to New York City just left five minutes ago, a local should be coming along soon though.

6. My favorite presents this Christmas were my two Beatles CDs, from my aunt Lois, my briefcase, from my girlfriend Cathy, and my subscription to <u>Road and Track</u> magazine, from my mother.

7. The travel book listed a number of good places to eat; the Ritz, the Waterfront, and the Park Palace.

8. His dissertation was accepted for publication, now all he had to do was finish it.

9. Peter and Brenda had an exciting announcement, they had decided to get married.

10. There was one objection to the plan: it wouldn't work if the security guards had time to sound the alarm.

14 Under the Gun

Writing Essay Examinations

Write about your worst experience in taking a test or examination. Why was it so bad? What could you have done to make things better?

Some courses require you to write in class, usually with a time limit. You may have exams, midterms, or finals that require written sections in which you must produce complete essays. Some English courses, perhaps the one you are in right now, require an end-of-term essay written in a timed situation in response to a prompt or reading. Such a test may serve as an entrance exam into a higher-level English course.

No matter what the circumstance, writing an essay in a short period of time is stressful. After all, you do not have time to do your best work. However, just like you can learn to write essays outside of class, you can learn skills that will help you succeed at in-class essay writing.

The Purpose of Timed Writing

One of the first things to be aware of is *why* in-class writing examinations are given. Essay examinations are given to test your ability to recall information, to organize information in a fresh way, to distinguish between important and unimportant material, and to understand relationships within a subject. You may expect essay examinations in such fields as history, political science, foreign languages, philosophy, and a wide array of social, cultural, and religious studies courses.

In English classes, essay examinations are sometimes given less as a test of your subject matter mastery and more as a test of your writing skills. An English essay examination may test your ability to think critically about written material, develop a thesis sentence, construct logically reasoned arguments, supply sufficient evidence, provide transitions, and express yourself in grammatically correct English.

Writing in Response to a Prompt

A **prompt** is an article or short essay that you are expected to read, understand, and be able to write an essay about. A frequent technique in English courses is to require that students read a prompt and then write essays in response to a question based on the prompt, all within a time limit.

Writing in Response to a Question

In some examinations, you will not have a prompt. Instead, the instructor will simply ask you to answer a question by writing an essay. In such a situation, you must be familiar with the subject matter ahead of time. Your instructor may allow you to consult a textbook (an *open-book* test) or may not (a *closed-book* test). Even in an open-book test, you must be familiar with the material so that you are not trying to learn about the subject during test time.

Succeeding at Essay Examinations

What is the best way to ensure success with essay examinations? First of all, remember that no special hints or techniques will make up for severe deficiencies in writing skills. There is no special trick that can negate trouble with grammar, spelling, or punctuation. These are skills that you must learn if you are to succeed at writing in English. Beyond that, however, there are ideas to keep in mind about how to approach essay examinations.

Reading the Prompt

If you are allowed to read the prompt before the start of the examination, do so. Look up in a dictionary every word that you do not know, and be sure that you understand the concepts or ideas brought up in the prompt.

Your instructor may devote class time to discussing the prompt before the examination. Take full advantage of this opportunity to clear up any questions you may have. Make sure that you understand what main points the author of the prompt is making, what the minor points are, what type of evidence is being used, how reliable and relevant that evidence is, and what objections exist to what is being said in the prompt.

If you are allowed to write on your prompt, do so. Underline or highlight significant passages, write in the margins definitions of any unfamiliar words, and circle passages you still do not understand. You may want to put a star next to any passage that seems suitable for quoting in your own essay.

Dealing with Anxiety

Like actors who have forgotten their lines, some students freeze on the day of an essay examination. A certain amount of stress and nervousness is understandable, perhaps even inevitable, but too much stress can be debilitating. How can you overcome stress?

Learn to relax. Since everyone has different means of relaxing, you should learn some relaxation techniques that work for you. Some people like to drink coffee, but for others that would be like throwing gasoline on a fire. Right before the test some people take out a magazine—something fun—just to give themselves a diversion. You might try breathing exercises, listening to music, or talking with other members of your class about something unrelated to the examination.

Avoid activities that are likely to create stress, including studying up to the very last minute. Rarely does last-minute studying help. Instead, you are likely to aggravate your anxiety, trying to cram too much into your head. You should stop studying well before the time of your examination and give yourself the opportunity to relax.

Once the test has started, of course, you may not able to do some of these relaxation techniques. Instead, if you feel too much stress building, take a slow, deep breath and exhale slowly. Close your eyes for one or two moments, and try to relax the muscles in your body. Roll your head around if necessary. In short, you can do quiet, unobtrusive relaxation exercises at your desk should you need to.

Test anxiety can be a grade killer. Don't let it get the better of you.

Responding to the Question

One very important and seemingly obvious bit of advice is to make sure that you *answer the question you have been asked*. Too often students get excited and write the paper they *want* to write rather than the paper they are *asked* to write. This can happen if a student has tried to anticipate the examination question, has prepared extensively only for that question, and then finds that a different question has been asked.

The best way to be sure that you answer the question is to remember this: your thesis sentence should answer the question. That will make it certain that there is no confusion about whether you have answered the question and whether the rest of your essay develops that answer fully. If your test question reads "Argue for or against requiring students to wear uniforms in public schools," your thesis sentence should respond to the question using many of the same words: *Students attending public schools should not be required to wear uniforms.*

Another key to answering the question asked is to look at the verb that dictates your response to the question. Many questions will require you to respond using at least one of the rhetorical modes. Here is a list of verbs and their purposes:

Verb	Purpose
Analyze	To break something down into parts or to show how something works, as in "Analyze the role of computers in the workplace."
Classify	To divide into categories based on a single, unifying principle, as in "Classify the different types of personalities found in our nation's leaders."
Compare	To examine the similarities between two items, as in "Compare the raising of children to the growing of houseplants."

Contrast	To examine the differences between two items or people, as in "Contrast the League of Nations with the United Nations."
Define	To give the meaning of a word, often an abstract term, as in "Define the term *justice*."
Describe	To tell how something looks or how something happened, as in "Describe the movements required to perform a pirouette."
Explain	To give information about something. This can be used with rhetorical modes, as in "Explain the causes of the Civil War."
Illustrate	To give examples of something, as in "Illustrate how modern medicine has made life better for the average person."
List	To create an array of items, either in parallel or in most important to least important or vice versa, as in "List the factors necessary for a successful business venture."
Trace	To show a process *or* to show causal relationships, as in "Trace the origins of ancient Greek culture" or "Trace the series of events that led to the start of World War I."

Outlining under Pressure

You might think that in a timed situation, outlining would be a luxury only the fastest writers could afford. Keep in mind, though, that failure to outline your essay before you begin writing can lead to writing an incoherent essay. In an incoherent essay, the points of support or controlling ideas may not relate to the thesis sentence, and the evidence may be irrelevant or even contradictory to the points you are trying to make.

Allow yourself anywhere from five to ten minutes at the start of the examination simply to think about the question and chart your response. Determine your thesis sentence and your three controlling ideas *before* you begin to write. This should be enough information for you to quickly sketch an informal outline in which you state your thesis sentence and three topics you will address. Such an informal outline might look like this:

Thesis: Students attending public schools should not be required to wear uniforms.

— Inhibits students' freedom of expression
— Skirts the real problems in public schools
— Will not substantially save on the costs of clothes

The point of writing an outline for yourself is to keep your essay on target throughout. You don't need to make a very detailed outline to do this, just enough to guide you along.

Beginning Your Essay

Your in-class essay should have all of the essential structures of the essay as discussed in Chapter 10, including an introduction, main body, and conclusion. Of great importance is your introduction, since it sets the tone for your whole essay. Remember to grab your reader's attention with a hook. Then provide a lead-in to your thesis that sets up the subject matter of your essay. If your essay examination is based on a question in response to a prompt, your lead-in should include the author's name and title of the prompt. Furthermore, if the question is directly based on the prompt, you may wish to provide a one- or two-sentence summary of it. That way, your thesis sentence will make more sense as a *response* to the prompt.

Using Evidence

One of the keys to being successful in an in-class essay is to use specific examples instead of gross generalities. If you are asked to respond to a prompt, one effective means of doing this is to find phrases or sentences in the prompt that you can quote in your own essay. If you receive your prompt before the examination day, you may be able to find other articles or essays on the same subject. Memorize several key phrases or sentences that you might use from those materials; you never know what might came in handy during the examination!

Some essay questions will allow you to respond based on your personal experience. If you do so, be sure that your use of personal experience is connected to the specific point you are trying to make. Avoid the tendency to drift into narrative. Remember that you are trying to prove your thesis sentence. Use examples as pieces of evidence, not as a substitute for analysis or observation.

Common Pitfalls to Avoid

Students who fail at essay examinations do so for a number of reasons besides a lack of writing skills. The following are a few common errors.

Rushing in Too Quickly

Too often, students receive the assignment and begin writing with barely enough time to consider the question. Try to spend anywhere from ten to twenty percent of your total time on prewriting activities. If you have fifty minutes to produce an essay, you can generally afford to spend the first five to ten minutes reading the question carefully and doing some quick prewriting, including forming a thesis sentence and sketching an informal outline. If you have more total time to write your examination, you can devote a greater amount of time to your prewriting activities.

Beginning Poorly

Never assume that the reader knows what you are talking about. Do not refer to the prompt before you have introduced its name, title, and summary. Otherwise, the reader is apt to be confused. Also, do not refer to your title as though it were a sentence in your essay. Consider it distinct from your paragraphs. Of prime importance is to set up the lead-in to your thesis sentence. Essays that begin with the thesis sentence or that provide evidence in the introduction generally do not fare well.

Lacking a Thesis Sentence

The lack of a thesis sentence in an essay will generally cause enormous troubles for you and your instructor. All essays must have a thesis sentence—even ones produced under timed circumstances. Your thesis sentence should be your answer to the question posed. Without a thesis sentence, your essay will not make any central point or argument; consequently, the essay will be a collection of observations with no direction or purpose.

Changing Your Mind

Another possible result of failing to prewrite effectively is that you may change your mind about your position as you are writing. The result may be that you begin arguing one side of an issue and end up arguing the opposite view. Sometimes, students are not even aware that they are doing this because they begin writing without any idea of where they are headed. Essentially they are just writing down thoughts as they come into their heads. Such an essay examination winds up looking more like a freewriting exercise than a reasoned response to a prompt.

Failing to Proofread

You should leave yourself time at the end of the period to proofread your essay. Because you are writing in a timed situation, you are more likely to make mistakes. Allow yourself the chance to fix them if possible. Try to make your corrections as neatly as you can—a simple straight line through words you wish to delete will be enough. Your instructor will appreciate seeing that you are capable of recognizing and fixing your own mistakes during an in-class essay examination.

Neatness Counts!

Poor handwriting can be a detriment to your grades. After all, if your instructor has difficulty reading your handwriting, she may simply lower your grade. When you write in a timed situation, the natural tendency is to write faster, which can cause your legibility to suffer. Be conscious of this problem, especially if you know from past experience that your handwriting is not particularly good.

Also, keep in mind the tips discussed in Chapter 13 about handwritten materials. Write on only one side of the paper, unless instructed otherwise. Even in examination books, commonly known as *blue books,* you should take care to use only one side of the paper. If your handwriting is particularly difficult to read, you may wish to skip every other line, as well. Bring several examination books with you on exam day so that you do not run out of paper.

Student Writing Assignment: Timed Essay

Your instructor will provide you with a prompt, either from this textbook or from another source, and will also give you a question based on the prompt. You have fifty minutes in which to write an essay in response to the question.

In essay examinations or competency exams, you will not have the opportunity to meet with a peer group to help you revise a rough draft and create a polished final draft. Therefore, the peer-editing guidelines have been removed from this Student Writing Assignment. Still, you may be able to read your essay sometime after the period has been completed, so a Your Choices: Timed Essay questionnaire has been included; you should think about the choices you made during the examination.

Start-Up Suggestions

Follow these steps before the timed essay examination.

1. Read the prompt carefully. Look up any words that are unfamiliar to you. Be sure that you understand all the concepts discussed in the prompt.
2. If you are given the prompt before the examination day, spend time in the library searching for additional material on the same topic. They may provide you with useful insights or evidence that you can quote in your essay.
3. Try to anticipate what questions you may be asked on the prompt. Then try to decide how you might respond to each question.
4. Write informal outlines for each of the possible questions you have anticipated.
5. Get a timer, set it to fifty minutes (or whatever time limit you know you will face), and do a practice run on your own.

Self-Revision Questions

Answer these questions after writing your essay examination.

1. Do you have a title?
2. Have you mentioned the author and title of the prompt in the introduction?
3. Have you summarized the content of the prompt in the introduction?
4. Do you have a thesis statement that answers the question asked?
5. Do you have three controlling ideas that logically relate to the thesis?
6. Have you remembered to use specific evidence and not just broad generalizations?
7. Have you quoted material from the prompt or from any other related material?
8. Have you provided adequate transitions?
9. Do you have an adequate conclusion?
10. Have you proofread your essay and checked grammar, spelling, and punctuation?

Submit your essay examination to your instructor.

Your Choices: Timed Essay

Answer these questions after you have completed the essay examination.

1. How did you choose your title?
2. How did you choose your thesis?
3. How did you choose your three controlling ideas?
4. How did you choose your method of development?
5. How did you choose what evidence to quote from the prompt?
6. Did you choose specific evidence or did you stay on a more general level?
7. How did you choose materials other than the prompt to use as evidence?
8. Did you make sure that each of your main body paragraphs had a wrap-up sentence?
9. Was your conclusion fully developed? Did you answer the question *So what?*
10. What technical errors did you have time to fix?

COMPUTER EXERCISE

If you have taken a practice fifty-minute in-class writing exam and you have handwritten it, type the finished exam on the computer. Pay attention to the following things:

1. Do you have a thesis sentence that answers the question asked?
2. Do you have topic sentences that help prove the thesis?
3. Do you have adequate development?
4. Is your essay complete, including a concluding paragraph?
5. Do you have many technical errors?

Now, take a second practice fifty-minute in-class writing exam, this time composing on the computer. Compare the results to the first practice exam, especially keeping in mind the preceding five questions. Try to determine whether you perform better composing your essays first by hand or by typing on the computer. If you find that you do better composing straight on the computer, check with your instructor to see if you can write your in-class exam in this fashion.

Essay examinations and competency exams are sometimes based on a student's ability to respond to a question based on a prompt. The following article is an actual prompt used in a competency exam.

The Inherent Need to Create Need
Jerry Mander

Advertising exists only to purvey what people don't need. Whatever people do need they will find without advertising if it is available. This is so obvious and simple that it continues to stagger my mind that the ad industry has succeeded in muddying the point.

No single issue gets advertisers screaming louder than this one. They speak about how they are only fulfilling the needs of people by providing an information service about where and how people can achieve satisfaction for their needs. Advertising is only a public service, they insist.

I have never met an advertising person who sincerely believes that there is a need connected to, say, 99 percent of the commodities that fill the airwaves and the print media. Nor can I recall a single street demonstration demanding one single product in all of American history. If there were such a demonstration for, let's say, nonreturnable bottles, which were launched through tens of millions of dollars of ads, or chemically processed foods, similarly dependent on ads, there would surely be no need to advertise these products. The only need that is expressed by advertising is the need of advertisers to accelerate the process of conversion of raw materials with no intrinsic value into commodities that people will buy.

If we take the word *need* to mean something basic to human survival—food, shelter, clothing—or basic to human contentment—peace, love, safety, companionship, intimacy, a sense of fulfillment—these will be sought and found by people whether or not there is advertising. In fact, advertising intervenes between people and their needs, separates them from direct fulfillment and urges them to believe that satisfaction can be obtained only through commodities. It is through this intervention and separation that advertising can create value, thereby justifying its existence.

Excerpted from "Four Arguments for the Elimination of Television" by Jerry Mander (Morrow/Quill). Reprinted by permission.

Consider the list of the top twenty-five advertisers in the United States. They sell the following products: soaps, detergents, cosmetics, drugs, chemicals, processed foods, tobacco, alcohol, cars, and sodas, all of which exist in the realm beyond need. If they were needed, they would not be advertised.

People do need to eat, but the food which is advertised is *processed* food: processed meats, sodas, sugary cereals, candies. A food in its natural state, unprocessed, does not need to be advertised. Hungry people will find the food if it is available. To persuade people to buy the processed version is another matter because it is more expensive, less naturally appealing, less nourishing, and often harmful. The need must be created.

Perhaps there is a need for cleanliness. But that is not what advertisers sell. Cleanliness can be obtained with water and a little bit of natural fiber or solidified natural fat. Major civilizations kept clean that way for millennia. What is advertised is *whiteness,* a value beyond cleanliness; *sterility,* the avoidance of all germs; *sudsiness,* a cosmetic factor; and *brand,* a surrogate community loyalty.

There is a need for tranquility and a sense of contentment. But these are the last qualities drug advertisers would like you to obtain; not on your own anyway.

A drug ad denies your ability to cope with internal processes: feelings, moods, anxieties. It encourages the belief that personal or traditional ways of dealing with these matters—friends, family, community, or patiently awaiting the next turn in life's cycle—will not succeed in your case. It suggests that a chemical solution is better so that you will choose the chemical rather than your own resources. The result is that you become further separated from yourself and less able to cope. Your ability dies for lack of practice and faith in its efficacy.

A deodorant ad never speaks about the inherent value of applying imitation-lemon fragrance to your body; it has no inherent value. Mainly the ad wishes to intervene in any notion you have that there is something pleasant or positive in your own human odor. Once the intervention takes place, and self-doubt and anxiety are created, the situation can be satisfied with artificial smells. Only through this process of intervention and substitution is there the prospect of value added and commercial profit.

The goal of all advertising is discontent or, to put it another way, an internal scarcity of contentment. This must be continually created, even at the moment when one has finally bought something. In that event, advertising has the task of *creating* discontent with what has just been bought, since once that act is completed, the purchase has no further benefit to the market system. The newly purchased commodity must be gotten rid of and replaced by the "need" for a new commodity as soon as possible. The ideal world for advertisers would be one in which whatever is bought is used only once and then tossed aside. Many new products have been designed to fit such a world.

Students were given the prompt two class meetings prior to the examination. They were told to take the prompt home and read it carefully. When they returned to class, they spent that period discussing the contents of the prompt. At the next class, they took the examination.

On examination day, students were given fifty minutes to respond to the following question based on the prompt:

> In Jerry Mander's article "The Inherent Need to Create Need," Mander argues that advertisers sell only what people do not need. Do you believe that advertising provides products that are truly in demand or that it creates needs where they otherwise do not exist? Respond, based on your own observations, knowledge, and reading.

Of the essays that were written that day, two examples are included. Here is the first, written by Student A:

The Inherent Need to Create Need

All of us are exposed to advertising every day. There's no getting away from it? But do we really need it? What really is need? Can we live without soap? I don't think so.

Jerry Mander says in his article that advertisers are selling only what people don't need, but I don't buy that because I see lots of things I need on TV or in magazines. Ok, maybe I won't die if I don't have them, but isn't life more about being happy? If we bought only what we truly needed to live, we wouldn't have very much at all, and I think a lot of people would be out of jobs because if you think about it a lot of jobs are involved in these things.

So I don't think that Jerry Mander is right at all. If he isn't even sure we need soap. I don't want to be near him. I like people who smell nice, not all sweaty.

He also misses out on the positive side of advertising. A lot of advertising is very original and entertaining. Some commercials are more entertaining than the TV shows they're on. It used to be people left the TV to go to the bathroom or get something to eat when commercials came on, now people stay and watch and leave during the shows!

So, all in all, Jerry Mander is wrong about advertising being bad. We need advertising to know what we want to buy.

This essay, written by Student A, would likely fail a competency exam for entrance into a transfer-level English course, and if it were given a letter grade, it would likely receive a D or F grade.

There are several specific problems with Student A's essay. We can examine several aspects:

- The title is not original to the writer but is the same title as Mander's article. You may think this is a minor point, and it is, except that this title signals to the reader that the writer has not thought enough about his own work to come up with an original one.

- The writer fails to mention the name of the author and the title of the prompt in the introduction, and, of course, fails to provide a summary of the work, as well.

- The introduction fails to provide a thesis sentence. *I don't think so* is not adequate to serve as a thesis sentence.

- The introduction asks too many questions when it should make statements.

- The writer confuses the issue by adding specifics (*Can we live without soap?*) instead of remaining at a more general level in the introduction.

- The essay lacks three controlling ideas. The writer knows enough to have five paragraphs in his essay, but the three main body paragraphs form no coherent argument. They do not relate to the same thesis (which is never explicitly stated) nor do the paragraphs build on each other.

■ The evidence is confusing. This is partly due to the lack of a strong thesis statement and partly due to the lack of three controlling ideas. The result is that observations are made throughout the main body, but they remain scattered. Occasionally, a good idea seeps through (such as questioning Mander's strict definition of *need*), but the essay never develops any of these thoughts.

■ The third paragraph includes a personal attack on Mander that is speculative and irrelevant.

■ The statements about the positive side of advertising are also irrelevant to Mander's argument. Mander is not questioning the technical quality or entertainment value of advertising. Instead, Student A needs to focus on what Mander is focusing on: the purpose and effect of advertising.

■ The grammar and punctuation in this essay are flawed, including run-on sentences, comma-spliced sentences, fragments, and awkward phrases.

Here is another essay, this one written by Student B in response to the same question and prompt:

I Need More Than I Really Need

Would you like to go back to living in caves, hunting every day for your food, and wearing untreated animal skins for clothing? At least your bare essentials would be met, right? While most people would agree that meeting our most basic needs is not enough, Jerry Mander proposes just that in his article "The Inherent Need to Create Need." He argues that advertisers sell the public products and services people do not really need. Mander, however, is wrong. Advertisers promote many products that improve the quality of life people lead, such as food products, medical products, and personal hygiene products.

Advertisers promote food products that help improve people's quality of life. Mander argues that advertisers push processed foods, not healthy foods, but, of course, Mander is wrong. Grocery stores compete with each other over the prices of tomatoes, uncooked ground beef, bread, and innumerable other food products that are very healthy. Stores advertise these products as a way to entice customers to shop at their stores rather than competitors'. They advertise chips and frozen TV dinners, as well, but a person can choose not to buy those products.

The advertising of medical products fills an important need. Who wants to live with pain? That seems to be Mander's universal solution. He even says to await "the next turn in life's cycle." This attitude suggests that pain is good. Well, pain is not always good, nor is a runny nose, sore throat, or bad cough. If a product can make a person feel better, why not use it? The logical extreme of Mander's position is to use no medicine at all, and I do not think many people would agree with that.

Personal hygiene may not be a biological necessity, but it is a social one. Sociologist Cynthia C. Strinberg wrote, "Humans are social creatures and must learn to accommodate each other." It's a lot nicer for people to wear deodorant than to assault everyone with bad body odor. Yes, this is not mandatory for personal survival, but in a practical world, we need it. Besides, clean is good—things like soap and detergent help keep people from spreading germs.

Advertisers may create need, but these needs are part of what can make life more enjoyable. While Mander may want to return to the caveman days where people had only their most basic needs met, most people prefer to have more fun. Healthy food, helpful drugs, and perfumed soaps are fine, as are many other products that are advertised. After all, if no one needs it, no one has to buy it.

Student B has written a far more successful essay and would likely be allowed entrance into transfer-level English if this were written for a competency exam. Here are several reasons why:

▪ The title is intriguing and fun. A good start never hurts.

▪ The introduction begins with a rhetorical question that most readers would answer in the negative, which is just what the writer wants. That leads into the presentation of the prompt, including the author's name, the title, and a brief summary of its main idea.

▪ The thesis sentence is clear and unambiguous and includes three controlling ideas that are logically connected to the claim.

▪ Each of the three main body paragraphs has a topic sentence that effectively introduces the topic of the paragraph and relates that topic back to the thesis.

▪ Evidence in each of the three main body paragraphs is clear, common, and specific. For example, most people can relate to grocery store advertising from their own experience, most people have had some occasion to use over-the-counter drugs, and most people can recognize the social value in pleasant body odors.

▪ The presence of material from an outside source (the quote from Strinberg) adds to the writer's credibility and shows good preparation.

▪ The conclusion is effective, restating the thesis and answering the question *So what?* with the implication that no one has to be a mindless pawn of advertisers.

▪ The sentences are well constructed, with good variety. Grammar, spelling, and punctuation are all in order.

Why did Student B write a better paper than Student A? To know for certain, we would have to ask how much preparation the two students did. Certainly, Student B looks as though she had a strong command of the topic. She had thought about the material well enough to have ready examples at hand. Also, Student B sketched an informal outline during the opening five minutes of the exam period. This was her informal outline:

Thesis: Advertisers promote many products that improve the quality of life people lead.
— *Food*
— *Drugs*
— *Hygiene*

That was all Student B needed to do to keep herself on track throughout her essay.

Student A, on the other hand, appears to have done very little preparation, did not sketch an informal outline before beginning the test, and did not formulate a thesis before beginning to write. Student A laid the groundwork for a poor essay by not preparing well.

GRAMMAR INSTRUCTION AND EXERCISES:
Using Quotation Marks

Whenever you use material from another source, you must indicate that to your reader. Quotation marks are used to signal the reader that the words being presented are rendered exactly as they were first spoken or written. Here are several circumstances and situations in which to use quotation marks.

1. ***Use double quotation marks to set off direct quotations. Use no quotation marks for indirect quotations.***

   Dr. Ho said, "I'm afraid you're going to die. It may take thirty or forty years, but you will definitely die."

   Brad sputtered, "The tan is everything though!"

Gail said that she was ready to move to Atlanta next week.

Colleen told her children that playing in the empty field was dangerous.

2. *Use single quotation marks to separate a quotation within a larger quotation.*

Janice laughed, "Oh, I can just see Hank asking 'But where did you hide the beer?' with that shocked look on his face!"

"Yes," said the young child, "my mother is not home right now, but I can't talk to you because she told me 'Never talk to strangers.'"

Several other punctuation marks are typically used with quotation marks, and you should be aware of how they are used.

1. *A comma is used to separate introductory or explanatory remarks from a quotation.*

Beth asked, "Is this all there is to eat?"

2. *A comma or period at the end of a quotation is placed inside the quotation mark.*

"There is a great danger that the foreign fishing trawlers will overfish the region," declared the local newspaper editorial.

FEMA director James Witt said, "The state of emergency has been lifted for three counties."

3. *A colon or semicolon is placed outside the quotation mark.*

According to Elaine Hadnot, the payout for workers' compensation claims "has reached epidemic proportions that threaten small businesses everywhere"; still, many workers fear that changes to the system will only hurt their financial and physical futures.

In the glory days of Las Vegas, nobody was more popular than the members of the self-styled "Rat Pack": Frank Sinatra, Dean Martin, Sammy Davis, Jr., Joey Bishop, and Peter Lawford.

4. *An exclamation point or question mark that is part of the quoted material is placed inside the quotation mark. One that is not goes outside the quotation mark.*

"Did you hit the fire hydrant?" asked Graham.

"Look out!" yelled Red.

Did Horace really say, "I miss my mommy"?

I told you not to sing "White Christmas"!

(See pages 395–97 for further discussion of quotation marks.)

EXERCISES Place quotation marks where appropriate.

1. The campaign manager reported that donations had fallen off dramatically since word of the scandal broke.

2. Uncle Dub announced, It's time to break out the champagne.

3. Once you take out the trash, said Kate, vacuum the living room.

4. Sal asked, Did Josh really lose to his grandmother at checkers?

5. Stop blowing the horn! yelled the mechanic.

6. I always wanted to use the line If you want me just whistle, said Davene, but the opportunity has just never happened.

7. Debbie's response to Mike's proposition was No!; as a result, Mike did not attend the prom.

8. The angry janitors said, We want our job title changed to Maintenance Engineer!

9. Did Scott really say Last year I earned $150,000?

10. Joseph announced that he was joining the navy to earn money for college.

Reviewing the Rules

A Guide to Grammar, Spelling, and Punctuation

Knowing how to use the English language effectively is essential for anyone wishing to succeed in college. When speaking, people rarely follow all the rules of grammar. Spoken English can violate any number of principles, especially when speakers are using slang or dialect. Standard written English, however—the kind required in most college classrooms—has specific rules and guidelines. As a writer, you should be aware that you stand a good chance of confusing your reader if your writing does not conform to these rules. As a student, you should be aware that most instructors stress the importance of standard written grammar, spelling, and punctuation. Becoming a successful, competent writer, therefore, means that you must master the fundamentals of the English language.

This guide will help you achieve that mastery over grammar, spelling, and punctuation. Some of the most basic rules are covered here. Many have already been covered in the Grammar Instruction and Exercises sections of earlier chapters, but additional rules and guidelines have been added here. In addition, new examples and exercises have been provided to give you assistance in understanding key concepts.

Parts of Speech

Every word in the English language belongs to one of the eight parts of speech. Many words can, in fact, serve as more than one part of speech. The parts of speech are noun, pronoun, verb, adjective, adverb, preposition, conjunction, and interjection. In the following pages you will learn to recognize and use all of them.

Nouns

Nouns name people, places, things, and ideas. **Common nouns** are the names of general people, places, and things. **Proper nouns** are the names of particular people, places, things, and ideas. **Collective nouns** name groups of people and things. Consider the following:

> **Erin** showed the **teacher** the **frog** in her **pocket.**
>
> Proper   Common   Common   Common
> noun   noun   noun   noun

> The **class** squealed with **delight** when the **frog** escaped from
>
> Collective   Common   Common
> noun   noun   noun
>
> **Mr. Perez** and hopped out the **door.**
>
> Proper noun   Noun

Verbs can often function in sentences as nouns; when this occurs, they are called **verbals.** Gerunds (the *-ing* forms of verbs) and infinitives (the *to* forms) are two types of verbals. Here is an example of each:

> **Waiting** is not easy. I have been waiting over three years for Oliver to leave.
>
> *Waiting* is a noun in the first sentence. It functions as the main verb of a verb phrase in the second sentence.

> Carol wants **to visit** the mountains in eastern Tennessee.
>
> The infinitive *to visit* is used as a noun because it names a thing—in this case, an activity.

Verbals may also function as adjectives or adverbs. (See pages 352–54 for further discussion of verbals.)

Pronouns

Pronouns are words that substitute for nouns. There are eight classes of pronouns.

   1. Pronouns that substitute for the names of one or more persons are called **personal pronouns.**

I, me, mine, my	it, its
you, your, yours	we, us, our, ours
he, him, his	they, them, their, theirs
she, her, hers	

While on tour, each member of the all-female choir is responsible for **her** own luggage.

I hope to see **you** at **our** open house this weekend.

We Americans have a tradition of celebrating the New Year by watching college football bowl games from morning until night.

   2. Pronouns that introduce dependent clauses are **relative pronouns.**

that	which	whichever	who
whom	whoever	whomever	whose

The words *that, which,* and *who* rename and refer to the nouns that they follow.

The recipe **that** we are using calls for three teaspoons of fresh ginger.

The silver mine, **which** had been abandoned over a century ago, was now a tourist attraction.

The archeologist **who** discovered the tomb fell victim to an ancient curse.

See pages 336–37 for a discussion of dependent clauses.

   3. Demonstrative pronouns indicate or point to the nouns they replace. When they immediately precede the nouns they point to, they are used as adjectives.

that	this
these	those

"We'll use **that** to make our escape," said the crook, pointing to a parked car.   Used as pronoun

These beans need to soak in water much longer.   Used as adjective

This is the magazine I used to read, but it no longer appeals to me since its editors tried a new format.   Used as pronoun

Mr. Farrell told us to load **those** bricks in the truck and take them to the construction site.   Used as adjective

4. Questions are asked by using **interrogative pronouns.**

who	which	whom
what	whose	

Who first sang "White Christmas"?

To **whom** does this lost puppy belong?

Which bracelet goes best with this blouse?

What gave you the idea that she would consider resigning?

Whose boots are in the mud room?

5. An **intensive pronoun** emphasizes its antecedent.

myself	yourself	himself	herself
itself	ourselves	yourselves	themselves

If you **yourself** want to go, fine, but I am staying here.

The crime **itself** was hardly unprecedented.

Even though she was raised in Nebraska, Marianne **herself** believed that moving back to Omaha would be a mistake.

6. **Reflexive pronouns** are the same words as intensive pronouns but rename or refer to their antecedents.

Marcus bought **himself** a computer screen-saving program.

She left the party by **herself**.

The activities of the congressmen left **themselves** open to charges of abuse of the taxpayers' money.

7. **Indefinite pronouns** do not refer to any particular people, places, things, or ideas.

all	any	anyone	anybody
anything	both	each	each one
either	every	everybody	everyone
everything	few	many	many a
more	most	much	neither
nobody	no one	none	nothing
one	other	others	several
some	somebody	someone	something

Anyone who finds broken glass on the floor should be careful not to step in it.

Many a race car driver has wanted to win the Indianapolis 500, but only a handful actually have.

Some view the world as a glass that is half empty; **others** see it as half full.

8. Reciprocal pronouns distinguish between the distinct or separate parts of plural nouns and pronouns.

one another   each other

The pilots congratulated **one another** on successfully completing their mission.

The couple looked at **each other** and started to laugh.

Verbs

Verbs are words that describe actions and states of being.

The driver **swerved** to get out of the way of the doe.   Action

Colleen **plays** the clarinet in the symphony.   Action

The spaghetti sauce **tasted** spicy.   State of being

The tailor **was** happy with his payment.   State of being

Verbs can also be described as transitive or intransitive. **Transitive verbs** take objects, and **intransitive verbs** do not.

Perry **watched** the dogs play together.   Transitive

Tom **painted** the bedroom white.   Transitive

Krista **marched** straight back to her bedroom.   Intransitive

Despite the gloomy weather, Heather **laughed** and **sang** with joy.   Intransitive

A **helping verb,** also known as an **auxiliary verb,** helps show the tense and mood of another verb. This other verb is referred to as the **main verb.** Taken together, a helping verb and its main verb form a **verb phrase.**

Beth **is moving** to a farm in upstate Michigan.
The auxiliary verb *is* helps the main verb *moving.*

Raymond's financial situation **has been** better in the past.
The auxiliary verb *has* helps the main verb *been.*

Last year's car models **were losing** value even as they sat on the lot.   The auxiliary verb *were* helps the main verb *losing.*

(For a discussion of verb tenses, see pages 346–48.)

Adjectives

Adjectives modify and describe nouns and pronouns.

The **rambunctious** child broke the **expensive** vase.

The **green** bicycle was found underneath the **aging** tree.

She feels **tired**.   The adjective *tired* describes the pronoun *she.*

Sometimes, nouns can serve as adjectives. When this happens, they are called **noun modifiers.**

The **computer** company reported its highest earnings of the decade last year.

Antonio wrote his **classification** paragraph on types of dishware.

(See pages 367–70 for further discussion of adjectives.)

Adverbs

Adverbs modify verbs, adjectives, and even other adverbs. Adverbs can often be made from adjectives by adding the suffix -*ly*.

Jeremy is a **slow** learner.   Adjective

Jeremy is learning **slowly**.   Adverb

An adverb explains the where, when, and how of a sentence.

"The buck stops **here**," said President Harry Truman.

Josephine **quickly** understood what the question implied.

Rosemarie fought **bravely** for her place in line.

(See pages 367–70 for further discussion of adverbs.)

Prepositions

Prepositions show the relationships between nouns and pronouns and the rest of sentences. Often, the relationships involve time or space. The following is a list of common prepositions:

about	above	according to
across	after	against
ahead of	along	along with
alongside	among	apart from
around	as	at
away from	because of	before
behind	below	beneath
between	beyond	but (as "except")
by	by means of	concerning
contrary to	concerning	despite
down	due to	during
except	except for	for
from	in	in addition to
in back of	in case of	in front of
in spite of	into	like
near	of	off
on	on account of	on top of
onto	out	out of
outside of	over	owing to
since	through	to
together with	toward	under
until	up	upon
with	with regard to	with respect to
within	without	without regard to
without respect to		

Jackie has been sitting there **since** twelve.

"I want to move **to** Brazil," moaned Terry.

This company hires **without regard to** race, ethnicity, religion, creed, or gender.

The ladybug landed **on** the flower **under** the fence **alongside** the street.

Conjunctions

Conjunctions link words, phrases, and clauses. Conjunctions come in three types: coordinating, correlative, and subordinating. **Coordinating conjunctions** link equivalent parts of sentences. There are seven coordinating conjunctions:

and	but	or	so
for	yet	nor	

Meriwether Lewis **and** George Rogers Clark explored the American Northwest.

The frame was worth over $200, **but** the painting inside it was awful.

You can see Hawaii this winter, **or** you can save your money and go to Europe next summer.

The crisis was getting worse, **so** the president held a news conference to answer questions.

Matthew wanted to go camping, **for** he had seen a program about the wilderness on TV.

The flood waters were rising, **yet** Susie wanted to stay in her home longer.

Rueben cannot speak French fluently, **nor** can he understand the Paris subway map.

Correlative conjunctions are pairs of coordinating conjunctions. They include:

either/or	neither/nor
not only/but also	both/and

Neither his ability to hit the fastball **nor** his desire to play baseball is enough to ensure that Fred will be signed by a professional team.

She lost **not only** her ownership of the land **but also** the money she invested in hog futures.

Subordinating conjunctions show the relationships between dependent clauses and independent clauses. Here is a list of common subordinating conjunctions:

after	although	as	as if
as though	because	before	even if
even though	how	if	in order that
once	provided that	since	so that
supposing that	than	that	though
unless	until	when	whenever
where	whereas	wherever	whether
which	while	why	

Since roses do well in the sun, we have planted several of them in the front yard.

I assume **that** my mother will remember my birthday.

Pedro still does not know **why** Rosa left him.

(See pages 336–39 for a discussion of dependent and independent clauses.)

Interjections

Interjections are words and expressions that show emotions and feelings but are not part of the grammatical structures of sentences. They are often followed by exclamation points or commas.

Blast! I failed my math test again!

Let me just suture this and—**oops!**—I dropped my scalpel in here somewhere.

Oh, I didn't know that piece of cake was for you.

EXERCISES   Using your dictionary, identify which parts of speech each of the following words can be. Each of the words listed here can be used as more than one part of speech. Write one sentence for each possible part of speech for each word.

Example: change

The cashier handed **the change** to the lady.   Noun

Gaston **changes** his hair style every six months.   Verb

flat	short	dirty	yes
perfect	good	quick	many
two	track	tie	spin
wall	yellow	thread	meet
form	conference	card	age

Sentence Patterns

English sentences have five basic patterns. A **sentence pattern** is a way in which a sentence can be written in English and still make sense. Every sentence consists of a subject and a predicate. The **subject** is the noun or pronoun that does the action or is described by the sentence, and the **predicate** is the verb and all the other words associated with the verb that describe the action of the sentence or the state in which the subject exists. The differences in the five patterns appear in the predicate. Here are the five patterns:

1. Subject-Verb
2. Subject-Verb-Direct Object
3. Subject-Verb-Indirect Object-Direct Object
4. Subject-Verb-Direct Object-Object Complement
5. Subject-Verb-Subject Complement

Subject-Verb

Most subject-verb sentences are short and simple. In the following sentences, the subject is indicated with the letter *S* and the verb with the letter *V.*

Ollie fished.
  S   V

Lot's wife looked back.
     S   V

Early every morning, the loud, braying burro trudged down the
                                     S   V
cobble-stoned alley.

Subject-Verb-Direct Object

A **direct object** is a noun or pronoun that receives the action of the verb. The direct object is the thing or person that is acted upon by the subject. The direct object is indicated with the letters *DO*.

The worker painted the wall.
     S   V   DO

The piano teacher touched the keys lovingly.
           S   V   DO

Rod drank the entire bottle of water.
S   V   DO

Subject-Verb-Indirect Object-Direct Object

In this sentence pattern, the **indirect object** is a noun or pronoun that does not directly receive the action of the verb. In the following sentences, each indirect object is indicated with the letters *IO*.

Joel threw Leroy the football.
S   V   IO   DO

Tony gave Marta a diamond ring.
S   V   IO   DO

Myths tell us secrets from the past.
S   V IO DO

One key to detecting an indirect object is to see if the sentence can be rewritten by moving the noun or pronoun to another spot in the sentence using a **preposition.**

Original:
The corrupt official offered the undercover agents bribes.

Rewritten:
The corrupt official offered bribes to the undercover agents.

Because the sentence can be rewritten by moving *the undercover agents* to the end of the sentence following the preposition *to,* you know that *the undercover agents* (or more strictly speaking, just the noun *agents*) is an indirect object in the original sentence.

Subject-Verb-Direct Object-Object Complement

An **object complement** is a noun or adjective that completes the meaning of the direct object by renaming or describing it. In the following sentences, each object complement is indicated with the letters *OC*.

> The judge declared her unfit as a parent.
> S   V   DO OC

> The confused natives made him king.
>   S   V   DO OC

> The editorial called the decision wrong.
>   S   V   DO   OC

Subject-Verb-Subject Complement

This pattern uses a **subject complement,** which is an adjective, noun, or pronoun that renames or describes the subject. The verb in this sentence pattern is always a **linking verb,** such as *is, feels, appears,* or *seems,* which describes a state of being or existence. In the following sentences, each subject complement is indicated with the letters *SC*.

> Glenn is an optometrist.
> S V   SC

> The brackets appear worn.
>   S   V   SC

> New York seems quiet this time of year.
>   S   V   SC

EXERCISE   Write a paragraph on a topic of your own choosing using each of the five sentence patterns at least once.

Sentence Types

A complete sentence is a complete thought. In order to form a complete sentence, you must have three elements:

1. A subject
2. A verb
3. A complete thought

What is a subject? The **subject** is the word or phrase that the sentence is about. The **complete subject** is usually a noun or a pronoun and all of its modifiers. The **simple subject** refers to the noun or pronoun only.

The First Lady stands as a role model for many women in her generation.

Earl McNeil was acquitted of the charge of shoplifting.

The elderly and infirm gentleman told his life's story to the eager young journalist.

A **verb** is a word showing an action or a state of being.

The professor **thought** about the student's question for a moment.   Shows action

Aaron Burr **shot** Alexander Hamilton in a duel.   Shows action

The tank accident **was** the private's fault.   Shows state of being

Your sister **is** so immature.   Shows state of being

A complete sentence must also express a complete thought. To determine if a sentence expresses a complete thought, you can look for certain clues. If your sentence begins with a subordinating conjunction, such as *since, when,* or *while,* you have created the expectation that something else must follow. The following sentence is incomplete because nothing follows it to complete the thought started with the subordinating conjunction *because.*

Because Becky lacks self-esteem.

What's wrong? The reader is waiting for more—What happened or what is the situation caused by Becky lacking self-esteem? The following sentence provides a complete thought.

Because Becky lacks self-esteem, she failed to stand up for herself when David demanded that she apologize for her actions.

There are four sentence types:

1. Simple sentences
2. Compound sentences
3. Complex sentences
4. Compound-complex sentences

Simple Sentences

A **simple sentence** is made up of one independent clause. An **independent clause** is a group of words that has a subject, a verb, and a complete thought. Thus, an independent clause can be a complete sentence.

> The fundamentals of macroeconomics are fairly easy to learn.

> The hunter found the ram's body near the crag.

> Only two letters on that issue were received by the newspaper editors.

Compound Sentences

A **compound sentence** is a sentence with two or more independent clauses. These clauses can be joined with a semicolon or with a comma and a coordinating conjunction. Joining independent clauses with a semicolon implies a close relationship between the clauses. A **conjunctive adverb**—such as *however, moreover,* and *therefore*—can often be used to help describe that relationship and join the clauses.

> The dinner party was a great success**, but** Yvonne felt exhausted by the end.
> **Two independent clauses joined by a comma and a coordinating conjunction**

> Many people have a hard time trying to stop smoking**;** to them, the nicotine patch can be helpful.
> **Two independent clauses joined by a semicolon**

> Life is a bowl of cherries**; however,** mine are out of season.
> **Two independent clauses joined by a semicolon and a conjunctive adverb**

Complex Sentences

A **complex sentence** contains an independent clause and at least one dependent clause. A **dependent clause** has a subject and a verb but does not express a complete thought. Therefore, a dependent clause cannot stand on its own as a complete sentence. A dependent clause is also marked by the presence of a **subordinating conjunction** or a **relative pronoun.**

> No one was admitted to the museum **because** the federal government had shut down.   **Subordinating conjunction**

The guard said **that** no one had passed through the gate for at least an hour.   Relative pronoun

Whoever holds the winning ticket will be set for life financially.

Relative pronoun

> *Note:* Sometimes the word *that* is omitted from a sentence when it introduces a dependent clause. The sentence is still a complex sentence.

The judge knew the witness was lying.

instead of

The judge knew **that** the witness was lying.

Mother thought Harold was a scoundrel.

instead of

Mother thought **that** Harold was a scoundrel.

Compound-Complex Sentences

A **compound-complex sentence** has an least one dependent clause and more than one independent clause.

> **Even though** Grandma had baked the Thanksgiving turkey by herself for years, Grandpa still wanted to help in the kitchen; he wound up burning the gravy.

> Sherry remembered a time from her childhood **when** she had played in that tunnel with friends, **but** now the tunnel seemed only damp and dirty.

> The chamber **that** held the electric chair was opened, **and** Rock saw **that** he must escape now or he would never get back to Montana alive.

EXERCISES   Rewrite each sentence, underlining the subject(s) once and verb(s) twice. Be aware that some sentences may have more than one subject or verb. Then identify whether a sentence is simple, compound, complex, or compound-complex.

1. She expected that Edith would have to wait at least twenty minutes.

2. Mr. Coates found that all of his assets had been confiscated by his creditors; his spendthrift ways had finally caught up with him.

3. That island is a well-known vacation spot, but I know one near it that is less crowded and more beautiful.

4. The yellow raft was adrift on the ocean.

5. A touch here and there will give you a new look, but your personality cannot be fixed so easily.

6. The four brothers had little in common except that they despised their father.

7. The evergreen trees are truly inspiring this time of year; I only wish I had remembered to bring my camera.

8. The star of the show was shocked that the critics panned his performance.

9. The outdoor Christmas lights were left up all year at the Anderson home because Elmer was too lazy put them up and take them down each holiday season.

10. Lane knew the time had come.

11. Katie found that digging ditches was hard work.

12. Norman knew that his time had come; nevertheless, he hoped the dental appointment would not prove too painful.

13. Luanne studied the sculpture of the goddess because she expected her art history instructor to include questions about it on the exam.

14. Neichung noticed that a piece of pie was missing.

15. While Winston was painting a seascape, she read her book on the art of origami.

16. Kim joined the sorority to make friends and to ensure that she would have a nice place to live near campus.

17. Although book binding is not a lucrative business, Marty wants to make it his life's work.

18. Randy demonstrated leadership when he led the group of campers out of the wilderness after they had run out of food and water.

19. Thomas's greatest wish is to attend the Mardi Gras in New Orleans.

20. When Maria found out that she had been accepted to graduate school, she first called her grandfather.

Sentence Fragments

A sentence fragment occurs when a group of words fails to express a complete thought. This can happen for three reasons. The fragment may:

1. Lack a subject
2. Lack a verb or verb phrase
3. Contain only a dependent clause and therefore fail to express a complete thought

To fix a sentence fragment, you must first determine what is missing.

Missing a Subject

A sentence that lacks a subject fails to answer the question Who or what is doing the action in the sentence?

Raced against the clock to finish the project.

Dreams of being reunited in the afterlife with Jerry Garcia.

Exhibited inappropriate behavior at the opera.

Each of these fragments needs a subject.

Brenda raced against the clock to finish the project.

My good friend Bob dreams of being reunited in the afterlife with Jerry Garcia.

The drunken billionaire exhibited inappropriate behavior at the opera.

Missing a Verb or Verb Phrase

A group of words that lacks a verb or verb phrase fails to describe the action or state of being in the sentence.

Original:

Seagulls nature's beach cleaners.

Two palms side by side in front of the archway.

The pilgrimage to Rome during the spring.

Rewritten:

Seagulls **are** nature's beach cleaners.

Two palms **swayed** side by side in front of the archway.

The pilgrimage to Rome **will be held** during the spring.

Another type of sentence may appear to contain a verb but actually contains only part of a verb phrase.

Original:

Chin studying to become a nurse.

Martin faking an injury on the basketball court.

The library holding over one million books.

Rewritten:

Chin **is** studying to become a nurse.

Martin **was faking** an injury on the basketball court.

The library **holds** over one million books.

Dependent Clause Only

A group of words containing only a dependent clause will fail to express a complete thought. In order to form a complete sentence, you must combine a dependent clause with an independent clause.

Original:

Since Gunther could no longer pay his medical expenses.

When the trumpets sounded.

While the horses waited in the paddock.

Rewritten:

Since Gunther could no longer pay his medical expenses, he feared his treatment would be stopped.

When the trumpets sounded, the king entered the room.

While the horses waited in the paddock, the jockeys were putting on their racing livery.

EXERCISES

Examine the following items for sentence fragments. Rewrite each sentence fragment so that it is a complete sentence. If an item is a complete sentence, indicate it with the letter *C*.

1. The suspect's defense attorney arriving late for meeting.

2. Since the creation of killer bees in a laboratory decades ago in Brazil, a great deal of mythology about them has developed.

3. The general, as well as the senior officers, in no danger of enemy fire.

4. Sean, like many other guitar players who thought of themselves as the next Jimi Hendrix.

5. The beauty of the garden that Traci had worked on so hard.

6. The meteorologist noted that the low pressure system quickly moving westward.

7. Art, an unexpected guest, creating problems with his obnoxious eating habits.

8. Tran moved to the college area to cut down on his time commuting.

9. Six miles which were all sand, cacti, and vultures hovering overhead.

10. The engine running after the ignition is turned off.

11. The counterfeit bills discovered in a bank vault.

12. Because the world needs people like you.

13. Nicholas Cage, an outstanding young actor working in the movies today.

14. The stables needing to be cleaned out.

15. On the stage were two gigantic elephants and only one tiny elephant trainer.

16. Since David spilled his drink on the rug.

17. And isn't there to say "hello" either.

18. The golf pro sank the putt, winning the tournament.

19. Out of film in this camera.

20. For instance, love poems.

Run-Ons and Comma Splices

Run-ons and comma splices are similar sentence problems: each occurs when a sentence continues beyond its natural conclusion. Instead of ending one sentence and starting another, the writer has joined or spliced two or more sentences without any punctuation (**run-on**) or with only a comma (**comma splice**).

My uncle Tony owns a series of books about the war in Vietnam I find it so interesting to read them.   Run-on

The reports that cow's milk may be dangerous to young children seem absurd at first, further research shows some disturbing findings.   Comma splice

Julia enjoyed listening to an interview with the creators of a hit TV program, she was surprised to learn how hard it is to find good scriptwriters.   Comma splice

Family traditions seem more important the older people get they hate to see cherished rituals disappear.   Run-on

To correct a comma splice or run-on, you have four choices: use a period, use a coordinating conjunction with a comma, use a semicolon, or make one independent clause dependent. Choose the one that will make the best sentence for your purpose.

Use a Period

Use a period to separate two independent clauses. This way, each independent clause becomes its own sentence. This method works best when the two sentences are logically sequential and need no additional modifications.

> My uncle Tony owns a series of books about the war in Vietnam. I
>
> find it so interesting to read them.

Use a Coordinating Conjunction with a Comma

Another way to tie two independent clauses together is to use a coordinating conjunction and a comma. The coordinating conjunction will give the meaning necessary to show the relationship between the two independent clauses. The seven coordinating conjunctions are *and, but, or, so, for, yet,* and *nor.* Learning to use them properly will help you to create meaning. Remember, this option is available to you with run-ons as well as with comma splices.

> The reports that cow's milk may be dangerous to young children
>
> seem absurd at first, **but** further research shows some disturbing
>
> findings.

Use a Semicolon

You can use a semicolon to link two independent clauses. This will pull the two clauses together, suggesting a stronger relationship than shown just by a period.

> Julia enjoyed listening to an interview with the creators of a hit TV
>
> program; she was surprised to learn how hard it is to find good
>
> scriptwriters.

You can also add a conjunctive adverb after the semicolon if additional help is needed in making the relationship clear. If you do so, be sure to use a comma after the conjunctive adverb. Conjunctive adverbs include words such as *however, moreover, therefore, consequently,* and *hence.*

> Julia enjoyed listening to an interview with the creators of a hit TV
>
> program; **however,** she was surprised to learn how hard it is to find
>
> good scriptwriters.

Make One Independent Clause Dependent

You can avoid joining two independent clauses improperly by changing one of the clauses into a dependent clause and adding a subordinating conjunction or relative pronoun.

> Family traditions seem more important the older people get **because** they hate to see cherished rituals disappear.
>
> **Since** Craig left home to join the navy, the house has seemed much quieter.

Be aware that the meaning of your sentence may change slightly depending on which clause you make independent and which one you make dependent.

EXERCISES   Examine the following items for run-on and comma-spliced sentences. Rewrite each run-on or comma-spliced sentence. If an item is correct, indicate it with the letter *C*.

1. The school system does not work, more emphasis should be put on the teaching of fundamentals.

2. Mrs. Barrett is a good role model because she is a librarian, another reason why she is a good role model is that she participates in the lives of children who come to the library.

3. Teenagers undergo rapid physical, social, and emotional development, they often experience a great deal of inner conflict.

4. One of my favorite memories of my grandmother was when she carefully handed me a box full of big-band albums, we played them for hours on an old phonograph.

5. Because men and women have so much trouble communicating at times, one wonders how the human race has managed to survive.

6. Mastodons, camels, ground sloths, and lions used to roam the Domenigoni Valley, now they are unearthed by scientists who study their ancient remains.

7. Corporate downsizing means that large companies lay off lots of employees in an effort to increase profits for their stockholders those people who lose their jobs face very difficult times.

8. Most scientists believe the Sierra Nevada mountain range is increasing in height, new discoveries suggest though that the mountains are actually shrinking.

9. Cellular phones have joined microwave ovens and VCRs as the latest technologies to move from being luxuries to necessities for many people one can only guess what advancement will come along next to be in such heavy demand.

10. Weather is what happens each day, climate is weather over a long period of time.

11. I went back to Milwaukee to see my old home, it didn't look as big as I remembered it.

12. Bernie found that being paid in cash had its disadvantages, for one thing, he had a hard time not spending whatever was in his pockets.

13. The library staff was looking forward to moving into the new library building; they knew they had a lot of work ahead of them, however.

14. Gabriel was hoping to get tickets to this year's Super Bowl, that did not happen.

15. The lawyer came up to the victims of the accident and handed them each her business card.

16. Children's toys today are often spin-offs of movies and television shows; this shows how crafty marketing directors have become.

17. The restaurant manager took the couple to their table, handed them menus, and asked if they wanted any drinks, he signaled for the waiter to come to the table to introduce himself.

18. The cat was outside making so much noise Frank got out of bed to see what was happening.

19. Sarah's hearing aid was not functioning, she didn't hear the phone ring.

20. Even though Melissa wanted the emerald ring, she was happy with the ruby one; either ring was worth more than one month's pay for her.

Verb Tenses

The Present Tense

The **present tense** is used for events either that are occurring now or that occur on a regular basis. When writing about literature, the present tense is used, even though the author may have died along ago.

> Today I **find** that I **can** no longer **remember** her name.

> Every afternoon I **listen** to the stock market report on the radio.

> Hemingway's male characters **contain** traits of the author himself.

The Past Tense

The **past tense** is used for events that have already occurred. If two or more events in the past occur at close to the same time, the past tense is used for both events.

> I **graduated** from high school three years ago.

> Jared recently **bought** a motorcycle, but he **failed** to purchase a helmet.

> The trial **ended** with a surprise verdict.

The Future Tense

The **future tense** is used for events that will happen at some future point in time.

> Katrina **will enroll** in a weight-loss program next Monday.

> Next New Year's Eve, I **will** not **wait** until the last minute to get dinner reservations.

> Diane **will earn** twice as much next year.

The Perfect Tenses

All three time frames—present, past, and future—can be described using the perfect tenses: present perfect, past perfect, and future perfect. The **perfect tenses** allow you to distinguish the time relationship between two or more events. The perfect tenses are formed by using a form of the verb *to have* with the past participle form of the main verb (the *-ed* form in regular verbs).

> Researchers **have discovered** that walking for an hour every day is great exercise.
>
> The *present perfect* shows an action that started in the past and continues to have an effect on the present.

> Marco **had stuffed** the letter of recommendation in the wrong envelope, but a clerk discovered the error.
>
> The *past perfect* shows an action completed in the past before another action in the past.

> Pauline **will have filed** her income tax forms by the time she leaves for vacation.
>
> The *future perfect* shows an action that will be completed in the future before another action.

The Progressive Tenses

The **progressive tenses** use forms of the verb *to be* and the **present participles** (or *-ing* forms) of the main verbs. All six verb tenses can be progressive.

> Allen **is hoping** to switch jobs with Chris.
>
> The *present progressive* shows an ongoing action in the present that may extend into the future.

> Carrie **was watching** her baby take a bath.
>
> The *past progressive* shows an ongoing action in the past that has been concluded.

> Tim **will be flying** to Paris next week on business.
>
> The *future progressive* shows an ongoing action in the future.

> Eileen **has been selling** men's clothing for over six years.
>
> The *present perfect progressive* shows an action that started in the past, continues in the present, and may extend into the future.

Before his tragic accident, Darius **had been planning** to audition for a part on <u>Baywatch</u>.

The *past perfect progressive* shows an ongoing action in the past that was completed before another action in the past.

By the end of the century, the virus **will have been afflicting** people for over twenty years.

The *future perfect progressive* shows an ongoing action that will continue into the future for a specific period of time.

EXERCISES   For each of the following verbs, write a sentence in which you include it the assigned verb tense.

1. print   Present
2. build   Past
3. throw   Future
4. tap   Present perfect
5. hunt   Past perfect
6. eat   Future perfect
7. switch   Present progressive
8. move   Past progressive
9. whisper   Future progressive
10. sing   Present perfect progressive
11. cook   Past perfect progressive
12. help   Future perfect progressive

Agreement in Tense, Voice, and Person

Verb tenses need to be used with consistency and accuracy. If you shift unnecessarily or unexpectedly, you risk losing your reader. There are three kinds of unnecessary shifts: in tense, in voice, and in person.

Use a Consistent Tense

Do not shift back and forth between time periods unnecessarily. Generally speaking, if you're writing in the present tense, stay with the present tense throughout, and if you're writing in the past tense, stay with the past tense throughout.

Original:

As Shelley **spoke** to her mother, Steve **hides** in the garage.

After Cathy **purchased** the outfit, she **takes** it home and **tries** it on.

Rewritten:

As Shelley **speaks** to her mother, Steve **hides** in the garage.

After Cathy **purchased** the outfit, she **took** it home and **tried** it on.

Use a Consistent Voice

There are two types of **voice:** active and passive. A sentence written in the **active voice** has a subject that performs the action of an active verb.

Roberto **threw** the ball.

A sentence written in the **passive voice** has an object that is acted upon by the passive verb. A passive verb is constructed by using a form of the verb *to be* and the past participle of the main verb.

The ball **was thrown** by Roberto.

Sentences written in the passive voice often omit the doer of the action.

The ball was thrown.

Avoid the passive voice in your writing when possible. It has a tendency to make your writing dull and wordy.

To stay consistent, make sure your verbs remain in the same voice throughout.

Original:

The speaker resumed her lecture after a question had been answered.

This sentence is awkward because it does not indicate who answered the question.

Rewritten:

The speaker resumed her lecture after she answered a question.

Use a Consistent Person

A shift in person occurs when you shift from one point of view to another. This usually happens when you forget to follow the point of view of the subject of your sentence. There are three persons, which can be expressed in both singular and plural.

	Singular	Plural
1st person	I	we
2nd person	you	you
3rd person	he, she, it	they

The most common faults are shifting between second and third person and shifting between singular and plural.

Original:

A person should avoid charging products on credit cards if **you** want to avoid high interest fees.

Shifts from third person to second person

I have often found in **my** own experience that **we** need to use more discipline and less leniency with pets.

Shifts from singular to plural

Rewritten:

People should avoid charging products on credit cards if **they** want to avoid high interest fees.

Note: The third person plural is used to avoid the use of *he or she* in the dependent clause.

I have often found in **my** own experience that **I** need to use more discipline and less leniency with pets.

EXERCISES   Rewrite each of the following sentences, correcting any errors you find in the consistent use of tense, voice, and person. If a sentence is correct, indicate so with the letter *C*.

1. As we walked into the auditorium, you could hear the stage crew arguing.

2. A student in a physical therapy program is likely to make a decent living after they graduate.

3. Bev was trying to stop her car, but then the telephone pole was hit.

4. The air conditioning had been fixed by workers who are employed by the manufacturer.

5. If Betty wanted to join the club, she should come to any of their meetings.

6. Overfishing off the coast of Mexico is leading to the destruction of an industry that employed thousands.

7. The retailer was doing well because they have quality products and excellent service.

8. Juanita and her father are very close, although he lived in Central America.

9. When you try to find a plumber in the Yellow Pages, a blurring array of ads for plumbers is sometimes found.

10. As you leave this room, a person can feel the warmth and generosity generated this evening.

11. Debra ate breakfast slowly, but lunch was eaten quickly by her.

12. Everyone should have their fortune told some time.

13. She lost her contact lens, and now she is trying to find it on the floor.

14. Children expect toys at Christmas, but they got lumps of coal instead.

15. He found out that if you want something done right, you should do it yourself.

16. I know from experience that if you watch what you eat and exercise regularly, I can stay trim.

17. The grumpy old man worked at the desk writing checks so the bills were paid.

18. Phillipe told his wife that he loves her.

19. Zora knows about the charges against her, but she denied them.

20. The hill was climbed by Hugh, and he is a hero because of that.

Verbals

Verbals are verb forms that function as other parts of speech, such as nouns, adjectives, and adverbs. Verbals come in three forms: participles, gerunds, and infinitives.

Participles

Participles may be either past or present, depending on their endings. **Past participles** in regular verbs are marked by *-ed* endings (in irregular verbs, the forms vary), and **present participles** end with *-ing*. Participles are used as adjectives within sentences.

> The **tired** clerk put up the **"closed"** sign twenty minutes early.
>
> The past participle *tired* modifies the noun *clerk,* and the past participle *closed* modifies the noun *sign.*

> The **fallen** tree was trimmed of its branches and cut into sections by the lumberjacks.
>
> The past participle *fallen* modifies the noun *tree.*

> The cat **sleeping** in the window belongs to Amanda.
>
> The present participle *sleeping* modifies the noun *cat.*

Gerunds

Gerunds are present participles that act like nouns.

> **Writing** is a difficult but rewarding process.
>
> The gerund *writing* is functioning as the subject of the sentence.

> Bob and Carol hate **staying** in motels.
>
> The gerund *staying* is functioning as the object of the verb *hate.*

To see the difference between participles and gerunds, look at the following sentences:

> Mark and Scott are **golfing** partners.
>
> *Golfing* is a participle since it functions as an adjective, modifying *partners.*

> **Golfing** is one of Mark's favorite activities.
>
> *Golfing* is a gerund since it functions as the subject of the sentence.

Infinitives

An **infinitive** is the *to* form of a verb, such as *to watch, to listen,* and *to understand.* Infinitives can act as nouns, adjectives, and adverbs.

Maurice's goal is **to sail** around the world.

Infinitive as noun

The woman **to ask** is away from her desk right now.

Infinitive as adjective, modifying *woman*

She smiled **to conceal** her anger.

Infinitive as adverb, modifying *smiled*

EXERCISES

Identify the participles, gerunds, and infinitives in the following sentences and describe whether each functions as a noun, adjective, or adverb.

1. A blend of French vanilla bean grounds and regular grounds caused the coffee to smell fabulous without being too sweet.

2. Thirty minutes is a long time to wait for a bus.

3. The designers were told to prepare for the fall show at least six months ahead of time.

4. Screaming, the patrons fled the burning theater.

5. Michael Jordan, no longer playing professional baseball, has resumed his stellar basketball career.

6. To play tennis without the latest equipment is to put yourself at a great disadvantage.

7. Dancing remains her favorite form of exercise.

8. The man to cast in this role is Brad Pitt.

9. The right to vote is taken for granted in the United States but not everywhere else.

10. Andrea wanted to sue her employer for harassment.

11. Sighing, Paul decided he had failed.

12. The exhausted mine worker walked back to his home.

13. The children, laughing and giggling, played with the hamster.

14. The hostess to copy the most is Martha Stewart.

15. Walking is actually an Olympic sport.

16. The boxing champion held a press conference to announce his retirement.

17. To climb the mountain called "Half Dome" in Yosemite was his goal.

18. The building to demolish is the one with the shattered windows.

19. Breaking the law is a serious matter.

20. Murray wanted to eat Chinese food for lunch.

Subject-Verb Agreement

Subjects and verbs must agree in number and in person. When there is confusion about the number of the subject, problems can arise. This can be seen in the following forms:

1. A **collective noun** signifies a group, such as a team, family, class, or flock. Collective nouns are singular in form.

> The **corporation** has said that it will be laying off forty thousand employees.

> A **school** of tuna was detected by sonar.

2. A **compound subject** consists of more than one noun or pronoun acting as a single subject. When the elements of a compound subject are joined by a comma or the coordinating conjunction *and*, the subject takes the plural form of the verb.

> **Gerald, Pat, and Ann** are now selling real estate in South Florida.

> **Dennis and his crew** are experts at sailing in international competition.

When the nouns or pronouns of a compound subject are joined by *or* or *nor*, the element of the subject closest to the verb determines whether the verb will be singular or plural.

> Neither his principal nor his teachers know what to do about Page's behavior.

Either Tisha Hendrickson or Edith Myers is going to play the part of Nora for this evening's performance.

Note: In *either/or* and *neither/nor* subject constructions, placing the singular noun in the first position and the plural noun second is generally preferred.

Slightly awkward:

Either the attendants or the best man is going to have to bail the groom out of jail before the wedding.

Preferred:

Either the best man or the attendants are going to have to bail the groom out of jail before the wedding.

3. A **subject complement** follows a linking verb and is usually a noun, pronoun, adjective, or group of words that functions as a noun or adjective. For instance, in the sentence *The problem is the broken timing belts,* the word *belts* is the subject complement. Remember, however, the subject determines whether a verb is singular or plural in your sentence, not the complement.

The **reason** that the lawsuit failed **is** that our lawyers are simply incompetent.

The **shipment is** 223 pounds overweight.

4. Subjects in sentences that begin with phrases such as *There is/are* or *Here is/are* follow these phrases and determine whether the verbs are singular or plural.

There **is** no **reason** to cancel our subscription.

Here **are** the **clues** we need to find the killer.

5. Do not be confused by any phrase or clause coming between the subject and its verb.

The **singers** in the choir **are** practicing three times a week for the spring concert.

The **package** that Susan placed under the stairwell **has** come from the Fergusons.

Examine the following sentences for subject-verb agreement errors. Rewrite each sentence that has an error. If a sentence is correct, indicate it with the letter *C*.

1. The jury were sequestered for over nine months.

2. My boss, as well as other managers, are implicated in a payroll tax scandal.

3. There is without any doubt certain crises that have to be handled with outside help.

4. Once again, the navy are asked to perform a difficult and courageous mission.

5. Either the stockboys or the cashier have to take a cut in pay.

6. The rabbits that my friend Dr. Newman owns are meant for food, not for pets.

7. The core issues in the next school board election center on the rights of parents to be involved in their children's education.

8. Someone on the losing team want the head coach fired.

9. Four nuns who do missionary work in Peru is coming to give a presentation to our class.

10. Every person in this room at the time are a suspect.

11. Neither the coaches nor the team want to fly back tomorrow.

12. Congress are scheduled to vote on a pay raise.

13. Many of the passengers wait patiently for a new flight.

14. The minister, along with his congregation, are flying to Israel this summer.

15. Each of the residents were told not to drink the tap water for two days.

16. Several of the customers complains of the price increase.

17. Here is a box of chocolates that someone left on the bench.

18. The new bass player and the old drummer wants to form their own band.

19. Each of the officers at the scene were interviewed by the investigators.

20. Neither brother know if the money will ever be inherited.

Pronoun-Antecedent Agreement

A pronoun and its antecedent must agree in person and in number. An **antecedent** is the noun for which the pronoun is substituting. If an antecedent is plural, then the pronoun must be plural; if the antecedent is singular, then the pronoun must be singular.

> The **cows** in the herd are being moved to **their** new grazing lands.

> **Nobody** who wishes to earn a good living in the future should
>
> ignore **his or her** education.

> **Both** contestants wore **their** helmets.

Some difficulty comes when there is confusion in determining the number of the noun or in identifying the correct noun as the antecedent. Here are a few tips:

1. A singular pronoun is used when the antecedent is an **indefinite pronoun** such as *anybody, anyone, each, every, everybody, everything, many a, neither, nobody, no one, one, somebody,* or *something.*

> **Many a** female golfer has Nancy Lopez as **her** role model.

> **Everything** is in **its** place.

> **Everyone** wants **his or her** fifteen minutes of fame.

> *Note:* In colloquial language, many people would prefer to use the plural pronoun *their* in the preceding sentence with the singular antecedent *everyone*. You should be aware that this is not acceptable in formal English.

2. A few indefinite pronouns are always plural: *both, few, many, others,* and *several.*

> **Few** waiters **have** ever been given a tip that large.

> **Many** of the movies made today **are** simply trash.

3. A few indefinite pronouns can be singular or plural, depending on the noun for which they are substituting: *all, any, more, most, none,* and *some.* The pronoun is singular when it substitutes for a **mass noun,** which names an item that cannot be counted. The pronoun is plural when it substitutes for a **count noun,** which names items that can be counted.

Most of the money **was** spent on rent.   *Money is a mass noun.*

Most of the towels **were** washed last week.   *Towels is a count noun.*

Some of the food **is** wasted in the process.   *Food is a mass noun.*

Some of the paperclips **were** under Claire's desk.   *Paperclips is a count noun.*

4. Nouns joined by *and* usually take a plural pronoun, except when both nouns refer to the same person or thing.

An officer **and** a gentleman, **he** exuded the confidence that comes from a life of integrity.

Officer and *gentleman* refer to the same person.

A workout fanatic **and** part-time brain surgeon, **she** lived a fairy-tale life.

Work-out fanatic and *part-time brain surgeon* refer to the same person.

Awareness of the rules of subject-verb agreement can be helpful for determining pronoun-antecedent agreement. If your antecedent is also the subject of the sentence, the verb in the sentence will reflect the person and number of the antecedent. Look at this sentence:

I will bet that the workers in the union do not waste its time worrying about a strike.

You can avoid being about confused about which word is the proper antecedent by ignoring phrases or clauses between the antecedent and the pronoun. In the preceding example, the correct antecedent is *workers,* not *union.* The clue is that the sentence uses the verb *do,* which is the third-person plural form, rather than *does,* which is the third-person singular. Therefore, you can determine that the correct pronoun is *their* (third-person plural), not *its* (third-person singular).

I will bet that the workers in the union do not waste their time worrying about a strike.

EXERCISES　　Examine the following sentences that may contain pronoun-antecedent agreement errors. Rewrite any sentence that has an error. If a sentence is correct, indicate it with the letter *C*.

1. Each of the vases are cracked down their side.

2. All of the sausages are homemade, and it tastes good.

3. The Senate committee has their last meeting of the session next Tuesday.

4. Neither the decathlete nor the wrestlers was able to open the pickle jar.

5. A firefighter who wants their equipment cleaned can do so behind the station house.

6. The pair lost their battle for third place in the men's doubles tournament.

7. Every child needs to have their immunizations properly administered and documented.

8. Either the fruitcake or the doughnuts should be served or it will go stale in the cupboard.

9. Some of the pebbles were rare because of their origins.

10. Many a motorcycle racer has crashed their bike during a contest.

11. Every computer diskette should have a label on it.

12. Each type of influenza has their own characteristics.

13. Someone lost their earring in the women's bathroom.

14. Most of the speakers at the conference want his or her own special room.

15. Some of the news articles were clipped out of the newspaper if it was about the space program.

16. A few of the patrols did not return to its base.

17. Anyone can join our club now if they want to.

18. Everybody should keep quiet or they may get shot.

19. All of the gentlemen were wearing his tuxedo.

20. The tribe went to court to get their land back.

Case Forms

Nouns and pronouns appear in different **cases,** or forms, depending on their functions in sentences. Nouns stay the same, whether they are used as subjects or objects, but they do change to show possession. Most singular nouns and plural nouns that do not end in *s* add an *'s* to show possession. A plural noun that ends in *s* adds an apostrophe to show possession. (See pages 400–02 for further discussion of the use of the apostrophe to show possession.)

Pronouns, however, are more complicated. Not only do most of them change form to show possession, but they also change form when they are used as subjects and as objects. Therefore, you need to know three case forms for pronouns: subjective, objective, and possessive.

Subjective Pronouns

Use the subjective case when a pronoun is a subject, a subject complement, or an appositive, which renames the subject. The following is a list of subjective pronouns:

Singular	Plural
I	we
you	you
he, she, it	they

Here are some examples of sentences that use subjective pronouns.

While **he** is asleep, **we** can sneak out of here.   Subject of clause

The first ones to accomplish the feat were Victor and **I.**
Subject complement

James, not **she**, will be asked to participate in the symposium.
Appositive renaming the subject

> ***Note:*** In some clauses ending with verbs, the verbs are implied rather than stated explicitly. You must still use the subjective pronoun if a verb is implied.

Sheila is thinner than **I.**   The implied verb is *am.*

Karen can eat a lot more than **he.**   The implied verb phrase is *can eat.*

Objective Pronouns

When a pronoun is used as an object in a sentence, the pronoun takes the objective case. The following is a list of objective pronouns:

Singular	Plural
me	us
you	you
him, her, it	them

Here are some sentences that use objective pronouns.

Miriam handed **him** the letter.   Indirect object

Wayne entered six local art competitions, winning three of **them**.   Object of the preposition

The court decided to hang the spies—Richard and **her**.
Appositive renaming the object

Although the cars trailing **him** were approaching quickly, Kyle was not afraid of losing the race.   Object of the verbal

Also use the objective case for a pronoun that acts as the subject of an infinitive.

The managers want **us** to take a pay cut.
Subject of the infinitive *to take*

Possessive Pronouns

When a pronoun has ownership of something, that pronoun takes the possessive case. The following is a list of possessive pronouns:

Singular	Plural
my, mine	our, ours
your, yours	your, yours
his, her, hers	their, theirs
its	

Remember that *it's* is a contraction for *it is*, not a possessive pronoun. Here are some examples of sentences that use possessive pronouns.

The weaverbird, found in Europe, is noted for **its** nest-building technique.

The senator gave **her** approval to release the statement to the press.

His weather forecasting left a lot to be desired.

Please pick up **your** packet on the way out of the auditorium.

A possessive pronoun is used before a gerund to show possession.

The attorneys argued for **her** retaining custody of the children.

His speaking in favor of the library expansion measure made a big impression on the voters.

Some possessive pronouns—*mine, ours, yours, his, hers,* and *theirs*—are used as substitutes for nouns that function as subjects or subject complements.

The best pie at the state fair was **ours**.

Yours is a philosophy based on greed and bigotry.

All these children are **mine**.

Who/Whom/Whoever/Whomever/Whose

Be sure to use the proper case for the relative pronouns *who, whom, whoever, whomever,* and *whose*. This is how they are used:

Subjective: who, whoever
Objective: whom, whomever
Possessive: whose

You must be able to determine how the relative pronoun is functioning in a sentence. Look at the following examples:

The police are looking for the man **who** robbed the liquor store last night. Subject of *robbed*

Beatrice wished to know **whom** Miguel had invited to the dance. Object of *Miguel had invited*

Whoever started the fire will be charged with arson.
Subject of *started*

Whomever you choose to marry will be fine with me.
Object of *you choose*

EXERCISES   Choose the correct form of the pronoun in each of the following sentences.

1. Sly wants to play tennis with Sandra instead of (I, me).

2. (Our, Ours) is a long and difficult journey.

3. (Whoever, Whomever) answers the phone had better take a message for (I, me).

4. After the fund-raiser for public television, Mr. Hart thanked (we, us) volunteers for our time.

5. The cable was sent to (we, us) workers (who, whom) were faced with layoffs.

6. Watching the opera was difficult because of (them, their) constant chatter throughout the performance.

7. No one warned me about (him, his) eating food with his mouth open.

8. The most beautiful couple on the dance floor was Catherine and (he, him).

9. Two people—Theresa and (he, him)—were chosen to take part in the magician's trick.

10. To (who, whom) did Sam send a birthday card?

11. The purse that the security guard found was (her, hers).

12. The mine was designed to maim (whoever, whomever) stepped on it.

13. Although Art is older than (I, me), he can still lift more weight.

14. (Whose, Who's) ball is this?

15. The only people who had not seen the movie were Chris and (I, me).

16. Gretchen can toss the discus farther than (she, her).

17. Spring break allows (we, us) students an opportunity to head out to the sun and act like fools.

18. Randall wants to recite poetry to (whoever, whomever) will listen.

19. Eve says that she will marry (whoever, whomever) she pleases and does not worry about what her parents think.

20. Baby Sophie does not want (her, hers) eating schedule disrupted.

Parallel Structure

Parallel structure requires that you use the same word type and order for items in a list, for comparisons and contrasts, and for use with correlative conjunctions.

Items in a List

Items in a list require parallel structure, whether written in sentence form, as a vertical list, or as an outline.

Sentence Form

Examine the following sentences and note what elements are parallel in each one.

Jessica just wanted **to drink** a cup of coffee, **to eat** her ice cream, and **to write** a letter to a friend.   Parallel infinitives

Leon spoke **confidently, firmly**, yet **quietly**.   Parallel adverbs

The car Elden bought was **sporty, powerful**, and **expensive**.   Parallel adjectives

Marina decided to move to Seattle **because it was cheaper than Los Angeles, because her friend David lived there**, and **because she had been offered a good job there**.   Parallel dependent clauses

Vertical List Form

A vertical list is a way of organizing information of the same type.

These items were found in the care package from home:
-- shaving cream
-- razors
-- a bar of soap
-- homemade chocolate chip cookies
-- photos of my family
-- a cassette tape with personal messages from my family
-- a check

Outline Form

Creating an outline can be an excellent prewriting technique. Each element within the outline should be parallel to other elements from the paragraph or essay.

<u>Title</u>: The Death Penalty Restores Justice
  - A. The Importance of Punishment
  - B. The Ultimate Penalty for the Ultimate Crime
  - C. The Fairness of Its Application
  - D. Our Society's Need for Closure

Comparisons and Contrasts

Sentences that make comparisons or contrasts between items, either directly or indirectly, must use parallel structure. Comparisons using conjunctions such as *but* or *and* must be parallel.

> Her first child was very sweet tempered, but her second was a monster.

Parallel structure is also required for direct comparisons or contrasts.

> The coach wanted his players to come to training camp already fit, not out of shape.

Correlative Conjunctions

The use of correlative conjunctions is a convenient way to employ parallel structure.

> The bank robbers wanted **either** all the cash in the drawers **or** the keys to the safe deposit boxes.

> **Neither** the driver **nor** the passenger saw the plane coming down out of the sky.

> The director decided that **not only** was he going to fire the star actress **but also** he would recast the role with a virtual unknown.

> She wanted to apologize **both** to her husband **and** to her children.

Rewrite any of the following sentences that contain faulty parallel structure. If a sentence is correct, indicate that with the letter *C*.

1. Chandler would neither attend the lectures nor study for the examinations.

2. Victor's goals in life were to remain in harmony with his surroundings, achieve inner peace, and he wanted to marry a very wealthy woman.

3. The president announced that he wanted to shrink the budget deficit, keep health-care programs funded, and reducing the tax burden on middle-class Americans.

4. Pamela has already started crawling, gurgling, and she can sit up by herself, too.

5. Yoko felt that living in a foreign country would be an inspiration and challenging.

6. The fur coat was warm, soft, and it was beautiful.

7. Blood donors can feel proud and also have some assurances about the importance of their good deed.

8. The stale chips and soda that was lukewarm were unappealing.

9. The boxes were packed tightly, stacked neatly, and then they were completely covered with a sheet.

10. Since Veronica did not yet know about Leanne's project and since Nancy did know, Leanne felt awkward when all three of them went to lunch together.

11. The cement walkway runs up the the front doorway; the side yard is where it turns to head to the backyard.

12. The personnel office is looking to hire someone with a good education and who has a good job history.

13. Chicago in the winter is cold and it has a lot of wind.

14. Roxanne is thin, and she moves gracefully.

15. Alejandro is a hard worker, a loving father, and he is a devoted husband, as well.

16. Kay would rather work in a restaurant than sitting in an office pushing papers.

17. Each month this woman's magazine either tells you how to have a loving marriage or ways to cheat on your spouse is discussed.

18. Dr. Thomas is a man of few words and he gives a lot of money to charity.

19. The clerk's duties were to open the store, to open the cash register, and stocking the shelves before customers arrived.

20. The color of the sauce, the smell of it, and how it tasted reminded me of my mother's cooking.

Adjectives and Adverbs

Adjectives are words that modify nouns and pronouns, and **adverbs** are words that modify verbs, adjectives, and other adverbs. As a writer, you should recognize that adjectives and adverbs can be single words, phrases, and even clauses.

You should be able to determine whether a word is an adjective or adverb by how it is used in a sentence. Adjectives answer the questions Which? What kind? and How many?

The **last** song on the album is my favorite.   Which?

The **golf** shirt is in the washing machine.   What kind?

Derrick managed to carry **six** pies in **one** trip.   How many?

Adverbs, on the other hand, answer the questions When? How? How often? Where? and To what extent?

The stakes race was run **last**.   When?

The cat stalked the mouse **quietly**.   How?

The wealthy family donated to charity **regularly**.   How often?

Place the books **there** on the shelf.   Where?

The blanket **partially** covered the body at the crime scene.   To what extent?

Adverbs can also modify adjectives and other adverbs.

> The subway system upgrades were **quite** expensive.
>
> Modifying the adjective *expensive*

> The postal service employee was working **rather** slowly.
>
> Modifying the adverb *slowly*

Beware of confusing adjectives with adverbs. Be sure not to use adjectives to modify verbs or verbals.

> Original:
>
> Martha must move **quick** if she does not want to be hit by the ball.

> Corrected:
>
> Martha must move **quickly** if she does not want to be hit by the ball.
>
> Use an adverb to modify the verb *move.*

> Original:
>
> If you want to dress **casual**, don't wear your diamond tiara.

> Corrected:
>
> If you want to dress **casually**, don't wear your diamond tiara.
>
> Use an adverb to modify the verbal *to dress.*

There is one exception to this rule: use an adjective to modify a verbal if the verbal is the subject of a sentence that uses a linking verb.

> Running is **healthy**.
>
> The adjective *healthy* modifies the verbal *running* preceding the linking verb *is.*

Good and Well

One particularly confusing set of adjectives and adverbs is *good* and *well*. *Good* is an adjective but often is misused as an adverb when the word *well* should be employed.

> Original:
>
> The Yankees didn't play very **good** tonight.

> Corrected:
>
> The Yankees didn't play very **well** tonight. Adverb modifying *play*

Good is an adjective when used after a linking verb (a verb that shows a state of existence) to describe the condition of the subject.

> The progress on the project is **good**.   Adjective describing *progress*

> Whitney Houston looks **good** in her latest movie.
> Adjective describing Whitney Houston's appearance

> The new sofa feels **good**.   Adjective describing the touch of the sofa

Well is used as an adverb and an adjective. When *well* is used as an adjective following certain linking verbs (such as *look, seem, be,* or *feel*), it means "in a state of good health."

> Lt. Frakes shoots **well** in marksmanship contests.
> Adverb describing how Lt. Frakes shoots

> Dugan sat up studying **well** into night.
> Adverb describing how long Dugan studied

> The labrador does not feel **well** after having undergone such an invasive operation.
> Adjective describing the labrador's state of health

EXERCISES

Rewrite the following sentences so that the adjectives and adverbs are used correctly. Indicate each correct sentence with the letter *C*.

1. Shaquille O'Neal plays basketball good.

2. The infants are crying too loud for me to hear you.

3. Merrilee feels badly about having been rude to her colleagues.

4. Doctors examine their patients careful before writing out prescriptions.

5. He admitted that his handwriting was bad.

6. The old woman was walking too slow for the driver of the bus to wait any longer.

7. She figured her gifts were fair economical.

8. The odd scientist thought that the chemistry lab smelled well even as others fled from the stench.

9. The cautious optimistic viewpoint held that things would at least get no worse.

10. My new car handles so good.

11. I was pleased to hear that you did so good on your test.

12. This restaurant is terrible: the service is slow, and the food tastes horribly.

13. When Crispin first spotted the deer, it was walking slow.

14. The red velvet drapes looked impressively behind the cherry wood furniture.

15. The mother scolded her children for playing too loud.

16. The lotion helps her skin feel smoothly.

17. The dinner smelled great and tasted deliciously.

18. Andre's midlife career change seemed dangerously.

19. The dog is feeling good now that the veternarian has given him some medication.

20. Since it was her first time on a solo flight, Christina flew careful.

Vocabulary

The Dictionary

It is doubtful that anyone knows how to spell every word in the English language. So, if you can accept that you will sometimes encounter words in your reading and writing with which you are unfamiliar or that you are unable to spell, then you can accept the need for a dictionary.

A dictionary can be your best friend, whether you are working as a reader or a writer. Unfortunately, you may make the mistake of using a dictionary only to check spelling. However, dictionaries have other uses.

Dictionaries give the meanings of words. Of course, there are ways of learning what a word means without using a dictionary. For instance, when you are reading, you can often determine what a word's meaning is by carefully studying the context in which it appears. Read this sentence:

The prices at the restaurant were quite expensive, but the serving sizes were Lilliputian.

If you do not know the word *Lilliputian,* you can guess by the context and tone of the sentence that it must mean something like "very small." Indeed, "very small" is one accepted definition of *Lilliputian.*

Prefixes, Suffixes, and Root Words

Sometimes, the context of a word is not enough to help you determine meaning. Many instructors encourage you to learn prefixes, suffixes, and the root meanings of words. This is valuable and insightful advice. For instance, if you were to encounter the word *metamorphosis* and you knew that the prefix *meta* means "a change of position or condition" and *morph* as the root means "form," you could determine that *metamorphosis* means "a change in form."

The following is a brief list of prefixes:

Prefix	Meaning	Example
ante-	before	antechamber
anti-	against	antidote
bi-	two	bicycle
circum-	around	circumnavigate
hyper-	beyond, super	hypersensitive
intra-	within	intramural
inter-	between	intersection
macro-	very large	macroeconomics
mega-	great	megaphone
micro-	very small	microscope
neo-	new	neologism
poly-	many	polygamous
post-	after	postpone
pre-	before	prepay
sub-	underneath	submarine
un-	not	unstoppable
uni-	one	uniform

The following is a brief list of suffixes:

Suffix	Meaning	Example
-able	capable of	unthinkable
-al	process of	dismissal
-al	of, relating to	sectional
-ant	one who	defendant
-er	one who	boxer
-hood	state, condition of	neighborhood
-ible	capable of	horrible

Suffix	Meaning	Example
-ion	process of	admission
-ish	of, relating to	Turkish
-ism	act, practice of	pacificism
-ist	one who	druggist
-ity	state, quality of	sanctity
-ive	tends toward	destructive
-ness	quality of, degree	happiness
-or	one who	director

The following is a brief list of root words:

Root	Definition	Example
bio	life	biology
ego	I, self	egotistical
hydro	water	hydroelectric
jur	law	jury
manu	hand	manual
polis	city	metropolis
psych	soul	psychology
script	to write	scripture
tele	distant	telescope
therm	heat	thermometer
veritas	truth	verifiable

Many dictionaries will give you the meanings not only of the word itself but also of the prefix, root, and suffix that comprise the word. Thus, by consulting a dictionary, you can learn both the word and its parts.

A dictionary can tell you the meanings of words you are unfamiliar with and whose prefixes, suffixes, and roots you do not know. When looking up a word in the dictionary, be sure that you are referring to the correct part of speech. The meanings of some words can vary from one part of speech to another. Even within one part of speech, however, you may find different meanings. Some dictionaries will supply you with sample sentences to show the various meanings of a word. Use these sample sentences as a test of the word you are looking up. Does that meaning make sense? *It is very important not to assume that the first definition listed in the dictionary is the one that applies to your situation.*

When you have found the correct meaning, write it down in the book or magazine in which you found the word. (Of course, do this only if the reading material belongs to you.) This will help you to memorize the meaning of the word.

Divide the following words into prefixes, roots, and suffixes. Define the parts using either a dictionary or the list provided earlier in this section.

1. transportation
2. mistaken
3. substandard
4. vocational
5. unnatural
6. macroeconomics
7. cooperation
8. conform
9. illegal
10. terrestrial
11. symphony
12. thermal
13. telepathy
14. circumstance
15. repellant
16. hyperbole
17. intraregional
18. bicameral
19. communion
20. posterior

Spelling

Spelling in English is chaotic. There are a few simple rules that you can follow, but they all have exceptions. You will probably do best to check your spelling with a dictionary whenever you are unsure about a word.

Some Simple Spelling Rules

The following rules will be valuable in assisting you in your spelling:

1. Many people remember the *ei* and *ie* rules by reciting an old rhyme:

   I before *E*
   except after *C*
   or when sounded like *A*
   as in *neighbor* or *weigh*.

Here are a few examples of words that follow this verse:

believe	grief	niece	thief	
ceiling	perceive	receive		
freight	neighbor	sleigh	vein	weigh

Here are a few exceptions: *ancient, either, foreign, leisure, weird.*

2. Drop the silent *e* when adding a suffix that begins with a vowel.

value	valuable		accuse	accusative
extreme	extremity		game	gaming
love	lover			

Here are a few exceptions: *courageous, dyeing, noticeable.*

When the suffix begins with a consonant, do not drop the silent *e*.

achieve	achievement	hate	hateful
nine	nineteen	hope	hopeless
tame	tamely		

Here are a few exceptions: *duly, ninth, wisdom.*

3. Double the final consonant when the consonant is preceded by a single vowel in a one-syllable word.

fat	fatter	hit	hitting
mat	matted	shop	shopping
top	topped		

In a word with more than one syllable, double the final consonant after a single vowel if the stress falls on the last syllable.

admit	admitted	begin	beginning
occur	occurrence	prefer	preferred
repel	repellant		

Here are some exceptions: *conference, preference.*

4. When a word ends in *y* appearing after a consonant, change the *y* to *i* when you add a suffix. Don't change the *y* to *i* if the suffix already begins with an *i*.

baby	babies	carry	carried (*but* carrying)
harry	harried	thirty	thirtieth
wary	warily		

If a word ends in *y* appearing after a vowel, do not change the *y*.

attorney	attorneys	boy	boyish
donkey	donkeys	play	played
tray	trays		

Here are some exceptions: *paid, daily, said.*

5. To form the plurals of most words, add an *s*:

books	shirts	lamps

To form the plurals of words that end in *s, ch, sh,* or *x,* add *es.*

bosses	dishes	churches	taxes

Some words ending in *f* or *fe* change the *f* to *v* in their plural forms:

half	halves	knife	knives
leaf	leaves	life	lives
wife	wives		

Here are some exceptions: *roofs, chefs, chiefs.*

Some words ending in *o* add *es* to form the plural if the letter before the *o* is a consonant.

cargo	cargoes	echo	echoes
hero	heroes		

A few words are the same for both singular and plural.

fish	deer
sheep	series

Some words form their plurals by changing their spellings.

Singular	Plural
child	children
foot	feet
man	men
tooth	teeth
woman	women

6. Some words that come from other languages form plurals that have to be learned. You will want to consult a dictionary if you are not certain.

Singular	Plural
basis	bases
crisis	crises
datum	data
hippopotamus	hippopotami
medium	media
parenthesis	parentheses
phenomenon	phenomena
syllabus	syllabi

Commonly Misspelled Words

The following is a list of commonly misspelled words:

ably	absence	abundance
academic	accept	accidentally
accommodate	accommodation	accompanied

accuracy	achieve	achievement
acknowledge	acquaintance	acquired
across	address	adequate
admittance	advertise	advertisement
advice	affect	affectation
aggravate	aging	all right
allowed	almost	altar
alter	altogether	amateur
analysis	analyze	anonymous
anxiety	apparatus	apparent
appearance	arguing	argument
arithmetic	athletic	audience
awkward	bachelor	basically
beautiful	becoming	beginning
believed	benefitted	boundary
breath	breathe	bureau
business	cafeteria	calendar
campaign	candidate	capital
capitol	career	carrying
ceiling	cemetery	certain
chef	chief	chosen
column	coming	committee
competent	competition	condemn
conscience	conscientious	conscious
continuous	critical	criticism
criticize	deceive	decision
definite	definitely	definition
dependent	desirable	desperate
devastating	development	difference
dining	disappear	disappoint
disastrous	disease	dissatisfied
divide	doesn't	echoes
effect	efficient	eighth
eligible	eliminate	embarrass
emphasize	enthusiastic	environment
equipped	exaggerate	excellent
exercise	exhaust	existence
explanation	familiar	fantasy
fascinate	February	fictitious
fiery	finally	financially
forehead	foreign	foremost
forth	forty	fourth
fulfill	gases	gauge

glamorous

grievance

guard

happiness

heroes

hygiene

imitation

incredible

innocence

intelligence

irresistible

it's

knowledge

legitimate

lesson

lightning

loneliness

losing

marriage

mileage

morale

musician

necessary

obstacle

occurred

omitted

parallel

personnel

possess

presence

probably

pronunciation

quantity

recede

relevant

repetition

ridiculous

salary

schedule

seize

sergeant

skeptical

stationary

government

grievous

guidance

harass

humorous

hypocrisy

immense

indefinite

inquiry

intercede

irritate

jealous

knowledgeable

leisure

library

likely

loose

maintenance

mathematics

mischievous

mountain

mysterious

ninety

occasion

occurrence

opposed

pastime

physician

preceding

prevalent

procedure

psychology

questionnaire

recommend

religious

restaurant

sacrifice

Saturday

science

separate

severely

sophomore

stationery

grammar

guarantee

happily

height

hurriedly

illegal

incidentally

independence

insistence

interfere

its

judgment

laboratory

lessen

license

literature

lose

maneuver

medicine

moral

muscle

naturally

noticeable

occasionally

omission

optimistic

permissible

pneumonia

prejudice

privilege

prominent

pursue

realize

rehearsal

reminiscence

rhythm

safety

scarcely

secretary

September

similar

specimen

studying

succeed	surprise	susceptible
technique	temperament	tendency
theory	therefore	thorough
throughout	truly	Tuesday
twelfth	unanimous	unnecessary
unusual	unusually	usage
using	vacuum	valuable
village	villain	visible
warring	weather	Wednesday
whether	whisper	whole
wholly	who's	whose
women	writing	written
yield	your	you're

EXERCISES   Correct the spelling errors in the following sentences. Pay special attention to errors in spelling that create other, unintended words.

1. Luckly, tellevision shows don't often affect me very much, because I was pretty agravatted the other day.

2. I was watching this horse, Cigar, which was raceing to beat Citation's record for consequitive wins.

3. All of a sudden, smoke started comeing out of my TV, and like that, the picture was gone.

4. I tell you, my spirits sanked low because I thought I'd losed my best friend, that TV.

5. After I bought my new TV, I started watching soap opras again.

6. I think societies conscience should not allow such embarassing fantasys on the air.

7. Last Febrary, I started watching one, and know I can not stop.

8. Its a fun pasttime, and the shows can be humorus, but frankly, in my judgement, they are usualy sophmoric and ridiclous.

9. On one show, everyone goes to eat at the same restuarant, as though there is only one in the whole city.

10. I know I should stop watching, but I am too exciteed when ever my show is on to miss it.

Capitalization, Abbreviations, and the Use of Numbers

Capitalization

Here are thirteen rules for capitalization:

1. Capitalize the first word in a sentence.

She had trouble with her new camera until she read the instruction manual.

Has the dog been fed yet?

> ***Note:***   If the first word in a sentence is a number, write the number out, unless the number represents a date.

Thirty-six people were injured in the train wreck.

1946 was a great year for having babies.

2. Capitalize the first word in a sentence that is quoted directly.

"Can you see the island?" asked the captain.

The detective asked, "Did you tell your husband about us?"

3. Capitalize the names of people, political and religious organizations, ethnic groups, languages, and nationalities. Capitalize any adjectives derived from them, as well.

Oakley Hall	Democrats
Catholicism	Spanish
England	Asian American
Africa	

4. Capitalize the names of relatives and professions when they precede people's names and when those people are addressed directly.

Uncle Dennis lives in the suburbs.

Professor Quintana writes poetry in his spare time.

"I love you, Mommy," said Sean.

5. Capitalize official titles when they precede people's names.

President Clinton	*but*	the president
Mayor Susan Golding	*but*	the mayor
Justice Thurgood Marshall	*but*	the justice
General Colin Powell	*but*	the general
Ambassador Lawrence	*but*	the ambassador
Senator Gramm	*but*	the senator

Titles that follow people's names are not capitalized.

Willie Brown, the mayor of San Francisco, is in Japan this week.

Jon Schnittke is vice president of this bank.

> *Note:* Exceptions to this rule are made for certain national and international figures, such as the President of the United States, the Pope, and other persons of high distinction.

Itzhak Rabin, the Prime Minister of Israel, was assassinated in 1995.

6. Capitalize the first and last words in a title and all other words except *a, an, the,* conjunctions, and prepositions.

The Marriage of Figaro	Healing through Meditation
Paris Is a Moveable Feast	Sex, Lies, and Videotape

> *Note:* You may also need to underline or place titles in quotation marks when you cite creative works in your own papers. See page 397 for the rule on underlining titles and page 396 for the rule about using quotation marks around titles.

7. Capitalize the names of streets, buildings, bridges, rivers, neighborhoods, cities, nations, specific geographical figures, schools, and other institutions.

Brenner Drive	Russia
the World Trade Center	Mount Everest
the Golden Gate Bridge	the University of Texas
the Missouri River	Apple Computers
Greenwich Village	World Wide Web
Milwaukee, Wisconsin	

8. Capitalize compass directions only when they refer to specific places or are parts of proper names.

the Pacific Northwest	the South Pole
East St. Louis	West Virginia

Note: Do not capitalize words that refer to directions.

To get to Reno from Los Angeles, you must travel north and west.

9. Capitalize the names of the days of the week, months of the year, and holidays.

Monday	Holy Week
Thursday	Yom Kippur
May	the Fourth of July
December	Mother's Day

10. Capitalize the names of particular historical events and eras.

the Gilded Age	the Great Depression
World War II	the Atomic Age

11. Capitalize the names of school subjects only if they are proper nouns or if they are used with course numbers.

biology	*but*	Biology 215
English	*but*	English 51
mathematics	*but*	Mathematics 10
Spanish	*but*	Spanish 101

12. Capitalize all references to supreme beings.

God	Jehovah
Providence	Allah
the Almighty	

Note: Capitalize pronouns that refer to supreme beings.

"I know that He watches over me always," said Hap to the congregation.

13. You may capitalize the first word of a sentence after a colon.

The mission had two goals: The invading force needed to be stopped and the defenders needed reinforcements from the rear.

Abbreviations

An **abbreviation** is a shortened version of a word. Capitalize abbreviations only when the words abbreviated are themselves capitalized. Periods are used with most abbreviations.

B.C.E.	Dr.
p.m.	Dec.
Mrs.	Ph.D.

Note: When an abbreviation appears at the end of a sentence, use only one period.

We were told to meet here at 2:30 p.m.

Some well-known abbreviations do not take periods.

USC	NFL
FBI	GOP

Acronyms are pronounceable words formed by abbreviations. Acronyms use all capital letters and no periods.

AIDS	UNICEF
ROM	NATO

Numbers

There are several rules involving the use of numbers in your writing.

1. If a number requires only one or two words, spell the number out.

over one hundred refugees	twenty-six students
fifteen semesters	five billion people

2. If a number requires more than two words, use numerals.

131 pieces of evidence	29.5 seconds
2 1/2 teaspoons of baking powder	1,939 one-dollar bills

3. When a sentence begins with a number, write the number out unless it signifies a year.

Six hundred thirty-seven lives were lost in the ferry accident.

1990 was the year I met the man I would marry.

4. Use numerals when telling time with *a.m.* or *p.m.* Write out the numbers for whole hours.

5:30 a.m.	ten o'clock
7 p.m.	midnight

5. Use numerals or write out amounts of money that can be stated in two or three words.

$3 trillion	three trillion dollars
$10	ten dollars
$.25 or (25¢)	twenty-five cents

6. Use numerals to describe addresses, apartment units, and zip codes.

10702 Dabney Drive, #92, San Diego, CA 92126

7. Use numerals for phone numbers, dates, and military units.

1-619-555-1248

the 7th Cavalry

A.D. 1962

8. Use numerals for statistics, ratios, and scores.

There has been more than a 15 percent decline in air pollution since the abolition of leaded gasoline.

The Notre Dame–Michigan State game ended with the score tied 10–10.

Dentists prefer this toothpaste over the competition by a 3–2 margin.

Rewrite the sentences, correcting any errors in capitalization, the use of abbreviations, or the use of numbers. If a sentence is correct, indicate that with the letter *C*.

1. nineteen sixty-eight was a tragic year in american history.

2. the chargers beat the raiders twenty-five to twenty.

3. unfortunately, my friend has hiv but at least he has not developed a.i.d.s.

4. dr. lionel z. demlinger's office in san diego is actually a front for the trafficking of illegal narcotics.

5. we contacted an agent of the fbi, but there was little she could do to stop mortimer.

6. the minister said that god was with us.

7. sally asserted, "the victorian loveseat is not worth less than one hundred twenty-five dollars."

8. "make sure you use at least 3 tablespoons of sugar or you won't even be able to swallow the stuff," warned grandmother.

9. buck was proud to have joined the eighty-second airborne.

10. if you watch the movie rio bravo, you'll see one of dean martin's best performances.

11. you can send me a fax at five-five-five-two-six-nine-seven.

12. I want to see you at ten hours and thirty minutes ante meridiem.

13. There has been a thirty-nine percent increase in the population of deer since the extinction of wolves in the area.

14. Larry wants to take the rolls royce out for a spin.

15. Deanna Waugh, a Professor in the engineering department, teaches engineering 202 to Sophomores.

16. we watched the president give his state of the union address on tv.

17. Bismarck is the capital of north Dakota.

18. Some Idiot turned on all the lights in the house!

19. Denise was sure to attend her local a.a. meeting weekly as part of her Treatment.

20. The secretary general of the united nations traveled to the war-torn region.

Punctuation

End Punctuation

The end of a sentence is marked with a period, a question mark, or an exclamation point.

The Period

The period is a neutral mark to be used at the end of a sentence. Use it if no particular emphasis is needed and no question is asked directly.

The keyboard was the latest model from IBM.

The senior citizens expressed concern over the delay in receiving their Social Security payments.

Lilly asked if the boys planned to stay for dinner.

(See the previous section, Capitalization, Abbreviations, and the Use of Numbers, to see how periods are used with abbreviations.)

The Question Mark

Use a question mark after a direct question.

Will the Red Sox ever win the World Series again?

Did you remember to take the clothes to the dry cleaners?

What is the equation for determining the circumference of a circle?

Be sure to include a question mark when you quote a direct question.

Simon asked, "Why did you punish me for something I didn't do?"

"Are you sure you cannot remember?" asked the special prosecutor.

Mimi inquired, "When is the party?"

(See pages 396–97 for further instruction on how to use punctuation with quotation marks.)

The Exclamation Point

The exclamation point is used to express a strong feeling or emotion. Exclamation points are often used with interjections.

I don't want to take a bath!

Careful!

Ouch! That's hot!

Yea! We're going to the park!

EXERCISES   Rewrite the following sentences using proper capitalization and end punctuation.

1. father bill, a catholic priest, asked the mourners to come forward to view the casket

2. my best class at santa barbara city college was an english class taught by professor daley

3. i have enjoyed traveling around europe and seeing wonderful sights such as the eiffel tower in paris, the lush countryside in switzerland, and the beaches of the algarve in portugal

4. my dentist asked me, "do you remember to floss every day"

5. fire fire there's a fire in the barn

6. "cold weather never kept us from delivering the mail before," said the postmaster general.

7. wanda thinks <u>singing in the rain</u> is the best movie musical ever

8. the speaker of the house of representatives has proven to be a controversial figure

9. all my relatives live in north carolina, which is just south of virginia

10. the ship keeps veering off course to the south, pushed by the tide

11. sharon traveled east all day in her honda before arriving in amarillo, texas, for the evening

12. Jean wants to go to a university, but she was turned down by both the university of florida and louisiana state university

13. help police i've been robbed

14. the cincinnati reds baseball team plays its home games at riverfront stadium

15. "well," asked tiffani, "if you didn't take the bracelet, then who did"

16. the place is losing money because it's a dump

17. The name of the pulitzer prize-winning novel is <u>the shipping news</u> by e. annie proulx

18. "i can't take it," explained terry "do i have to keep trying until i lose my sanity"

19. elie cohen, m.d., loved to sing "love me tender" while performing surgery

20. having been raised in denver, renee said that her childhood dream had been to be an olympic skier

Internal Punctuation

Internal punctuation includes marks such as commas, colons, semicolons, quotation marks, underlining, parentheses, brackets, dashes, hyphens, and apostrophes.

Commas

Here are fifteen rules for using commas:

1. Use a comma to separate independent clauses joined by a coordinating conjunction.

The boxes are too large to carry, so Ben brought the forklift.

The lecture was quite interesting, but Todd was too tired to listen.

Tabitha wrote a letter to her grandmother, and her father helped her seal the envelope.

2. Use a comma after an introductory dependent clause.

Because the ponies were hungry and cold, we had to stop for the evening.

While Penny wandered through the museum, David attended the seminar.

After May scooped up the dirty clothes, she threw them into a basket.

3. Use a comma after a modifying word, phrase, or clause at the start of a sentence.

Quietly, Keisha watched through the window.

Late last winter, Janet came to visit.

After seeing the zoo, Alex felt a new appreciation for nature.

4. Use a comma after a transitional word, phrase, or clause at the start of a sentence.

In other words, there will be no supper tonight.

However, there is no need to panic.

5. Use a comma after an introductory request or command.

Look, he can walk now.

Remember, lock all the doors before you leave.

6. Use commas to separate three or more items in a series.

In this package I received the computer, a monitor, a keyboard, and some software.

Davey ate a hamburger, french fries, and shake.

> ***Note:*** Some writers prefer that the final comma be omitted. Check with your instructor to see if he or she has a preference.

Davey ate a hamburger, french fries and shake.

7. Use commas to set off interrupting elements.

It was Tracy, not Alice, who had stolen his heart.

Colin, as well as Malcolm, had been drinking too much to drive home safely.

8. Use commas to set off direct addresses and words such as *please, yes,* and *no.*

Mr. Bennett, your prescription is now ready.

Yes, I do want some bananas.

9. Use commas to set off nonessential elements in a sentence.

Mayor Jordan, who posed nude in the shower, lost his campaign for reelection.

The lights, which are on at the moment, were quite costly to install.

10. Use commas to set off elements that qualify, contrast, or make exception with the rest of the sentence.

What this meal needs is more salt, not garlic.

His usual fee was $300 an hour, but not this time.

11. Use commas to separate coordinate adjectives.

The greedy, violent gangster finally met his end.

Keith lived in a seedy, broken-down neighborhood.

12. Use a comma to set off quoted material.

The attorney asked, "Did you kill the victim?"

"It's a beautiful day," announced the young boy.

13. Use a comma between the day of the month and the year, as well as after the year, when you write down a complete date.

September 1, 1939, was the day Hitler invaded Poland.

I will never forget January 27, 1978, because of the terrible tragedy that befell me that day.

14. Use commas to separate elements in an address.

160 Gould Street, Needham Heights, Massachusetts

1600 Pennsylvania Avenue, Washington, D.C.

15. Use commas to prevent misreading.

Original:

While he wrote Betty Lou worked in the garage.

Rewritten:

While he wrote Betty, Lou worked in the garage.

While he wrote, Betty Lou worked in the garage.

Original:

To serve the turkey will need to be juicy.

Rewritten:

To serve, the turkey will need to be juicy.

EXERCISES   Rewrite the following sentences, adding commas wherever needed. Indicate each correct sentence with the letter *C*.

1. A fund-raising organization is suing a wealthy couple contending that they failed to pay a $2 million pledge to a charity drive.

2. At present getting access to the Internet is rather simple.

3. The victim described as a woman in her sixties was struck by the truck at the intersection of Helmer and Sunset.

4. I want this package sent to 387 Pinewood Place Memphis Tennessee.

5. According to published police reports the shooting started when gang members started a fight with security guards.

6. Mom I need to borrow five dollars.

7. Poor guy he hurt his arm climbing a tree in the garden trying to rescue the neighbor's cat.

8. Look you do it your way and I'll do it mine.

9. "Come back over here" said Diego.

10. A man who stood in his doorway with a shotgun after calling the police for help was shot by a police officer who responded to the call.

11. The letter obtained by the newspaper said that cigarette companies added nicotine to cigarettes.

12. Five large churches joined to form a company to market products to their members.

13. "I think I've probably got one of the best jobs in town" said Craig.

14. Aerial photos computers and math formulas go into the making of the population count.

15. "Well it's time to head back inside" said Ron.

16. Yesterday Al left to try his luck in Atlantic City.

17. Until now the debate about raising the speed limit has been about potential traffic accidents but more people are looking at the effects of increased speed on air pollution.

18. A snowstorm is expected to move into northern Indiana on Thursday dropping up to six inches of snow.

19. Under the old policy campers were allowed to make reservations up to eight weeks in advance.

20. He wanted to be elected president, not vice president.

Colons

Colons have several possible uses:

1. To introduce a list or quotation.

   Follow these steps if you suspect your child has swallowed poison:
   1. Identify the poison or poisonous substance.
   2. Try to determine the amount taken.
   3. Call your local Poison Control Center for any treatment you should administer at home.
   4. Call ahead to the nearest hospital emergency room.
   5. Drive carefully to the hospital.

Thomas Jefferson wrote: "We hold these truths to be self-evident; that all men are created equal; that they are endowed by their creator with certain unalienable rights; that among these are life, liberty, and the pursuit of happiness."

There were several dignitaries in attendance: the mayor, the entire town council, two local representatives from Congress, and a student of the month from Fawn Elementary School.

2. To set off a phrase, summary, or explanation.

The message was frightfully clear: publish or perish.

After hours of searching, they found the cause for the malfunction: the machine was unplugged.

This decade has seen another technological advance become the latest cultural phenomenon: the Information Highway.

3. To announce an important statement or question.

The radio program was interrupted to convey the message: Japan had surrendered.

The terrorist note contained an explicit threat: a bomb would explode somewhere in the city if the prisoners were not freed.

Carla had to ask herself the question: Would it ever stop snowing in Boston?

Note: Do not place a colon between a verb and its objects or between a preposition and its objects.

Original:

My two favorite authors are: James Joyce and Virginia Woolf.

Rewritten:

My two favorite authors are James Joyce and Virginia Woolf.

Original:

On this trip, Jerome will be traveling to: Cincinnati, Cleveland, and Pittsburgh.

Rewritten:

On this trip, Jerome will be traveling to Cincinnati, Cleveland, and Pittsburgh.

4. To separate hours from minutes.

4:35 p.m.

12:01 a.m.

5. To use after salutations at the starts of business and formal letters.

To Whom It May Concern:

To Ms. Daves:

Semicolons

There are three uses of semicolons:

1. To join two independent clauses, especially to show a close relationship between the clauses.

The young nurse was a native of Ireland; the young doctor was English but had studied at Trinity College in Dublin.

Some of the questions were designed to increase the witness's credibility; however, the jury seemed unimpressed.

They all agreed on the goal; they disagreed on the way to achieve the goal.

2. To separate items in a series when the items contain commas or are unusually long.

The university regents include several unusual members: Jay Nathe, who was appointed for his legal expertise but blocked the establishment of a law school; Cecil Madison, a rich contributor to the governor's campaign; Timothy Callahan, an activist from the sixties who still wore his hair long; and Catalina Garcia, an ex-big city mayor turned rancher.

The tribal council supported gaming for the following reasons: they believed that the games would be run honestly and without any interference from criminals; they estimated that the members of the tribe stood to triple or quadruple their personal incomes; and they reasoned that the only credible alternative for land use on the reservation was as a toxic waste site, a conclusion that pleased no one.

3. To join independent clauses before a coordinating conjunction when one or both clauses contain internal punctuation.

Before the Hubble Telescope was repaired, scientists were very disappointed with its photographs; but now they are pleased, even ecstatic, about what they have seen.

Mama, not Julian, works at the gas company; and Papa has a job selling furniture, not auto parts.

EXERCISES

Rewrite each of the following sentences, using correct punctuation. If a sentence is correct, indicate that with the letter *C*.

1. Vicki speaks English at school, at home, however, she speaks Ukrainian.

2. During our trip to Asia we visited Tokyo, Kyoto, and Hiroshima in Japan, Peking, Shanghai, and Tientsin in China, and Seoul and Pusan in South Korea.

3. Karen faced a dilemma whether to continue in school or stop and take the job offer.

4. Only one thing kept Kurt from an acting career a complete lack of talent.

5. I will have to pass Chemistry 110 this year, or the school will kick me out of my major.

6. Grace wanted to drive quickly through the mountains, that turned out to be a bad idea.

7. No one asked me to dance, it was the worst night of my life.

8. I have relatives all over the country Phoenix, Arizona, Milwaukee, Wisconsin, Chicago, Illinois, and Houston, Texas.

9. With her gift certificate, Kay bought: two sets of towels, one throw rug, a shower curtain, and a toilet seat cover.

10. At last, the news came the company got the contract.

11. The most influential teachers in my life were: Mrs. Sims, Mr. Tysell, and Mr. Waxman.

12. Isaac could no longer stand the heat, he had to turn on the air conditioning before he passed out.

13. Judy was hard to find, it was harder still to persuade her to come back home.

14. The three things you must have on a backpacking trip are: your own water, a good sleeping bag, and a change of socks.

15. Spain is known for its wine, flamenco music, and bullfights, however, its romantic image belies the thoroughly modern industrial country it has become.

16. Chip saw the handwriting on the wall: His dismissal was inevitable.

17. From the lounge at the top of the building, Rod and Lisa could see: the miles and miles of Nebraska farmland.

18. The worst meal I ever ate in my life had: undercooked liver, cold potatoes, and wine that had turned sour.

19. The conversations between men outside of work usually deal with three things: money, sex, and sports.

20. The guests of honor included Jenny Langan, from the central office in Atlanta, Bobby Troyka, from the Kentucky district branch, and Pat Salinger, from Spokane, covering all the Northwest.

Quotation Marks

Whenever you use material from another source, you must indicate that fact to your reader. Quotation marks are used to signal the reader that the words quoted are rendered exactly as they were first spoken or written. Here are several circumstances and situations in which to use quotation marks.

1. Use double quotation marks to set off direct quotations.

"I like driving a Yugo," insisted Nancy.

Dub said, "Somebody had better catch that thief before I get hold of him."

Mai shouted, "Don't open that door!"

2. Use single quotation marks to set off a quotation within a larger quotation.

Andrew said with a laugh, "I love Dana Carvey's imitation of Ross Perot, especially when he says 'Now that's a shame.'"

"Did Merry really say 'Paul's kind of cute'?" asked Paul nervously.

"I just don't think that shouting 'Boogie-down!' is appropriate at a debutante ball," said Mrs. Purcell.

3. Use double quotation marks to enclose the titles of short works such as short poems, songs, articles, sections from newspapers, essays, short stories, and chapter titles.

My local paper has a regular section called "National Update."

Dylan Thomas's poem "Do Not Go Gentle" is very stirring.

"The American Scholar" is an insightful essay by Ralph Waldo Emerson.

Several other punctuation marks are typically used with quotation marks:

1. Commas are used to separate introductory and explanatory remarks from quotations.

Lisa remarked, "Taking a cruise is my favorite idea for a vacation."

Part of the will read, "I leave all my worldly goods to my parakeets."

Lara noted, "I am smart, aren't I?"

2. Commas and periods at the ends of quotations are placed inside the quotation marks.

"Please send the tractor-pull tickets directly to my home," said Diane.

"I feel so bad about last night," said Matthew sincerely, "and I would like to have the chance to make it up to you."

"The symphony's season is coming to a close," said Jill. "I'd like to see its last performance."

3. Colons and semicolons are placed outside quotation marks.

My third-grade classroom had a "community center": it was just an area where we could all sit down on the floor.

My favorite Beatles' song is "Rain"; Ringo's drum playing is especially good on that one.

Whenever I told my father about my ideas, he always said, "That will never work"; eventually, I just stopped telling him about them.

Underlining

You should underline words in your papers for several reasons. Here are two of the most common:

1. Underline the titles of long works, such as books, plays, newspapers, magazines, journals, movies, and long poems, and the names of ships, airplanes, and trains.

Monet's Table is an excellent book to have on your coffee table.

The production of **Hamlet** at the City Theater was rather disappointing this year.

Todd let his subscription to **The Atlantic** expire because he thought its articles were becoming too political.

2. Underline a word in a sentence for greater emphasis.

The police were told **not** to stop the looting.

My mother made me drive the **station wagon** instead of the Mercedes on my first date with June.

Northwestern's only loss was to Miami **of Ohio**, not the University of Miami in Florida.

> ***Note:*** If you are using a computer or word-processing system that allows you to change fonts, at your instructor's discretion you may use *italics* instead of underlining.

Parentheses

Parentheses are used to enclose commentary or extra information that is not essential to a passage. Such information may include the year of an event or a person's life span. Be careful not to use parentheses where a pair of commas should be used.

William Seward (1801–1872) played an important role in some of the most important events before, during, and after the Civil War.

By 1800, Newcastle was an important financial city (the first banks were established in 1755), with a growing industrial base.

Brackets

Brackets are used to show that a word has been changed or added by the author to clarify quoted material.

Joyce writes, "[Tennyson] is a rhymester."

"Some [of the Bosnian Serbs] are resisting the peace agreement," wrote Conklin.

"One [of the experimental cars] has a keyless door," announced the flyer.

Dashes

The dash is used to break into either a quotation or your own writing. It has the power to interrupt the flow of writing, so it should be used carefully. Consider the following:

1. Dashes can be used to show a change in thought or an interruption in a conversation.

We have to go back because we forgot—oh never mind. Let's just go on.

George started, "I was wondering—"

"George," interrupted Muriel, "please leave me alone."

2. Dashes can be used to make parenthetical remarks even stronger.

F. Lee Bailey—one of the most famous lawyers in America—began his career in startling fashion.

All of the best painters—Rembrandt, Cezanne, Manet, Monet, Picasso, and Matisse—are represented in this collection.

3. Use a dash to set off a single word or concluding remark.

When he got out of prison, he wanted to do only one thing—golf.

The black sheep of the family—Bill—has become active in local politics.

He knew where to find her—at the bank!

4. Use a dash to set off an introductory series.

Italian, Chinese, Mexican—these three types of ethnic cuisine are featured in a large number of the restaurants in America.

Ed, Bernie, and Richard—not one of them can carry a tune in a bucket.

Hyphens

There are several rules with hyphens, such as the following:

1. Use hyphens after the prefixes *ex-*, *self-*, and *all-*.

ex-wife

self-inflicted

all-encompassing

2. Use hyphens after prefixes that come before proper nouns and adjectives.

anti-Catholic	pre-Mayan
pro-Greek	trans-European
un-American	

3. Use hyphens between compound modifiers acting as single adjectives preceding nouns.

tight-lipped witness

pea-green sea

win-win situation

4. Use hyphens between fractions and compound numbers from twenty-one to ninety-nine.

seventy-two   two-thirds

one-half   forty-four

Apostrophes

The apostrophe is used to show possession, to form contractions, and to indicate that letters or numbers have been omitted. Here are several rules to remember.

1. Use the apostrophe and an *s* to show possession with a singular noun or indefinite pronoun.

the bicycle's wheels

Terry's father

someone's wallet

> ***Note:*** If a proper name already ends in *s* in singular form, you may add *'s* or just the apostrophe, depending on how difficult the word would be to pronounce.

Ted Williams' records

Williams's records is acceptable but is somewhat awkward to pronounce.

Charles's painting was destroyed.

2. Use only an apostrophe when a plural noun ends with an *s*.

the girls' toys

the horses' stables

the marchers' demands

3. Use an apostrophe and an *s* if the plural noun does not end with an *s*.

men's league

children's playground

women's club

4. Use an apostrophe for both elements of a compound construction if appropriate.

Troy Aikman's and Dan Marino's styles of playing quarterback are quite different.   Two different quarterbacks

Ben and Jerry's Ice Cream is out of this world!   One brand of
ice cream

5. Use apostrophes to form contractions and to indicate that letters or numbers are missing.

I'm afraid I can't fill your order.

You're going to have to come back tomorrow.

He is a product of the '60s.

Note: Do not use an apostrophe with the possessive form of a pronoun.

Possessive pronouns:

its   hers   yours   ours   theirs   whose

Contraction:

it's   Meaning "it is"

EXERCISES   Rewrite the following sentences, using correct internal punctuation. If a sentence is correct, indicate that with the letter *C*.

1. Michelle cried oh no when she found that the picnic baskets lid had been taken off and all the food was gone.

2. Dede was told to meet her agent at 430 pm in the lounge of Saint Marks Bowling Alley.

3. My dream involved tiny mice, a motorcycle gang, and, no wait, that wasn't a dream, that really happened.

4. The most important thing a hero must have is; courage.

5. I just cant seem to get that conversation off my mind.

6. Vanilla, chocolate, or strawberry, who can make such difficult choices?

7. Use one and one half teaspoons of baking soda, three quarters of a cup of flour, and one fourth of a cup of sugar.

8. She has a wonderful private collection of preColumbian art.

9. The three gentlemen (Manuel, Tony, and Lawrence) have decided to go into business together.

10. Parker noted, Many of them were unable to adapt to the rapidly changing climate.

11. I've been meaning to read the book War and Peace in my spare time.

12. There's a column in the newspaper called My Life in the Suburbs that runs three times a week.

13. When Gertrude Stein said There's no there, there she was referring to Oakland.

14. Jay said that his goat was sick.

15. The sauces's flavors were all wrong.

16. The robber had only one thing in mind, diamonds.

17. The exJet quarterback is now peddling muscle relaxants.

18. My yellow brown dog is named Rusty.

19. Attendance is mandatory, said the instructor, because if youre not here, you cant learn.

20. Ulysses's wife, named Penelope, waited twenty years for the Greek hero to return home.

Readings

What is the single-best thing that you can do on your own to help improve your writing? Read as much as possible. Good writers are good readers. Reading will expose you to new ideas, new structures, and new ways to use language. Reading also will allow you to see what other writers have done before. You may be inspired by what you read, you may reject it, or you may even want to emulate it. Most of all, reading will give you ideas that you can use in your own writing.

Reading someone else's work exposes you to the finished product of another writer's efforts. Although a finished work reveals little about the process that created it, you can still learn about writing from it. Examine the writing and ask yourself: How does this author use language? How difficult is the vocabulary? Does the author use long, complicated sentences or short, simple ones? Are the paragraphs long, like in a textbook, or short, like in a newspaper? What rhetorical modes does the author use? How would you describe the structure of the work?

The works presented in this section are intended to perform two functions: to serve as models for writing that are discussed in class and to serve as the basis for additional writing assignments. The readings come from a variety of sources, such as autobiographies, popular magazines, journals, newspapers, and even other textbooks. You will find differing styles, from formal to colloquial; differing ways to support a thesis, from using personal experience to using academic research; and differing tones, from friendly and personal to distant and impersonal. Some may appeal only to a specific audience; others will have a very broad appeal. Some pieces are fairly short, and others are much longer. A few are excerpts of larger works that could not be presented in their entirety. Each of the readings has something to contribute to your own writing, from either its content or its writing style.

To assist you with the reading selections, you will find several features:

■ ***Questions Before the Reading:*** These questions are designed as prereading questions. You may wish to answer one or all of the questions. It would be a good idea to keep your answers in the same journal where you store your Journal Exercises. Perhaps the questions will bring out some ideas that you will want to develop later in a writing assignment.

■ ***Vocabulary Highlights:*** Each reading selection has a boxed section of Vocabulary Highlights. The words in this section may be unknown to you, or you may be unfamiliar with the particular definition used in the reading. You will want to take note of these words before you begin reading and refer to them as you read *only if necessary.* Look up in a dictionary any additional words that you do not understand based either on context clues or the words' prefixes, suffixes, and roots. You may wish to handwrite those words and their definitions in the Vocabulary Highlights section for future reference.

■ ***The Reading:*** The readings will vary in difficulty. Some are quite easy, and others may be challenging. Be sure to follow some simple advice when you read:

1. Find a quiet place where you will not be disturbed. It is best to read the entire selection without being interrupted.
2. Budget your time. Reading is more than glancing at letters and words, which often happens if you do not allow enough time to read the selection carefully. Remember, understanding the reading selection is what matters most.
3. Read with a pen or pencil in hand. Do not be afraid to mark up your textbook. Making margin notes or underlining passages can be very helpful. Circle words you do not understand so that you can look them up later.
4. Reread the selection later. If you got very little out of your first reading, do not be discouraged. Just make sure you budget time to read the selection again. Even if you understood a lot from one reading, you will find that you understand even more the second time through.

■ ***Responding to the Reading:*** This is the first set of questions following the reading; they are designed to be answered based on a close reading of the selection. *Close reading* means that you are paying attention to the meaning and nuances of what is said in the reading. The answers to these questions can all be found in the reading itself.

■ ***Questions Beyond the Reading:*** This is the second set of questions following the reading; they ask you to consider ideas that go beyond what was actually said in the selection. The answers to these questions must come from your own knowledge or experience. These questions can be developed into paragraph- or essay-length responses, and they may even require that you do some additional reading, as well.

Narration, Description, and Example

Questions Before the Reading

1. To what extent do you believe racism affects education in the United States?
2. What were some of your first experiences in a library like?

VOCABULARY HIGHLIGHTS

denunciation	an accusation of crime or wrongdoing
patronize	to do business with a commercial establishment
solidarity	union or fellowship, especially between members of a group
Jim Crow	the practice or policy of segregation and discrimination against Blacks

The Library Card

Richard Wright

1   One morning I arrived early at work and went into the bank lobby where the Negro porter was mopping. I stood at a counter and picked up the *Memphis Commercial Appeal* and began my free reading of the press. I came finally to the editorial page and there was an article dealing with one H. L. Mencken. I knew by hearsay that he was the editor of the *American Mercury,* but aside from that I knew nothing about him. The article was a furious denunciation of Mencken, concluding with one, hot, short sentence: Mencken is a fool

Chapter XIII from *Black Boy* by Richard Wright. Copyright, 1937, 1942, 1944, 1945 by Richard Wright. Copyright renewed 1973 by Ellen Wright. Reprinted by permission of HarperCollins Publishers, Inc.

2   I wondered what on earth this Mencken had done to call down upon him the scorn of the South. The only people I had ever heard denounced in the South were Negroes, and this man was not a Negro. Then what ideas did Mencken hold that made a newspaper like the *Commercial Appeal* castigate him publicly? Undoubtedly he must be advocating ideas that the South did not like. Were there, then, people other than Negroes who criticized the South? I knew that during the Civil War the South had hated northern whites, but I had not encountered such hate during my life. Knowing no more of Mencken than I did at that moment, I felt a vague sympathy for him. Had not the South, which had assigned me the role of a non-man, cast at him its hardest words?

3   Now, how could I find out about this Mencken? There was a huge library near the riverfront, but I knew that Negroes were not allowed to patronize its shelves any more than they were the parks and playgrounds of the city. I had gone into the library several times to get books for the white men on the job. Which of them would now help me to get books? And how could I read them without causing concern to the white men with whom I worked? I had so far been successful in hiding my thoughts and feelings from them, but I knew that I would create hostility if I went about this business of reading in a clumsy way

4   I weighed the personalities of the men on the job. There was Don, a Jew; but I distrusted him. His position was not much better than mine and I knew that he was uneasy and insecure; he had always treated me in an offhand, bantering way that barely concealed his contempt. I was afraid to ask him to help me to get books; his frantic desire to demonstrate a racial solidarity with the whites against Negroes might make him betray me.

5   Then how about the boss? No, he was a Baptist and I had the suspicion that he would not be quite able to comprehend why a black boy would want to read Mencken. There were other white men on the job whose attitudes showed clearly that they were Kluxers or sympathizers and they were out of the question.

6   There remained only one man whose attitude did not fit into an anti-Negro category, for I had heard the white men refer to him as a "Pope lover." He was an Irish Catholic and was hated by the white Southerners. I knew that he read books, because I had got him volumes from the library several times. Since he, too, was an object of hatred, I felt that he might refuse me but would hardly betray me. I hesitated, weighing and balancing the imponderable realities.

7   One morning I paused before the Catholic fellow's desk.

8   "I want to ask you a favor," I whispered to him.

9   "What is it?"

10   "I want to read. I can't get books from the library. I wonder if you'd let me use your card?"

11   He looked at me suspiciously.

12   "My card is full most of the time," he said.

13   "I see," I said and waited, posing my question silently.

14   "You're not trying to get me into trouble, are you, boy?" he asked, staring at me.

15   "Oh, no, sir."

16   "What book do you want?"

17   "A book by H. L. Mencken."

18   "Which one?"

19   "I don't know. Has he written more than one?"

20   "He has written several."

21   "I didn't know that."

22   "What makes you want to read Mencken?"

23   "Oh, I just saw his name in the newspaper," I said.

24   "It's good of you to want to read," he said. "But you ought to read the right things."

25   I said nothing. Would he want to supervise my reading?

26   "Let me think," he said. "I'll figure out something."

27   I turned from him and he called me back. He stared at me quizzically.

28   "Richard, don't mention this to the other white men," he said.

29   "I understand," I said. "I won't say a word."

30   A few days later he called me to him.

31   "I've got a card in my wife's name," he said. "Here's mine."

32   "Thank you, sir."

33   "Do you think you can manage it?"

34   "I'll manage fine," I said.

35   "If they suspect you, you'll get in trouble," he said.

36   "I'll write the same kind of notes to the library that you wrote when you sent me books," I told him. "I'll sign your name."

37   He laughed.

38   "Go ahead. Let me see what you get," he said.

39   That afternoon I addressed myself to forging a note. Now, what were the names of books written by H. L. Mencken? I did not know any of them. I finally wrote what I thought would be a foolproof note: *Dear Madam: Will you please let this nigger boy*—I used the word "nigger" to make the librarian feel that I could not possibly be the author of the note—*have some books by H. L. Mencken?* I forged the white man's name.

40   I entered the library as I had always done when on errands for whites, but I felt that I would somehow slip up and betray myself. I doffed my hat, stood a respectful distance from the desk, looked as unbookish as possible, and waited for the white patrons to be taken care of. When the desk was clear of people, I still waited. The white librarian looked at me.

41   "What do you want, boy?"

42   As though I did not possess the power of speech, I stepped forward and simply handed her the forged note, not parting my lips.

43   "What books by Mencken does he want?" she asked.

44   "I don't know, ma'am," I said, avoiding her eyes.

45   "Who gave you this card?"

46   "Mr. Falk," I said.

47   "Where is he?"

48   "He's at work, at M _____ Optical Company," I said. "I've been in here for him before."

49   "I remember," the woman said. "But he never wrote notes like this."

50   Oh, God, she's suspicious. Perhaps she would not let me have the books? If she had turned her back at that moment, I would have ducked out the door and never gone back. Then I thought of a bold idea.

51   "You can call him up, ma'am," I said, my heart pounding.

52   "You're not using these books, are you?" she asked pointedly.

53   "Oh, no, ma'am. I can't read."

54   "I don't know what he wants by Mencken," she said under her breath.

55   I knew now that I had won; she was thinking of other things and the race question had gone out of her mind. She went to the shelves. Once or twice she looked over her shoulder at me, as though she was still doubtful. Finally she came forward with two books in her hand.

56   "I'm sending him two books," she said. "But tell Mr. Falk to come in next time, or send me the names of the books he wants. I don't know what he wants to read."

57   I said nothing. She stamped the card and handed me the books. Not daring to glance at them, I went out of the library, fearing that the woman would call me back for further questioning. A block away from the library I opened one of the books and read a title: *A Book of Prefaces*. I was nearing my nineteenth birthday and I did not know how to pronounce the word "preface." I thumbed the pages and saw strange words and strange names. I shook my head, disappointed. I looked at the other book; it was called *Prejudices*. I knew what that word meant; I had heard it all my life. And right off I was on guard against Mencken's books. Why would a man want to call a book *Prejudices?* The word was so stained with all my memories of racial hate that I could not conceive of anybody using it for a title. Perhaps I had made a mistake about Mencken? A man who had prejudices must be wrong.

58   When I showed the books to Mr. Falk, he looked at me and frowned.

59   "That librarian might telephone you," I warned him.

60   "That's all right," he said. "But when you're through reading those books, I want you to tell me what you get out of them."

61   That night in my rented room, while letting the hot water run over my can of pork and beans in the sink, I opened *A Book of Prefaces* and began to read. I was jarred and shocked by the style, the clear, clean, sweeping sentences. Why did he write like that? And how did one write like that? I pictured the man as a raging demon, slashing with his pen, consumed with hate, denouncing everything American, extolling everything European or German, laughing at the weaknesses of people, mocking God, authority. What was this? I stood up, trying to realize what reality lay behind the meaning of the words . . . Yes, this man was fighting, fighting with words. He was using words as a weapon, using them as one would use a club. Could words be weapons? Well, yes, for here they were. Then, maybe, perhaps, I could use them as a weapon? No. It frightened me. I read on and what amazed me was not what he said, but how on earth anybody had the courage to say it.

62   Occasionally I glanced up to reassure myself that I was alone in the room. Who were these men about whom Mencken was talking so passionately? Who was Anatole France? Joseph Conrad? Sinclair Lewis, Sherwood Anderson, Dostoevski, George Moore, Gustave Flaubert, Maupassant, Tolstoy, Frank Harris, Mark Twain, Thomas Hardy, Arnold Bennett, Stephen Crane, Zola, Norris, Gorky, Bergson,

Ibsen, Balzac, Bernard Shaw, Dumas, Poe, Thomas Mann, O. Henry, Dreiser, H. G. Wells, Gogol, T. S. Eliot, Gide, Baudelaire, Edgar Lee Masters, Stendhal, Turgenev, Huneker, Nietzsche, and scores of others? Were these men real? Did they exist or had they existed? And how did one pronounce their names?

63   I ran across many words whose meanings I did not know, and I either looked them up in a dictionary or, before I had a chance to do that, encountered the word in a context that made its meaning clear. But what strange world was this? I concluded the book with the conviction that I had somehow overlooked something terribly important in life. I had once tried to write, had once reveled in feeling, had let my crude imagination roam, but the impulse to dream had been slowly beaten out of me by experience. Now it surged up again and I hungered for books, new ways of looking and seeing. It was not a matter of believing or disbelieving what I read, but of feeling something new, of being affected by something that made the look of the world different.

64   As dawn broke I ate my pork and beans, feeling dopey, sleepy. I went to work, but the mood of the book would not die; it lingered, coloring everything I saw, heard, did. I now felt that I knew what the white men were feeling. Merely because I had read a book that had spoken of how they lived and thought, I identified myself with that book. I felt vaguely guilty. Would I, filled with bookish notions, act in a manner that would make the whites dislike me?

65   I forged more notes and my trips to the library became frequent. Reading grew into a passion. My first serious novel was Sinclair Lewis's *Main Street*. It made me see my boss, Mr. Gerald, and identify him as an American type. I would smile when I saw him lugging his golf bags into the office. I had always felt a vast distance separating me from the boss, and now I felt closer to him, though still distant. I felt now that I knew him, that I could feel the very limits of his narrow life and this had happened because I had read a novel about a mythical man called George F. Babbitt.

66   The plots and stories in the novels did not interest me so much as the point of view revealed. I gave myself over to each novel without reserve, without trying to criticize it; it was enough for me to see and feel something different. And for me, everything was something different. Reading was like a drug, a dope. The novels created moods in which I lived for days. But I could not conquer my sense of guilt, my feeling that the white men around me knew that I was changing, that I had begun to regard them differently.

67   Whenever I brought a book to the job, I wrapped it in newspaper—a habit that was to persist for years in other cities and under other circumstances. But some of the white men pried into my packages when I was absent and they questioned me.

68   "Boy, what are you reading those books for?"

69   "Oh, I don't know, sir."

70   "That's deep stuff you're reading, boy."

71   "I'm just killing time, sir."

72   "You'll addle your brains if you don't watch out."

73   I read Dreiser's *Jennie Gerhardt* and *Sister Carrie* and they revived in me a vivid sense of my mother's suffering; I was overwhelmed. I grew silent, wondering about the life around me. It would have been impossible for me to have told anyone

what I derived from these novels, for it was nothing less than a sense of life itself. All my life had shaped me for the realism, the naturalism of the modern novel, and I could not read enough of them.

74   Steeped in new moods and ideas, I bought a ream of paper and tried to write; but nothing would come, or what did come was flat beyond telling. I discovered that more than desire and feeling were necessary to write and I dropped the idea. Yet I still wondered how it was possible to know people sufficiently to write about them? Could I ever learn about life and people? To me, with my vast ignorance, my Jim Crow station in life, it seemed a task impossible of achievement. I now knew what being a Negro meant. I could endure the hunger. I had learned to live with hate. But to feel that there were feelings denied me, that the very breath of life itself was beyond my reach, that more than anything else hurt, wounded me. I had a new hunger.

75   In buoying me up, reading also cast me down, made me see what was possible, what I had missed. My tension returned, new, terrible, bitter, surging, almost too great to be contained. I no longer felt that the world about me was hostile, killing, I knew it. A million times I asked myself what I could do to save myself, and there were no answers. I seemed forever condemned, ringed by walls.

76   I did not discuss my reading with Mr. Falk, who had lent me his library card; it would have meant talking about myself and that would have been too painful. I smiled each day, fighting desperately to maintain my old behavior, to keep my disposition seemingly sunny. But some of the white men discerned that I had begun to brood.

77   "Wake up there, boy!" Mr. Olin said one day.

78   "Sir!" I answered for lack of a better word.

79   "You act like you've stolen something," he said.

80   I laughed in the way I knew he expected me to laugh, but I resolved to be more conscious of myself, to watch my every act, to guard and hide the new knowledge that was dawning within me.

81   If I went north, would it be possible for me to build a new life then? But how could a man build a life upon vague, unformed yearnings? I wanted to write and I did not even know the English language. I bought English grammars and found them dull. I felt that I was getting a better sense of the language from novels than from grammars. I read hard, discarding a writer as soon as I felt that I had grasped his point of view. At night the printed page stood before my eyes in sleep.

82   Mrs. Moss, my landlady, asked me one Sunday morning:

83   "Son, what is this you keep on reading?"

84   "Oh, nothing. Just novels."

85   "What you get out of 'em?"

86   "I'm just killing time," I said.

87   "I hope you know your own mind," she said in a tone which implied that she doubted if I had a mind.

88   I knew of no Negroes who read the books I liked and I wondered if any Negroes ever thought of them. I knew that there were Negro doctors, lawyers, newspapermen, but I never saw any of them. When I read a Negro newspaper I never caught the faintest echo of my preoccupation in its pages. I felt trapped and occasionally, for a few days, I would stop reading. But a vague hunger would come over me for books,

books that opened up new avenues of feeling and seeing, and again I would forge another note to the white librarian. Again I would read and wonder as only the naive and unlettered can read and wonder, feeling that I carried a secret, criminal burden about with me each day.

89   That winter my mother and brother came and we set up housekeeping, buying furniture on the installment plan, being cheated and yet knowing no way to avoid it. I began to eat warm food and to my surprise found that regular meals enabled me to read faster. I may have lived through many illnesses and survived them, never suspecting that I was ill. My brother obtained a job and we began to save toward the trip north, plotting our time, setting tentative dates for departure. I told none of the white men on the job that I was planning to go north; I knew that the moment they felt I was thinking of the North they would change toward me. It would have made them feel that I did not like the life I was living, and because my life was completely conditioned by what they said or did, it would have been tantamount to challenging them.

90   I could calculate my chances for life in the South as a Negro fairly clearly now.

91   I could fight the southern whites by organizing with other Negroes, as my grandfather had done. But I knew that I could never win that way; there were many whites and there were but few blacks. They were strong and we were weak. Outright black rebellion could never win. If I fought openly I would die and I did not want to die. News of lynchings were frequent.

92   I could submit and live the life of a genial slave, but that was impossible. All of my life had shaped me to live by my own feelings and thoughts. I could make up to Bess and marry her and inherit the house. But that, too, would be the life of a slave; if I did that, I would crush to death something within me, and I would hate myself as much as I knew the whites already hated those who had submitted. Neither could I ever willingly present myself to be kicked, as Shorty had done. I would rather have died than do that.

93   I could drain off my restlessness by fighting with Shorty and Harrison. I had seen many Negroes solve the problem of being black by transferring their hatred of themselves to others with a black skin and fighting them. I would have to be cold to do that, and I was not cold and I could never be.

94   I could, of course, forget what I had read, thrust the whites out of my mind, forget them; and find release from anxiety and longing in sex and alcohol. But the memory of how my father had conducted himself made that course repugnant. If I did not want others to violate my life, how could I voluntarily violate it myself?

95   I had no hope whatever of being a professional man. Not only had I been so conditioned that I did not desire it, but the fulfillment of such an ambition was beyond my capabilities. Well-to-do Negroes lived in a world that was almost as alien to me as the world inhabited by whites.

96   What, then, was there? I held my life in my mind, in my consciousness each day, feeling at times that I would stumble and drop it, spill it forever. My reading had created a vast sense of distance between me and the world in which I lived and tried to make a living, and that sense of distance was increasing each day. My days and nights were one long, quiet, continuously contained dream of terror, tension, and anxiety. I wondered how long I could bear it.

<table>
<tr><td>

**Responding
to the
Reading**

</td><td>

1. Why does Wright choose to ask Mr. Falk and not one of the other men for permission to forge his name to get books out of the library?
2. Examine the passage where Wright is discovering the new names and ideas in Mencken's writing. What kind of effect does it have on him, and why?
3. Why does Wright feel trapped at the end of "The Library Card"?

</td></tr>
<tr><td>

**Questions
Beyond the
Reading**

</td><td>

1. There is an old maxim that reads, "When ignorance is bliss, 'tis folly to be wise." How does that apply to "The Library Card"? Explain.
2. How has learning and education opened new worlds for you? Be specific.
3. The Jim Crow laws under which Wright lived are no longer in effect, but racism is still present in the United States. Do you feel that race influences the type of education one gets? Why or why not? Be specific.

</td></tr>
</table>

<table>
<tr><td>

**Questions
Before the
Reading**

</td><td>

1. Have you had a close but nonromantic friendship with a member of the opposite sex?
2. What benefits are there to having a nonromantic friendship with a member of the opposite sex?

</td></tr>
</table>

VOCABULARY HIGHLIGHTS

borscht	a soup containing beets
fervid	showing great warmth or intensity
vitriolic	severely critical or sarcastic

A Friend for All Seasons

Karen Stabiner

1   My friends have girlfriends from day camp, from second grade, from nursery school. I, on the other hand, have Harry. We have known each other for 30 years. He is my oldest friend.

2   I do not have old girlfriends—although I wish I did, just as I wish I were two inches taller or marginally less moody, more of a regular gal. But I inherited from my mother a tendency to take everything personally, and from my father, a dogged ambition; the combination made for a cut-and-run adolescence.

"A Friend for All Seasons," by Karen Stabiner in *The New York Times Magazine,* January 21, 1996, p. 19. Copyright © 1996 by The New York Times Company. Reprinted by permission

3   Which is not to say I was an outcast. Just that I was in a hurry, wary of becoming comfortable.

4   This made Harry the perfect pal. He defied category—interested equally in magic tricks, poetry and alcohol. He was mysterious without any of the flirty baggage that made other boys so complicated. Harry told me he would be dead before 40, like the other men in his family. He did not have time for the usual teen-age rituals.

5   We were sarcastic and restless. And we were comfortably mismatched, which may have been the key to our longevity. He still remembers the "lunch from another planet" that my mother served when he dropped by one summer afternoon—cold borscht with sour cream, an unremarkable meal in our Jewish home. I found his quiet, dark, fatherless house—I cannot recall his mother's feet making any sound as they hit the floor—a comforting escape from my combustible family.

6   We went for endless bicycle rides along Lake Michigan. I appeared in one of Harry's poems ("damned deodand of bike and Jewess"), which I immediately tucked into my wallet, and subsequent wallets, for years. While I cannot lay my hands on the poem right now, I know it is in this house somewhere.

7   When I picked the wrong college, Harry, a sophomore at a men's school nearby, showed up for a big football weekend so I would have a date for the scheduled festivities. And he believed that I might become a writer—no big deal today, maybe, but a minority opinion at the dawn of the women's movement.

8   He is the only person with whom I have been falling-down drunk—six whisky sours, the Orange Bar, Syracuse, 1968. I may be the only person who knows he used to have a manual typewriter at his bedside so he could record his dreams the instant he woke up. I liked to listen to his dreams. I led such a matter-of-fact existence—Rice Krispies, matching kilts and knee socks. Harry was my escape.

9   At this point in the narrative my husband smirks. He thinks this is all polite euphemism. He refers to Harry as "'my wife's high-school boyfriend."

10   Yes and no. We dated a little during Harry's senior year, and the summer after he graduated. And there was a fervid interlude when we were both in college, long nights of sexual brinkmanship in a deserted fraternity house. He said please, I said no. I changed my mind and he held back. We were never lovers.

11   This is where the story usually ends. People don't know how to be friends with someone who never wanted them or doesn't want them anymore. But Harry and I were lucky. Somehow we understood that this was not rejection. It was fumbling, of the late-teen-age, presexual revolution variety. Nothing personal; a rehearsal for later life.

12   We escaped with our affections intact—but three years later, we had a disagreement on a topic neither of us remembers and retreated to opposite sides of the country.

13   The annual transcontinental phone calls began in the mid-70's. Steadfast as ever, Harry would call late at night with a grocery list of questions, and we would talk until we caught up. I called him once, when an abrasive first marriage made me wonder whether I had ever been a decent person; Harry was the only one with a historical perspective. He showed up in Los Angeles in 1978 in a rumpled summer suit and with a swollen jaw, the result of emergency dental work. When he came back in

1985 we were both better off: I had a second sweet husband and a new book; he had a computer software company and a businessman's dark blue suit.

14   Then, in 1990, he and his new wife stopped by on their way to see a doctor in San Diego. Harry had made it to just past 40, but barely. He had already undergone open-heart surgery; he had pills, he was on a no-fat diet, but still his arteries threatened to close up.

15   It had been 20 years since I had kissed him, and we never had the kind of wonderfully sloppy physical relationship that women have so easily with each other. But I wanted to do something. Harry once extracted me from a vitriolic family picnic, and then sat with me while I sobbed about the great injustice of being born. Now I listened to him crack wise about the coronary Roto-Rooter—and I did not know what to do to rescue him.

16   So I handed him our then-infant daughter. I was one of those loopy late moms who believe our children personify nothing less than hope, promise and magic. Maybe Sarah's invincibility would rub off on Harry. Given the careful vocabulary of our friendship, it was all I could think of to offer.

17   Go ahead, sneer. Six years later, Harry has just become a father himself. We allow ourselves a sweet joke here: perhaps some day Sarah and young William will meet and fall in love. We like, now, to talk about the passage of time—Harry, who always thought he had too little of it, and me, still eternally in a hurry.

18   Our friendship exists at more of an emotional distance than I imagine it would be between old female friends. We visit the past for entertainment and its charm—but never long enough to make judgments about what we did or did not do. The important thing at this point is to maintain, because there is so much at stake: Harry has known me longer than any other woman in his life (except his mom), and I have known him longer than any man except my dad.

19   My husband has a friend named Harry who lives down the street and is our daughter's godfather, and recently Sarah wanted to figure out how to distinguish one Harry from the other. Calling them new Harry and old Harry seemed wrong, since they both have been our friends for decades. We settled on "our Harry," for her godfather, and "my Harry" for my friend.

20   He, however, calls Sarah's godfather "the other Harry," wishing to assert his pre-eminence in the field.

21   That's O.K. with me.

Responding to the Reading

1. Why does Stabiner say that she and Harry were "comfortably mismatched"?
2. Why were Stabiner and Harry able to remain friends after they rejected each other as lovers?
3. Why does Stabiner hand her baby daughter to Harry?

Questions Beyond the Reading

1. Stabiner states that people who reject each other romantically seldom end up as friends. Do you agree or disagree? Explain.
2. What is important about the sharing between friends of private rituals and experiences?

3. Stabiner states that her friendship with Harry is less emotional than old friendships between female friends are. How do you feel friendships differ between males and females?

4. What role does friendship play in your life? Use specific examples.

Questions Before the Reading

1. Do you like to go out in nature for walks? Why or why not?

2. How do you handle disposing of your own trash when you are on a walk or a picnic?

3. How much trash do you see in public places?

VOCABULARY HIGHLIGHTS

tryst	a secret meeting of lovers
dell	a small, wooded valley
garish	crude or tasteless; showy
tawdry	cheap and showy

A Forest Mystery

There's garbage in them thar hills

Katie Letcher Lyle

1   Each spring, I mushroom near the Blue Ridge Parkway, stopping my car day after day along the road to search the deep ravines off the ridge for morels—those elusive, swooningly delicious fungi. I eat some and freeze the rest for later.

2   But I really go for deeper reasons: there is an annual tryst with the world that I must make, a reunion with Nature after the astonishing rebirth of the winter landscape. In addition to mushroom hunting, I go to enjoy the parkway, to see whether the shadbush is blooming, to find out whether the bloodroot has appeared and to note when the first trillium lifts its white petals. I almost hold my breath for the rare sight of a showy pink orchid. I listen for the cheerful call of a Carolina wren, the scratchy song of a scarlet tanager and the distant drumbeat of a pileated woodpecker. I've been doing this since I was 10, nearly half a century ago.

3   When I meet others in the woods, they are always good-natured and polite. It is hard to figure out who they are, since we wear flannel shirts and jeans, boots or sneakers. We go our separate ways, respecting each other's territories. Some smoke while they are in the woods, which makes me nervous, for forest fires start easily in the dry duff of dead and fallen trees. Usually the spring woods are damp or even wet, for which I give thanks as I watch a man flick his cigarette over a fallen limb into a tangle of grapevine. He doesn't even check to see that it's safely out.

4   However, we are unfailingly polite; we nod but rarely speak. If and when we do, it is to say what a nice day it is, or to ask, "found any?" or to answer, "a few." We smile and go our solitary ways. Rapists and murderers, I like to think, do not hunt morels in the mountains of Virginia.

5   My impression is that we are all there because we love tramping through the spring woods, and because we love what we find and see and hear. I believe we share a reverence for the places we are privileged to visit. We would no more trample a wild orchid than we would purposely run over a dog. I think they, as I do, watch for deer and raccoon tracks. We are often miles from highways, in places where humans don't regularly go, and have trudged down or up dangerous boulder-choked hillsides and braved gnats, mosquitoes, ticks and even snakes to be where we are. Our journeys are not without peril.

6   So why is it that some of these people, who seem just like me, will toss rubbish from their cars or litter the woods with potato-chip bags, aluminum cans and wads of paper napkins? It isn't just owners of shiny Volvos and Lincolns who are reluctant to soil their slick upholstery. I've also seen paper bags and plastic cups spewing out of the windows of old Toyotas and battered trucks.

7   Some of these otherwise good people leave McDonald's wrappers and plastic deep in the woods, damaging dells of May apple and jack-in-the-pulpit. Can it be they are not jarred by the sight of tattered bags and half-eaten sandwiches in these sacred places, not dismayed to find broken pop bottles and bent beer cans all over the tender green woods?

8   I think of the ugly Americans who trash everything they touch, who enjoy vandalizing a cemetery or a carwash, simmering in their own misguided angers fueled by abuse or poverty. I understand destroying public places where these people, mostly young, feel their disenfranchisement most keenly. I don't condone it; but I do understand it. I sympathize with their rage at a world that won't take them into consideration in any meaningful way, that won't give them their share because of the circumstances they were born to. I also understand their frustration at never having been able to get ahead. They are acting out, but tragic as it is, there is a reason.

9   Yet many of these gentle spring motorists and hikers who choose the parkway over the Interstate, quality over speed, and who seek gorgeous scenery or the delicate fungi that hide in the underbrush are so careless. Why?

10   There seems to be no angry statement in the scattered papers, the beer bottles, the discarded used diapers, the pink plastic bag slowly rolling along the ground in the spring breeze, that holds, when one checks it out, nothing more than a plastic spoon. It's not even the drunken stupidity of college kids winding miles of toilet paper around trees on the campus, making needless work for whoever has to clean it up. That can be explained away by youthful ignorance and mob mania.

11   No, this trash is not the have-nots ruining the world for the haves. It's not misdirected adolescent humor. There is something in the American mentality that doesn't see anything wrong with tossing rubbish—or anything that is inconvenient to carry—into a lovely forest or along a scenic highway. Some Americans simply don't care about ugliness (as long as it's not in their cars). As with many issues in our society, the assumption is that others will clean up our messes.

12   We clearly view the natural spaces we have left differently from Europeans. I believe we are the only civilized country in the world that doesn't have a cabinet-level position that deals with land-use planning. I recall from a trip I took years ago how Germans who hiked through the Black Forest picked up debris as they went along to ensure that their woods remained clean; in America we act as we have acted for centuries, as if there were still virgin space to move into once we've used up what we have.

13   Each year thousands of tourists visit Colonial Williamsburg for its beauty. Yet these same people tolerate and patronize the miles of garish commercial strips—abysmal concrete landscapes studded with every vain and tawdry thing we materialists ever dreamed of—that line every entrance to that lovely historic town of restored gardens and houses. Apparently, few see the irony.

14   Similarly, how could anyone sensitive enough to hunt mushrooms be so unaware? It's a mystery I can't fathom.

Responding to the Reading

1. Why does Lyle call her experiences of searching for mushrooms an annual "tryst"?
2. What is it about throwing trash in the woods that bothers Lyle so much?
3. What does Lyle mean by the phrase "ugly Americans"?
4. What does Lyle suspect is the reason Americans are so careless with their trash?

Questions Beyond the Reading

1. Lyle states that the mushroom hunters share a "reverence" for the woods. In your experience, what other places inspire reverence, and why?
2. Lyle says that most people assume that others will clean up their messes. Is this true in your experience? Explain, using specific examples.
3. At the close of her essay, Lyle asks, "How could anyone sensitive enough to hunt mushrooms be so unaware [of how they dispose of their trash]?" How would you answer her question?

Questions Before the Reading

1. How important were books and reading in your home when you were growing up?
2. What early memories do you have of libraries?
3. How have your reading habits today been influenced by your childhood reading habits?

Learning to Listen

Eudora Welty

1   I learned from the age of two or three that any room in our house, at any time of day, was there to read in, or to be read to. My mother read to me. She'd read to me in the big bedroom in the mornings, when we were in her rocker together, which ticked in rhythm as we rocked, as though we had a cricket accompanying the story. She'd read to me in the diningroom on winter afternoons in front of the coal fire, with our cuckoo clock ending the story with "Cuckoo," and at night when I'd got in my own bed. I must have given her no peace. Sometimes she read to me in the kitchen while she sat churning, and the churning sobbed along with *any* story. It was my ambition to have her read to me while *I* churned: once she granted my wish, but she read off my story before I brought her butter. She was an expressive reader. When she was reading "Puss in Boots," for instance, it was impossible not to know that she distrusted all cats.

2   It had been startling and disappointing to me to find out that story books had been written by people, that books were not natural wonders, coming up of themselves like grass. Yet regardless of where they came from, I cannot remember a time when I was not in love with them—with the books themselves, cover and binding and the paper they were printed on, with their smell and their weight and with their possession in my arms, captured and carried off to myself. Still illiterate, I was ready for them, committed to all the reading I could give them.

3   Neither of my parents had come from homes that could afford to buy many books, but though it must have been something of a strain on his salary, as the youngest officer in a young insurance company, my father was all the while carefully selecting and ordering away for what he and Mother thought we children should grow up with. They bought first for the future.

4   Besides the bookcase in the livingroom, which was always called "the library," there were the encyclopedia tables and dictionary stand under windows in our diningroom. Here to help us grow up arguing around the diningroom table were the *Unabridged Webster,* the *Columbia Encyclopedia, Compton's Pictured Encyclopedia,* the *Lincoln Library of Information,* and later the *Book of Knowledge.* And the year we moved into our new house, there was room to celebrate it with the new 1925 edition of the *Britannica,* which my father, his face always deliberately turned toward the future, was of course disposed to think better than any previous edition.

5   In "the library," inside the mission-style bookcase with its three diamond-latticed glass doors, with my father's Morris chair and the glass-shaded lamp on its table beside it, were books I could soon begin on—and I did, reading them all alike and as they came, straight down their rows, top shelf to bottom. . . .

6   To both my parents I owe my early acquaintance with a beloved Mark Twain. There was a full set of Mark Twain and a short set of Ring Lardner in our bookcase, and those were the volumes that in time united us all, parents and children. . . .

7   I was presented, from as early as I can remember, with books of my own, which appeared on my birthday and Christmas morning. Indeed, my parents could not give

Reprinted by permission of the publishers from *One Writer's Beginnings* by Eudora Welty, Cambridge, Mass.: Harvard University Press, Copyright © 1983, 1984 by Eudora Welty.

me books enough. They must have sacrificed to give me on my sixth or seventh birthday—it was after I became a reader for myself—the ten-volume set of *Our Wonder World.* These were beautifully made, heavy books I would lie down with on the floor in front of the diningroom hearth, and more often than the rest, volume 5, *Every Child's Story Book,* was under my eyes. There were the fairy tales—Grimm, Andersen, the English, the French, "Ali Baba and the Forty Thieves"; and there were Aesop and Reynard the Fox; there were the myths and legends, Robin Hood, King Arthur, and St. George and the Dragon, even the history of Joan of Arc; a whack of *Pilgrim's Progress* and a long piece of *Gulliver.* They all carried their classic illustrations. I located myself in these pages and could go straight to the stories and pictures I loved. . . .

8   I believe I'm the only child I know of who grew up with this treasure in the house. I used to ask others, "Did you have *Our Wonder World?*" I'd have to tell them *The Book of Knowledge* could not hold a candle to it.

9   I live in gratitude to my parents for initiating me—and as early as I begged for it, without keeping me waiting—into knowledge of the word, into reading and spelling by way of the alphabet. They taught it to me at home in time for me to begin to read before starting to school. I believe the alphabet is no longer considered an essential piece of equipment for traveling through life. In my day it was the keystone to knowledge. You learned the alphabet as you learned to count to ten, as you learned "Now I lay me" and the Lord's Prayer and your father's and mother's name and address and telephone number, all in case you were lost. . . .

10   Ever since I was first read to, then started reading to myself, there has never been a line read that I didn't hear. As my eyes followed the sentence, a voice was saying it silently to me. It isn't my mother's voice, or the voice of any person I can identify, certainly not my own. It is human, but inward, and it is inwardly that I listen to it. It is to me the voice of the story or the poem itself. The cadence, whatever it is that asks you to believe, the feeling that resides in the printed word, reaches me through the reader-voice. I have supposed, but never found out, that this is the case with all readers—to read as listeners—and with all writers, to write as listeners. It may be part of the desire to write. The sound of what falls on the page begins the process of testing it for truth, for me. Whether I am right to trust so far I don't know. By now I don't know whether I could do either one, reading or writing, without the other.

11   My own words, when I am at work on a story, I hear too as they go, in the same voice that I hear when I read in books. When I write and the sound of it comes back to my ears, then I act to make my changes. I have always trusted this voice. . . .

12   Long before I wrote stories, I listened for stories. Listening for them is something more acute than listening *to* them. I suppose it's an early form of participation in what goes on. Listening children know stories are there. When their elders sit and begin, children are just waiting and hoping for one to come out, like a mouse from its hole. . . .

13   When I was five years old, I knew the alphabet, I'd been vaccinated (for smallpox), and I could read. So my mother walked across the street to Jefferson Davis Grammar School and asked the principal if she would allow me to enter the first grade after Christmas.

14   "Oh, all right," said Miss Duling. "Probably the best thing you could do with her."

15   Miss Duling, a lifelong subscriber to perfection, was a figure of authority, the most whole-souled I have ever come to know. She was a dedicated schoolteacher who denied herself all she might have done or whatever other way she might have lived (this possibility was the last that could have occurred to us, her subjects in school). I believe she came of well-off people, well-educated, in Kentucky, and certainly old photographs show she was a beautiful, high-spirited-looking young lady—and came down to Jackson to its new grammar school that was going begging for a principal. She must have earned next to nothing: Mississippi then as now was the nation's lowest-ranking state economically, and our legislature has always shown a painfully loud reluctance to give money to public education. That challenge brought her.

16   In the long run she came into touch, as teacher or principal, with three generations of Jacksonians. My parents had not, but everybody else's parents had gone to school to her. She'd taught most of our leaders somewhere along the line. When she wanted something done—some civic oversight corrected, some injustice made right overnight, or even a tree spared that the fool telephone people were about to cut down—she telephoned the mayor, or the chief of police, or the president of the power company, or the head doctor at the hospital, or the judge in charge of a case, or whoever, and calling them by their first names, told them. It is impossible to imagine her meeting with anything less than compliance. The ringing of her brass bell from their days at Davis School would still be in their ears. She also proposed a spelling match between the fourth grade at Davis School and the Mississippi Legislature, who went through with it: and that told the Legislature. . . .

17   Jackson's Carnegie Library was on the same street where our house was, on the other side of the State Capitol. "Through the Capitol" was the way to go to the Library. You could glide through it on your bicycle or even coast through on roller skates, though without family permission.

18   I never knew anyone who'd grown up in Jackson without being afraid of Mrs. Calloway, our librarian. She ran the Library absolutely by herself, from the desk where she sat with her back to the books and facing the stairs, her dragon eye on the front door, where who knew what kind of person might come in from the public? SILENCE in big black letters was on signs tacked up everywhere. She herself spoke in her normally commanding voice; every word could be heard all over the Library above a steady seething sound coming from her electric fan: it was the only fan in the Library and stood on her desk, turning directly onto her streaming face.

19   As you came in from the bright outside, if you were a girl, she sent her strong eyes down the stairway to test you: If she could see through your skirt she sent you straight back home: you could just put on another petticoat if you wanted a book that badly from the public library. I was willing; I would do anything to read.

20   My mother was not afraid of Mrs. Calloway. She wished me to have my own library card to check out books for myself. She took me in to introduce me and I saw I had met a witch. "Eudora is nine years old and has my permission to read any book she wants from the shelves, children or adult," Mother said. "With the exception of *Elsie Dinsmore,*" she added. Later she explained to me that she'd made this rule because Elsie the heroine, being made by her father to practice too long and hard at the piano, fainted and fell off the piano stool. "You're too impressionable, dear," she told me. "You'd read that and the very first thing you'd do, you'd fall off the piano stool."

"Impressionable" was a new word. I never hear it yet without the image that comes with it of falling straight off the piano stool.

21   Mrs. Calloway made her own rules about books. You could not take back a book to the Library on the same day you'd taken it out: it made no difference to her that you'd read every word in it and needed another to start. You could take out two books at a time and two only: this applied as long as you were a child and also for the rest of your life, to my mother as severely as to me. So two by two, I read library books as fast as I could go, rushing them home in the basket of my bicycle. From the minute I reached our house, I started to read. Every book I seized on, from *Bunny Brown and His Sister Sue at Camp Rest-a-While* to *Twenty Thousand Leagues under the Sea,* stood for the devouring wish to read being instantly granted. I knew this was bliss, knew it at the time. Taste isn't nearly so important; it comes in its own time: I wanted to read immediately. The only fear was that of books coming to an end.

Responding to the Reading

1. Write a paragraph about the importance of Welty's parents in fostering her interest in reading.
2. How do the three female role models (Welty's mother, Miss Duling, and Mrs. Calloway) influence Eudora Welty?
3. Why do you think Welty says that "the alphabet is no longer an essential piece of equipment for traveling through life"?

Questions Beyond the Reading

1. Welty implies that there is a relationship between the love of reading and education. Do you agree or disagree? Use specific examples to explain.
2. Welty's father buys the new edition of the *Britannica* because he feels it will be superior to the older version. This reflects his overall optimistic view of progress and the future. Do you share his view that progress is generally for the better? Give specific examples.
3. Today, books compete with television for a child's attention. What do books have to offer that television does not, and what does television have to offer that books do not? Explain with examples.

Definition and Classification

Questions Before the Reading

1. What limits do you believe exist on the pursuit of happiness?
2. What is your definition of the word *right* in the sentence "I have the right to do that"?
3. What are good reasons to end a marriage when both parties have made a vow that includes "to death do us part"?

VOCABULARY HIGHLIGHTS

virility	having masculine strength; capable of procreation
correlative	so related that each implies the other
august	inspiring awe or reverence
sanction	permission for an action
tautology	needless repetition of an idea in different words
teetotaler	one who does not drink alcohol
transient	staying only a short time
amours	lovers or love affairs
conjugal	of marriage or the relationship of husband and wife
monogamous	being married to one person; showing sexual faithfulness within marriage
carte blanche	full power to do what one wishes

We Have No Right to Happiness

C. S. Lewis

1   "After all," said Clare, "they had a right to happiness." We were discussing something that once happened in our own neighborhood. Mr. A. had deserted Mrs. A. and got his divorce in order to marry Mrs. B., who had likewise got her divorce in order to marry Mr. A. And there was certainly no doubt that Mr. A. and Mrs. B. were very much in love with one another. If they continued to be in love, and if nothing went wrong with their health or their income, they might reasonably expect to be very happy.

2   It was equally clear that they were not happy with their old partners. Mrs. B. had adored her husband at the outset. But then he got smashed up in the war. It was thought he had lost his virility, and it was known that he had lost his job. Life with him was no longer what Mrs. B. had bargained for. Poor Mrs. A., too. She had lost her looks—and all her liveliness. It might be true, as some said, that she consumed herself by bearing his children and nursing him through the long illness that overshadowed their earlier married life.

3   You mustn't, by the way, imagine that A. was the sort of man who nonchalantly threw a wife away like the peel of an orange he'd sucked dry. Her suicide was a terrible shock to him. We all knew this, for he told us so himself. "But what could I do?" he said. "A man has a right to happiness. I had to take my chance when it came."

4   I went away thinking about the concept of a "right to happiness."

5   At first this sounds to me as odd as a right to good luck. For I believe—whatever one school of moralists may say—that we depend for a very great deal of our happiness or misery on circumstances outside all human control. A right to happiness doesn't, for me, make much more sense than a right to be six feet tall, or to have

a millionaire for your father, or to get good weather whenever you want to have a picnic.

6   I can understand a right as a freedom guaranteed me by the laws of the society I live in. Thus, I have a right to travel along the public roads because society gives me that freedom; that's what we mean by calling the roads "public." I can also understand a right as a claim guaranteed me by the laws, and correlative to an obligation on someone else's part. If I have a right to receive £100 from you, this is another way of saying that you have a duty to pay me £100. If the laws allow Mr. A. to desert his wife and seduce his neighbor's wife, then, by definition, Mr. A. has a legal right to do so, and we need bring in no talk about "happiness."

7   But of course that was not what Clare meant. She meant that he had not only a legal but a moral right to act as he did. In other words, Clare is—or would be if she thought it out—a classical moralist after the style of Thomas Aquinas, Grotius, Hooker and Locke. She believes that behind the laws of the state there is a Natural Law.

8   I agree with her. I hold this conception to be basic to all civilization. Without it, the actual laws of the state become an absolute, as in Hegel. They cannot be criticized because there is no norm against which they should be judged.

9   The ancestry of Clare's maxim, "They have a right to happiness," is august. In words that are cherished by all civilized men, but especially by Americans, it has been laid down that one of the rights of man is a right to "the pursuit of happiness." And now we get to the real point.

10   What did the writers of that august declaration mean?

11   It is quite certain what they did not mean. They did not mean that man was entitled to pursue happiness by any and every means—including, say, murder, rape, robbery, treason and fraud. No society could be built on such a basis.

12   They meant "to pursue happiness by all lawful means"; that is, by all means which the Law of Nature eternally sanctions and which the laws of the nation shall sanction.

13   Admittedly this seems at first to reduce their maxim to the tautology that men (in pursuit of happiness) have a right to do whatever they have a right to do. But tautologies, seen against their proper historical context, are not always barren tautologies. The declaration is primarily a denial of the political principles which long governed Europe: a challenge flung down to the Austrian and Russian empires, to England before the Reform Bills, to Bourbon France. It demands that whatever means of pursuing happiness are lawful for any should be lawful for all; that "man," not men of some particular caste, class, status or religion, should be free to use them. In a century when this is being unsaid by nation after nation and party after party, let us not call it a barren tautology.

14   But the question as to what means are "lawful"—what methods of pursuing happiness are either morally permissible by the Law of Nature or should be declared legally permissible by the legislature of a particular nation—remains exactly where it did. And on that question I disagree with Clare. I don't think it is obvious that people have the unlimited "right of happiness" which she suggests.

15   For one thing, I believe that Clare, when she says "happiness," means simply and solely "sexual happiness." Partly because women like Clare never use the word "happiness" in any other sense. But also because I never heard Clare talk about the "right" to any other kind. She was rather leftist in her politics, and would have been

scandalized if anyone had defended the actions of a ruthless man-eating tycoon on the ground that his happiness consisted in making money and he was pursuing his happiness. She was also a rabid teetotaler; I never heard her excuse an alcoholic because he was happy when he was drunk.

16   A good many of Clare's friends, and especially her female friends, often felt—I've heard them say so—that their own happiness would be perceptibly increased by boxing her ears. I very much doubt if this would have brought her theory of a right to happiness into play.

17   Clare, in fact, is doing what the whole western world seems to me to have been doing for the last forty-odd years. When I was a youngster, all the progressive people were saying, "Why all this prudery? Let us treat sex just as we treat all our other impulses." I was simple-minded enough to believe they meant what they said. I have since discovered that they meant exactly the opposite. They meant that sex was to be treated as no other impulse in our nature has ever been treated by civilized people. All the others, we admit, have to be bridled. Absolute obedience to your instinct for self-preservation is what we call cowardice; to your acquisitive impulse, avarice. Even sleep must be resisted if you're a sentry. But every unkindness and breach of faith seems to be condoned provided that the object aimed at is "four bare legs in a bed."

18   It is like having a morality in which stealing fruit is considered wrong—unless you steal nectarines.

19   And if you protest against this view you are usually met with chatter about the legitimacy and beauty and sanctity of "sex" and accused of harboring some Puritan prejudice against it as something disreputable or shameful. I deny the charge. Foam-born Venus . . . golden Aphrodite . . . Our Lady of Cyprus . . . I never breathed a word against you. If I object to boys who steal my nectarines, must I be supposed to disapprove of nectarines in general? Or even of boys in general? It might, you know, be stealing that I disapproved of.

20   The real situation is skillfully concealed by saying that the question of Mr. A.'s "right" to desert his wife is one of "sexual morality." Robbing an orchard is not an offense against some special morality called "fruit morality." It is an offense against honesty. Mr. A.'s action is an offense against good faith (to solemn promises), against gratitude (toward one to whom he was deeply indebted) and against common humanity.

21   Our sexual impulses are thus being put in a position of preposterous privilege. The sexual motive is taken to condone all sorts of behavior which, if it had any other end in view, would be condemned as merciless, treacherous and unjust.

22   Now though I see no good reason for giving sex this privilege, I think I see a strong cause. It is this.

23   It is part of the nature of a strong erotic passion—as distinct from a transient fit of appetite—that it makes more towering promises than any other emotion. No doubt all our desires make promises, but not so impressively. To be in love involves the almost irresistible conviction that one will go on being in love until one dies, and that possession of the beloved will confer, not merely frequent ecstasies, but settled, fruitful, deep-rooted, lifelong happiness. Hence *all* seems to be at stake. If we miss this chance we shall have lived in vain. At the very thought of such a doom we sink into fathomless depths of self-pity.

24   Unfortunately these promises are found often to be quite untrue. Every experienced adult knows this to be so as regards all erotic passions (except the one he himself is feeling at the moment). We discount the world-without-end pretensions of our friends' amours easily enough. We know that such things sometimes last—and sometimes don't. And when they do last, this is not because they promised at the outset to do so. When two people achieve lasting happiness, this is not solely because they are great lovers but because they are also—I must put it crudely—good people; controlled, loyal, fairminded, mutually adaptable people.

25   If we establish a "right to (sexual) happiness" which supersedes all the ordinary rules of behavior, we do so not because of what our passion shows itself to be in experience but because of what it professes to be while we are in the grip of it. Hence, while the bad behavior is real and works miseries and degradations, the happiness which was the object of the behavior turns out again and again to be illusory. Everyone (except Mr. A. and Mrs. B.) knows that Mr. A. in a year or so may have the same reason for deserting his new wife as for deserting his old. He will feel again that all is at stake. He will see himself again as the great lover, and his pity for himself will exclude all pity for the woman.

26   Two further points remain.

27   One is this. A society in which conjugal infidelity is tolerated must always be in the long run a society adverse to women. Women, whatever a few male songs and satires may say to the contrary, are more naturally monogamous than men; it is a biological necessity. Where promiscuity prevails, they will therefore always be more often the victims than the culprits. Also, domestic happiness is more necessary to them than to us. And the quality by which they most easily hold a man, their beauty, decreases every year after they have come to maturity, but this does not happen to those qualities of personality—women don't really care twopence about our *looks*—by which we hold women. Thus in the ruthless war of promiscuity women are at a double disadvantage. They play for higher stakes and are also more likely to lose. I have no sympathy with moralists who frown at the increasing crudity of female provocativeness. These signs of desperate competition fill me with pity.

28   Secondly, though the "right to happiness" is chiefly claimed for the sexual impulse, it seems to me impossible that the matter should stay there. The fatal principle, once allowed in that department, must sooner or later seep through our whole lives. We thus advance toward a state of society in which not only each man but every impulse in each man claims *carte blanche*. And then, though our technological skill may help us survive a little longer, our civilization will have died at heart, and will—one dare not even add "unfortunately"—be swept away.

Responding to the Reading

1. Write a paragraph in which you explain what Lewis means by "Natural Law."

2. Write a paragraph in which you discuss whether you agree with Lewis that sexual happiness makes the towering promise that "one will go on being in love until one dies."

3. Write a paragraph in which you agree or disagree with Lewis's assertion that unfaithfulness in marriage invariably is more hurtful to the woman than to the man.

1. Do you agree with Lewis's claim that marriage should be forever, regardless of the circumstances? Explain why or why not.
2. Lewis published this article in the early 1960s. Have changes since then (such as the invention of reliable birth control, the advent of the women's movement, and the return of women to the work force) changed the validity of his essay? Explain.
3. Lewis argues that the unbridled pursuit of happiness will eventually lead people to throw away their morals to pursue all avenues of happiness, not just sexual. Do you think that this has happened? Explain.

---

1. Do you consider yourself more of a city person or a country person? Why?
2. What kinds of activities do you like to do to relax?

VOCABULARY HIGHLIGHTS

riverine	of or related to rivers
biosphere	the part of the earth's crust, waters, and atmosphere capable of supporting life
frotteurism	the practice of rubbing against another person for sexual excitement
paraphiliac	preference or addiction to unusual sexual practices
scatologia	preoccupation with excretement or obscenity
estrangement	the state of being emotionally turned away from
benign	showing or caused by kindness
dicta	sayings or insights (plural of *dictum*)
biodiversity	the varied forms of life that exist in the biosphere
reciprocity	mutual giving or feeling
paradigm	an example serving as a model
indigenous	originating in a particular region or country

The Nature of Serenity

Theodore Roszak

1   I recently attended a meeting of the International Rivers Network, a San Francisco-area environmental group. The featured speaker was Dan Beard, head of the U.S. Bureau of Reclamation. After detailing the ways in which big dams have devastated natural watersheds and riverine cultures, he ended with an appeal: "Somehow

we have got to convince people that projects like this are crazy." There was applause all around.

2   "Crazy" . . . In the presence of environmental horrors, the word leaps to mind. Depleting the ozone is "crazy," killing off the rhinos is "crazy," destroying rain forests is "crazy." Our gut feeling is immediate, the judgment made with vehemence. "Crazy" is a word freighted with strong emotion.

3   Inflicting irreversible damage on the biosphere might seem to be the most obvious kind of craziness. But when we turn to the psychiatric literature of the modern Western world, we find no such category as ecological madness.

4   The American Psychiatric Association lists more than 300 mental diseases in its *Diagnostic and Statistical Manual.* Among the largest of *DSM* categories is sex. In mapping sexual dysfunction, therapists have been absolutely inspired. We have sexual aversion disorder, female sexual arousal disorder, hypoactive sexual desire disorder (male and female), gender identity disorder, transient stress-related cross-dressing behavior, androgen insensitivity syndrome, fetishism, transvestic fetishism, transvestic fetishism with gender dysphoria, voyeurism, frotteurism, pedophilia (six varieties), and paraphiliac telephone scatologia.

5   Granted, the *DSM* bears about the same relationship to psychology as a building code bears to architecture. It is nonetheless revealing that the volume contains only one listing remotely connected to nature: seasonal affective disorder, a depressive mood swing occasioned by seasonal changes. Even here, nature comes in second: If the mood swing reflects seasonal unemployment, economics takes precedence as a cause.

6   Psychotherapists have exhaustively analyzed every form of dysfunctional family and social relations, but "dysfunctional environmental relations" does not exist even as a concept. Since its beginning, mainstream Western psychology has limited the definition of mental health to the interpersonal context of an urban industrial society: marriage, family, work, school, community. All that lies beyond the citified psyche has seemed of no human relevance—or perhaps too frightening to think about. "Nature," Freud dismally concluded, "is eternally remote. She destroys us—coldly, cruelly, relentlessly." Whatever else has been revised and rejected in Freud's theories, this tragic sense of estrangement from nature continues to haunt psychology, making the natural world seem remote and hostile.

7   Now all is changing. In the past 10 years, a growing number of psychologists have begun to place their theory and practice in an ecological context. Already ecopsychology has yielded insights of great value.

8   For one thing, it has called into question the standard strategy of scaring, shaming, and blaming that environmentalists have used in addressing the public since Rachel Carson wrote *Silent Spring.* There is evidence this approach does more harm than good—especially if, as ecopsychologists suggest, some environmentally destructive behavior bears the earmarks of addiction.

9   Take consumption habits. In ecopsychology workshops, people frequently admit their need to shop is "crazy." Why do they buy what they do not need? A common answer is: "I shop when I'm depressed. I go to the mall to be among happy people." Buying things is strictly secondary—and in fact does little to relieve the depression.

10   Some ecopsychologists believe that, as with compulsive gamblers, the depression that drives people to consume stems not from greed but from a sense of emptiness. This void usually traces back to childhood experiences of inadequacy and rejection; it may have much to do with the typically middle-class need for competitive success. The insecurity born of that drive may grow into a hunger for acquisition that cannot be satisfied even when people have consumed so much that they themselves recognize they are behaving irrationally.

11   If the addiction diagnosis of overconsumption is accurate, then guilt-tripping the public is worse than futile. Faced with scolding, addicts often resort to denial—or hostility. That makes them prey for antienvironmentalist groups like the Wise Use Movement, which then persuade an aggravated public to stop paying attention to "grieving greenies" and "ecofascists" who demand too much change too quickly.

12   As every therapist knows, addictive behavior cannot be cured by shame, because addicts are already deeply ashamed. Something affirmative and environmentally benign must be found to fill the inner void. Some ecopsychologists believe the joy and solace of the natural world can itself provide that emotional sustenance. Some, therefore, use wilderness, restoration projects, or gardens as a new "outdoor office."

13   "Nature heals" is one of the oldest therapeutic dicta. Ecopsychologists are finding new ways to apply that ancient insight. Over a century ago, Emerson lamented that "few adult persons can see nature." If they could, they would know that "in the woods, we return to reason and faith. There I feel that nothing can befall me in life, no disgrace or calamity . . . which nature cannot repair."

14   Why have therapists made so little of this obvious resource? When highly stressed people are asked to visualize a soothing scene, nobody imagines a freeway or a shopping mall. Rather, images of wilderness, forest, seascape, and starry skies invariably emerge. In taking such experiences seriously, ecopsychologists are broadening the context of mental health to include the natural environment. They are hastening the day when calling our bad environmental habits "crazy" will be more than a rhetorical outburst. The word will have behind it the full weight of considered professional consensus.

15   This, in turn, could be of enormous value in opening people to our spiritual, as well as physical, dependence upon nature. The time may not be far off when environmental policymakers will have something more emotionally engaging to work with than the Endangered Species Act. They will be able to defend the beauties and biodiversity of nature by invoking an environmentally based definition of mental health. We might then see an assault upon endangered species or old-growth forest as an assault upon the sanity of a community, upon children, or upon our species as a whole.

16   In devastating the natural environment, we may be undermining a basic requirement of sanity: our sense of moral reciprocity with the nonhuman environment. Yet ecopsychology also offers hope. As ecocidal as our behavior may have become, our bond with the planet endures; something within us voices a warning.

17   Ecopsychologists have begun to detect in people evidence of an unspoken grieving for the great environmental losses the world is suffering. Sometimes, indeed, clients themselves demand to have that sense of loss taken seriously in their therapy. In a letter to *Ecopsychology Newsletter,* one reader reports how she con-

fessed her anxiety for our environmental condition to her psychiatrist. "I felt depressed that things had gotten so bad I could no longer drink tap water safely." Her therapist, all too typically, dismissed her feelings as an "obsession with the environment." That judgment eventually drove the client to seek help elsewhere and finally toward a commitment to the environmental movement.

18   Denying the relevance of nature to our deepest emotional needs is still the rule in mainstream therapy, as in the culture generally. It is apt to remain so until psychologists expand our paradigm of the self to include the natural habitat—as was always the case in indigenous cultures, whose methods of healing troubled souls included the trees and rivers, the sun and stars.

19   At a conference titled "Psychology As If the Whole Earth Mattered," at Harvard's Center for Psychology and Social Change, psychologists concluded that "if the self is expanded to include the natural world, behavior leading to destruction of this world will be experienced as self-destruction."

20   Such an intimate connection with the earth means taking our evolutionary heritage seriously and putting it in an ecological framework. Ecopsychology reinforces insights from naturalists like E. O. Wilson, who suggests that we possess "an innately emotional affiliation with all living organisms"—biophilia—that inclines us toward fostering biodiversity.

21   If our culture is out of balance with nature, everything about our lives is affected; family, workplace, school, community—all take on a crazy shape. For this reason, ecopsychology does not seek to create new categories of pathology, but to show how our ecological disconnection plays into all ensuing ones. For example, the *DSM* defines "separation anxiety disorder" as "excessive anxiety concerning separation from home and from those to whom the individual is attached." But no separation is more pervasive in this Age of Anxiety than our disconnection from the natural world.

22   Freud coined the term reality principle to designate that objective order of things to which the healthy psyche must adapt if it is to qualify as "sane." Writing in a preecological era, he failed to include the biosphere. Ecopsychology is seeking to rectify that failure by expanding the definition of sanity to embrace the love for the living planet that is reborn in every child.

Responding to the Reading

1. Why does Roszak object to the use of the word *crazy* to describe environmental devastation?
2. Why does Roszak believe that the strategies of "scaring, shaming, and blaming" that environmentalists have used are questionable?
3. Roszak believes that our destruction of nature is similar to other addictive behavior. Why?
4. What does Roszak believe is behind the appeal of groups like the Wise Use Movement?

Questions Beyond the Reading

1. Roszak claims that a middle-class lifestyle generates a need for competitive success that cannot be satisfied. Do you agree or disagree? Explain.
2. Do you agree or disagree with the saying "Nature heals." Explain.

3. Roszak claims that nature is relevant to our emotional health. Do you agree or disagee? Explain.

4. Roszak states that "no separation is more pervasive in this Age of Anxiety than our disconnection from the natural world." Do you agree or disagree? Explain.

5. Do you personally feel disconnected from nature. If so, what can you do to reconnect with it? If not, describe what benefits you get from being connected with nature.

Questions Before the Reading

1. Do you have access to the Internet? If so, what features do you use?
2. What types of games do you enjoy playing?

VOCABULARY HIGHLIGHTS

vicariously	feeling or enjoying by imagining oneself as participating in the experiences of others
epigram	a witty or pointed saying or poem
placate	to appease by making concessions
malcontents	people who are dissatisfied with the prevailing conditions

---

Godhood: Not All Fun and Games
Don't get stuck in a MUD
Kristina Harris

1   It isn't easy being a goddess—I know; I've tried. Several years ago I joined the Information Superhighway and took the ramp marked MUD, or Multi-User Domain. These electronic role-playing adventure games, which have cropped up all over the Internet and local Bulletin Board Services, have been known to drain the lifeblood of hapless players who stumble across them. For the uninitiated, MUDs are a bit like videogames; but instead of graphic images, your screen will display something like this: "You have stumbled through a wooden archway into a damp, stone chamber. You shiver as you listen to the dripping of the moisture from above. Remains of an ancient tapestry hang on the east wall. There is a large iron door to the north and a dark staircase leading downward."

2   From these descriptions, a player must decide where to "go," and by entering simple commands (north, south, east, west) can move about and explore this realm. In some rooms monsters, ranging from abominable snowmen to zombies (depending

on the setting of the game), reside. They may have bits of information or valuable treasures to aid the quest, or they may be deadly foes. Simply slaying monsters can, however, become boring, if not for two additional elements: other players and The Gods.

3   One reason these games are so addictive is the player interaction. In "cyber-space," games afford anonymity and the chance to act the role of a different age, race or even sex. Players soon discover the exhilaration of setting out on a quest, slaying evil monsters or joining other adventurers and experiencing victory over incredible odds. Many players spend hours (even days) on line, attempting to pump up their characters' experience to the highest possible level. The pursuit of greater strength, more powerful weapons, additional protective armor and magical items for the char-acter drives the player onward. Because the game is played not only against the com-puter program but also against people, it is constantly changing.

4   Player-interaction dynamics are fascinating. Users may team up their charac-ters with others in the game, talk to them, attack them—even kill them. Knowing that these characters are the personas of others like themselves adds spice to the game. Violent actions may develop into electronic feuds where several users band to-gether to "kill" a player who has wronged them.

5   What makes these games enticing is that they are a step up from chat and e-mail. Not only is it possible to assume whatever personality you want, but you can also act any way you want. You can kill without ever seeing blood, roar threats or cross swords without ever breaking into a sweat. You can be an Arnold Schwarzenegger look-alike or a wise old sorceress unleashing forces of magic. With MUDs and other on-line multiplayer games, you can live vicariously in a new uni-verse and even attain godhood, thereby achieving omnipotence.

6   Many people identify so strongly with their characters that if one of them is maligned or killed they threaten to cancel their account with the on-line service. Some Mudaholics have even threatened legal action if a beloved alter ego is lost, since they believe that the (sometimes costly) hours spent building up a character have been wasted. These overly involved players become enraged when something happens to them and behave as if the wrong inflicted upon their game persona had really happened.

7   Even with the stimulus of player interaction, one can put only so many hours into playing the game before the same old dungeons lose their charm. Enter The Gods. Gods are players with the power to create, design and edit parts of the game program; it's like simultaneously trying to write a science-fiction novel and filming an episode of "Cops in Cyberspace."

8   We gods have absolute power in the game environment. Did your character die? I can resurrect him. Is a nasty monster rampaging through the town? I can delete it. Did you run out of places to explore? I can create new domains with some quick programming.

9   The power of godhood can be even more addictive than just playing the game. No matter how powerful you become, I can eliminate you. I can create monsters who will speak to you, diabolical traps that rob you of your money or your life, or carnivo-rous plants to devour you. For those who please me, I can create generous rewards. Power tends to corrupt, and absolute power . . . well, we all know the epigram. It is

often extremely difficult for game gods to refrain from harassing players with whom they have personality conflicts or enhancing the attributes of those who praise them.

10   A real problem with godhood is that mortals constantly appeal to your divine mercy at the first hint of trouble. The most fascinating thing about these appeals is that most of the people do not send electronic mail saying, "I was playing this game, and my character was deleted somehow. Could you check into the program?" Quite the contrary; most of the messages I get are often frantic, "I'm DEAD! Elrich Storm-slasher killed ME! I demand you resurrect me and return my long sword!"

11   The pleasing thing about divinity is that goddesses don't have to listen to demands. Generally, the "virtual deity" will restore an afflicted player—if only because it's simpler than ignoring him. Nothing ruins a goddess's day quite as much as the threat of a lawsuit. Gods therefore have three major functions: to continually create new worlds to explore, to rescue mortals who get into trouble and to placate malcontents.

12   With great power comes greater responsibility, and the hours spent in creation are often outnumbered by the hours spent dealing with unhappy players who seem to have forgotten that this is a game. If I had it to do again, I think I'd stick to being a mortal—but with good magic and heavy armor. Being Lord of the Universe can be fun, but the hours are generally lousy. Godhood is definitely not all it's cracked up to be.

Responding to the Reading

1. Why does Harris refer to herself as a "goddess"? Why is this appropriate?
2. According to Harris, why do people become so wrapped up in their game playing?
3. Why does Harris say "Godhood is definitely not all it's cracked up to be"?

Questions Beyond the Reading

1. How does playing games in a Multi-User Domain differ from ordinary game playing? In your opinion, which is better? Why?
2. Harris says that people identify strongly with their characters. Why is this so? Is there any danger in this identification? If so, what?
3. Harris starts to cite the epigram "Power tends to corrupt, and absolute power tends to corrupt absolutely." How is this epigram appropriate in ways that go beyond game playing?

Comparison and Contrast

Questions Before the Reading

1. Have you ever known anyone with a physical disability? How did that person manage his or her daily life with the disability?
2. Do you feel you are making good use of your time? Why or why not?

> **VOCABULARY HIGHLIGHTS**
>
> *atrophied*   having wasted away (as with a bodily organ)
> *gratification* satisfaction or pleasure
> *exacerbated*   having increased the bitterness or severity of something

Losing My Sight Made Me See
I realized too late how much time I had wasted

Terrence Kennell

1   When I entered the hospital in June of 1991, to have maxillofacial surgery, I had little concern whether or not all would go well, or reason to fear otherwise. The surgery also included exploration of the optic canal due to a lifelong bone disorder that was thought to be a probable threat to the optic nerve. I awoke from the surgery to near darkness, able to see only faint shadows and outlines. Somehow, the optic nerve had been damaged. It wasn't long thereafter that the nerve atrophied completely and I slipped into total darkness.

2   The shock of losing my sight did not hit me right away. My faith led me to believe that what had happened was simply temporary and that it was just a matter of time before I would see again. After all, blindness wasn't me. I had too many hopes and dreams to accomplish, things I wanted to do, places to go. And besides, I knew nothing about being blind. Such a thought, for me, meant life was over.

3   As I lay in the hospital, I couldn't resist the feelings of regret that hung over me. I quickly became angry with myself as I looked back on a life that—though still young—appeared to be half-filled with youthful indifference. It seemed to me that I had done very little with what was now a lot of valuable time and the wasted days of earlier years had suddenly come to an account. The future appeared to be over, and all I had for nearly three decades of living were nagging feelings of regret.

4   I get very concerned when I hear and read about the widespread apathy that is said to exist among the young and how so many are idling their time away. Their goals and expectations amount to little more than a search for instant gratification. Ambition is hurriedly disappearing among them. It is what the author Thomas French, in his book "South of Heaven: A Year in the Life of an American High School . . . ," refers to as a "withering of curiosity."

5   Looking back on the once idle course of my own past, I know how easy it is to slip into a do-nothing way of life. I grew up in the heart of the Mississippi Delta, where a person's existence begged for direction and the civil-rights legacy was a mainstay. I came from an impoverished family worsened by an absent father. My poor health together with a lack of opportunity—exacerbated by racial prejudices—left little doubt that living required much hard work and determination to make it any better. Despite all these reasons for diligence, my indifference persisted.

6   At the time of the loss of my sight at the age of 28, it seemed I had somehow managed to spend nearly 10 years doing little or nothing. The years from mid-teens to mid-twenties, not only for me but for most of those who moved along with me, were full of an almost instinctive desire for self-gratification and an oblivion to anything tomorrow. Even college bore little expectation and proved to be a continuation of the time before, resulting in academic dismissal and, finally, a failure to graduate.

7   When I did become focused—several years before the surgery—I found starting a career to be no small feat. I had hoped to make my way as a writer, editor and book publisher. It wasn't long before I realized that getting started was filled with difficulties. Having a degree may not necessarily open a door of opportunity, but not having one will definitely close it. Without my degree, most publications I spoke with would not consider me for an interview. It was only after offering to do some work for free as a stringer for the local paper—and a great deal of pleading with many others for a tryout—that I succeeded in landing a job as a copy editor with a newspaper. I later worked as a book editor. Shortly after I lost my sight, my employer informed me that my job had been filled by someone else.

8   Now my horizons represent new and unfamiliar struggles—days and things once taken for granted have long since been given due value and meaning. The previously unknown world of the disabled has served to remind me of the immediacy of life and just how fragile it really is. It also has brought many changes and adjustments. I find it difficult to get used to the absence of the sweet faces of family and friends, beautiful seasonal days and moonlit nights, the printed words of a favorite book. I even miss taking a hectic drive on South Florida's I-95.

9   Everyday tasks have had to be relearned. I attended the state's rehab center to learn necessary skills for daily living and how to become mobile by using a cane. I later returned to the center to receive valuable training in adaptive computer technology.

10   My employer's perception about my loss of sight proved to be typical of what I found as I began to step back into society. I was amazed to find out how uninformed most people are about blindness, especially concerning the capabilities of blind people, what we can do or cannot do. At first, family and friends tried to do every little thing possible for me. For others, it means a lot of false assumptions, such as thinking they cannot speak to me directly but must do so to whomever I happen to be with. And for too many employers, it means assuming that I have discontinued to be a worthwhile investment. I can attest to this by all the doors I have knocked on for nearly three years; and by the 70 percent of disabled Americans who are unemployed.

11   As for myself, I have come to believe that life still has a great deal to offer and all the things that really matter remain with me. My dreams haven't faded. I would like to work as a writer, perhaps to marry, have a family and own a home. And above all, to rightly relate to others and live in a fulfilling way as I strive to become an integral, contributing part of the community.

12   It is understandable that when we're young we think that time is on our side and the world waits for us. But only when it is somehow abruptly interrupted do we realize it "just ain't so." Maybe if young people could see, firsthand, the struggles and challenges of the disabled, it would stir in them an awareness of the urgency of

life—to pursue dreams and to realize what God has given them. I write these words not as a moralistic effort to pick on today's youth, nor to be overly critical of them. But rather to offer a few words to the wise: "There is no time to waste."

Responding to the Reading

1. Why does Kennell say that at first, the thought of being blind meant that his life was over?
2. Why does Kennell say that being disabled has reminded him of "the immediacy of life and just how fragile it really is"?
3. Kennell's essay belongs to a long tradition of literature that has the theme of *carpe diem,* meaning "seize the day." How does Kennell motivate the reader to take action now and not put life off until later?

Questions Beyond the Reading

1. Kennell states that he hears that the young are apathetic. Do you agree or disagree? Explain.
2. Despite the newfound difficulties associated with his blindness, Kennell ends his essay on a positive, hopeful note. How do you see the plight of the disabled and their opportunities for the future?
3. What can you do to make your time more valuable and productive?

Questions Before the Reading

1. Have you ever owned a dog? If so, describe your relationship with it.
2. Describe your reaction to the idea of treating dogs for psychological problems.

VOCABULARY HIGHLIGHTS

dotage	feebleness of mind, usually from old age
psychotropic	affecting mental activity
hierarchical	a ranked system of persons or things
desensitization	the state of being unable to feel or perceive
quid pro	one thing in return for another

Dr. Sigmund Doolittle

Jeffrey Kluger

1   If you're in the market for a dog, think twice before making that dog a dachshund No doubt there are millions of happy dachshund owners who would disagree, but millions of happy dachshund owners never met Sossi.

From Jeffrey Kluger, © 1996 The Walt Disney Co. Reprinted with permission of *Discover* magazine.

2   Sossi was a dachshund of indeterminate age that lived next door to my family during the late 1960s and, given the rancor she inspired among her neighbors, was lucky to see the 1970s. The first problem with Sossi—one that, granted, wasn't her fault—concerned her looks. When choosing a dog, most dachshund enthusiasts set their aesthetic standards low—and well they should. Given the canine industry's obsession with breeding and bearing, it takes some courage to select a dog that looks as though at least one root of its family tree is firmly planted in the Jimmy Dean sausage factory. Sossi, small at birth and throughout her life, took the distinctive dachshund body type even further, appearing less like a huggable household pet than a sort of high-speed kielbasa with feet. But Sossi's worst feature was not her wurst feature.

3   If part of a dog's job in the whole interspecies domestication deal involves keeping the human's home safe from intruders, Sossi was evidently bucking for employee of the month. To be sure, a home guarded by 11 pounds of mobile luncheon meat is not exactly impregnable, and Sossi must have known that, deciding that what she couldn't accomplish with her bulk she would accomplish with her bark. Rising at least 15 minutes before sunrise, she would spend up to 11 hours a day standing in her front yard and barking in a high, piercing register at any unfamiliar person she detected within the tristate area. As Sossi got older, she grew even more cantankerous, routinely barking not just at strangers but at family members, friends, cats, plants, furniture, and on one memorable occasion, a fresh loaf of Roman Meal sandwich bread. Eventually, Sossi became so antisocial she simply retreated to the attic, took her meals in her room, and spent much of her dotage looking out her window and alternately barking at passersby and yelling at neighborhood kids to turn down that confounded rock and roll.

4   Sossi's snappish temperament is not uncommon among dogs, and it is by no means the only behavioral quirk the canine personality can exhibit. For every breed of dog available, there is a breed of dog dysfunction never mentioned in the owner's manual. Nowadays human beings are beginning to realize that their best nonhuman friends have psyches that are every bit as complex as their own—and every bit as in need of understanding. More and more, the person providing that understanding is Dr. Nick Dodman.

5   Dodman is the director of the Tufts University Animal Behavior Clinic in Grafton, Massachusetts, and the author of the upcoming book *The Dog Who Loved Too Much: Tales, Treatment, and the Psychology of Dogs.* The acknowledged leader in the admittedly narrow field of dog psychology, Dodman has spent much of his career studying the canine mind and has developed a wide range of methods for curing what ails it. The way Dodman sees it, troubled dogs, like troubled humans, can respond to a variety of psychotherapeutic protocols, including behavior modification regimens and even the use of psychotropic medications like Anafranil and Prozac. While many pet owners may doubt whether treatment of this kind is ever right for a patient that would just as soon chew a couch as lie down on it, Dodman, a dog lover himself, is not among them.

6   "As people who own and study dogs discover," Dodman says, "keeping a dog healthy is far more complicated than it seems. The old idea that a dog with behavioral problems is just being obstinate is falling out of favor. In its place, people are beginning to accept that a misbehaving dog is usually a troubled dog, and a troubled dog needs care."

7   While Dodman has identified a wide range of canine personality disorders in his years in practice, he believes that all the emotional problems dogs exhibit tend to fall into one of three broad categories: aggressive behavior, fearful and anxious behavior, and compulsive behavior. Of the three, aggressive behavior poses the biggest problem.

8   Twelve thousand years ago, when humanity's Ice Age House Pet Selection Committee was first considering candidates for domestication, the dog must have seemed an unlikely applicant:

9   NAME: Dog.

10   TURN-ONS: Meat.

11   FAVORITE FOODS: Meat

12   LEISURE ACTIVITIES: Stalking and killing things to get meat.

13   CLOSEST RELATIVE TO CONTACT IN CASE OF EMERGENCY: The wolf.

14   Despite such a questionable résumé, however, it was the dog that was first invited into humanity's collective home, and for both species, the cohabitation took some getting used to. Dogs in the wild tend to congregate in highly structured, extremely hierarchical packs, with dominant and submissive members constantly jockeying for position through threat displays, intimidation, mock fighting, and, frequently, real fighting. Human beings, who fancy themselves a good deal more socially sophisticated than this, are no strangers to such power-play behavior, but we generally express it a bit more subtly—and it's a good thing, too. The day Newt Gingrich nips Dick Gephardt on the neck in order to assert his congressional dominance is the day I apply for a Canadian passport. When the more socially direct dog comes to live with the more socially discreet human, however, there are bound to be conflicts.

15   "Dogs think of themselves as members of the family," Dodman says, "and as such, they immediately try to determine where they fit in the hierarchy of the pack. Often the dog concludes that it ranks number two or even number one and will snap at humans it considers its subordinates, growl at them if they try to touch its food, and generally make it its business to threaten at least some of the people in whose home it's been invited to live. Understandably, humans see this as inappropriate."

16   Just as troubling as the hostile dog—if a good deal less dangerous—is the anxious dog. One of the things pet owners appreciate most about the canine species is its open adoration of the human species. Unlike cats, which insist on a credit check and at least three personal references before agreeing to come live with you, dogs thrive on the company of people. Some dogs, however, thrive too much and can suffer extreme separation anxiety when left alone.

17   In most cases, the symptoms of separation anxiety are easy to spot, usually beginning with a dog that's very clingy when the owners are home, whimpery when they prepare to leave, and so distressed when they're gone that it may damage lamps or furniture or even begin urinating throughout the house. Certainly, as social protest goes, this form of free speech is not exactly the stuff of op-ed pages, but faced with even the most trenchant George Will commentary and a Labrador retriever urinating on the living room rug, I know what would get my attention. In addition to growing terrified when faced with separation, anxious dogs can also develop fear of strangers, inanimate objects, and even noises like thunder.

18   More perplexing than both canine anxiety and canine aggression are canine compulsions—specifically compulsive tail chasing and paw licking and chewing. For most people, few activities call the intellectual wattage of the entire canine species into greater question than the sight of a dog chasing its tail. Though even the most devoted dog owners do not pretend that their pets have the brainpower of an Oxford Fellow, they do expect them to be smarter than an oxford shirt. Dodman explains, however, that tail chasing, as well as paw licking, is not an intellectual problem but a psychological one.

19   "Many dogs chase their tails on occasion," he says. "For a handful, however, those occasions become more and more frequent until tail chasing becomes all they do. Compulsive licking, which leads to 'lick granuloma,' is even more unpleasant. Dogs that do this pick a spot on their bodies, generally on their left foreleg, and systematically lick and gnaw it until the fur in that area is lost and the skin underneath becomes infected."

20   While compulsive disorders—as well as anxiety and aggression—generally resist the ministrations of even the most dedicated pet owners, things change considerably when a professional like Dodman gets involved. Of all three categories of illness, anxiety disorders appear to respond best to treatment, and separation anxiety may respond best of all.

21   To treat a dog with separation problems, Dodman recommends a two-pronged approach, consisting of what he terms systematic desensitization accompanied by counterconditioning. Dogs suffering from separation anxiety are remarkably adept at reading their owners' unspoken cues and in some cases may be aware that you're preparing to leave the house long before you ever do. If the moment you step into the shower to get ready for a dinner date, your dog starts whimpering, you know you're in trouble; if when you walk toward the closet to pick out something to wear, it takes to its bed, unplugs the phone, and places a cold compress on its head, you're in *big* trouble. To combat this, Dodman prescribes a series of planned departures that accustom the dog to all the stimuli that cause it distress. For dogs that become anxious when they hear you pick up your car keys, for example, Dodman recommends a series of key-jingling exercises that, if repeated often enough, ultimately cause the sound to lose its power. When key jingling is no longer a problem, you would next tackle coat donning or front door opening, advancing to the point at which you actually leave the house.

22   "Eventually," Dodman says, "you expose your dog to a series of planned departures during which you leave the house for a few minutes at a time, staying away longer and longer until your dog grows accustomed to the idea of your being gone."

23   Similar habituation can be used, Dodman believes, to treat other canine anxieties, including fear of people and fear of noises. But what if such training isn't effective? In these cases, Dodman believes, the answer may be less habituation than medication.

24   Ever since the introduction of the antidepressant Prozac in the mid-1980s, the search for the magic psychotropic bullet has accelerated dramatically. While nobody in the pharmaceutical industry has yet introduced festive, Barney Rubble–shaped

Anafranil for the K-through-12 crowd, the idea of chemical treatments for people with emotional disorders has gained increasing acceptance. As it has, animal doctors have begun to discover that the same drugs can work for *dogs* with emotional disorders as well.

25 "The dog mind may be less sophisticated than ours," he says, "but the brain is just as chemically complex. In the case of anxious human beings, who always have the option of trying to talk their problems through, we still sometimes prescribe drugs. In the case of dogs, who don't have that option, shouldn't medication make even more sense?"

26 When faced with an anxious dog that is otherwise untreatable, Dodman may use BuSpar. Similar to Valium—which is so commonly prescribed for people, it is now being used as a garnish in many fine West Coast restaurants—BuSpar mimics the effects of the neurotransmitter serotonin. A chemical essential for regulating mood, serotonin can be produced in different quantities in the brain at different times, leading to impulsiveness or aggression when levels are low, and a sense of well-being when levels are sufficient. BuSpar works by binding to the same sites on brain cells to which serotonin binds, mimicking the neurotransmitter's action and supplementing it when natural concentrations drop too far.

27 Says Dodman: "I don't say BuSpar should be the first treatment tried; but as a sort of chemical shoehorn to help ease a dog into more traditional therapy, it can work remarkably well."

28 The same yin-and-yang, medicate-and-train option is available for aggressive dogs as well. In treating a dog that sees itself as the alpha member of the family pack, Dodman first prescribes a protocol he refers to as the Work for a Living program, in which the dog learns that everything it gets from the family—food, love, attention—must be paid for in some small way.

29 "If an aggressive dog comes up to a member of the family and indicates that it wants to be petted or fed, it almost always gets petted or fed," he says. "But why should it?"

30 Instead of such automatic compliance, Dodman recommends that when a dog requests food or attention, you respond with an instruction like "Sit" or "Stay." If the dog obeys, it should be rewarded with what it is seeking. If it looks at you with slit eyes, rolls a toothpick ominously around on its tongue, and suggests that maybe you're the one who ought to be thinking about sitting, you probably need to start over from the top.

31 In some cases, of course, no amount of repetition is sufficient to help the dog get with this quid pro program. When behavioral treatments have failed and the dog is still so convinced of its own household dominance that it's begun changing the locks and having its own premium cable channels installed, the medicinal option might again be the best. In these cases, the drugs that bring about the most promising results appear to be the members of the Prozac family, including Anafranil, Zoloft, and Prozac itself. These medications work not by mimicking serotonin but by preventing excess amounts of the chemical from being reabsorbed by brain cells, thus making more available in the synapses between cells, where the real signal-sending activity of the brain takes place.

32   "In dogs that don't respond to behavioral training," Dodman says, "these so-called serotonin re-uptake inhibitors can lead to a reduction in aggression about 75 percent of the time."

33   For dogs with compulsive disorders, the pharmacological option might be most important of all. Tail chasers can sometimes be helped with a program of human attention and intervention in addition to being given more exercise and a better diet, but no pet owner is vigilant enough to catch the chasing activity every time it occurs.

34   Paw licking is even harder to cure, with existing treatments involving little more than bandaging the affected area or outfitting the dog with a large plastic collar that attaches to its collar and flares up around its head, denying it access to the wound long enough to allow the leg to heal. This, however, works only as long as the apparatus is in place, and when it is it can actually *increase* anxiety. Many is the cone-wearing canine that has run home in tears at the end of the day because all the other dogs in the park were pointing and chanting, "Carvel-head! Carvel-head!" while clutching their sides in laughter. In these cases medication may be the only answer.

35   "Human beings with obsessive-compulsive disorder have been helped by drugs in the Prozac family," Dodman, says, "which relieve the anxiety that helps drive the compulsions. In dogs the drugs can work the same way."

36   To be sure, nobody, Dodman included, wants to be responsible for a whole generation of medicated dogs that have sacrificed their essential canineness to the prescription pad. Nor does anyone want to rely too long on reconditioning or other animal equivalents of talk therapy if they're not working at all. But even the most conservative dog doctors would agree that when you're providing emotional counseling to a member of the family who still has to be reminded not to drink from the toilet or eat the living room throw pillows, your treatment can't afford to be too subtle. For the anxious Akita or the despondent Doberman, a little medication may turn out to be the only way to prevent Ol' Blue from remaining Moody Blue.

Responding to the Reading

1. Kluger starts his essay with the story of a dachshund named Sossi. What is the point of his story?
2. Dr. Nick Dodman classifies dog personality disorders into three categories. What are they and how is each characterized?
3. What is the importance of understanding a dog's sense of hierarchy?
4. Why does Dr. Dodman believe that medication is sometimes necessary for the treatment of psychologically disturbed dogs?

Questions Beyond the Reading

1. Kluger states, "For every breed of dog, there is a breed of dog dysfunction." What dysfunctional behavior have you noted in dogs? How have you treated or dealt with such behavior?
2. How do the types of treatments Dodman suggests for dogs compare and contrast with treatments for humans? Explain.
3. Many people would suggest that treating dogs for psychological problems is a waste of time and money. What is your opinion? Explain.

Cause/Effect

1. What famous natural or historical landmarks have you visited? How did you feel when you visited them?
2. How do you see the balance of wanting to preserve historically important sites and wanting to exhibit those sites to the public?

VOCABULARY HIGHLIGHTS

draconian	rigorous, harsh, or cruel
notoriously	as is very well known, especially unfavorably
unscrupulous	unprincipled; without morals
suffice	to satisfy a need

The Four Corners Dilemma
Should we hide history's treasures to keep them safe?

Barry Meier

1   Fall in the Southwest is the time of long shadows that mute the sandstone mesas, bleached red by sun and time. Each year a quiet descends on the Four Corners, where snow may soon cover the area's archaeological treasures, providing a natural defense from what may be their greatest enemy: the tourists who love them too much.

2   Some American Indian ruins in the Four Corners (where the borders of Arizona, Colorado, New Mexico, and Utah meet) are today obscured by more than snows; they are left off some maps entirely. Abuse by tourists has become so critical that the federal government has taken the rather draconian step of asking cartographers to remove archaeological sites from maps in order to hide them from travelers.

3   Archaeologists and preservationists justify censorship as a necessary shield for the fragile treasures they don't have the manpower to oversee. But critics question the wisdom of putting historic sites in the exclusive custody of a few bureaucrats and experts. In a nation with a notoriously short memory, that strategy could eventually disconnect millions from a cultural history that is already quite vague.

4   Scattered throughout the Four Corners are the ruins left by the ancient Anasazi people, who abandoned the area in the 1300s. For seven centuries their remnants were left virtually untouched. But as more and more Americans discover that the Anasazi artifacts rival those of the Greeks or the Maya, they have visited the ruins in record numbers. In the absence of adequate security, visitors have com-

Reprinted with permission from Barry Meier.

mitted such mindless offenses as camping and building fires inside the highly vulnerable Anasazi structures.

5   Federal officials and the Navajo tribe, which has hundreds of ruins on its sprawling reservation, have asked the Automobile Club of Southern California to remove Anasazi sites from its popular "Indian Country" road map of the Southwest. Places slated to disappear include Cutthroat Castle and the Hackberry, Horseshoe, and Cajon ruins, all of which are unguarded, outlying parts of Hovenweep National Monument, an archaeological park that straddles the border of Colorado and Utah.

6   Officially, park authorities say that the action is being taken to ensure that travelers register before visiting the sites so that they may be instructed in basic archaeological etiquette. But there is also an unstated hope—that once a site is removed from the map, many tourists will simply drive by it.

7   As irresponsible tourists multiply, the traveler's door to the past is closing in all too many places. In France, for example, most tourists to the famous cave paintings at Lascaux must now content themselves with reproductions rather than the real thing. And some Anasazi ruins, their ancient stones and sticks coated in a high-tech plastic to prevent damage by visitors, have taken on the look of theme parks.

8   Looting has long plagued the Four Corners, a panorama of forested peaks, deep gorges, rugged canyons, and desert plains. Military parties probing the Southwest in the mid-19th century found the Anasazi sites, which attracted souvenir hunters. In 1884 a San Francisco newspaper described the scene at a site near Flagstaff, Arizona. "We dug for an hour," one amateur archaeologist reported, "and found beans, gourds, reeds, arrows, bowstrings, coarse cloth [and] a child's sandal."

9   Today, professional looters pay local residents to dig up unexcavated Anasazi sites. The resulting haul quietly makes its way through unscrupulous dealers to private collectors or galleries. But even more damaging to the Anasazi heritage is the sheer volume of well-meaning tourists.

10   The number of visitors to Mesa Verde National Park, near Durango, Colorado, has reached 750,000 annually—a 100 percent increase in 10 years. With thousands of tourists daily inspecting such ruins as the Balcony House—a structure built of stone, dried clay, and sticks inside a cave carved into a canyon wall—even the most watchful park rangers cannot prevent damage.

11   Little is known about the Anasazi; even their name, which supposedly means Enemy Ancestors, was given to them by the Navajo. But the signatures of their culture, such as paintings of abstract animals and flute-playing spirit figures, which appear on canyon walls throughout the Four Corners, suggest a society both elegant and mysterious.

12   Those eager to explore such mysteries have touched rock paintings and inadvertently left behind oils from their hands, which damage the ancient works of art. As a result, visitors to some Anasazi sites have begun to face new limits on visiting hours and other restrictions. At Mesa Verde this summer, for example, officials started requiring tourists to have tickets, in an effort to control their numbers.

13   Some experts believe that the surge of interest in the Anasazi reflects a long-overdue appreciation for America's prewhite past. They maintain that tourism may benefit archaeological sites rather than endanger them.

14   "Overall, tourism is very positive because it raises public awareness of these cultural resources," argues Mark Michel, president of the Archaeological Conservancy, a group in Albuquerque, New Mexico, that works to protect historic sites.

15   On another front, a battle has been under way for several years over whether to pave a 22-mile-long dirt road leading to Chaco Canyon National Historic Park, near Nageezi, New Mexico.

16   Archaeologists believe that Chaco Canyon was one of the epicenters of Anasazi culture, where as many as 6,000 people lived 900 years ago. Set on a desert plain and surrounded by canyon walls, its major building complexes, such as Pueblo Bonito, rose four stories.

17   Park officials at Chaco Canyon have long held that its bumpy entrance road, which can take on the consistency of cake batter during a sudden summer downpour, has served as a natural tourist barrier, holding down visitation to manageable levels. But as the population in the surrounding countryside has steadily grown, residents have put increasing pressure on local officials to improve the road.

18   Butch Wilson, the park superintendent, estimates that, if the road is completely paved, the number of annual visitors to Chaco Canyon will jump to 500,000, from some 90,000 today.

19   Similar problems have emerged at virtually every major Anasazi site in the Four Corners. And in some cases, the economic needs of hard-pressed Indians are playing a critical role.

20   At Canyon de Chelly (pronounced deh-SHAY) National Monument, on the Navajo reservation near Chinle, Arizona, many Navajos work as drivers or guides on two-and-a-half-ton trucks that ferry tourists to Anasazi sites. A few years ago, however, government archaeologists began to fear that the impact from the heavy trucks was undermining some archaeological sites.

21   A proposal by park-service officials to limit the number of trucks led to complaints from some local Navajos, who saw their livelihoods threatened. Some older tourists also claimed it would be impossible for them to see some of the canyon's most distant attractions.

22   Park-service officials announced this year that they would freeze the number of trucks rumbling into the canyon at a level slightly above the current rate. The way visitation is increasing (doubling in six years), some future visitors will find themselves left out.

23   The guiding principle of responsible tourism has long been to leave a place as one finds it, but admirable sentiments alone no longer suffice. Exploration of the past requires a new set of attitudes, including the willingness to view replicas instead of the real thing and the acceptance of the fact that the survival of a place may depend on our not visiting it at all.

Responding to the Reading

1. Why do you think Meier describes America as "a nation with a notoriously short memory"?
2. Who were the Anasazi and why are they important today?
3. Why does Meier cite the example of the cave paintings at Lascaux?
4. What "new set of attitudes" is Meier calling for?

**Questions
Beyond the
Reading**

1. Meier states that some maps no longer carry directions to famous historical sites in an effort to preserve them from the abuse of tourists. In your opinion, is this a good idea? Why or why not?
2. Meier shows how tourism can be both a blessing and a curse for historical sites. How do you feel about making historical sites readily accessible to tourists? Explain.
3. Argue for or against the policy of keeping tourists from historical sites that exist in fragile environments.

**Questions
Before the
Reading**

1. What do you do when you're bored?
2. How do you like to spend your spare time?

VOCABULARY HIGHLIGHTS

apathy	lack of interest or concern
incessantly	without stopping
acculturated	having adopted the traits and patterns of another group
stagnant	sluggish or dull

Action as the Antidote to Boredom

Leo F. Buscaglia

1   There is a disease that afflicts infants known as marasmus, which literally means wasting away. Its cause is believed to be lack of stimulation of the senses, and it can lead to death.

2   We adults have been known to suffer from boredom that has its own wasting-away consequences—apathy, despair, passivity, depression—that often leads to physical problems. Boredom also seems to be a root cause of such social problems as juvenile delinquency, vandalism, drug addiction, and suicide.

3   The effects of boredom may be less obvious among older people. We may not realize, for instance, that individuals who are afraid to take risks, who complain incessantly, who are constantly fatigued, who have little self-esteem, may be suffering from a lack of stimulation in their lives.

4   We can understand how assembly-line workers, housekeepers and others who perform monotonous, repetitive tasks can become listless and apathetic at times. Occasional boredom is something we all confront. Chronic boredom, however, is a signal that something fundamental is missing in our lives.

Reprinted with permission of Leo Buscaglia.

5   Perhaps it reflects a reluctance to involve ourselves deeply in life or in relationships with others. Or perhaps it is an unconscious resistance to change. It is safe to say that whatever is behind these feelings, the solution must come from within. Others cannot provide what is missing, be it excitement, imagination or variety.

6   We can bring an end to boredom by activating our own strengths, by doing something that has meaning for us and enhances our good feelings about ourselves. In a sense we cure boredom by unbalancing our lives, giving up the security of the way we live, taking risks and accepting challenges.

7   But as with all meaningful change, there are obstacles to overcome. A survey conducted for a magazine recently asked: "Which of the following items give you the most pleasure and satisfaction in life?" The list included: friends, helping others, vacations, hobbies, reading, marriage, sexual relationships, food, sports, religion and watching TV. The hands-down winner was television watching.

8   One may conclude from such a survey that we have become acculturated to boredom by the mechanization of our push-button lives. We have become spectators rather than participants, exercising our fingers more and more and our minds and bodies less and less.

9   But rather than give credence to one more despairing conclusion about the human condition, I suggest we take responsibility for our boredom and do something about it. Boredom is a form of anger without enthusiasm. In other words, it is a passive state. Bored people complain about things without feeling they must change them.

10   They hold on to unrewarding jobs, continue in stagnant relationships, resisting the risk of change. They place the blame for their discontent on others for failing to spark their interest or engage their enthusiasm.

11   It becomes essential, then, that we take action against this monotony. We can do something for others, set fresh goals, follow our fantasies, give rein to our imaginations, learn new skills, strive for more spontaneity.

12   We can become more aware of the boring demands and routines that fill our lives. We can listen more and talk less. We can throw ourselves into some work or cause we believe in.

13   As Nietzsche wrote, "Isn't life a hundred times too short for us to bore ourselves?"

Responding to the Reading

1. What does Buscaglia say are the causes of boredom?
2. What does Buscaglia say are the effects of boredom?
3. How does Buscaglia define *boredom?*
4. How does Buscaglia suggest we combat boredom?

Questions Beyond the Reading

1. Buscaglia suggests that boredom has been a root cause of many social problems. Do you agree or disagree? Why?
2. Buscaglia suggests that we must unbalance our lives to cure boredom. What risks does unbalancing involve? Give examples.

3. How does the mechanization of our lives contribute to boredom? Explain.
4. How do you avoid boredom or "being in a rut"? Explain with examples.

---

1. Do you consider yourself a neat person or a sloppy one?
2. How important are clothing and behavior in public?
3. What assumptions do you make about strangers, based on their appearance?

VOCABULARY HIGHLIGHTS

unkempt	not neat or tidy
disheveled	marked by disorder or disarray
spool	a cylindrical device on which thread or string is wound
pauper	a person without any means of support except begging or charity
namby-pambyism	the state of being weakly affected or without firm methods or policy

The Decline of Neatness

Norman Cousins

1   Anyone with a passion for hanging labels on people or things should have little difficulty in recognizing that an apt tag for our time is the Unkempt generation. I am not referring solely to college kids. The sloppiness virus has spread to all sectors of society. People go to all sorts of trouble and expense to look uncombed, unshaved, unpressed.

2   The symbol of the times is blue jeans—not just blue jeans in good condition but jeans that are frayed, torn, discolored. They don't get that way naturally. No one wants blue jeans that are crisply clean or spanking new. Manufacturers recognize a big market when they see it, and they compete with one another to offer jeans that are made to look as though they've just been discarded by clumsy house painters after ten years of wear. The more faded and seemingly ancient the garment, the higher the cost. Disheveled is in fashion; neatness is obsolete.

3   Nothing is wrong with comfortable clothing. It's just that the current usage is more reflective of a slavish conformity than a desire for ease. No generation has strained harder than ours to affect a casual, relaxed, cool look; none has succeeded more spectacularly in looking as though it had been stamped out by cookie cutters.

The attempt to avoid any appearance of being well groomed or even neat has a quality of desperation that suggests a calculated and phony deprivation. We shun conventionality, but we put on a uniform to do it. An appearance of alienation is the triumphant goal, to be pursued in oversize sweaters and muddy sneakers.

4   Slovenly speech comes off the same spool. Vocabulary, like blue jeans, is drained of color and distinction. A complete sentence in everyday speech is as rare as a man's tie in the swank Polo Lounge of the Beverly Hills Hotel. People communicate in chopped-up phrases, relying on grunts and chants of "you know" or "I mean" to cover up a damnable incoherence. Neatness should be no less important in language than it is in dress. But spew and sprawl are taking over. The English language is one of the greatest sources of wealth in the world. In the midst of accessible riches, we are linguistic paupers.

5   Violence in language has become almost as casual as the possession of handguns. The curious notion has taken hold that emphasis in communicating is impossible without the incessant use of four-letter words. Some screenwriters openly admit that they are careful not to turn in scripts that are devoid of foul language lest the classification office impose the curse of a G (general) rating. Motion-picture exhibitors have a strong preference for the R (restricted) rating, probably on the theory of forbidden fruit. Hence writers and producers have every incentive to employ tasteless language and gory scenes.

6   The effect is to foster attitudes of casualness toward violence and brutality not just in entertainment but in everyday life. People are not as uncomfortable as they ought to be about the glamorization of human hurt. The ability to react instinctively to suffering seems to be atrophying. Youngsters sit transfixed in front of television or motion-picture screens, munching popcorn while human beings are battered or mutilated. Nothing is more essential in education than respect for the frailty of human beings; nothing is more characteristic of the age than mindless violence.

7   Everything I have learned about the educational process convinces me that the notion that children can outgrow casual attitudes toward brutality is wrong. Count on it: if you saturate young minds with materials showing that human beings are fit subjects for debasement or dismembering, the result will be desensitization to everything that should produce revulsion or resistance. The first aim of education is to develop respect for life, just as the highest expression of civilization is the supreme tenderness that people are strong enough to feel and manifest toward one another. If society is breaking down, as it too often appears to be, it is not because we lack the brainpower to meet its demands but because our feelings are so dulled that we don't recognize we have a problem.

8   Untidiness in dress, speech and emotions is readily connected to human relationships. The problem with the casual sex so fashionable in films is not that it arouses lust but that it deadens feelings and annihilates privacy. The danger is not that sexual exploitation will not create sex fiends but that it may spawn eunuchs. People who have the habit of seeing everything and doing anything run the risk of feeling nothing.

9   My purpose here is not to make a case for a Victorian decorum or for namby-pambyism. The argument is directed to bad dress, bad manners, bad speech, bad human relationships. The hope has to be that calculated sloppiness will run its

course. Who knows, perhaps some of the hip designers may discover they can make a fortune by creating fashions that are unfrayed and that grace the human form. Similarly, motion-picture and television producers and exhibitors may realize that a substantial audience exists for something more appealing to the human eye and spirit than the sight of a human being hurled through a store-front window or tossed off a penthouse terrace. There might even be a salutary response to films that dare to show people expressing genuine love and respect for one another in more convincing ways that anonymous clutching and thrashing about.

10 Finally, our schools might encourage the notion that few things are more rewarding than genuine creativity, whether in the clothes we wear, the way we communicate, the nurturing of human relationships, or how we locate the best in ourselves and put it to work.

Responding to the Reading

1. Why does Cousins say that people who attempt to dress casually actually appear to be "stamped out by cookie cutters"? Explain.
2. What does Cousins mean by "the violence of language"?
3. Why does Cousins maintain that overexposure of sexuality leads not to lust but to the deadening of feeling? Explain.
4. In the next-to-last paragraph, Cousins refers to "bad manners, bad dress, bad speech, bad human relationships." What does he mean by *bad* in each instance?

Questions Beyond the Reading

1. Cousins says that people's sloppy appearance is indicative of an overall sloppiness in society. Do you agree or disagree? Explain.
2. Some opponents of Cousins would claim that movies do not create behavior but merely reflect behavior that already exists. Do you agree or disagree? Explain.
3. In the final paragraph, Cousins calls upon schools to encourage "genuine creativity." What do you think *genuine creativity* is? Give examples.

Questions Before the Reading

1. What is the worst grade you ever received in a class? Did you feel that you deserved that grade?
2. What are the responsiblities of a student versus those of a teacher for a student's performance in a course?

VOCABULARY HIGHLIGHTS

merit	deserved respect or praise
banal	boring and pointless
sundry	miscellaneous
delineated	specifically portrayed or described in words
egress	a means of exiting

What Our Education System Needs Is More F's

Carl Singleton

1   I suggest that instituting merit raises, getting back to basics, marrying the university to industry, and the other recommendations will not achieve measurable success [in restoring quality to American education] until something even more basic is returned to practice. The immediate need for our educational system from prekindergarten through post-Ph.D. is not more money or better teaching but simply a widespread giving of F's.

2   Before hastily dismissing the idea as banal and simplistic, think for a moment about the implications of a massive dispensing of failing grades. It would dramatically, emphatically, and immediately force into the open every major issue related to the inadequacies of American education.

3   Let me make it clear that I recommend giving those F's—by the dozens, hundreds, thousands, even millions—only to students who haven't learned the required material. The basic problem of our educational system is the common practice of giving credit where none has been earned, a practice that has resulted in the sundry faults delineated by all the reports and studies over recent years. Illiteracy among high-school graduates is growing because those students have been passed rather than flunked; we have low-quality teaching because of low-quality teachers who never should have been certified in the first place; college students have to take basic reading, writing, and mathematics courses because they never learned those skills in classrooms from which they never should have been granted egress.

4   School systems have contributed to massive ignorance by issuing unearned passing grades over a period of some 20 years. At first there was tolerance of students who did not fully measure up (giving D's to students who should have received firm F's); then our grading system continued to deteriorate (D's became C's, and B became the average grade); finally we arrived at total accommodation (come to class and get your C's, laugh at my jokes and take home B's).

5   Higher salaries, more stringent certification procedures, getting back to basics will have little or no effect on the problem of quality education unless and until we insist, as a profession, on giving F's whenever students fail to master the material.

6   Sending students home with final grades of F would force most parents to deal with the realities of their children's failure while it is happening and when it is yet possible to do something about it (less time on TV, and more time on homework, perhaps?). As long as it is the practice of teachers to pass students who should not be passed, the responsibility will not go home to the parents, where, I hope, it belongs. (I am tempted to make an analogy to then Gov. Lester Maddox's statement some years ago about prison conditions in Georgia—"We will get a better grade of prisons when we get a better grade of prisoners"—but I shall refrain.)

7   Giving an F where it is deserved would force concerned parents to get themselves away from the TV set, too, and take an active part in their children's education. I realize, of course, that some parents would not help; some cannot help. However, Johnny does not deserve to pass just because Daddy doesn't care or is ignorant. Johnny should pass only when and if he knows the required material.

8   Giving an F whenever and wherever it is the only appropriate grade would force principals, school boards, and voters to come to terms with cost as a factor in improving our educational system. As the numbers of students at various levels were increased by those not being passed, more money would have to be spent to accommodate them. We would not be accommodating them in the old sense of passing them on, but by keeping them at one level until they did in time, one way or another, learn the material.

9   Insisting on respecting the line between passing and failing would also require us to demand as much of ourselves as of our students. As every teacher knows, a failed student can be the product of a failed teacher.

10   Teaching methods, classroom presentations, and testing procedures would have to be of a very high standard—we could not, after all, conscionably give F's if we have to go home at night thinking it might somehow be our own fault.

11   The results of giving an F where it is deserved would be immediately evident. There would be no illiterate college graduates next spring—none. The same would be true of high-school graduates, and consequently next year's college freshmen—*all* of them—would be able to read.

12   I don't claim that giving F's will solve all of the problems, but I do argue that unless and until we start failing those students who should be failed, other suggested solutions will make little progress toward improving education. Students in our schools and colleges should be permitted to pass only after they have fully met established standards; borderline cases should be retained.

13   The single most important requirement for solving the problems of education in America today is the big fat F, written decisively in red ink millions of times in schools and colleges across the country.

Responding to the Reading

1. Singleton states that the widespread giving of F's would "open every major issue related to the inadequacies of American education." What are those inadequacies?
2. Why does Singleton suggest that giving F's will force parents to get involved in their children's education?
3. Why does Singleton say that other solutions will not work until teachers start awarding more F's?

Questions Beyond the Reading

1. Singleton claims that a basic problem with the U.S. educational system has been the giving of credit where none has been earned. Based on your experience, do you agree or disagree? Explain.
2. Singleton makes the connection between the "failed student" and the "failed teacher." How would you define a *failed teacher?*
3. Singleton assumes that awarding grades for performance in school is a good idea. Do you agree with this assumption? Why or why not?
4. If Singleton's proposal was adopted, what effect would it have on U.S. schools?

1. What is your own practice of using profanity?
2. How do you feel about the use of profanity in public places or in the media?

VOCABULARY HIGHLIGHTS

myriad	an infinitely great number
profusion	liberal use; abundance
benumbed	made to lack feeling or be inactive
brasseries	restaurants
gratuitous	without reason or justification
sentient	able to perceive by the senses
chaste	pure; free from obscenity
bowdlerize	to remove offensive language
rigorous	strict or severe
fervent	showing great warmth or intensity
transcendent	going beyond ordinary experience, thought, or belief

F-Word March

Stephen Chapman

1   The F-word is hard to avoid these days, and if you really want to avoid it, stop reading now. It came out of the mouths of a prosecutor and a defense lawyer in a hearing leading up to O. J. Simpson's trial as they read from transcripts of testimony, and CNN didn't even bother to bleep it. It showed up in the novel that won Britain's Booker Prize last year, James Kelman's *How Late It Was, How Late,* which uses myriad forms of the term in such profusion that even ordinarily benumbed critics complained. It made up nearly all of Hugh Grant's first dozen lines in *Four Weddings and a Funeral*—you remember, when he woke up, realized he had overslept and had to rush to the church.

2   You can hear it just about anywhere, in places where it never surfaced before—on the bus, in the checkout line, at the dinner table. It may have even crept into church by now. It was also at the center of *People of Texas* v. *Mary E. Conn.* The defendant, a Houston attorney, lost her composure one day when her wire-rimmed nursing bra set off a metal detector in the county courthouse, not for the first time. She responded with "a whole string of bad words," reported the *New York Times,* "most of them six- and seven-letter variants of a four-letter emphatic vulgarity." A deputy sheriff took offense and arrested her for disorderly conduct through the use of vulgar language, which is a misdemeanor in Texas.

3   Her defense was that this "emphatic vulgarity" is part of the background noise of the halls of justice. "That particular word is so commonly used in all the criminal courthouses I've ever practiced in that you don't even notice it when a person says it," said a local attorney who testified in her behalf. "It's used like punctuation."

Reprinted with permission from *The American Spectator,* January 1996 issue.

Conn's lawyer elicited testimony that the district attorney himself employs the word frequently. She herself asserted under oath that a judge had used it from the bench. The jury took 20 minutes to acquit. So it is official: In Texas, you-know-what and its derivatives do not constitute vulgar language.

4   Nor in much of the rest of the country. When I was in high school, just a brief generation ago, one of my classmates was notorious for his inability to complete a sentence without deploying a certain obscenity, sometimes three or four times, in noun, verb, adjective, and adverb form. Nowadays, he could hold court in plenty of upscale brasseries without attracting notice from his fellow patrons.

5   Hollywood, which used to take special care to safeguard our morals, now reflects and amplifies any declining standards in the populace at large. Half the dialogue in *Scarface* consisted of one rough-and-ready Anglo-Saxon expletive. Even wholesome stars feel no obligation to act wholesome off-screen. Harrison Ford, the modern version of the all-American male, sprinkled the term through an interview last year with *Vanity Fair:* "You don't have to f - - - with me. . . . You cannot get where I got without luck. Bags of it. F - - -ing *bags* of it. . . . I came into a business that was completely f - - - ed. . . . I was like a f - - - ing *snake* that grew a new tail. . . . Might as well have the hat on my f - - - ing head." This from an actor who in his films, the magazine noted, "has shied away from gratuitous sex."

6   So has Marisa Tomei, who played a hot number in *My Cousin Vinnie* without baring anything more than a thigh. Her modesty, however, ends at her mouth. In a session with *Movieline,* she repeatedly indulged in her favorite modifier: "No f - - - ing way. . . . It is f - - - ing fun. . . . He has a great f - - - ing sense of humor . . . people who are so f - - - ing brilliant."

7   No sentient adult would expect chaste language from anyone playing or coaching big-time sports. The average professional athlete, if he were barred from using expletives, would find it impossible to construct a sentence. Here, too, though, there is evidence of generational change. Indiana University basketball coach and perpetual sorehead Bobby Knight carpet-bombs his players' ears with every bad word known to English-speaking man. But when John Feinstein recorded his pronouncements faithfully in *A Season on the Brink,* Knight was angry that the author had not troubled to do some discreet bowdlerizing. Philadelphia Phillies slugger Lenny Dykstra, on the other hand, published an autobiographical work, *Nails,* which reads just about like most ballplayers talk. A certain utility infielder of a cuss word shows up, oh, every sentence or two.

8   Perhaps the First Couple's long-standing infatuation with the movie crowd explains its own fondness for the word. Bob Woodward reported in *The Agenda* that, upon hearing his advisers say he had to reduce the deficit to reassure Wall Street, Bill Clinton was incredulous: "You mean to tell me that the success of the program and my reelection hinges on the Federal Reserve and a bunch of f - - - ing bond traders?" At the end of a lengthy phone conversation in which he tried in vain to persuade Senator Bob Kerrey to vote for his first budget reconciliation plans, the president finally ran out of patience, not to mention eloquence. "F - - - you!" he bellowed. Richard Nixon got in trouble for swearing on the White House tapes even though all his expletives were deleted. Clinton's words were reported in all their glory, and nobody cared.

9   But he may not be the real trashmouth in the family. A former Arkansas state trooper told this magazine that when Clinton was governor, his wife once threw a fit when the American flag was not raised at a sufficiently early point in the day. "Where is the goddamn f - - - ing flag?" she demanded. "I want the goddamn f - - - ing flag up every f - - - ing morning at f - - - ing sunrise!"

10   Now that sort of rigorous profanity, wedded to fervent patriotism, could be said to achieve something transcendent. But most of the uses of the term are greatly deficient in creativity and passion. I would not dream of suggesting there is anything wrong with the word itself; I treasure a good emphatic vulgarity as much as anyone—well, maybe not as much as the First Lady. But the risk in the prevailing overuse is that this most forceful of obscenities will be drained of its historic power. A four-letter synonym for fellatio used to be reserved for extreme circumstances and banned from polite company. Now newspapers will quote someone saying that this or that sucks. It may be only a matter of time before the f-word also becomes mainstream.

11   And then we might as well not have it. If you use this term whenever a "hell" or "damn" would do the job of emphasizing irritation or exasperation, what do you turn to on those occasions when you want to escalate your rhetoric? It's like trying to settle a trade dispute by dropping an H-bomb: If it doesn't work, you're out of options.

12   As the word becomes more and more commonplace, people eventually cease to notice it—as they have in the Houston County Courthouse. So we will no longer be able to deploy it to get someone's attention. Then we will be forced to develop novel forms of expression to let people know when we are nearing the end of our rope. Personally, I've gotten results with "dag nab it."

Responding to the Reading

1. Why does Chapman say that the F-word no longer constitutes vulgar language in the state of Texas?
2. What is the effect of giving examples of the use of the F-word by famous people?
3. Why does Chapman say that "most of the uses of the term [the F-word] are greatly deficient in creativity and passion"?
4. Chapman concludes that "we might as well not have [the F-word]." Why?

Questions Beyond the Reading

1. Chapman says that the use of profanity has greatly increased in just a generation. Why do you think this is so, and what is the effect of this?
2. In your opinion, does the frequent use of profanity lessen the power of profanity? Why or why not?
3. Where and under what circumstances, if any, do you feel it is acceptable to use profanity?

Process

Questions Before the Reading

1. Are you more of an optimist or a pessimist? Why?
2. What examples of optimists do you find in your life, and why do you think these people are optimistic?

> **VOCABULARY HIGHLIGHTS**
>
> *crudités*   bite-sized raw vegetables served as appetizers
> *soufflé*   a light, baked dish made fluffy with beaten eggs

Think Positive: How to Be an Optimist

An upbeat outlook isn't just something you're born with.
The latest research shows it's a skill anyone can master.

Tamara Eberlein

1   If you'd asked me six months ago, I'd have said *optimism* means having faith I'd make it through the week without a child getting sick or a major appliance breaking down. And I'd have claimed to be an optimist myself, because despite the fact that my kids are constantly catching colds and my fridge is forever going on the fritz, I continue to make plans that assume no such setbacks.

2   Then I saw the movie *Apollo 13,* and I realized that positive thinking is a lot more than blind faith, and its power over people's lives is pretty awesome. Just watch Ed Harris as the mission control leader: Here's a guy who, despite every indication to the contrary, insists there's a way to eke out enough power from a wounded spacecraft to bring three astronauts back to earth—and then figures out how to *do* it, using little more than socks, spit, and bubble gum.

3   I want to become more like him, I decided. And fortunately, I *can*. The latest research shows that optimism isn't simply a trait a person is born with—or without. It's a skill anyone can master.

4   But first let's clear up a few misconceptions. "Optimism is not about constant elation, or being lucky enough to escape disappointment," says David G. Myers, Ph.D., professor of psychology at Hope College in Holland, MI. And it has nothing to do with feeling entitled to wealth and well-being. In fact, an attitude of entitlement without a sense of responsibility only leads to frustration. "Most of us live with a level of material comfort undreamed of half a century ago," Myers says. "But because we think we deserve home computers and brand name athletic shoes, we feel cheated if we don't automatically get them. It's the same with relationships. Our grandparents didn't expect endless ecstasy from marriage, and their marital satisfaction was higher."

5   So what *is* optimism? "It's a habitual way of explaining your setbacks to your-self," explains Martin E. P. Seligman, Ph.D., a psychology professor at the Univer-sity of Pennsylvania and author of *Learned Optimism* and *The Optimistic Child*. Here's how it works:

6   • The pessimist believes bad events stem from permanent conditions ("I lost the tennis match because I'm a lousy player"), and good events from temporary ones ("My husband brought me flowers because he had a good day at work"). The opti-mist, however, attributes failure to temporary causes ("I lost the match because I was exhausted today"), and favorable situations to enduring causes ("He brought me flowers because he really loves me").

7   • The pessimist allows a disappointment in one area of her life to pervade the rest. Say she's laid off from work The pessimist not only feels bad about losing her job, she also starts to worry that her husband has lost interest, her kids are out of control, and her house is a wreck. The optimist doesn't let one setback contaminate her whole life. "Okay, so at the moment I don't have a job," she thinks. "My husband and I are still close, my kids made the honor roll, and my garden's the envy of the neighborhood."

8   • When things go wrong, the pessimist blames herself even if she wasn't at fault. If another driver dents her parked car, she chides herself for parking in a stupid spot. The optimist ascribes such trouble to a fluke—"Darn, a dent! Oh well, every-body has bad luck occasionally"—or as evidence that she needs a new approach—"Next time I'll park in the far lot where there are fewer cars."

9   It boils down to *control*. While the optimist feels she's in charge of her life, the pessimist feels helpless and, therefore, hopeless.

10   "The thought, *Nothing I do matters,* prevents the pessimist from trying to im-prove her situation," Seligman notes. "So, confronted by a setback, she just gives up." Her first soufflé is a flop? She quits her cooking class. Her first pregnancy ends in miscarriage? She's too afraid of heartbreak to try to conceive again.

11   Optimists, however, persist in the face of failure because they "believe in themselves," says New York City psychologist Penelope Russianoff, Ph.D. That's why, as we've often heard, optimists fare better in almost every aspect of life.

12   "Professionally, the pessimist's lack of perseverance may lead her to achieve less than her talents warrant," Seligman says. In contrast, optimists often achieve *beyond* their apparent potential. "Studies show that the level of hope among fresh-men more accurately predicts college performance than do SAT scores or high-school grades," says C. R. Snyder, Ph.D., director of clinical psychology at the Uni-versity of Kansas in Lawrence.

13   Hopeful people enjoy greater social success as well, while pessimists may let friendships wither rather than work through misunderstandings.

14   Small wonder, then, that pessimists are prone to depression. But they're also more susceptible to physical ills, from colds to cancer to heart disease. "An opti-mistic outlook encourages people to stick to health regimens and seek medical advice when sick," Seligman explains. "There's strong evidence, too, that optimism bol-sters the immune system."

15   Psychologists believe optimism and pessimism are habits we learn as children, and our parents are our primary role models. When a water pipe broke and flooded the rec room of your brand-new home, did your mother lament, "Why did I pick such

a lousy house? Who knows how we'll pay for the damage?" Or did she declare, "Our contract guaranteed everything would be in perfect condition. I'll have the builder fix the plumbing and replace the furniture"?

16   The kind of criticism you received as a child also influenced your outlook. Say you failed a math quiz. If you were told, "You didn't pay attention during the lesson on fractions," you learned to see the causes of failure as temporary. But if you heard, "You don't have a head for numbers"—a permanent weakness beyond your control—you were steered down the path of pessimism.

17   Luckily, learned habits can be unlearned. A variety of techniques can boost your optimism level, whether you're a hard-core naysayer, or someone who's occasionally susceptible to the defeatist power of pessimism (who isn't?). Below, a ten-step program to help you to think positive.

When Is Pessimism a Good Thing?

Does optimism mean you should never find fault with yourself when you do mess up? Suppose I run up a huge debt on my credit cards. Am I suppose to gripe, "Why do those card companies allow people such huge credit limits? It's their own fault if no one can pay them back."

"No, no, no," Seligman answers. "Being an optimist *doesn't* mean dodging responsibility. It means admitting you made a mistake, learning from it, and finding ways to fix it."

"Another pitfall of optimism is that it can loosen our grasp on reality, so we don't take sensible precautions," Myers warns. "The so-called optimist who cheerfully shuns seat belts, denies the effects of smoking, or rushes into a mismatched marriage reminds us that blind optimism, like pride, may go before a fall."

So how do we know when to think like an optimist and when not to? "Ask what the cost of failure is in the particular situation," answers Seligman. If the cost is low, try optimism. The shy person deciding whether to initiate a conversations risks only rejection. But when the cost is high, optimism is the strategy of fools. For the partygoer who says, "I'm sober enough to drive home," optimism could prove fatal.

Challenge Your Negative Thoughts

18   • **Find the inaccuracies.** Suppose you're late getting to work. Rather than berating yourself—"I'm always late. I have the worst punctuality record in the company"—try to remember when you were last late. Yesterday? No, eight weeks ago. Are you really the least punctual? Consider your coworker who's been late three times this month.

19   • **Don't always blame yourself.** Are you late because you lazed in bed? No, your teenager emptied the car's tank last night, so you had to make an emergency stop for gas.

20   • **Consider the consequences.** "I'm going to get fired," you moan. Not likely. Imagine the worst case scenario if you must, but then picture the *best*. Maybe the boss gets caught in traffic and arrives even later than you. Finally, envision the *most likely* scenario: The boss scowls as you scurry to your desk—embarrassing, but far from fatal—and by five o'clock she's forgotten the whole incident.

21   • **Instead of brooding, look for a solution.** Maybe you can appease the boss by working through lunch. Strategize, too, on how to prevent a recurrence. Tell your teen to fill the tank whenever he uses the car. Leave the house ten minutes earlier to allow for unforeseen delays. "Think of failure as the result of a faulty strategy, not some character flaw," says Seligman. "Then, instead of feeling helpless, you can take action."

Rehearse the Role

22   • **Picture yourself a winner.** "In experiments, people who imagine themselves succeeding outperform those who expect to fail," explains Myers. Suppose you're afraid you'll blow your diet at your niece's wedding. Before the big day, visualize yourself passing up crab puffs in favor of crudités. Anticipate the problems you might encounter—"Yikes, they're serving cheesecake!" Then imagine your ideal response: "Quick, Harry, dance with me so I don't go near that dessert table." By the time you face the real challenge, your mental rehearsals will have given you confidence and willpower.

23   • **Act like an optimist.** Suppose you were recently divorced. A friend arranges a dinner party to which she's also invited an eligible man. The pessimist in you moans, "He probably won't be interested in me anyway." Now ask yourself what the optimist would do. Put on that little black dress friends say is so flattering? Do it!

24   "Advising people to act positively sounds like telling them to be phony," Myers admits. "But when we step into any new role—perhaps our first day playing parent, boss, or teacher—an amazing thing happens. The phoniness gradually subsides, and the new role and the accompanying attitude begin to fit us as comfortably as an old pair of jeans."

Give Yourself Credit

25   • **Acknowledge past successes.** Make a list of all the good things that have happened to you, Russianoff suggests. Then analyze each as the result of your own efforts. Your vacation photographs were superb not because cameras today are designed for dummies, but because you are skilled at lighting and composition. Your garden party was a great success, not because the weather was nice, but because of your preparation and social skills.

26   • **Celebrate achievements.** Share good news with friends and family. And don't forget to reward yourself: "I fixed that hole in the wall without having to call the carpenter. Now I'll treat myself to a manicure." Taking pride in your accomplishments builds your sense of self-worth.

Set Goals

27   Optimism, Snyder says, "requires both willpower *and* way power, the means to achieve your goals."

28   • **Choose goals wisely.** Be sure your goal is your own. Maybe your father did always dream you'd take over the family hardware store, but if you love books more than drill bits, you'll be happier as a librarian. Guard against disappointment by striving to improve in various arenas—family life, friendships, career, recreation. The woman who achieves her goal of running a marathon is less demoralized at being passed over for a promotion.

29   • **Be specific.** Vague plans to do more for the community have less chance of succeeding than do vows to volunteer once a week at the soup kitchen.

30   Break down larger goals into smaller objectives to keep from being paralyzed by the enormity of your task. "With each interim goal you reach," says Snyder, "you see progress. You feel energized and excited about what's to come." And that is the mark—and the power—of an optimist.

Responding to the Reading

1. Eberlein states that optimism is "a skill anyone can master." What does she mean by that?
2. According to Eberlein, what is the importance of control?
3. Why does C. R. Snyder say that optimism requires both "willpower and way power"?

Questions Beyond the Reading

1. Eberlein reports that David G. Myers, Ph.D., suggests "an attitude of entitlement without responsibility only leads to frustration." Do you agree or disagree? Explain.
2. Compare and contrast the attitudes of optimists and pessimists.
3. Eberlein presents a list of ways to challenge negative thinking. Can you think of any additional methods to add to that list? Explain.

Questions Before the Reading

1. In your experience, how important is someone's situation in life to his or her health?
2. Describe your own expriences with stress and how you cope with it.

> **VOCABULARY HIGHLIGHTS:**
>
> *camaraderie*   good fellowship
> *protocommunity*   an original or essential community

The Healing Powers of Community
How Creating Community Can Enrich— Even Prolong—Your Life

Carolyn R. Shaffer and Kristen Anundsen

1   In the early 1960s, a small town in Pennsylvania became the focus of attention for scores of medical researchers. The community of Roseto appeared unremarkable in every way except one: Its inhabitants were among the healthiest people in the

United States. The rate at which they died of heart disease was significantly lower than the national average, and they exhibited greater resistance to peptic ulcers and senility than other Americans.

2   When researchers searched for clues to the Rosetans' health and longevity among the usual array of factors, they came up empty-handed. The folks in Roseto smoked as much, exercised as little, and faced the same stressful situations as other Americans. The residents of this closely knit Italian-American community practiced no better health habits than their neighbors. So why were they so healthy?

3   The answer surprised the researchers. After extensive testing, they learned that the Rosetans' remarkable health was linked to their strong sense of community and camaraderie. The town was not so ordinary after all. "More than that of any other town we studied, Roseto's social structure reflected old-world values and traditions," says Dr. Stewart Wolf in a booklet summarizing the study that he directed. "There was a remarkable cohesiveness and sense of unconditional support within the community. Family ties were very strong."

4   Developments since the initial study underscored this conclusion. As young Rosetans began to marry outside the clan, move away from the town's traditions, and sever emotional and physical ties with the community, the healthy edge Roseto held over neighboring towns began to lessen until, by the mid-1970s, its mortality rates had climbed as high as the national average.

5   While you cannot, and for many reasons would not want to, recreate the patriarchal, religion-bound, old-world traditions that helped keep Rosetans healthy, you can discern the positive qualities of social interaction that contributed to their health and take steps to nourish these qualities in various areas of your life.

6   An important reason to seek functional or conscious community, even proto-community, is that it can keep you healthier in many respects. The Roseto findings are far from unique. Contemporary medical psychological and sociological literature overflows with studies that point to the life-prolonging, even life-saving qualities of interpersonal support. For example:

7   • Dr. Dean Ornish, a California specialist in coronary heart disease, developed a treatment program with support groups that surprised even him and his colleagues with its positive results: Chest pains diminished or went away entirely, severe blockages in coronary arteries reversed, and patients became more energetic. In Ornish's study, which was partially funded by the National Institutes of Health, patients lived together for a week in a retreat, then met two evenings every week for four hours.

8   "At first," Ornish writes in *Dr. Dean Ornish's Program for Reversing Heart Disease*, "I viewed our support groups simply as a way to motivate patients to stay on the other aspects of the program that I considered most important: the diet, exercise, stress management training, stopping smoking, and so on. Over time, I began to realize that the group support itself was one of the most powerful interventions, as it addressed what I am beginning to believe is a more fundamental cause of why we feel stressed and, in turn, why we get illnesses like heart disease: the perception of isolation.

9   "In short, anything that promotes a sense of isolation leads to chronic stress and, often, to illnesses like heart disease. Conversely, anything that leads to real intimacy and feelings of connection can be healing in the real sense of the word: to

bring together, to make whole. The ability to be intimate has long been seen as a key to emotional health; I believe it is essential to the health of our hearts as well."

10   • The University of Michigan's Dr. James House and two fellow sociologists concluded, from their own studies and those of others, that there is a clear link between poor social relationships and poor health. "It's the 10 to 20 percent of people who say they have nobody with whom they can share their private feelings, or who have close contact with others less than once a week, who are most at risk," the researchers declared. This risk extends to life itself. In fact, House reports, the people with the weakest social ties have significantly higher death rates—100 percent to 300 percent for men, 50 percent to 150 percent for women—than their counterparts who are more socially integrated in terms of marital and family status, contacts with friends, church memberships, and other group affiliations.

11   • A study at St. Luke's–Roosevelt Hospital and Columbia University in New York City revealed that, for people with heart disease, living alone is a major independent risk factor comparable to such factors as previous heart damage and heart rhythm disturbances. The data indicate that heart attack patients living alone are twice as likely as others to suffer another heart attack, and more likely to die of an attack, within six months.

12   "What's particularly significant is the magnitude of the effect," said clinical psychologist Nan Case, co-author of the study. "We know that emotions and [social] integration have an effect, but we never knew it could come close to the physiological factors in heart disease."

13   • A team of Stanford Medical School psychiatrists, led by Dr. David Spiegel, found that metastatic breast cancer patients who joined support groups lived nearly twice as long as those receiving only medical care.

14   • At Ohio State University, psychologist Janice Kiecolt-Glaser and her colleagues discovered, in comparing thirty-eight married women with thirty-eight separated or divorced women, that the married women had better immune functions than the unmarried women.

15   Several studies suggest that it is not the number of personal contacts that affects people's health, but the degree to which people perceive that they have someone they can turn to. Social networks do not always feel like community. Unhappy marriages, alcoholic families, and other dysfunctional relationships can actually damage a person's health. Psychologists at the University of Washington concluded that even supportive actions and words do not necessarily translate into perceived support. "It all depends on whether your social support comes from someone you believe truly loves, values, and respects you," concluded one of the researchers, Dr. Gregory Pierce.

16   Psychologist Robert Ornstein and physician David Sobel believe that human beings evolved as social animals, and that our brains are programmed to connect us with others in order to improve our chances of survival. When the brain detects signals of isolation or emotional imbalance, it transmits these signals to other parts of the body. The way you interact with family members, co-workers, and others in your social sphere is translated by brain mechanisms into changes in hormone levels and in neurotransmitters.

17   "People need people," the researchers conclude in *The Healing Brain*. "Not only for the practical benefits which derive from group life, but for our very health

and survival. Somehow interaction with the larger social world of others draws our attention outside of ourselves, enlarges our focus, enhances our ability to cope, and seems to make the brain reactions more stable and the person less vulnerable to disease."

Responding to the Reading

1. Why do Shaffer and Anundsen say that one would not want to "recreate the patriarchal, religion-bound, old-world traditions that helped keep Rosetans healthy"?
2. Shaffer and Anundsen quote a number of different authorities in this essay. Are they all credible, reliable sources? Explain.
3. Shaffer and Anundsen note that not all social networks are positive. What can go wrong?
4. According to this article, how can one's social health be translated into physical health?

Questions Beyond the Reading

1. This article suggests that there is a close relationship between one's mental well-being and one's physical health. Based on your personal experiences, cite some examples of this relationship.
2. Shaffer and Anundsen suggest that more attempts to create community will lead to better health. What communities do you belong to, and how do they contribute to your own feeling of mental well-being?
3. Shaffer and Anundsen report that dysfunctional relationships can damage a person's health. From your own experience, do you agree or disagree? Explain.

Questions Before the Reading

1. How important is getting good grades to you?
2. Describe the methods that you use to learn the material in a class.

VOCABULARY HIGHLIGHTS

abstract   theoretical; apart from a specific object or concrete reality
neuron   a nerve cell

Note: The following reading is from Chapter 5 of the book *How to Get the Most Out of College*. At times, the text refers to passages in earlier chapters. Although such references may be distracting, the content of the material should be clear. As part of their research for this book, the authors interviewed sixty current freshmen, juniors, and seniors of different ages, ethnicities, and national origins. The names and quoted comments you will read in this article come from those interviews.

Maximizing Learning from Courses and Classes

Arthur W. Chickering and Nancy K. Schlossberg

1   We hope that you have been able to identify some clear purposes for your college education. We hope these are important enough so there are things you really want to learn, skills and areas of competence you want to strengthen, personal characteristics you want to develop further. If you have decided on a major, we hope that decision adds fuel to the time, energy, money, and emotion you are ready to invest.

Learning, Not Grades

2   Your long-run pay-offs depend on what you learn that lasts. They depend on progress you make in developing the knowledge, abilities, and personal characteristics you have specified. Those pay-offs will *not* depend upon the grades you get by memorizing pages of lecture notes and highlighted textbook readings. We know that's hard to believe. Getting good grades and maintaining a high grade point average seem to be the most important reasons for studying, for spending long hours in the library, for psyching out the professor, for figuring out what is likely to be on exams and staying up all night cramming for them. It's hard to believe that grades are not important after college when parents, professors, and other students see them as critical evidence of success or failure.

3   But, since the 1950s there have been numerous studies correlating the relationships between grade point average and many diverse indicators of post-college success: income level, career success, graduate school performance, happiness, personal adjustment and mental health . . . you name it. Over the years, several persons have summarized this research. All these summaries say that grades are poor predictors of whether someone will be successful in work and living a good life. One of the most recent found, across a large sample of studies, no overall relationship between grades and adult achievement in the workplace.

4   If you don't believe us, you can, as they say, look it up. The recent report is by Robert Brest, "College Grade Point Average as a Predictor of Adult Success: A Meta-Analytic Review and Some Additional Evidence," in *Public Personnel Management, Vol. 18,* No. 1, 1989, pp. 11–22.

5   There is one exception: If you hope to enter a highly selective graduate school immediately after graduation, then your grade point average *is* important. These schools, because of their large number of applicants, use GPAs as an efficient way to make a first cut. So if that's your next step after college, you need to shoot for high grades.

6   Of course, if your grades are so poor you flunk out and don't complete college, it is a different story. The critical distinction is whether or not you graduate. Once you've got your degree in hand, your grades have little consequence for your long-term happiness and success.

7   We emphasize these points about grades because we want to help you maximize your learning and personal development, acquire knowledge, develop skills,

and build personal characteristics that will serve you well throughout life, across a wide range of situations. Unfortunately, much classroom teaching and many course requirements do not result in learning that lasts. If you really want to learn, often you will need to invest time and energy in ways not required by the teacher. Or you may be required to take courses that are so badly taught you cannot learn effectively. Then the wisest choice may be to put in only the minimum amount of time and energy necessary to get by. Use the time and energy saved for other areas where the learning is important to you and leads to outcomes of lasting value.

8　　Some experienced, thoughtful students have become clear about these trade-offs. Remember Victoria's comment, "Sure, you can work for a grade but the idea is to really learn something." And her description of her fiance who got C's and D's but who is "very successful," making a good living and happy about what he does.

9　　Li Peng, for example, said, "Right now grades are more important to students than what they've learned. Right now you gotta get this kind of grade to make your parents happy, yourself happy, and your teachers happy. So the grades are more important than what you learned. I used to think that as long as I got a good grade I didn't really care what I learned. Because all they ever told me was, 'Just get this grade and you'll be okay.' I don't believe in that now. Now I feel successful if I understand what I've studied."

10　　"What advice do you have for other students about getting the most out of their academic program?"

11　　"Get your priorities straight first. If you want to be what you want to be, you are gonna have to work on it. If you're not really working on it that means you're not really into it. You don't have any motivation. So you might as well get out of it. Don't worry about your grades. Just try to learn whatever you can because a lot of people think too much about grades and not enough about what they are actually getting out of their studying."

12　　If what we're saying, and if Victoria's and Li Peng's orientations sound like heresy, so be it. Listen to these students describe their courses and studies and you'll understand why we take this apparently extreme position.

13　　MIKE: "In class it is mostly listening to the lecture on whatever topic we happen to be considering. Just taking notes is the core of the class. We'll receive homework assignments. Lately we've been getting a lot of theory-related classes, which is a lot of homework and textbook-oriented work. You just kind of show up, make sure you get the information, and just do what you can with it. It requires a lot of reading and a lot of memorization."

14　　REBECCA: "Generally it's a lecture course where we read and then are tested on the information. I generally hold off on the reading until three or four days before the exam. Then I will read everything, study my notes, and things like that. I think it is easier for me to remember all the information, that way."

15　　How much would you guess Rebecca has actually learned? How much will she retain three months, six months, a year later? If she gets an A in this course, how much value will that kind of learning contribute to her working knowledge later in life?

16　　Lou Ann has a more systematic approach to assimilating the information. "Basically, what I do is take the test deadlines and say, 'Okay, I have ten chapters for this test.' So I read all the chapters and start reviewing them. Then every time I go to class I take what he lectures in class and go back and study it together with the book. So I learn it in units, almost, so that when the test gets here I don't spend three days before cramming. That's how I learn. That's the learning process, memorizing. So that's that."

17   These comments from Mike, Rebecca, and Lou Ann are consistent with studies of college teaching. Most teaching involves heavy use of lectures. Teachers, on the average, spend about 80 percent of class time lecturing to students who are paying attention only about half the time. But the major problem is how much and how quickly students forget the content of the lectures. Within a few months, at least 50 percent of the content has evaporated. One study gave students a summary of the lecture, let them use their notes, and tested them immediately after the lecture. The students had retained only 42 percent of the content. When they were tested a week later, they retained only 17 percent.

18   Here again, if you are skeptical about this research, you can do your own experiment. Pull out a mid-term or final exam from last semester. Sit down and take it cold. No reviewing notes or readings, no discussion with others, no preparation. See how you do. If you score more than 50 percent, your retention rate is outstanding. Or perhaps you have been using the material in other courses or other activities since then to keep it fresh. Or maybe it is an area of special interest to you where you've kept on learning. But we will bet you a dollar to a doughnut that if you try that for five different exams at random, your retention will be closer to 20 percent, perhaps less.

19   Our basic point here, and it is fundamental to this chapter, is that memorizing rarely creates learning that lasts. If you keep on using the ideas, concepts, and skills, then they will stick with you and become integrated. But if you simply memorize them to pass an exam and then go on to other courses or unrelated activities, you may have obtained a good grade—but not much else. If you really want to learn the material effectively, so it will serve you in the future, you need to do more.

Experiential Learning

20   To help you toward learning that lasts we want to tell you about David Kolb's "experiential learning theory." Strictly speaking, all learning is "experiential," so it may be helpful to begin with some simple definitions. The dictionary says "learning" is to gain in knowledge, understanding, or skill, by study, instruction, or experience. "Experience" is actually living through an event or events, actual enjoyment or suffering, and thus, the effect on judgment or feelings produced by personal and direct impressions. So "experiential learning" includes knowledge, understanding, and skills as well as judgment and feelings. It includes the educational processes of study and instruction as well as actually living through events. It recognizes that both joy and suffering often accompany significant learning. When the Bible says that "Abraham knew Sarah," it is not talking about memorizing abstract concepts. It is talking about full-fleshed, active, "experiential" knowing.

21   According to Kolb, most learning occurs through a four-stage cycle. You start with some experiences. You think about these, reflect on them, make observations about them. As these experiences accumulate in relation to particular events, activities, persons, and areas of interest, you begin to develop some concepts, maybe a

The Experiential Learning Model

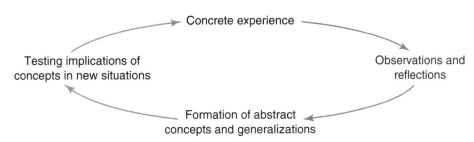

hunch or a "theory," which seem to explain what is going on or why something seems to happen in recurring fashion. These concepts become the basis for how you think or how you act the next time you encounter a similar experience.

22   Take an obvious example. The first time you come on campus, the layout of the buildings is unclear. The location of classrooms or offices within buildings may be confusing. You are uncertain how to get from the admissions office to your advisor, to where you pay your bills, to the cafeteria, and so forth. You begin to walk around. You may look at a campus map and try to figure out what's where. You develop an initial impression of how to get from A to B to C. You try out a route, and usually, perhaps after a bit of wandering around and asking questions, you find what you're looking for. You may stop to think about where you turned wrong, what would have been a more direct route. On the basis of these reflections you refine your own internal "map." The next time you need to get from A to B or B to C, you make fewer wrong turns. Pretty quickly you can find your way everywhere on campus. You know all the shortcuts and, down to a minute or two, how long it takes you to go from one class to another, from the student union to the library, and so forth. If for some reason you need to go to a faculty member's office, or to some particular place you've never been before, you find it much more efficiently than you would have the first day. You can do that because you have accumulated experiences and developed a rich set of concepts that help you cope with the new unknown.

23   Or take a more complex, more academic example. In school you had social studies courses that taught you the basics about the United States government, the division of powers among the executive branch, the legislature, and the Supreme Court. You go to Washington, DC, perhaps on a class trip, or with your children, and see the White House and the Capitol. Perhaps you visit your local senator or congressional representative, or attend a session of Congress. Your experiences make more vivid and clear those abstract concepts. The idea of "division of powers" takes on added reality, added richness. You won't forget it so easily.

24   Not all learning is conscious. The "experiential learning cycle" can apply to unconscious learning as well. You grow up living in a community where persons of certain backgrounds—who perhaps speak English poorly, or come from a different country, or have a different skin color—collect the garbage, maintain the streets, do the dirty work and manual labor. You may see similar persons sleeping in the streets. You may pick out news about robberies or violence committed by some such persons. Before long, you begin to assume that all such persons are stupid, irresponsible, dangerous, can't be trusted. You avoid them. Your experiences get more and

more selective. Your assumptions get reinforced. And you have become, without really being aware of it, prejudiced toward, biased about, such persons.

25   Other examples of unconscious learning involve what's called "psychomotor coordination": riding a bicycle, throwing a ball where you want, shooting a basket, stroking a tennis ball, driving a car, swimming. You usually start with experiences and observations. Sometimes you get some basic instructions. But the real learning occurs through practice, practice, practice. That's how it gets built in, how the skills get honed, how your repertoire expands.

26   We know from neurological research that our brain is a mass of interconnected neurons. Every sensation we receive, every move we make, every emotion we feel, every thought we think, every word we speak, involves a network of those interconnections. The fundamental thing we need to do, to achieve learning that lasts, is connect the new learning with one of those pre-existing networks. Whether it is a new physical skill, a new emotional experience, a new piece of information, a new set of concepts, if it doesn't get connected it won't last long. It's like the internal map of the campus. Once we have it well developed, we can plug in new locations easily and quickly; in the future, we will remember clearly how to get there.

27   Kolb's experiential learning theory describes how those networks are built. Effective learning has four basic ingredients that call for four different abilities. You must be able to enter new experiences openly and fully, without bias. You must then try to stand back from those experiences, observe them with some detachment, and reflect on their significance. Next you need to develop a logic, a conceptual framework, a "hypothesis," that makes sense of your reflections and observations. Finally, you need the ability to apply these concepts, to test their implications through action, to use them to solve problems, and to try out appropriate behaviors. This testing kicks off a new, better-informed, better-skilled, more sophisticated cycle.

28   Note that there are some critical consequences of this approach when it is well used. First, it attaches major importance to testing ideas through action. When ideas are tested in action, their significance is greater than when they are simply memorized or left as unexamined abstractions. An idea taken as a fixed truth gives no cause for further thought; an idea as a working hypothesis must undergo continual scrutiny and modification. That, in turn, creates pressure to formulate the idea itself accurately and precisely.

29   Second, when an idea is tested for its soundness or its consequences, the results must be acutely observed and carefully analyzed. Activity not subject to observation and analysis may be enjoyable, but it usually doesn't add much to learning, to greater clarification, or to new ideas or improved skills. We often have the same experiences over and over, and still don't learn from them. That's because we do not take time for reflection and analysis.

30   Third, reflection and analysis require discrimination and synthesis. We have to make distinctions about the elements of our experience. We also need to synthesize the relationships among them. So when we talk about Kolb's experiential learning theory, we are sharing this complex set of interactions.

31   A good football coach uses all four elements. Players have the *concrete experience* of playing the game: missing blocks, making clean tackles, running a faulty pass pattern, getting mousetrapped, executing a perfect option play. They *reflect* between

games on what worked and what didn't, reviewing video tapes and discussing how to improve. They use *abstract conceptualization* to get the plays down pat and to visualize their own moves. The next game provides the context for *active experimentation* and triggers another cycle.

32   When we asked Sara Jane what advice she would give students about getting the most out of their academic program, she unwittingly illustrated how part of Kolb's cycle worked for her: "Definitely attend your classes. You may get notes from someone, but when you attend classes you get a lot of examples from your teacher and she'll help you understand. Then attend any study groups you can, review what you learn each day, and be prepared for class. I find it easier, if I'm supposed to read something for class, to read it after the teacher lectures 'cause I'll understand it more rather than reading before and tuning myself out 'cause I don't understand. My mind will wander. But if they lecture about it I understand it more from them talking about it and then reading the material."

33   Sara Jane likes to start with the experience of her classes, even if she can get the notes from someone else. She gets a lot of examples from the teacher, which helps make things concrete. Then she joins study groups where she can review the class. She likes to do the reading after the lectures because then she will understand it more and won't "tune out" of the class. So she really has described a sequence that involves the first three elements of Kolb's cycle: the concrete experiences from the lecture examples, the reflection with fellow students in the study groups, and then the basic concepts through the readings.

34   Our point is, the more often the full cycle of concrete experiences, reflective observations, abstract concepts, and testing in action occurs, the more powerful the learning and the greater likelihood it will remain useful in the future.

Responding to the Reading

1. Why do Chickering and Schlossberg say that grades are not important, only graduating is?
2. What do Chickering and Schlossberg mean by *experiential learning?* Explain how the Experiential Learning Model applies to your typical learning experiences in a classroom.
3. What is the relationship among *concrete experience*, *reflection*, *abstract conceptualization*, and *active experimentation?*

Questions Beyond the Reading

1. In your opinion, what is the difference between getting good grades and learning the material in a class? Explain.
2. Chickering and Schlossberg state that about 80 percent of class time is used for lecturing in a typical class. Is this good or bad? Why?
3. How would you teach a writing course that relied on the Experiential Learning Model? Give specific examples of activities you might use.

Glossary

abbreviation   A shortened version of a word.

abstract word   A word that represents an idea, emotion, or quality.

acronym   An abbreviation of a long term; can be used as a pronounceable word.

active voice   The form of a transitive verb in which the doer of the verb is emphasized.

adjective   A word that modifies or describes a noun or pronoun.

adverb   A word that modifies or describes a verb, adjective, or other adverb.

analogy   A comparison between two unlike or unrelated people, objects, processes, or events that is made in order to understand difficult concepts, events, or processes.

antecedent   A word or group of words for which a pronoun substitutes.

antonym   A word that has a meaning opposite to the meaning of another word.

argument   The attempt to advance a point of view or thesis.

argumentative writing   Writing in which the emphasis is on argument.

attacking the messenger   A logical fallacy that ignores the substance of what a person says and instead criticizes or draws attention to the character of the person.

audience   The expected reader(s) of the author's paper.

auxiliary verb   See **helping verb.**

begging the question   A logical fallacy that assumes something in a statement that has not yet been proven.

brainstorming   A prewriting technique that relies on free association of ideas. Brainstorming can involve writing down ideas in the form of a list or in a form that lacks organization. The second form can lead to **mapping.**

case   The different forms that nouns and pronouns can take, depending on their functions within a sentence. The three cases are subjective, objective, and possessive.

cause   A rhetorical mode that investigates the reason(s) an event or action occurred.

chronological order   A method of arrangement in which the writer begins at one point in time and proceeds in sequence.

claim   The writer's opinion or statement about a writing subject. The claim is usually found in the thesis sentence.

classification   A rhetorical mode that discusses how things of the same type are grouped into categories by some unifying principle.

clustering   A prewriting technique in which lines are drawn between different items related to the same subject or topic. The items are usually placed inside boxes or circles.

collective noun   A noun that names a group of people or things.

common noun   A noun that names general people, places, or things.

comparison   A rhetorical mode that examines areas of similarity between two persons, places, things, or ideas.

complete subject   The simple subject and all other modifiers associated with it.

complete thought   In a sentence, when the logic of the words is executed properly.

complex sentence   A sentence that has at least one dependent clause and one independent clause.

compound sentence   A sentence that has two or more independent clauses.

compound subject   A subject that consists of two or more nouns or pronouns.

compound-complex sentence   A sentence that has at least one dependent clause and more than one independent clause.

concession   An acknowledgment that there are different points of view than those expressed by the writer.

concrete word   A word that represents something that can be perceived by the physical senses.

conjunction   A word that joins two or more words, phrases, or clauses.

conjunctive adverb   A word that establishes an adverbial relationship between independent clauses or complete sentences. Conjunctive adverbs are often used to create compound sentences; semicolons are used to join the sentences.

connotation   The emotional associations and implications of a word.

contrast   A rhetorical mode that examines the differences between two people, places, things, or ideas.

controlling ideas   The concepts used to support a thesis sentence. They are usually stated in the topic sentences of an essay's main body paragraphs but are sometimes included as part of the thesis sentence itself.

coordinating conjunction   A word that joins equally independent clauses or parallel elements in a sentence.

correlative conjunctions   Pairs of coordinating conjunctions that place extra emphasis on the relationship between the coordinated parts.

count noun   An item that can be counted.

creative writing   Writing in which the main purpose is to entertain. It is based on originality of thought or expression and is usually fictitious; includes short stories, novels, poems, plays, feature films, TV shows, and even song lyrics.

crystalline word   The key word of a sentence, paragraph, or essay that expresses the central idea or message of the work.

deduction   A method of logic in which a conclusion is drawn from two premises, major and minor.

definition   A rhetorical mode that presents something's distinguishing characteristics or limits.

demonstrative pronoun   A pronoun that indicates or points to the noun it replaces.

denotation   The dictionary meaning of a word.

dependent clause   A group of words that has a subject and predicate but cannot stand on its own as a complete sentence.

description   A rhetorical mode that presents something's physical details or characteristics.

dictionary   A book containing the words in a language, arranged in alphabetical order; usually provides meanings, pronunciations, and etymologies.

direct object   The noun or pronoun that receives the action of a verb.

effect   A rhetorical mode that examines the results or potential results of an action or event.

emotional blackmail   A logical fallacy in which a writer appeals to a reader's feelings in ways that are misleading or unfair; used to avoid rational argument.

essay   A written work of at least several paragraphs on a single subject; presents and supports a thesis.

example   A rhetorical mode that emphasizes particular instances or samples of a thing, idea, or event.

expository writing   Writing in which the primary purpose is to explain, instruct, or expound on something.

external forces   Factors that shape the author's writing that come from outside the author, such as its purpose, audience, and subject.

false analogy   A logical fallacy in which an analogy is used to confuse or mislead the reader.

faulty authority   A logical fallacy in which a person misuses his or her authority on one matter to speak on another.

free association   The flow of one's ideas free of any conscious attempts to mold or organize them.

freewriting   A prewriting technique that relies on free association. It is done within a set time period and involves writing down all ideas that come into one's mind, left to right, across the page. Focused freewriting involves keeping the mind focused on a general subject.

future perfect   See **perfect tenses.**

future perfect progressive   See **progressive tenses.**

future progressive   See **progressive tenses.**

future tense   Used for events that will happen at some later time.

gerund   A present participle used as a noun. See **verbal.**

hasty generalization   A logical fallacy in which a person arrives at an erroneous conclusion by using too small of a sample.

helping verb   A verb that helps show the tense or mood of another verb; a form of the verb *to be, to have,* or *to do.*

hook   An opening statement in an essay, designed to catch the reader's attention.

indefinite pronoun   A pronoun that does not refer to a particular person or thing.

independent clause   A group of words that has a subject and predicate and can stand alone as a complete sentence.

indirect object   A noun or pronoun indirectly involved in the action of a sentence.

induction   A method of logic that arrives at a general conclusion based on the observation of specific examples or instances.

inference   A statement based on the observation of statistical data or arrived at on the basis of another statement believed to be true.

infinitive   The *to* form of a verb; also known as the *base form* or the *dictionary form.* When used as a verbal, the infinitive can function as a noun, adjective, or adverb.

innuendo   A logical fallacy in which an indirect suggestion, often of a derogatory nature, is made about someone or something.

intensive pronoun   A pronoun that emphasizes a preceding noun or pronoun.

interjection   A word or phrase expressing emotion or physical sensation; it has no grammatical relationship to the rest of the words in a sentence.

internal forces   Factors that shape an author's writing that are generated from within, such as family background, spiritual or philosophical beliefs, personal experiences, academic or personal interests, and hopes, goals, and dreams for the future.

interrogative pronoun   A pronoun that is used to ask questions.

intransitive verb   A verb that does not take a direct object; action is limited to the subject.

jargon The language restricted to members of a certain field or profession.

journal A written record of reflections on one's life and times.

lead-in See **hook.**

letter A piece of written personal or business correspondence of relatively short length.

linking verb A verb that describes a state of being or existence.

listing A prewriting technique that involves organizing items, usually vertically and without sentences.

logical fallacy A breakdown in the logical thinking process.

looping A prewriting technique in which the writer uses ideas generated in one prewriting session as the basis for another.

main verb The verb in a verb phrase that indicates the action or state of being.

mapping A prewriting technique done after a brainstorming session. It involves drawing circles or boxes around items and then drawing lines to connect related items.

mass noun An item that cannot be counted.

narration A rhetorical mode that emphasizes telling a story.

noun A word that names a person, place, thing, or idea.

noun modifier A noun functioning as an adjective.

object complement A noun or pronoun that completes the meaning of a direct object by renaming or describing it.

objective Showing no bias or opinion in one's writing.

outlining A prewriting technique that arranges ideas within a paragraph or essay according to their relationships. Types include scratch, or informal, outlines and formal outlines.

paragraph A group of sentences that discuss the same topic.

parallel structure The construction of a series of words, phrases, or clauses using the same word types and orders.

participle Either past or present; it can be used alone as a verbal or joined by a helping verb to form either the perfect or progressive tenses. When used as a verbal, a participle functions as an adjective. See **past participle, present participle,** and **verbal.**

passive voice The form of a transitive verb in which the object of the verb is emphasized and the doer of the verb is deemphasized.

past participle Marked in a regular verb by the *-ed* ending; the form varies in irregular verbs. The past participle is used with a form of the helping verb *to have* to create the perfect tenses and with a form of the helping verb *to be* to create the passive voice; can also be used alone as a verbal.

past perfect See **perfect tenses.**

past perfect progressive See **progessive tenses.**

past progressive See **progressive tenses.**

past tense Used for events that have already occurred.

perfect tenses Used to indicate completed actions; include past perfect, present perfect, and future perfect.

personal diary The record of the daily events of one's life.

personal pronoun A pronoun that refers to a person or thing.

persuasion The attempt to change a reader's views about something or to motivate a reader to take a course of action.

persuasive writing Writing in which the main purpose is to persuade.

points of support See **controlling ideas.**

predicate The verb and all other words associated with it that describe the action of the sentence or the state in which the subject exists.

premise A statement or assertion that one is certain is true. Two premises, one major and one minor, are used in a syllogism. The major premise is a general statement or assertion, and the minor premise is a specific instance or example of what was related in the major premise.

preposition A word that shows the relationship between its object and something else in the sentence.

present participle Marked by the *-ing* ending; used with a helping verb to create the progressive tenses. Can also be used alone as a verbal.

present perfect See **perfect tenses.**

present perfect progressive See **progressive tenses.**

present progressive See **progressive tenses.**

present tense Used for events that are either happening now or that occur on a regular basis.

prewriting Activities that are done prior to drafting a paragraph or essay; designed to enhance the writer's ability to generate and organize ideas. They include such techniques as brainstorming, freewriting, listing, mapping, outlining, asking questions, and journal writing.

process A rhetorical mode that discusses either how something is made or what something is made of.

progressive tenses Used to indicate ongoing action. They include present progressive, past progressive, future progressive, present perfect progressive, past perfect progressive, and future perfect progressive.

prompt A reading on which a timed essay assignment is based.

pronoun A word that substitutes for a noun.

proper noun A noun that names a particular person, place, or thing.

purpose The reason the author is writing a paragraph or essay. The three main purposes in writing are to entertain, to instruct, and to persuade the reader. Most writing has elements of all three purposes, but a particular piece of writing will usually emphasize one more than the other two.

qualifier Words that provide reservations about a statement.

rational basis The reasons that support a thesis sentence, expressed through the controlling ideas.

reciprocal pronoun A pronoun that refers to the separate parts of a plural noun.

reflexive pronoun A pronoun that renames or reflects back to a noun or pronoun.

relative pronoun A pronoun that introduces a dependent clause that functions as an adjective.

sentence pattern The way in which elements of a sentence (such as subject, verb, and object) can be ordered coherently.

series A sequence of causes or effects.

signpost An announcement to the reader of what to expect next.

simple sentence A sentence that consists of one independent clause.

simple subject The single noun or pronoun that serves as the subject of a sentence.

slang The most restrictive form of language in which only members within a group understand the meanings of certain terms.

slippery slope A logical fallacy that predicts that because of one event, an entire sequence of later events, usually undesirable, is inevitable.

spatial order   A method of arrangement in which the writer shows the physical relationships between people or things.

stages   The phases of a process.

style   How language is used.

subject   The noun, pronoun, or noun phrase that receives the action of the verb or whose state of being is described in a sentence. Also, the general area of inquiry with which the author's paper is concerned.

subject complement   A noun or adjective that follows a linking verb and renames or describes the subject.

subjective   Showing bias or opinion in one's writing.

subordinating conjunction   A word that joins a dependent clause with an independent clause.

syllogism   A deductive argument based on three propositions: a major premise, a minor premise, and a conclusion.

synonym   A word that has a meaning similar to that of another word.

thesis   The main idea or opinion of an essay.

thesis sentence   The sentence in an essay that states its main idea or opinion.

topic   A narrowed or limited aspect of the subject.

topic sentence   The sentence in a paragraph that states its main point or idea.

transition   A word or phrase that serves as a guidepost for the reader, indicating what to expect next.

transitive verb   A verbs that transfers the action to a direct object.

verb   A word that shows an action or state of being.

verb phrase   A group of words consisting of helping verbs and the main verb.

verb tense   The form used to indicate the time an action or state of being occurred or existed.

verbal   A verb form that functions as a noun, adverb, or adjective in a sentence. A verbal can be a gerund, participle, or infinitive.

voice   The form of a transitive verb in a sentence that indicates whether the emphasis is given to the doer of an action or the object acted upon. There are two voices: active and passive.

Index

Note: A boldface number indicates a page on which the subject is used as a key term.

474